WE LIVED THERE TOO

WE

KENNETH LIBO / IRVING HOWE

LIVED THERE TOO

*In their own words and pictures—pioneer Jews
and the westward movement of America*

1630–1930

ST. MARTIN'S/MAREK

NEW YORK

DESIGN BY HELEN BARROW

Library of Congress Cataloging in Publication Data

Libo, Kenneth.
    We lived there too.

    1. Jews—West (U.S.)—Addresses, essays, lectures.
2. Frontier and pioneer life—West (U.S.)—Addresses,
essays, lectures. 3. West (U.S.)—Ethnic relations—
Addresses, essays, lectures. 4. West (U.S.)—History—
Addresses, essays, lectures. I. Howe, Irving. 1920–
II. Title.
F596.3.J5L53   1984   978/.004924   84-11787
ISBN 0-312-85866-3

10 9 8 7 6 5 4 3 2

CONTENTS

9. *Religious Adjustments*

10. *Emerging Communities*

11. *Secular Influences*

In the preparation of this work, which began in 1978 and continued until 1984, many libraries and archives were visited and many scholars consulted who with unstinting generosity gave of their time and knowledge. We would like to thank in particular Jacob Rader Marcus, director of the American Jewish Archives at Cincinnati; Isidore S. Meyer, Editor Emeritus of *American Jewish History*; Norton B. Stern, editor of the *Western States Jewish Historical Quarterly*; and Rabbi Floyd S. Fierman of El Paso's Temple Mount Sinai for meeting with us and discussing their many outstanding publications, without which it would be difficult to imagine what the state of American Jewish scholarship would be like today.

Repeatedly, the following invaluable works proved especially helpful: *American Jewry • Documents • Eighteenth Century*, by Jacob Rader Marcus; *The Jews of the United States: 1790–1840, A Documentary History*, edited by Joseph L. Blau and Salo W. Baron; *Adventures in Freedom: Three Hundred Years of Jewish Life in America*, by Oscar Handlin; *Jews and Judaism in a Midwestern Community: Columbus, Ohio, 1840–1975*, by Marc Lee Raphael; *Mordecai M. Noah: Jacksonian Jew*, by Jonathan Sarna; *Strangers Within the Gate City: The Jews of Atlanta, 1845–1915*, by Steven Hertzberg; *The Making of an Ethnic Middle Class: Portland Jewry Over Four Generations*, by William Toll; *Architects of Reform: Emanu-El of San Francisco, 1849–1980*, by Fred Rosenbaum; *Zion in America*, by Henry L. Feingold; *Our City: The Jews of San Francisco*, by Irena Narell; *House of Harmony: Concordia-Argonaut's First 130 Years*, by Bernice Scharlach; *Jewish Roots in Arizona*, by Joseph Stocker; *The Standard Club of Chicago, 1869–1969*; *100 Years of Jewry in San Antonio*, by Frances R. Kallison; *Dakota Diaspora: Memoirs of a Jewish Homesteader*, by Sophie Trupin with Anne Moose; *The History of the Jews of Philadelphia*, by Edwin Wolf 2nd and Maxwell Whiteman; *The History of the Jews of Milwaukee*, by Louis J. Swichkow and Lloyd P. Gartner; *History of the Jews of Los Angeles*, by Max Vorspan and Lloyd P. Gartner, and *A Jewish Tourist's Guide to the U.S.*, by Bernard Postal and Lionel Koppman.

We also owe special debts of gratitude to Abraham Peck and Fannie Zelcer of the American Jewish Archives; Nathan M. Kaganoff, librarian of the American Jewish Historical Society at Waltham, Massachusetts; and Ruth Kelson Rafael, archivist of the Western Jewish History Center at Berkeley, California, for helping us to find our way through the incredibly rich collections of Judaica Americana housed in these three institutions.

This book would have been all the less complete had we not benefited from the pioneering efforts of Jeanne Abrams of the Rocky Mountain Historical Society at Denver; Molline Cassman of the Omaha Section of the National Council of Jewish Women; Lora Meyer of the Jewish Historical Society of Oregon; and Lillian Krantz-Sanders of the Oral History Project of Kansas City, Missouri. Without their collective work, together with that of Ruth Rafael, Norton Stern, and their associates in the field of oral history, it would have been impossible for us to explore certain crucial aspects of our shared American heritage.

We are equally grateful for the guidance, hospitality, and expertise furnished by Carol Gendler of the Omaha Jewish History Project; John Livingston of the University of Denver; Everett E. Cooley of the University of Utah; Blaine P. Lamb of Arizona State University; Elsa Freudenthal Altshool, Carmen Freudenthal, E. J. Stern, and John, Francis, and Nellie Hernandez of Las Cruces, New Mexico; Howard Shorr of Theodore Roosevelt High School and Stephen E. Breuer of the Wilshire Boulevard Temple in Los Angeles; Ralph Hancock of San Diego; Mary Sarber of the El Paso Public Library. Also, special thanks to Brenda Weisberg Meckler of Phoenix, Arizona; Mrs. Bert Fireman of Douglas, Arizona; Lawrence Pratt of Hays, Kansas; Ruth Fischlowitz Marget and Dan Makovsky of St. Louis, Missouri; Frank Adler of Kansas City, Kansas; Charles H. Elias of Little Rock, Arkansas; Roy P. Drachman of Tucson, Arizona; Leo Lewinson and Israel Carmel of Albuquerque, New Mexico; Adele Stern and Saul Viener of Richmond, Virginia; Michael H. Cardozo of Washington, D.C.; Edward J. Bristow and Myron Brinig of New York City; Jeanne Bornstein and Jerry Wertkin of the Museum of American Folk Art in New York City; Carl Bibo of Santa Fe, New Mexico, and Allen and Cynthia Mondell, creators of the superb documentary film *West of Hester Street.*

It is a pleasure to acknowledge a deep sense of gratitude to Andor Braun, stalwart friend and teacher, for patiently and perseveringly reading through early drafts of this book and offering a wealth of suggestions, and to Helen Barrow, book designer *par excellance.* Also, special thanks to Judy Cohen Sandman for being a sharp and persistent critic of an early draft, and to Peter Shen and Alphe Casper for their many useful suggestions.

It has been our privilege to benefit from a number of invaluable suggestions from Richard C. Wade, Distinguished Professor of History at the City University of New York, and Moses Rischin, Professor of History at San Francisco State University. We hope that our efforts convey in some way our sincere appreciation for their enormous contributions in the fields of American urban and regional history.

Finally, a word of gratitude to the godmother of this book, Joyce Engelson, an editor of insight and fortitude who provided help, encouragement, and patience all along the way.

In this book of documents and pictures we have tried to tell the story of those Jews who, together with other pioneers of differing ethnic and cultural backgrounds, settled on or near the American frontier and, in the process of meeting and mingling there, contributed to the emergence of a distinctly American way of life. Our story begins with the migration of Sephardim and Ashkenazim (Jews of Spain and Germany and their descendants) in the seventeenth and eighteenth centuries, when the eastern edge of America in a very real sense was the western frontier of Europe. From this starting-off point we follow Jewish settlers from central Europe in their push inland in the 1800s to the Ohio Valley and the upper reaches of the Mississippi River; to the Old Southwest, the Great Plains, and the Pacific coast; from the Rocky Mountains to the High Sierras. Our story concludes with the migration west of hundreds of thousands of East European Jews in the late nineteenth and early twentieth centuries.

We believe what these Jews accomplished is as significant in its own way as the collective experience of those Jews who settled in the large American cities of the Northeast around the turn of the century and about whom so much has justifiably been written. We say this in recognition of the courage and stamina it took to risk their lives by traveling across a vast ocean and then to decide to go on, beyond the known American Jewish world. By so doing a new era in Jewish history was brought about, an era—despite its many regrettable shortcomings—of egalitarianism and brotherhood with Gentiles that arose out of a pressing need to work together in civilizing the wilderness. It is with this in mind that we have attempted to bring together here a collection of documentary materials which, at the very least, particularizes the extraordinary achievements of these people.

It may interest our readers to know something about how this book was put together. Most of the documents were collected in the course of a number of trips taken through every section of the country. Wherever we traveled, we had the good fortune to meet and spend time with people from all walks of life who often went out of their way to help us find just the right picture or account from a local newspaper, a family album, an unpublished memoir, a long neglected book. Sometimes we found what we were looking for in the attic of an old house or the back room of a dilapidated store. At other times we sifted through priceless materials in public and private collections, in archives and libraries, for weeks and months at a time. We also talked with a number of old-timers who made us appreciate the courage and human understanding it took to bring a little Jewish life to sparsely settled areas of this country where, before their arrival, Jews had rarely if ever been seen by the people among whom they had elected to live.

Much of what we came across is simplicity itself, honest and heartfelt accounts of hope and suffering, as evidenced in the recollections of Sarah Thal, a North Dakota homesteader's wife who found herself caught between the Laws of *Kashruth* and the dictates of nature, and Anna Solomon, who with her husband, Isadore, founded the frontier town of Solomonville, Arizona. Other accounts by people like Abraham Isaacson, a small-town Southern merchant, and Oscar Straus, the first Jew to occupy a post in the cabinet of an American President, reveal that larger gift C. Wright Mills once called "the sociological imagination." Equally important are the impassioned speeches of David Einhorn, Ernestine Rose, and other major Jewish social reformers who force us to feel the same outrage that motivated them to cry out against cruelty and injustice. We have also included a number of translations from the Yiddish in which we have tried to show the lively interest that immigrant writers and poets took in their newly adopted land. See especially the selection from I. J. Schwartz's epic poem, *Kentucky* (p. 150), Yehoash's paeon to the Colorado Mountains (p. 309), and Isaac Raboy's account of the experiences of a North Dakota Jewish cowboy (p. 288).

The pictures accompanying these accounts are meant to show what Jewish pioneers in a variety of situations looked like, as well as what America looked like to them. Wherever possible, we have tried to convey through images a sense of movement, immediacy, vitality; a feeling of being right in the middle of things; an understanding of precisely what it was like to be a Jewish pioneer at a number of different stages in the history of the American West.

Because we deal with so many different experiences within a period covering three centuries of American history, it is impossible in a book of this kind to get as far beneath the surface of life as we would have liked. However, we hope that at least we have cleared the air of a number of stereotypical notions about Jews who went west (not everyone was a merchant or peddler, for example) and thus prepared the way for future scholars to delve more deeply into both the individual and collective achievements of the people whose words and deeds fill the pages of this book.

A final note: This book is the result of an editorial collaboration. We have consulted with each other in the preparation of all its parts, but we would like to make clear the main division of labor. Irving Howe is responsible for the Introduction and Epilogue, while Kenneth Libo is responsible for the documentary materials and interconnecting passages.

THE EDITORS

THE AMERICAN EXPERIMENT
by Irving Howe

FOR AT LEAST TWO THOUSAND YEARS, *wandering and migration have been an integral part of Jewish experience. Often enough this was due to the harassment, persecution, and expulsions to which Jews were subjected in the Christian world. Migration came to serve as a strategy for survival, what one historian has called "the escape valve of Jewish history." But with time these enforced upheavals must also have produced a psychology of restlessness, and for at least some Jews frequent journeying from country to country became a habit, perhaps even a source of pleasure.*

Of the three thousand Jews living in the United States in 1790, some had come for the familiar reasons—to escape harassment, to find livelihood, to worship unmolested. Probably the majority came for such reasons. But others had more personal motives. Insofar as we can judge from surviving letters and documents, these early settlers—many of them Sephardim, that is, descendants of Jews who had settled in Spain and Portugal—were a hardy group of men and women. If a good number were merchants looking for snug corners in the coastal towns, a few were merchant-adventurers ready to risk life on the frontier in order to trade with Indians.

Like at least some of the early Christian settlers, the Jews who came to the colonies saw the New World as a place where they could move—more easily, they hoped, than in the Old World—into affluence, comfort, position. That they also found in America a certain liberality of spirit toward their religion in most (though by no means all) of the colonies was an added incentive, a pleasing major benefit.

This liberality of spirit was at least as much a result of the practical circumstances prevailing in the colonies as it was of any belief in the principle of religious toleration. Except for Boston, there was no coastal town in colonial America where any single religious or ethnic group exerted a clear predominance. In New Amsterdam (later New York), there were as early as 1643, according to the historian Lawrence Raesly in his Portrait of New Amsterdam, *"eighteen different languages spoken," and the "diversity of religions, all exercised privately excepting Calvinism, was equally surprising . . . Roman Catholicism, English Puritanism, Lutheranism, Anabaptism," and so on. The same held true, in varying degrees, for colonial Rhode Island, Pennsylvania, South*

Carolina, and Georgia. The very diversity of religious devotion made for a certain tolerance in practice if not principle; the difficulties of exercising a strict discipline within a given colony or, still less plausibly, over all the scattered colonies also helped. What helped still further was that in 1740 Great Britain enacted a Naturalization Law which encouraged emigration to the colonies by enabling aliens, after seven years of residence, to become British citizens. This gave Jews the right to vote in the British colonies even though they could not yet do so in the mother country. Still, to avoid too rosy a picture, I should add that the colonial Jews were steadily subject to the threat of disfranchisement at the whim of colonial authorities, who in day-to-day affairs pretty much held all the power in their hands. One can speak of a liberality of spirit in the colonies only with some discounts and qualifications.

The Jews emigrating to colonial America enjoyed the fruits of this tolerance, yet they can hardly be said to have crossed the Atlantic with a high sense of mission, some idea that they were fulfilling an obligation of Jewish faith. The Puritans, at least in the seventeenth century, had fervently believed they were the bearers of an "errand into the wilderness." In the unspoiled land they would create "a new Israel," a theocratic society in which a purified Christianity would shape the whole of existence. But the children of Abraham—or the scatter of them who made their way to the colonies—were happily free of any burdens of historic mission. They were not zealots, they were not grandiose. What they wanted was a little space for themselves. We who, for good reasons, are inclined these days to be suspicious of zealotry, may well feel a certain admiration for their good sense.

In the history of the United States as a nation, these early Jewish settlers have only a modest importance. We can all remember from our school years the stories about Jewish merchants supplying Washington's hard-pressed armies; perhaps we may also remember that he had a loyal adjutant who was Jewish. But you could write a respectable history of the United States in the seventeenth and eighteenth centuries without giving more than a few paragraphs to the Jews. For that matter, you could write a history of the Jews in those centuries without more than a passing mention of Jewish settlers in the New World.

The Jews scattered across the colonies at the time of the Revolution had no communal organization binding them from Georgia to New England. The internal structure of particular synagogues could be as tight as those the Jews in Europe had worked out, or been forced to work out. As long as there was only one congregation in each community, the local Elders could exert control over rituals and mores, holding the threat of excommunication over the heads of those whose participation was slack or opinions were heterodox. But each congregation had to get along independently, even though the Sephardic ritual and liturgy dominated synagogue practice throughout the colonial period. Yet despite a strict inner discipline, one can detect the beginnings of that local autonomy which has characterized Jewish life in America. Distance helped. What the Jews of Charleston did was pretty much their own business; what the Jews of New York did was their own business too. Inevitably, this led to gradual differences in communal structure and styles of worship.

Some Jews in early America—we cannot know how many—dropped away from the local synagogues and faded into the Gentile population. But most kept a measure of Jewish commitment, and this meant to know something about the history of one's people. It meant to know that back in Europe, despite the stirrings of the Enlightenment, Jews generally lived as, at best, a tolerated alien minority which lacked whatever civil rights the Christian populace had managed to acquire. As they came here, the Jews must immediately have been struck by the fact that some of the leading political figures, those soon to become the founding fathers of the young republic, were espousing a doctrine of universal liberty and religious toleration. This doctrine was of course violated in practice, as all such doctrines are; Negroes were enslaved and Jews and Catholics suffered discrimination in several colonies. But even the least self-aware Jew could not fail to grasp how important it was that the doctrine, the guiding norm of tolerance, had been put forward in public life.

If the Jews did not press for their rights as a strongly disciplined group within the new country, they did speak up loudly when they saw an opportunity. In August 1790, President Washington visited Newport, Rhode Island, and the Jewish community of that town, fairly substantial by the standards of the day, sent him an "Address" praising his service as "Chief Magistrate" of a "government erected by the majority of the people—a government which to bigotry gives no sanction." Washington graciously replied by noting that in the new republic, "all possess alike liberty of conscience," and then repeating, a shade less elegantly, the phrase of the Newport Jews: "The government," he said, "gives to bigotry no sanction."

Symbolically, at least, this was a moment of great importance in both the history of the nation and the history of the Jews. Generations of American Jews, if they felt ill-treated, could always point to the exchange at Newport as a buttress for their case. Later national and state administrations, to be sure, would continue to pursue both the policies and practices of racial prejudice; and a good many social and economic institutions would indulge a barely disguised anti-Semitism long after "any trace of bigotry" had formally been removed from government. But what mattered most was that the principle of toleration had been articulated by the "Father of Our Country," as it would be by John Adams, Jefferson, and Madison. All of their statements, footnotes as it were to the Bill of Rights, permitted the first major "emancipation" enjoyed *by Jews in the modern world. Surely there is something emblematic—charming, also—in the story that when a parade was organized in 1789 in Philadelphia to celebrate the new Constitution, one of the refreshment tables at the end of the parade route served food conforming to Jewish dietary laws.*

These early settlers continue to hold our interest for reasons as simple as they are fundamental—reasons of human curiosity, that fellow feeling one has upon striking up an acquaintance with ancestors. We read the letters of the Gratz family, for instance, wondering what might lie behind their words, what was the price in tension and effort as they went about finding a place for themselves in the new, unfamiliar world of colonial America.

We see the ways in which the experiences of these first Jewish settlers contain the seeds of the later experiences of Jews in America—for instance, the anxiety of a woman like Abigail Franks that her daughter may marry a Gentile (already, the intermarriage problem!) and the hesitation of Jews to become involved in American politics lest it make them a target of prejudice and enmity (see the extremely interesting section on page 53).

These Jewish settlers were not particularly learned in Judaic texts or secular knowledge; they were only moderately pious; and they made little contribution to the formative thought or culture of the republic. Mostly, they seem to have lacked the intensity of belief and introspectiveness of mind that, rightly or wrongly, we associate with modern Jewish life. But they also lacked some of the flaws, the nervous excesses we have come to associate with modern Jewish life. In word and picture, they give off an aura of self-assurance, stability, and strength. They worked hard; they accepted the obligations of citizenship; they held their families together, sharing in the gains and costs of being pioneers. If they left no books or thoughts worth remembering, they did establish themselves as independent Americans in the New World—distinctive, indeed, for being in many ways like other Americans. Here at last, despite some handicaps and prejudices imported from Europe, it was possible for Jews to stand erect, as it had often not been possible in Europe. Here they could be equals among free men.

IT IS IN 1838 that the United States enters, so to say, Jewish history. This is the year of the first large-scale migration of European Jews to the New World—not just as individuals but in organized groups from Germany. Until then there had been scattered, sometimes chance journeys; now there was a structured and purposeful Jewish effort to find a new home. Again, if this was not an event of the first magnitude for the history of the United States, it certainly was for the future of the Jews. For here begins one of the two great migrations of European Jews in the modern era, indeed, one of the two great modern experiments in Jewish self-determination.

The migration of the German Jews breaks conveniently into two phases. First there comes, during the 1830s, a group from Bavaria, mostly small-town Jews both poor and culturally limited. Lacking capital or skills, many of these people live as peddlers, fanning out across the South and Midwest, and gradually settling down in a multitude of American towns. Starting in the 1840s, a second group of German Jews comes to the United States: it is better educated, more affluent, and includes a small number that had thrown in its lot with the German democratic revolution of 1848 and must now flee to political exile. This second wave of German Jews brings some experience in commerce, which helps prepare them for careers as businessmen, both large and small, in America.

Between 1840 and 1880, it is estimated, the Jewish population in the United States increased from 15,000 to 250,000, with most of these newcomers arriving from Germany. For the first time the Jews became a felt presence in such cities as New York, St. Louis, San Francisco, Cincinnati, Philadelphia, and Baltimore. Raised in a tradition of communal organization, they soon set up a network of synagogues, centers, fraternal societies, and cultural groups. In the smaller cities and sometimes the countryside they improvised, for a time, a rough balance between participating in the social and cultural life of the already established Gentile German community and creating their own, distinctively Jewish institutions. In the larger cities they were numerous and self-confident enough to keep mostly to themselves, sustained as they were by the network of extended German-Jewish families that in strength and intricacy resembled clans or tribes.

These families often formed not merely groupings of kinship but economic structures. One brother, barely established in a little business, would send for another brother; cousin for cousin; and the result was often a complex chain in which personal relations could hardly be distinguished from business relations. Here is a characteristic example from the memoirs of Joseph Hays:

> About two weeks after I had been in Cleveland I became impatient to get out and earn money for myself. My brother Kaufman . . . sent me out to a printing office to buy a large pasteboard box covered with black oilcloth and straps. When I returned with it, Kaufman selected my first stock. . . . Next morning bright and early Kaufman gave me a paper upon which was written the necessary questions and answers which I needed in selling goods, getting money changed, and obtaining food and lodging. . . . [Days later] after my supper I emptied my money bag on the table. My sister Yetta helped me count it. She laughed and encouraged me as she stacked the money, and said, "Du wirst noch ein Kotzen sein [You will be a rich man someday]."

But a word of caution. There is a legend that persists to this day among American Jews that all the German-Jewish immigrants, upon coming to this country, achieved rapid economic success and then smoothly integrated themselves into American middle-class life. As with most legends, this has a grain of truth to it, but hardly more than a grain. Trudging from village to village in the sparsely populated reaches of the country and not always encountering a cordial welcome, many of the early German-Jewish peddlers were quite poor. Wanting to establish a secure family life, perhaps having accumulated some savings, they would settle after a time in one or another town, to set up a clothing or dry goods store and scratch out a living. They profited, of course, from the expansion of the country, but often rather slowly and only through the steady exertion of that industriousness for which they were noted. In turn, they contributed to the transformation to commercial capitalism that was taking place in nineteenth-century America by introducing more sophisticated mechanisms of trade and credit than were commonly known in outlying parts of the country. A study by William J. Parish illustrates this point:

> *The fact that wherever there was hope for commerce in New Mexico, there was most likely to have been a German Jewish merchant . . . certainly holds more significance than merely that of a ubiquitous business man. The Jewish pueblo trading post; the Jewish sutler; the Jewish storekeeper . . . the Jewish sedentary merchant of the cities . . . the Jewish drummer . . . in total these businessmen had both social and economic influence far beyond their numbers.*
>
> *The goods he possessed or commanded, and the understanding and sympathy that came with his cosmopolitanism, brought easy access to every door. His solid education and his acuteness in its use made it second nature for him to exert leadership in family and community problems. Solomon Floerscheim, while traveling the countryside in the collection of sheep accounts, became widely known as "Doctor" because of his commonsense application of a minimum of medical knowledge. All these merchants were scribes for a population that was more than half illiterate.*

At about this time there begins the rise of major German-Jewish fortunes in the large cities, as well as of a solid German-Jewish middle class. Prosperous burghers, strongly devoted to maintaining family ties, not often troubled by intense religious or political convictions, devoted to a mild version of traditional German culture, these people lived by a code of hard work, personal moderation, and social respectability. By the end of the nineteenth century, writes Barry Supple in an important study, the German-Jewish business families had coalesced into a homogenous elite within but distinct from the larger society of New York City. All were wealthy, most were connected with the financial world; they went to the same clubs, attended the same synagogues, chose their friends and wives from within their own limited circle, were connected with the same philanthropic and communal activities. . . .

[Binding these families and clans] was an attitude imported from the Old World: that of family solidarity and unity. For the Seligmans, the Guggenheims, and [Jacob] Schiff, Friday night was family night—a time when children and grandchildren gathered in the patriarch's house. "I have made it a rule," wrote Schiff in 1890, "to spend Friday evening exclusively with my family, and I can under no circumstances vary from this."

The German-Jewish immigrants were not, of course, exclusively peddlers and storekeepers, on the one hand, nor financiers, on the other. Many settled into a wide range of trades and businesses. Especially important is the clothing industry, which in the second half of the nineteenth century was being transformed from hand sewing to machine manufacture. German Jews took a dominant place within this industry, quick to see the advantages offered by the relatively small capitalization required for opening a garment shop. Within a few decades they would be edged out by East European Jews, but meanwhile the clothing industry provided a major stepping stone in their economic rise.

PERHAPS the single major achievement of the German Jews in America was in the area of religion. By the late eighteenth century the Enlightenment, or Haskala, had already made considerable encroachments upon German-Jewish orthodoxy. Intellectual figures like Moses Mendelssohn proposed a new way of life for those who wished to be both Jews and rationalist humanists. Secular studies would be introduced in Jewish education; long-encrusted rituals, taken to be mainly superstitions, would be cut away from religious services; the synagogue would be granted both a new dignity and the aesthetics of organs and choirs. Jewish life, in a word, would be "modernized," so that in substance and style it would more closely approach the life of cultivated and secularized Germans. Out of this tradition arose "Reform Judaism" as a distinctive religious tendency among the German Jews. Some of Reform, as Nathan Glazer writes, did indeed consist of "a largely opportunistic desire to adapt to Western norms," and was attacked on these grounds by the beleaguered Orthodox (as later, in our time, it would be sneered at by Jewish intellectuals who chose not to pray but implied that if they did pray, they would do so only in the ways of authentic orthodoxy). But to stop with Glazer's description would be a little unjust. For there was genuine thought and useful innovation in Reform, a seri-

*ous wish to separate the kernel of faith from the crust of superstition. A move-
ment in Germany called* Wissenschaft des Judentums *dared for the first time
to approach the sacred texts and historical practices of Judaism from a critical
point of view, somewhat as Ludwig Feuerbach and David Strauss would approach Christianity. One result was the discovery that such Reform innovations as preaching, upon which the Orthodox heaped scorn, could find a
sanction in the Jewish past. All in all, then, the Reform tendency simplified
and aestheticized Jewish services, stressed Biblical imperatives over Talmudic
interpretations, and insisted that Jewish life, both communal and religious,
had to change in accord with changing historical circumstances.*

*By the 1840s and 1850s, a transplanted Reform started to win a foothold
with the German-Jewish community in the United States, and very soon afterward it gained a large following. For some time the religious life of the German Jews was polarized between orthodoxy and Reform. One reason why
orthodoxy proved to be vulnerable among them, writes Lucy Dawidowicz, was
that in the United States "there was no sufficiently strong bulwark of traditional Judaism to withstand Reform's onslaughts. There were no venerable institutions of Jewish learning and no great Talmudists [in the United States] to
retard, if they could not altogether halt, the pace of Reform, which often
meant the abandonment of traditional observance."*

*Reform Judaism was fortunate in having as leader and spokesman Isaac
Mayer Wise, a rabbi not distinguished for scholarship but charged with energy, optimism, and shrewdness. Almost intuitively, Wise understood how
Reform could best adapt itself to American circumstances and thereby help its
followers remain Jews—seldom pious, seldom learned, yet unmistakably Jews.
At least part of what D. H. Lawrence writes about Benjamin Franklin—that
he "had no concern, really, with the immortal soul. He was too busy with social man"—seems also to have been true about Wise. Under his realistic and
level-headed guidance, the quantity of Hebrew in the prayers was reduced and
English translation substituted. The separation of men and women within the
synagogue was brought to an end. Such measures were practical and cohesive:
they made sense. For the German-Jewish middle class, as its circumstances
improved, Reform created a communal-religious life that was dignified yet
made no extreme demands on one's soul or spirit, and that narrowed the differences in style between the services of Jews and those of surrounding Protestant
communities.*

*Remember that by and large these Jews did not, like many of the later East
European immigrants, consider themselves to be in galut, or "exile." The idea
that Jews lived in the Diaspora—central to the whole of Jewish life since the
fall of the Second Temple—had gradually weakened among the German Jews
so that now, pleased with their new country, they saw the United States as*

their natural home. They tended to shift their interests toward the realm of culture, bringing music, books, and intellectual enlightenment to the towns and cities in which they lived—this was a way to be at once good Jews, good Germans, and now, good Americans. Even back in Germany they had regarded Judaism as primarily a structure of faith and observance; it was not, as for the Jews of eastern Europe, an encompassing culture, a total way of life. In the long run, as its opponents have charged, Reform may have provided a smoothly planed slope down which one could easily slip away from both Judaism and Jewish life. Indeed, by the 1870s, there appeared in New York a group of Reform Jews, led by Felix Adler, who decided that since Reform stressed universal moral values and hoped to ground belief in reason, there was no longer any need to maintain a distinctive or Jewish community. These people formed the Ethical Culture Society, which has since devoted itself to a humanist ethic and a somewhat bleached piety. But the main effect of Reform during the nineteenth century was to strengthen, not weaken, the bonds of the Jewish community. It created new institutions, increased the number of active congregants, and in 1875 established a rabbinical school, the Hebrew Union College of Cincinnati, which would become a major center of Jewish learning.

PERHAPS *the most notable fact about the German-Jewish settlement was that it did not remain confined to a few Eastern cities. Frequently mobile and adventuresome, the German Jews spread out across the entire nation, thereby rendering the Jews a nationwide community. By the 1870s or so, there was barely an American town without its little gathering of Jews. In many of these they soon established synagogues or temples, or if their number was too small for that, they would regularly travel for holiday services to the nearest city. When the eastern European Jews started to arrive later in the nineteenth century and some of them occasionally drifted into the smaller towns, they were not treading completely unmarked territory. A Jewish welcome—helpful if not always warm—was usually waiting for them.*

It would be hazardous to offer a simple generalization about the reception these German Jews met in the United States. Only occasionally, if we can trust their own memoirs and recollections, did they encounter open hostility or rejection; rarely if ever the open evidences of the "Hep! Hep!" riots they had sometimes suffered in Europe. Most of the time they were received in the Midwestern and Southern towns with a quizzical mixture of amiability and suspicion. Protestant Americans, relatively isolated in small towns, had often not so much as seen a living Jew; they were curious about these "sons of Abraham," and only the more fanatical among them expressed fears of alien contamination. Some of the Midwestern Protestants were descendants of the New England Puritans, in whose imaginations the Jews had always held a promi-

nent, if anomalous, position. What is more, the German Jews proved fairly easy "to take," certainly easier than the East European Jews a few decades later. The German Jews spoke German, and that enabled them to blend with other "Dutchmen." They were rarely religious zealots or flaming radicals. They did not make their "Jewishness" into a hermetic or total way of life. They wore no strange religious costumes nor insisted upon "outlandish" rituals. Friendly, they yet maintained an inner communal discipline. They established temples that, in certain respects, were not so different in style and appearance from Protestant churches—indeed, they sometimes used abandoned churches for their temples. And, most important of all, they were sober, hardworking people whose values meshed pretty well with those of sober, hardworking Protestants.

For the German Jews the Civil War brought a moral test, and they passed it about as well as most other people in the United States. A small group of survivors from the revolution of 1848 enlisted in the Union Army, enthusiastic in their support of the anti-slavery cause. Some merchants in the South joined with old-line Southern Jews in support of the Confederacy. The rabbis responded across the entire spectrum of possibility, one of them, the distinguished David Einhorn, being forced to leave his Baltimore congregation and move to Philadelphia because he was so outspoken a critic of slavery, while another, Morris Raphall of New York, offered a cumbersome half-apology for slavery. The shrewd Isaac Mayer Wise, triumphantly Americanized, found ways to trim and duck. The Jews did not, as a body, take a firm stand on the slavery issue, perhaps because they really had no nationwide agency through which to do so, and perhaps because each local community felt obliged to go along, or seem to go along, with the dominant sentiments surrounding it. When a fervent young woman like Ernestine Rose threw herself into the cause of abolition, she had to step outside the Jewish community. It was not a community prepared for the fervor or high idealism of abolitionism.

The German Jews had many qualities that native Americans could admire. In the cities, German Jews created an elaborate structure of hospitals, nurseries, charities, clinics, and schools, and this must have appealed deeply to that part of the Protestant population that still held firm to the ethic of "providing for your own." (Carl Schurz, the Gentile German leader, noted in 1871 an astonishing proliferation in New York City alone of Jewish social welfare agencies, adding that the German Jews "constitute less than a third, probably no more than a fourth of the total German population [yet give] three times as much for its charitable institutions as the Germans. . . .")

In the cities and smaller towns, the German Jews played a valuable part in maintaining cultural institutions—as the patrons and devotees of opera, library, lecture circuit, musical recital. Especially in the smaller towns, which were often culturally deprived, the German Jews helped acquaint their neigh-

bors with the virtues and pleasures of glee clubs, school orchestras, chamber music groups. All of this was worthy, solid, and sustaining—though it was not necessarily, or at least uniquely, Jewish. For the German Jews had neither a strong tradition of, nor a strong interest in, the idea of a distinctive Jewish culture, self-sustaining and historically rooted, which would touch upon every segment of communal and personal life. Their whole view of Jewishness was less intense and, if you wish, less fanatical than that of the East European Jews. They wanted to keep intact a portion of the old German-Jewish ways they had brought across the Atlantic; they wanted to maintain a version of the Judaic faith; but meanwhile they also wanted to find a place for themselves in American life through commercial success and cultural adaptation. It was their peculiar triumph—yet perhaps not wholly a triumph—that they managed simultaneously to achieve all of these objectives.

We tend to think of American pioneers as austere figures, living at the edge of settlement, experiencing great dangers and hardships, gradually conquering forest and plains. And there is of course a measure of truth in this perception. But it is good to remember that the German Jews, moving into towns where they might constitute a tiny and perhaps suspect minority, were also pioneers in their own ways. They opened stores rather than cleared the land, they wore business suits rather than linsey-woolsey; but the experience of migration, the shock of new ways of life and speech, the difficulties of adapting to unfamiliar settings, were as real and hard for them as for the earlier pioneers. There are different modes of heroism in the world, some dramatic and others mild, and one suspects a certain righting of the historical balance would result if we acknowledged that the settlement of the German Jews across the nation had its touches of heroism too.

WITH the mass migration of East European Jews that starts in the 1880s, we come to the major source of Jewish settlement in this country, indeed, to a major source of Jewish energy in our century. I cannot pretend in a few pages to pack in the material to which I have devoted a large book, World of Our Fathers, *but a few central points should be sketched here.*

For the East European Jews, the second half of the nineteenth century may be said to have formed one of those critical moments in human affairs when the accumulated mounds of historical inertia melt away and a path is cleared for new possibilities. A great burst of long-suppressed communal energies, half-guilty yearnings to break into the modern world, eagerness to embrace new and alien ideas, the flowering of a rich inner life marked by controversy and polemic, in short, a collective renewal of social and cultural life—all these coincide during the last several decades of the nineteenth century. A powerless people struggles to make its own will and purpose a substi-

tute for power; a suppressed people unable to make a revolution in history makes out of its yearnings a revolution in being.

Part of this forms, of course, another episode in the history of nineteenth-century nationalism in Europe. But one also wonders whether there is another instance, so poignant and dramatic, of a people lifting itself up through sheer decision, even desperation—another instance, I mean, of a people seeking to transcend its wretched circumstances through the sheer workings of the mind.

This passion for transformation finds two major outlets. First, there is a thrust toward cultural renewal. The disabilities of life in eastern Europe are taken for granted, yet within these cramped circumstances the Jews seek a kind of vertical liberation—a transcendence variously defined as religious or cultural but actually encompassing the two. Second, there is an enormous physical movement, mostly to America and a little to Palestine.

This passion for transformation seizes the liveliest portions of the East European Jewish community, filling them with hopes for freedom or at least relief, with yearnings for deliverance or at least a little more bread, with visions of a new Jewish life or at least a new Jewish character. The dream of creating through collective will a new Jewish character—active not passive, subject not object, erect not bowed, combative not acquiescent, self-defining not trembling—is shared by all the secular Jewish movements, whether Zionist, socialist, or folkist. And with it goes the chimera all of them also share: that it may yet be possible to achieve a "normal" Jewish life.

Like all other peoples in Europe, the Jews could not resist the power of romanticism, the most influential world outlook of the past two centuries. Romanticism penetrates the minds of younger Jews in Kiev, Vilna, and Warsaw, leading to radically new outlooks regarding the idea of nationhood, the conflicts of social classes, the possibilities of the individual self, indeed, just about everything that might be expected on this earth short of the coming of the Messiah.

Some years ago, in an essay I wrote for the catalogue of an exhibit organized by the Jewish Museum of New York, I suggested—no doubt a little fancifully—that the migration of East European Jews to America resembled "a collective utopian experiment." There had, after all, been systematic discussions among such Jews as to whether they should migrate to America, with the rabbinical authorities and the handful of wealthy merchants usually saying no and secularist Jews often saying yes. (A recent major work of scholarship, Jonathan Frankel's Prophecy and Politics, shows in rich detail the extent to which the issue of migration excited and split the East European Jewish community during the 1880s.) Now, for suggesting that the migration of the East European Jews to America resembled a collective utopian experiment, I was amiably rebuked by Professor Robert Alter, who wrote that most of the immigrants had barely been literate, they had come here for personal reasons, to escape the armies of the czar or in search of bread, and it was grandiose to speak of these simple people as coming to America in behalf of a shared, indeed, an exalted Jewish end. Well, I accepted this chastisement . . . but I was not convinced.

For what I came to believe in the course of writing World of Our Fathers is that the distinction between collective enterprise and personal goals was not, for the Jews, nearly so clear or precise as we may suppose. When your barely literate Jew, with his few scraps of Hebrew and his kitchen Yiddish, ran away from pogroms to sweat and sometimes starve in the slums of Chicago or New York, or to wander, lonely and anxious, to innumerable small towns, he was indeed thinking of himself—but he was thinking of himself as a Jew. It was characteristic of Jewish life that a sense of collective fate should become implanted in the consciousness of almost every Jew, whether well- or ill-lettered. You could not grow up a Jew, at least until recent decades in America, without having a keen sense that, for better or worse, you occupied a distinctive place in the scheme of things.

In any usual sense, of course, the migration of the East European Jews can hardly be called a "collective utopian experiment." Yet I found some confirmation for my hyperbole in the memoirs of Abraham Cahan, the Yiddish writer and editor who played a central role in the Jewish immigrant experience:

> Each new wanderer, ruined by a pogrom or seeking to improve his lot or caught up in the excitement of the exodus, thought he was trying to better his own condition only. . . . But soon every emigrating Jew moving westward realized he was involved in something more than a personal expedition. Every Jew . . . came to feel he was part of an historical event in the life of the Jewish people. Ordinary Jews became as idealistic and enthusiastic as intellectuals. Even Jewish workers and small tradesmen who had managed fairly well [in the old country] sold their belongings and joined . . . the move westward to start a new Jewish life. They did so with religious fervor and often with inspiring self-sacrifice.

Cahan, I believe, was entirely right. The Yiddish-speaking intellectuals like Dubnov and Zhitlovsky spun their theories; the Yiddish-speaking workers sang "Vos mir zenen zenen mir, aber iden zenen mir [Whatever we may be we may be, but Jews are what we are]." Theory and folk sentiment came together.

Now I am not saying that this sense of a special, even unique history was a direct cause of the migration of the East European Jews and, a little later, of their entry into American society and culture. Yet it was a major condition. It made the Jews self-conscious, it made them ambitious, it made them wary, it made them eager; it also made them wonder whether those goods of the alien *world they had been so intent upon acquiring were in fact worth acquiring. Psychologically, it enabled them to go.*

The sociologist W. I. Thomas has remarked, in a brilliant phrase, that the process of Americanization was devoted to "the destruction of memories" among the immigrants. Now, with peasants from the Balkans or farmers from Scandinavia, this may not have been too difficult a task, since some of these people had already been excluded from the cultures of their home countries. But the East European Jews, though already subject by the late nineteenth century to the shocks of the Enlightenment and no longer the religiously uni- fied people they had been for centuries past, still wanted, in their deepest per- suasions, to resist that "destruction of memories." An Italian or a Pole might submit to it and retain his religion, even a fair portion of his received customs, for he was, after all, a Christian coming to a Christian country. But a Jew sub- mitting to a "destruction of memories" ceased, in effect, to be a Jew. That this actually happened to a considerable number of immigrant Jews we know, but it did not happen to the Jews as a whole.

Let me put the matter more concretely. The East European Jews were dif- ferent from all other ethnic groups—and, indeed, from the earlier Sephardic and German-Jewish contingents—in that they brought with them their intel- lectuals. By and large, the others did not. The Jews didn't bring them all at once: In the first great wave of immigration, during the 1880s and 1890s, the Jews who came over tended to be ill-lettered, the social flotsam and jetsam of the shtctl, *the adventurers and the adventurous. But after the turn of the cen- tury when, for example, the important Yiddish writer Abraham Reisen comes to America and, a few years later, the gifted Yiddish poets calling them- selves* Di Yunge (*the Young Ones) also appear, there occurs an event of major importance in American Jewish history: a gradual reunification of the Yiddish- speaking intelligentsia, both religious and secular, with the masses of Yiddish- speaking immigrant workers.*

This point can hardly be overstated. An Italian professor of art in Florence or history in Bologna seldom had any reason to come to America. Those who came from Italy were the dispossessed, the landless peasants of the South, who barely had any relation with Italian high culture in the first place. But among the East European Jews there were very few professors—the czar had made sure of that. The Yiddish-speaking intelligentsia consisted of journalists, teach- ers, party spokesmen, and plain luftmenshen *who had no more reason to re- main in eastern Europe than the Jewish masses did. So they came here also, often working in the same shops as the ordinary people and living next door in the same tenements. This meant that immigrant Jewish life was to be remark- ably enriched, as it had never been in earlier decades. The new freedom of America enabled the Yiddish intelligentsia to express and to "live out" the vi-*

sions and ideologies it had accumulated in eastern Europe. It enabled the Yiddish intelligentsia to fulfill itself in the arts, so that those among the next generation, children of the slums, who were ambitious to become writers and artists came not from a deprived immigrant milieu cut off from its Old World cultural sources, but from a thriving and feverishly brilliant immigrant milieu that had kept its culture, had indeed brought it to flowering.

But still more. The Yiddish culture which the immigrant Jews brought over—an unstable mixture of religious custom and memory, newfound secular notions, radical theories—was itself in a state of extreme ferment, what might be called creative decomposition. A boy or girl growing up on the East Side didn't, as a rule, receive a fixed or rigid heritage; he or she was not often subject to the kind of strict Orthodox upbringing that Isaac Bashevis Singer has described in the memoirs of his Warsaw youth. Here everything was in flux, open to debate, so that such youngsters encountered a touch of rabbinic orthodoxy, a smattering of socialist ideology, a smidgin of Yiddish culture, all mixed up into a stew of excitement. Cultures sometimes reach their peaks of creativity just when they are starting to come apart. The Talmudic quickness of debate, the ferocious intensity of belief, the preference for open expression of feeling as against repressive gentility—all these strains of eastern European Jewish life, shifting during the last few decades of the nineteenth century in a secular and radical direction, would be carried over into American culture, there to reach both a climax of fulfillment and a drop into vulgarity.

Partly by training but also a little through sheer luck, the East European immigrant Jews proved to be reasonably well adapted to the styles and rhythms of American society. But not right away. It took some time, and paradox though it may seem, the fact that it had to take some time contributed to the success of their adaptation.

Newly arrived immigrant groups can bring with them at least two kinds of handicap. The first is a rigid determination to maintain themselves as a self-sufficient alien enclave within American society, resisting both genuine opportunities and delusionary enticements. The second is an excessive eagerness to race into the American mainstream, so that ethnic distinctiveness fades too quickly or is, at least, greatly weakened. Now, the first handicap means that the immigrant group, even while necessarily losing a portion of its Old World traditions, fails to establish a vital relation with the culture of the New World. It lives in a kind of sterile limbo, no longer sustained by the old yet unable to "catch on" with the new. The second handicap causes too rapid an assimilation (as, for instance, the ease with which the Irish in the nineteenth century took over urban political machines), and this may, in turn, lead to a loss of social and cultural opportunities that could become available only after a period of shared stumbling and learning in the New World.

More perhaps by intuition than policy, the East European Jews managed to avoid both of these extreme paths. Coming here in the late nineteenth century, they largely kept to themselves in the big cities and smaller towns, suffering terrible hardships in the sweatshops and as wandering peddlers, finding it very difficult to connect with, even understand, American political ways, and barely grazing American culture. But by the turn of the century, their morale sustained by the strong communities improvised in the American cities by both the religiously Orthodox and politically radical minorities, the immigrant Jews were somewhat better prepared to find a place for themselves in America. They were creating their own subculture, in which Yiddish was the common language, and this gave them a touch of dignity, a warrant for self-esteem. They did not have to feel, like so many other immigrants, totally lost in the chaos of America. By keeping themselves somewhat apart they were in fact preparing to break into the outer, the Gentile American world.

I would not, even in so condensed a summary, want to make this process seem without tension, conflict, pain, and loss. It was nothing of the sort. The immigrant Jews, bringing with them a centuries-old discipline in self-denial, were experts at the postponement of pleasure in order to achieve a better life later on—a better life for their children, seldom for themselves. Still, the tacit persuasion that the Jews had to stick together at least for a time, in their own streets and behind the shield of their own institutions, enabled them to gather strength for that breakthrough into America, "the land of opportunity," which all but the most zealous of the Orthodox and most doctrinaire of the radicals wanted to make. Historically speaking, their timing was right: they sensed when it was necessary to stay together and when it might be convenient to move apart.

If one looks at the central institutions established by the East European immigrant Jews—the trade unions, the landsmanshaften *(societies based on descent from the same European town or area), the political leagues and parties—it becomes clear that they were marked by an uneasy mixture of coherence and flexibility. I find in this mixture a keen intuition on the part of the immigrants. Their institutions were coherent enough to provide both material protection and cultural support, yet also flexible enough to enable them to begin a social rise after consolidating themselves in the immigrant quarters. The institutions the Jewish immigrants were improvising all served as a kind of home away from home. And this in at least two senses: away from the home of the old country, still remembered and even yearned for though rarely a place anyone wanted to go back to; and away from the home of the tenements in which they now lived, wretched, airless, cramped. The Jewish unions had of course to be bargaining agencies, but they were also social centers, political forums, and training schools for young people preparing to break into intellec-*

tual and sometimes professional life. Even so seemingly parochial an institution as the landsmanshaft, despite its nostalgic ties with the shtetl, helped Jews adapt themselves to America. It provided everything from immigrant versions of the native fraternal societies to "doing a little business" at meetings, business especially handy for insurance agents, young doctors without patients, melamdim doomed to pupils, Yiddish book salesmen, and other entrepreneurs.

The immigrant subculture in the large cities was at once tight and loose, strong in inner discipline yet somewhat anarchic in institutional life. Intuitively—and rightly—most immigrants resisted any notion of a kehillah (communal structure) that would speak for the entire community; they sensed that they needed enough organization to avoid chaos but not so much as to be shackled by a domineering leadership. By 1915, Horace Kallen was already writing about the "pluralism" of Jewish life in America, and while most of the immigrants knew nothing about either Kallen or his phrase, they in fact were steadily inching toward a pluralistic view of Jewish life, without severe boundaries or strict lines of command or theological and ideological rigidities.

Is it not a similar mixture of attitudes—a nervous resistance to Americanization together with a fierce eagerness to share its benefits—that accounts for the cultural achievements of the sons and daughters of the Jewish immigrants? And here again both the Orthodox and socialist segments of the immigrant world—minorities resisting success in its vulgar sense, clinging to their radically different versions of Jewishness, profoundly ambivalent about the whole American experience—endowed their children with a strong critical sense. A strong critical view of commercial values together with a growing appreciation of the American creed of equal opportunity: all this enabled the Jewish writers, artists, intellectuals, and critics both to express their own version of Melville's "No, in Thunder" and also to embrace what was best in the native tradition of democratic fraternity.

A large portion of the Jewish immigrants from eastern Europe was proletarianized soon after its arrival in this country. In fact, the first major Jewish working class appears in the large American cities, perhaps a shade before a Jewish working class is formed in Lodz and Warsaw. For immigrants without a long experience behind them of working-class life, immigrants often physically weak and malnourished, this enforced proletarianization constitutes a trauma. It was a trauma made all the more severe because it coincided with a physical uprooting from places of birth and being thrust into the strange precincts of a Protestant culture in the United States. This trauma may partly account for the militancy, the frequent heroism, and the radical idealism that marked the Jewish working class; it may also partly account for the passionate intensity with which the Jewish working class wished, so to say, to abolish itself by find-

ing an escape from the grimness of the shops. At once ready for a combative self-defense and alert to the possibilities of social escape, buoyed by the feverishly brilliant culture of Yiddish now being improvised in the New World yet acutely alive to the opportunities America offered them and their children, the immigrant Jews paid with the sweat and blood of self-sacrifice for the lives their children would make.

WE LIVED THERE TOO

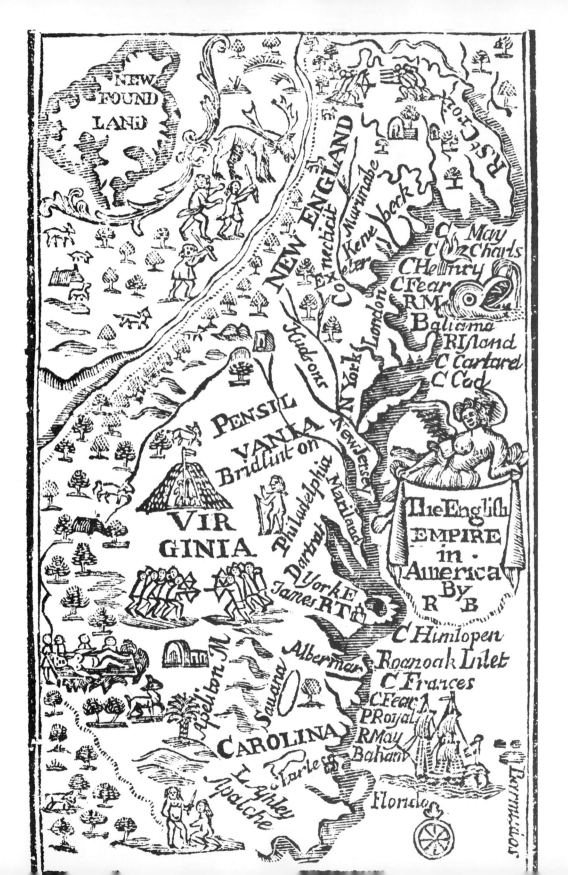

PART ONE
SEPHARDIM AND ASHKENAZIM
1630–1830

☙ THE FIRST JEWS *to settle in America did not come in large numbers as did the Puritans and the Cavaliers. Nor were they provided with a place of their own as the Quakers were in Pennsylvania and the Catholics in Maryland. No landholding companies enticed them with promises of generous subsidies. No government sponsored them. They arrived with little more than a special set of beliefs, sensitivities, skills that enabled some of them to negotiate their way into a new world, a new way of life with abilities others didn't have. It was a condition that led to the establishment of economic enclaves of considerable importance in the five major colonial towns of New York, Philadelphia, Newport, Charleston, and Savannah at a time when the population of America was overwhelmingly rural. What is clear even at this early stage is the complex nature of the collective Jewish experience in America. For already there are those who stay east and those who go west, those who come with special privileges and those who suffer discrimination, those who care about the faith of their fathers and those who do not, those who remain uprooted and those who transplant themselves.*

1
Confronting a New World

THE FIRST TO COME

ON AUGUST 3, 1492, one day after the decree expelling every avowed Jew from Spain was executed, Columbus set sail for the New World. At least one Jew was on board, Luis de Torres, an interpreter. The first European to set foot on American soil, de Torres was a descendant of a long line of Sephardim (Jews of Spain and Portugal) who, from the time of the Arab conquests in the eighth century to the reigns of the great kings of Aragon and Castile five hundred years later, had lived in peace and prospered among their Moslem and Christian neighbors.

It was a golden age in which Sephardim were encouraged by enlightened rulers to enter every known field of endeavor. Medicine, astronomy, law scholarship, poetry, commerce, architecture, music—Jews achieved prominence in all of these areas. In time an intellectual aristocracy came into being superior to that of any period in Jewish history since the days of the prophets.

Not until the onset of Christian fanaticism in Spain early in the thirteenth century did conditions for Jews begin to deteriorate. A climax was reached in 1391 when a wave of massacres swept through the entire peninsula, as a result of which large numbers of Jews accepted baptism in order to escape death. In 1478, the Spanish Inquisition was introduced against Jews who accepted Christianity outwardly but still remained Jews at heart. Called *Marranos*, derived from the Spanish word meaning "swine," they risked their lives by remaining true to their faith. After their expulsion from Spain in 1492, some found refuge in North Africa and the Turkish Empire while others fled to Portugal only to be expelled once more. A few then went on to Amsterdam where the Dutch, Protestants who themselves had suffered under the yoke of Catholic Spain, welcomed them.

By the middle of the seventeenth century, Amsterdam had a population of over two thousand Jews. The city had already become a major center of Jewish scholarship; however, what we would call freedom of expression was unwelcome. The unorthodox thinkers Uriel da Costa and Baruch Spinoza were both excommunicated for contradicting the religious establishment.

Wherever Sephardim settled in western Europe—in Hamburg and London, Bordeaux and Venice—they erected rigid social barriers, not only to separate themselves from Christians but also from German and Polish Jews (Ashkenazim) who had begun moving west in the seventeenth century. Convinced that theirs was the superior culture, even though by now Ashkenazim had produced great centers of learning, the Sephardim in these cities had little to do with those who refused to conform to their social habits, literary fashions, and religious traditions.

International merchants, they did a brisk trade in such New World commodities as sugar and tobacco, cotton and indigo. These products were the backbone of a colonial economy that Jews from western Europe with ready capital at their disposal were instrumental in developing, not only as traders and shippers but also as owners and managers of plantations in the New World. The records of the Inquisition suggest that there were Marranos in Mexico as early as 1528. By the end of the sixteenth century there was not a major Iberian settlement in the New World without at least one person of Jewish origin. They and those who followed introduced new ideas, new techniques, particularly in the sugar industry.

On the Portuguese island of São Tomé, off the west coast of Africa, Jews were among the first plantation owners to set up sugar factories on a large scale. They then brought sugar cane to Madeira and other islands farther north, and from there to Brazil, a Portuguese colony which by the seventeenth century had become the largest sugar-producing land in the world. By now many Jewish sugar planters, mill owners, and brokers were active in the industry, not only in Brazil but also in Jamaica, Curaçao, and Barbados.

Jews were among the first settlers in Brazil, where they lived freely and openly as Jews until the union of Spain and Portugal in 1580. Then came the rigors of the Inquisition. Only after the state of Pernambuco was conquered by the Dutch in 1630 were Jews *qua* Jews allowed back into Brazil. Soon a vigorous community numbering close to a thousand people came into being in the harbor city of Recife, complete with a synagogue, a rabbi, doctors, lawyers, peddlers, merchants—and even a main street called *Rua dos Judeos* (Street of the Jews). Once more a Jew did not have to fear being a Jew in the New World.

But in 1654 the Portuguese reconquered Brazil. Fearing the worst, the Jews fled Recife—either to Holland or to Dutch, French, or English colonies in the Caribbean where, by now, Jews were allowed to settle in small numbers. A total of sixteen ships were used to transport Jewish and Dutch colonists from Recife to their destinations. Fifteen arrived safely; however, the sixteenth was captured by a Spanish pirate ship only to be overtaken once more by a French privateer, the frigate *St. Charles.* After much negotiating, the master of the *St. Charles* agreed to bring the twenty-three Jewish men, women, and children on board as far as New Amsterdam, a Dutch West India Company trading outpost, for 900 guilders in advance and 1,600 on arrival.

As New Amsterdam came into view with its gallows and weather-

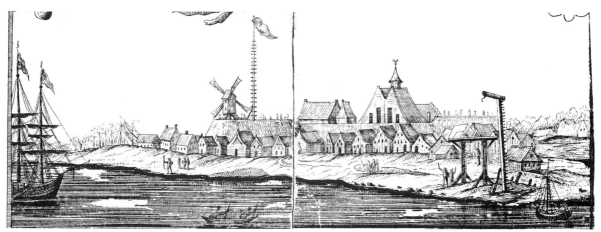

New Amsterdam, the way it looked to the first group of Jewish settlers in 1654.

beaten wooden houses dominating a raw, windswept landscape, these Jews were overcome with feelings of foreboding. They had reason to be, for New Amsterdam was still a frontier settlement filled with brawling sailers and rough-looking fur traders. Upon arrival, suit was brought against them by the master of the *St. Charles* for payment of the balance owed him and his crew. With no ready cash at their disposal, the newcomers were taken by force to the local *Stadt Huys* (courthouse) where a magistrate instructed that their goods be put up for auction and that two of their number, David Israel and Moses Ambrosius, be placed under civil arrest to ensure full payment.

Meanwhile, Peter Stuyvesant, governor of the colony, had started a campaign to drive the Jews out of New Amsterdam. Already predisposed by a strict Calvinist upbringing to look upon Jews as killers of Christ, Stuyvesant was disturbed by rumors from the Dutch West Indian island of Curaçao, where he was also governor. Just a few years before the arrival of the *St. Charles*, a boatload of Jews had come to Curaçao from Holland to oversee the cultivation of tobacco, indigo, and other crops, but were said instead to be exporting horses and lumber in addition to selling goods to the other colonists at exorbitant prices. Accepting these rumors at face value, Stuyvesant felt all the more inclined to address the following remarks to the colony's directors in Amsterdam:

. . . The Jews who have arrived would nearly all like to remain here, but learning that they (with their customary usury and deceitful trading with the Christians) were repugnant to the inferior magistrates, as also to the people having the most affection for you; the Deaconry also fearing that owing to their present indigence they might become a charge in the coming winter, we have, for the benefit of this weak and newly developing land, deemed it useful to require them in a friendly way to depart; praying also most seriously in this connection, for ourselves as also for the general community of your worships, that the deceitful race—such hateful blasphemers of the name of Christ—be not allowed further to infect and trouble this new colony, to the detraction of your worships and the dissatisfaction of your worships' most affectionate subjects.

IN RESPONSE TO Stuyvesant's attempts to get them to leave, the newcomers addressed an urgent appeal to their kinsmen in Amsterdam in the hope that they might help them in some way. It was in response to this appeal that the Jews of Amsterdam addressed the following petition to the directors of the colony:

. . . through lack of opportunity all cannot remain here [in Holland] to live. And as they cannot go to Spain or Portugal because of the Inquisition, a great part of the aforesaid people must in time be obliged to depart for other territories of their High Mightinesses the States-General and their Companies, in order there, through their labor and efforts, to be able to exist under the protection of the administrators of your Honorable Directors, observing and obeying your Honors' orders and commands.

It is well known to your Honors that the Jewish nation in Brazil have at all times been faithful and have striven to guard and maintain that place, risking for that purpose their possessions and their blood.

Yonder land is extensive and spacious. The more of loyal people that go to live there, the better it is in regard to the population of the country as in regard to the payment of various excises and taxes which may be imposed there, and in regard to the increase of trade, and also to the importation of all the necessaries that may be sent there.

Your Honors should also consider that the Honorable Lords, the Burgomasters of the City, and the Honorable High Illustrious Mighty Lords, the States-General, have in political matters always protected and considered the Jewish nation as upon the same footing as all the inhabitants and burghers. . . .

Your Honors should also please consider that many of the Jewish nation are principal shareholders in the Company.

UNWILLING TO OFFEND their own shareholders, the colony's directors rejected Stuyvesant's request, although from the tone of their response it is clear that they would have preferred to have acted otherwise.

We would have liked to effectuate and fulfill your wishes that the new territories should no more be allowed to be infected by people of the Jewish nation, for we foresee therefrom the same difficulties which you fear, but after having further weighed and considered the matter, we observe that this would be somewhat unreasonable and unfair, especially because of the considerable loss sustained by this nation, with others, in the taking of Brazil, as also because of the large amount of capital which they still have invested in the shares of this Company. Therefore, after many deliberations, we have finally decided that these people may travel and trade to and in New Netherland and live and remain there, provided the poor among them shall not become a burden to the Company or to the community, but to be supported by their own nation. You will now govern yourself accordingly.

    ◆§ ALTHOUGH IN Holland Jews were protected from religious and economic discrimination, under Stuyvesant's regime they were not allowed initially to pray in public, own property, employ Christian help, work at certain trades, or travel about freely. Jews were denied even the right to stand guard against Indian attacks on the grounds that they were "not admitted or counted among the citizens, as regards trainbands [forces of citizen soldiers] or common citizens' guards, neither in the illustrious City of Amsterdam nor (to our knowledge) in any city in the Netherlands."

At first, Jews were actually barred by law from doing anything more than defending themselves during an Indian attack. Deciding to test the law, Asser Levy, a native of Amsterdam, together with Jacob Barsimson petitioned for the right to stand guard like other settlers. Though they were turned down initially, in 1655 Levy acquired this right, thus opening the way for full citizenship rights for Jews in the New World.

A sense of what conditions were like for Jews in those early days is conveyed by the following courtroom drama involving "Nicasius de Silla, in his quality as sheriff of this city, plaintiff," and David Ferera, a Jewish peddler accused of the grave offense of demanding prompt payment from a customer.

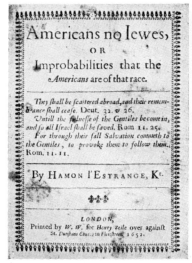

Americans no Jewes, *a pamphlet published in England in 1652 in response to the popularly held notion that the American Indians were descended from the Ten Lost Tribes of Israel.*

NICASIUS DE SILLA, IN HIS QUALITY AS SHERIFF OF THIS CITY, PLAINTIFF, VS. DAVID FRERE, DEFENDANT

July 3, 1656. David Frere [sic], a Jew, brought by order a certain chest with clothes to the house of Dirck van Schelluyne, Bailiff of this city, on condition that the Jew aforesaid should receive satisfaction therefor that evening, or at furthest next day. But . . . the above mentioned Jew was not willing to be contented with that but would have immediate payment or take the things back. Paying no attention to all the Bailiff's admonitions, warnings and protests he has . . . come with a cart before the Bailiff's dwelling and removed the chest therefrom, making use moreover of many words in his tongue, in presence of the Bailiff. . . . such proceedings, such unbecoming opposition and disturbance to the duties of the Bailiff . . . cannot be permitted but must be punished. The Sheriff having ex officio taken cognizance thereof, in support of justice, he concludes that the assigned beaver skins (which the Jew aforesaid claims as his pay) shall remain confiscated for the Sheriff, that the said Jew shall be publicly whipped at a stake and banished forth from the province of New Netherland, and that he provisionally shall go into close confinement. . . .

Defendant David Frere appears with an interpreter, Joseph de Koster, in court, requests copy of the demand to answer thereunto in writing by the next court day.

By the court it is, by plurality of votes, ordered and adjudged that defendant David Frere be imprisoned in the City Hall of this City and be

granted copy of the demand to answer thereunto in writing on the next court day.

EXTRAORDINARY MEETING HELD AT REQUEST OF DAVID D'FRERE

July 4, 1656. Joseph d'Coster [sic], interpreter for the prisoner David Frere, appears in court, insisting that defendant Frere be released from confinement under sufficient bail. When it was asked if Frere was ready to answer to the demand, he answered No since he could not do so without an attorney or writing, requesting time thereto until next Monday.

The court, by plurality of votes, orders and decides that David Frere shall remain in confinement until the case shall be definitely disposed of. The above Frere was notified on the part of the court through Joseph D'Coster, as interpreter, to prepare his defence to the demand and deliver the same to the Secretary.

SHERIFF DE SILLA REQUESTS COURT TO PRONOUNCE SENTENCE

July 13, 1656. Burgomasters and Schepens [magistrates] of the city of Amsterdam in New Netherland, having paid attention to the demand and conclusion of the Sheriff as well as the written answer and acknowledgment of the prisoner David Frere, and having maturely weighted everything material, have, after due deliberation, condemned, as they hereby do, the said David Frere for his aforesaid committed offence to pay a fine of eight hundred guilders . . . and to remain confined until the said moneys be paid.

TO THE GREAT HONORABLE LORDS, DIRECTOR GENERAL, AND HIGH COUNCILORS OF NEW NETHERLAND

July 24, 1656. David Ferera, Jew, residing here . . . frankly confesses his ignorance of Dutch laws and customs and lack of knowledge of the language, and therefore not knowing to have sinned so greatly . . . he . . . humbly requests of your Honors to please issue a writ of appeal. . . .

Your Honors' humble servant,
David Ferera
Joseph D'Acosta

PARTIES ORDERED TO CHOOSE ARBITRATOR

July 26, 1656. . . . the Honorable Director General and Council of New Netherland have ordered, to prevent costs and so dispatch the suit quickly, that parties under due compromise shall each choose an arbitrator . . . to the decision of whom, their chosen arbitrators, parties declare to submit themselves, to abide by the same and accomplish it, under bond of three hundred guilders to be forfeited by whoever shall not accept the same. . . .

Pursuant to the above deed of compromise, the arbitrators met together . . . and gave as their decision that the aforesaid David Ferere shall pay for the behoof of the Sheriff N. de Silla the sum of one hundred and twenty guilders and defray besides the costs of suit, estimated at fifty guilders, together with the costs incurred by this appearance.

THOUGH THREATENED with banishment, Ferera, as far as we know, was allowed to remain in New Amsterdam. There are no further incidents of this nature recorded in local court records—an indication, perhaps, of the success of Ferera and his supporters in protecting themselves from Christians inclined to disavow their financial obligations to Jews.

⋙ HOSTILE ATTITUDES toward Jews were by no means unusual in those days. In Spain and Portugal, Jews were still being burned at the stake for refusing to renounce their faith. In Poland in 1648 and 1649, over 100,000 Jews were murdered and their communities destroyed by Chmielnicki's bloodthirsty Cossacks. In England after hundreds of years of banishment, Jews were still forbidden legal entry. Nor were they any more welcome in colonial Virginia where the Church of England held sway.

The situation was just as grim in Puritan New England. Convinced that they had been chosen by God to establish a New Jerusalem on Massachusetts soil, the Puritans looked upon the Jews as a fallen people who could redeem themselves only by adhering to the Mosaic laws out of faith in Christ. To be sure, Puritans were capable of occasional acts of charity. In 1648 Solomon Franco, a merchant-adventurer from Amsterdam, was given a stipend of several shillings a week to tide him over in Boston while waiting for a ship to take him back to Holland. However, had Franco wanted to stay on, he would have had to become a Christian. Not until much later in the century were avowed Jews permitted to settle where Puritans were in power.

⋙ IN 1664 THE ENGLISH captured New Amsterdam, then a settlement of some one thousand five hundred inhabitants, and renamed it after King Charles II's brother, the Duke of York, to whom the king ceded all the land between the Connecticut and Delaware rivers. In the same year the presence of a group of Marranos in London was officially recognized by the king. Henceforth, Jews were allowed by the English to settle in the new colony. Nonetheless, laws were subsequently passed denying Jews in New York the right of public worship. As late as 1685 this right was granted only "to those that professe faith in Christ." Somehow Jews managed to circumvent such laws, for as early as 1692 mention is made in a public document of a Jewish house of worship in New York. In a map dated 1695 a site on Beaver Street is referred to as "the Jewes Synagogue." By now there were twenty or so Jewish families, comprising over 2 percent of the city's population. Though insignificant numerically, these Jews were already a force to be reckoned with in commercial affairs.

Near what is now Chatham Square, a "Jews Burying Place . . . in length about 52 feet, and Breadth about 50 feet" had been granted under Dutch rule. Among those interred there was Rachel Rodriquez Marques. She and her son Isaac were among the first of Bernard Baruch's ancestors to reach these shores.

Arriving in New York sometime before 1700, he [Marques] established himself as a shipowner whose vessels did business with three continents. He was a contemporary of the legendary Captain William Kidd . . . [whose] widow lived across the street from Isaac Marques. She [Captain Kidd's widow] was accepted in the best circles and eventually remarried a well-to-do, respected citizen.

Marques' choice of the city and his calling suggest a keen business judgment. New York at that time extended only two or three streets north of its wooden wall [near today's Wall Street]. Still, it was a bustling place of 3500 inhabitants. Its boom-town character was largely the result of the liberal attitude to maritime affairs, including piracy, taken by the Royal Governor of the colony, Benjamin Fletcher. . . .

Under Governor Fletcher, New York came to rival Newport and Charleston as a remarkably convenient place to dispose of seaborne commerce, with no embarrassing questions asked as to a cargo's origin. It has been said that under Fletcher's administration nearly every shipowner operating out of the city was suspected of piracy.

It would be colorful if I could claim descent from a pirate. Alas, the documentation I have assembled prevents my doing this. All available evidence indicates that Isaac Marques kept his salt-water ventures on the starboard side of the law. One bit of circumstantial data supporting this conclusion arises from the fact that a year after he became a freeman of the city, piracy suddenly went out of fashion. This was due to the arrival of a new governor, the Earl of Bellomont, who, reversing Fletcher's policies, launched a vigorous anti-pirate drive. One victim of this campaign was Captain Kidd.

Bellomont's reforms upset the carefully built-up business organizations of some of New York's foremost citizens, including several friends of my ancestor. But Marques himself does not seem to have been affected, if one may judge from the growth of his fortune and the fact that his name nowhere appears in the black books of the crusading Bellomont. . . .

The earliest document relating to my first American ancestor that I have been able to find is dated September 17, 1697. On that day Isaac mounted the City Hall steps, stood before the Mayor and Aldermen of the Corporation, and after due examination and the payment of five pounds, was made a freeman of the city. This gave him the right to vote in local elections. It also required him to serve in the militia. . . .

He is said to have owned three ships. I have found record of only one, the *Dolphin*, which appeared to have two regular runs—one, New York to England and back; the second, New York to England, then to the African slave coast, the West Indies, and home, the famous triangular trade route.

New York's City Hall in 1678.

Sometimes the run was made directly from Africa to New York, for slave labor was being widely introduced into the colony. . . .

His surviving papers indicate that Isaac moved in a wealthy and influential circle. His . . . home stood only a block from the mansion of Abraham DePeyster, a former mayor. Nicholas Roosevelt, the sugar importer, served as alderman of the ward.

The witnesses signing Isaac's will were Ebenezer Willson, a mayor of the city, Rip Van Dam, the first native-born American to act as governor of the colony, and William Peartree, who rose from seaman to master of a ship, traded in slaves, and later . . . establish[ed] the city's first free school.

This will, dated October 17, 1706, opens with a curious flourish: "Being . . . bound on a Voyage to Jamaica in the West Indies and Considering the certainty of death and the uncertain Time of the Coming of the same. . . ."

The will then spells out Isaac's testament. He directed that a slave be purchased as a maid for his mother, who also shared in his estate. The remainder of the estate was to be divided equally among the wife and two children Easter and Jacob. Easter was also to have "Fifty pounds to Buy her a Jewel at her age of Eighteene yeares or marriage with her mothers consent."

With this will the documentary record of Isaac Marques comes to an abrupt end.

Bernard Baruch

⤳ MERCHANTS LIKE Marques often outfitted Jewish peddlers, who then traveled from hamlet to hamlet either by foot or on horse, laden with everything from cotton goods and cutlery to trinkets and notions, small tools, and other hardware. Although by no means as common a sight on colonial highways and byways as the Yankee peddler, by the middle of the eighteenth century the "Jew Pedlar" had already become a part of the comic and anecdotal literature of a yet-to-be-born nation.

PHILADELPHIA. *March 13, 1753.* We have an account from the Country of the following comical affair, which lately happen'd. A Jew Pedlar went into a House where he offered his goods for sale, but the good Man being out, and all his Family, except his Wife, who told the Pedlar that she could not buy any Thing, for her Husband had got the Key of the Money: The Pedlar then finding that the Woman was entirely alone, offer'd to make her a Present of a Piece of Calicoe upon Condition of her giving up her Charms to him: The Bait was very alluring, for the Thoughts of sporting with a young Man, and having a new Gown in the Bargain, made her readily yield to his Desires; he accordingly gave her the Calicoe, and after taking a Repast in the Banquet of Love, went about his Business; but had not gone far before he met with her Husband, and having some knowledge of him said, "Sir, I have sold your wife a very cheap Piece of Calicoe, and on six Months Credit," with that the poor man stood amaz'd, and said, "I wonder at my wife's ill Conduct in running me in Debt, when she knows that I have a considerable Sum of Money to pay in a few Months Time, and can't tell how to make it up." He then persuaded the Pedlar to go back and take his piece of Calicoe, which he readily consented to, and when they came to the House, he ordered his Wife to give the Pedlar his Calicoe again, which she did after privately concealing a Coal of Fire in it; the Pedlar took his Calicoe and put it in his Pack (which was a Wallet slung across his Shoulders) so march'd off, pleas'd with the Thoughts of his Success; but for his sweet Meat he soon found sour Sauce; he not suspecting the Cheat, jogg'd along till he met with a Countryman, who seeing his Pack on Fire (and which was just then ready to blaze) cry'd, "Hay, Friend, from whence came you?" *"From Hell,"* replied the Pedlar; "so I perceive," says the Countryman, "by the Flames at your Back." The Pedlar then look'd behind him, and to his great Surprize found all his Goods on Fire, which made him stamp and rave like a mad Man, and curse his Folly in cuckolding the poor Man.

Pennsylvania Gazette

COLONIAL FAMILIES AND CLANS

⤳ IN THE WAKE OF the Chmielnicki massacres of 1648 and 1649 a centuries-old pattern of Jewish migration shifted from an eastward to a westward movement, with Polish Ashkenazim fleeing to neighboring Germany. Mostly petty traders and artisans, some settled in Hamburg

New York merchant Moses Levy at the height of his career, c. 1720.
Museum of the City of New York

and Frankfurt while others went on to Amsterdam, London, and even farther. So many came to America that by the second quarter of the eighteenth century there were more Ashkenazim in New York than Sephardim.

One of the most enterprising Ashkenazim to make his way to New York during these early years was Moses Levy. Born in Germany in 1665, Levy traveled to New York from London as a young man and by 1700 was living in Manhattan's Dock Ward with his brother Samuel, their wives Rycha and Rachel (who were sisters), and their growing families. With fewer than one hundred Jews in the entire colony, there was no Jewish community outside of the Sephardi-dominated congregation.

Thus, early Ashkenazi arrivals were left with the choice of conforming to the ways of the Sephardim or fending pretty much for themselves.

As for Levy, he was busy doing business. Taking full advantage of commercial contacts in London and the West Indies, Levy soon became so successful in the export-import trade that he built a ship and named it *Abigail* after his favorite daughter. With the emergence of a diversified economy, Levy grew increasingly involved in the larger operations of jobbing and wholesaling, leaving much of the small trade to shopkeepers. Business was so good that by 1711 Levy had accumulated enough savings to join several other prominent Jewish merchants in contributing to a fund for the completion of a spire for Trinity Church. Four years later the New York Assembly passed a bill naturalizing all persons of foreign birth in the colony having "lands, tenements, and hereditments." This law entitled Levy to the same rights of trade extended to native-born Englishmen. Perhaps to show off his New World status, Levy posed for his portrait at the height of his career looking every bit the proper English gentleman. Yet he never abandoned his faith. On the contrary, Levy became president of New York's pioneer congregation, Shearith Israel, in 1728, the year of his death.

By then almost twenty years had elapsed since Jacob Franks, the son of a London "Jew broker," came to live with the Levys. Levy could not have asked for a better husband for his daughter Abigail. After a satisfactory arrangement was worked out by a *shadchen* (a professional matchmaker) who happened to be in New York at the time, Jacob and Abigail were married. They had nine children, not a large number in those days. (Abigail herself was one of twelve children.) As soon as they could afford to, they moved into a neighborhood on the east side of town where members of their family mixed freely with DeLanceys, Livingstons, DePeysters, and Bayards. By now a successful merchant in his own right, Jacob prospered by trading in a wide range of commodities—tea, iron, guns, rice. Of great help to him were his sons Naphtali in London and David in Philadelphia. Naphtali was in charge of buying goods for sale in the colonies, selling goods shipped from the colonies, and, most important of all, obtaining military contracts from the British government and keeping them in force. With the help of a younger brother, Moses, and *mishpocheh* (kinfolk) in London, Naphtali succeeded in providing Jacob and David with over £750,000 in military contracts during the French and Indian War, an enormous amount in those days.

Much of what we know about the Franks family comes to us from letters Abigail wrote to Naphtali during the 1730s and '40s. The picture we get of Abigail from her correspondence is of a conscientious mother worrying over her children's welfare, in particular their education, a serious problem in America for Jews at a time when instruction was largely in the hands of Christian clergymen. Abigail resolved the problem by sending her children to the best Christian tutors available (her son Moses was a classmate of the governor's son), and also to Mr. Lopez, a *melamed* (teacher) employed by Shearith Israel. Herself the product of two cultures, Abigail wrote in the style of Addison and Steele (popular English essayists of their day) on everything from matters pertaining to "our strict Judaical method" to "learning mathematics at Mr. Malcolm's."

LETTERS FROM ABIGAIL FRANKS TO HER SON NAPHTALI

July 9, 1733. I have so often recommended you to be wary in your conduct that I will not again make a repetition but this I must recommend to you not to be so free in your discourse on religion and be more circumspect in the observance of some things, especially your morning devotions, for though a person may think freely and judge for themselves, they ought not to be too free of speech nor to make a jest of what the multitude in a society think is of the last consequence.... You wrote me some time ago you was asked at my brother Asher's to a fish dinner but you did not go. I desire you will never eat anything with him unless it be bread and butter, nor nowhere else where there is the least doubt of things not done after our strict Judaical method, for whatever my thoughts may be concerning some fables, this and some other fundamentals I look upon the observance of conscientiously, and therefore with my blessing I strictly enjoin it to your care.

October 7, 1733. Moses is learning mathematics at Mr. Malcolm's who tells me he will go through it with an abundance of ease, and be perfect in very little time. Phila learns French, Spanish, Hebrew, and writing in the morning, and in the afternoon she goes to Mrs. Brownell's. She makes a quick advance in whatever she learns. Mr. Lopez tells me he is surprised at her advancement in Spanish. I intend to send for some patterns for her to work upon next summer.

June 15, 1735. Your sister Richa has begun to learn on the harpsicord and plays three very good tunes in a month's teaching. Her master is one Mr. Pachelbel. Mr. Malcolm says he is excellent. Moses . . . profits very much in his drawing and has begun to learn to paint upon glass which he does very well.

Abigail Levy Franks, whose husband, Jacob, was elected parnass (*president*) *of New York's Congregation Shearith Israel in 1743, the year their daughter Phila eloped with a DeLancey.*
American Jewish Historical Society, Waltham, Massachusetts

December 3, 1736. Your brother Moses is in great want of a German flute. The one he brought from Philadelphia he was obliged to return to the owner. Therefore he begs you would apply to his uncle Mr. Aaron Franks to let him have the pleasure to play on one of his for he hears he plays on that instrument. Though Moses has had no master, he is the best.

October 25, 1737. . . . the continued confirmation of your good state of health and good will gives me a vast pleasure. I have sent you two kegs of pickles. One is a 15 gallon filled with pepper and the other ten with mangoes, peaches and a few pepper to fill up the cask. When you receive them take the peaches and mangoes from the pepper and put fresh vinager to them and that will take of the strength of the pepper. . . . I have nothing

else but conclude with my prayers for your long life and happiness, dear child.

November 9, 1740. . . . I shall give you a short account of my short journey to the Jerseys where I . . . was five days with Mr. Seixas and am very glad I took the resolution to go for it has very much altered my opinion of him. I was surprised to find a person of his temper so much mended and capable to conform with so much ease to the station of life he has entered into—I mean with regard to keeping a small country store and attending those trifling people with so much patience. I believe Mr. Pecheco will scarce think his nephew would ever have weighed a pound of sugar in the Jerseys with a contented mind.

June 21, 1741. Your father is very full of business. I never knew the benefit of the Sabbath before but now I am glad when it comes for his sake that he may have a little relaxation from that continual hurry he is in. In short it's a very great fatigue and makes him very peevish to those he employs. In the family he is of the same good nature. Still, I often when I hear him loud amongst them take part against him and then it's over for a while.

December 5, 1742. Now pray tell me, do you expect your sisters to be nuns? For unless they can meet with a person that can keep them a coach and six, I suppose they must not think of changing their condition. I am no stickler for marrying at a moment's warning. Neither would I consent to any worthless body that makes an appearance. But if chance should present a worthy person (though there is no prospect of it here) . . . there is David Gomez who for some years has had an inclination for Richa, but he is such a stupid wretch that if his fortune was much more and I a beggar no child of mine, especially one of such a good understanding as Richa, should ever have my consent, and I am sure he will never get hers.

June 7, 1743. I am now retired from town and would from my self (if it were possible to have some peace of mind) from the severe affliction I am under on the conduct of that unhappy girl [Phila]. Good God, what a shock it was when they acquainted me she had left the house and had been married six months. I can hardly hold my pen whilst I am writing it. It's what I never could have imagined especially after what I heard her so often say: that no consideration in life should ever induce her to disoblige such good parents. I had heard the report of her going to be married to Oliver Delancey, but as such reports had often been of either of your sisters I have no heed to it further than a general caution of her conduct which has always been unblemished, and is so still in the eye of the Christians who allow she has disobliged us but has in no way been dishonorable, being married to a man of worth and character. My spirits were for some time so depressed that it was a pain to me to speak or see anyone. I have overcome it so far as not to make my concern so conspicuous, but I shall never have that serenity nor peace which I have so happily had hitherto. My house has been my prison. Ever since I had not heart enough to go near the street door. It's a pain to me to think of going again to town, and if . . . it was in my power to leave this part of the world, I would come away in the first man of war that went to London.

◄ᥫ THERE WERE OTHER incidents every bit as unpleasant for Abigail. One evening a few years after his marriage to Phila, Oliver in the company of a few of his "gentlemen rake" friends attacked a young Jewish bride who had recently arrived from Holland. "Their faces blacken'd and otherwise disguised," they broke all the windows in the newly married couple's house and then entered and "tore everything to pieces; they swore they would lie with the woman, Oliver saying that because she was like Mrs. Clinton [the governor's wife] he would have her likeness." Only the influence of the DeLancey clan kept the unruly Oliver from going to jail.

As voters, Jews also came under attack. In 1737, during an argument that arose over the outcome of a New York Assembly election, William Smith, a Puritan lawyer who later became Chief Justice of New York, declared in an impassioned speech that an apparent majority had been gained through Jewish votes, but that since Jews were responsible for the death of Christ, they should not have been allowed to vote in the first place. Smith's speech caused staid legislators to weep while others nearby wanted at once at attack the Jews. (By now there were some three hundred in the city.) Without further ado, the Assembly passed a resolution that Jews "ought not to be admitted to vote for representatives in this colony." The resolution remained unrepealed until the Revolutionary War.

In Pennsylvania, Jews were effectively barred from holding public office until 1790. Conditions were no better in Rhode Island, where the Superior Court held that no Jew could hold any office or vote in choosing others. When in 1775 the General Assembly of Rhode Island asked all those "suspected of being inimical to the United American Colonies" to sign an oath of loyalty to the Revolutionary cause, Moses Michael Hays, an ancestor of the twentieth-century poet Robert Lowell, responded by professing "the strongest principles and attachments to the just rights and privileges of this my native land" as well as his whole-hearted support for the war as a "just one"; however, he declined to sign the oath. Instead, Hays, who as a Jew still could not vote, addressed a petition to the General Assembly of Rhode Island, demanding "the rights and privileges due other free citizens." As far as we know, Hays's petition was ignored.

PHILA WAS NOT the only child of Abigail's to stray from the fold. A few years after her marriage into the DeLancey clan (for whom Delancey Street on New York's Lower East Side is named), Phila's brother David moved to Philadelphia and married Margaret Evans, an Episcopalian with social connections. In 1748, David and Margaret joined Philadelphia's exclusive City Dancing Assembly. He was the second Jew to join.

As far as we know, David never became a member of Philadelphia's Congregation Mikveh Israel—a congregation made up largely of Yiddish-speaking Jews with whom he probably did not feel at ease. In any case, he did not instruct his children in the tenets of Judaism. Instead, they were baptized with their father's approval and brought up as Christians, as were so many of Abigail's grandchildren that by 1800 every one of them in America was a Christian. David, meanwhile, continued making annual contributions to his parents' synagogue in New York, and even attended services there on occasion.

COLONIAL SEPHARDIM as a rule fared better in holding on to their Jewish ties. Lewis Moses Gomez, a contemporary of Moses Levy who served many times as *parnas* (president) of Shearith Israel, had six sons. Of the five who reached adulthood, all married Jewish women and remained observant Jews for the rest of their lives. One of Gomez's sons, David, was a licensed *shochet* (ritual slaughterer). Another, Benjamin, was a *mohel* (circumciser) who also served as *parnas* of Shearith Israel. A third son, Mordecai, married the local *chazzen*'s (cantor's) daughter and, after the death of his father, became the undisputed head of the Jewish community in New York. No fewer than twenty-two Gomezes were laid to rest in the old Jewish cemetery at Chatham Square. One of the last to be buried there before the cemetery was filled to capacity was Mordecai's son Moses, who served for many years as clerk of Shearith's board of trustees. When Moses died in 1826 at the age of eighty-two, he was the oldest member of a congregation that his family had been leaders of for over one hundred years. In that year Moses' kinsman Isaac Gomez, Jr., wrote a short history of his family, an abstract of which follows.

My great great grandfather, Isaac Gomez, was a favorite at the Spanish Court, and particularly noticed by the King. When the Inquisition formed a plan to confiscate his estate on account of his being a Jew, the King, having found it out, informed him by letter, on which information he sent his wife and infant son Moses to France with a considerable property in money and jewels as well as plate. But before he could escape the Inquisition laid hold of him and made him a prisoner for fourteen years. Whether they liberated him or he made his escape I am not informed, but at the end of the fourteenth year he got over to France. He after that had two daughters. One married and went to Leghorn. Her name and connections I know not. The name of the other daughter was Leonora.

In respect and gratitude to the King of France, whose country being the asylum of his family, my great grandfather added to the name of his son that of Lewis. He (Lewis Moses Gomez) married Miss Esther Marchado by whom he had six sons—namely: Jacob, Mordecai, Daniel, David, Isaac and Benjamin. I am not well informed if it was not the Huguenot persecution that caused him to quit France for England but I am led to believe it was. How long he remained in England I know not but believe it was but a short time before he obtained a letter of denization from the Crown of

England (which I have now in my possession) for him and his family to reside in America, granting him and his family all the privileges of one of the most favored subjects, which was a matter of high importance as the Jews were far from being on the same footing with the people of the Christian faith. The privileges granted to him and his family were to hold land in fee simple [ownership of land with unrestricted rights of disposition] and to hold offices both civil and military, equal to the most favored subject. With this protection he came to this country about one hundred and twenty or thirty years ago, it being in the reign of Queen Anne.

FROM THE PAGES OF THE *NEW YORK GAZETTE*

October 29, 1729. All persons who shall have occasion for good Stone-Lime next Spring or Summer, may be supplyed with what Quantity they shall have occasion for, by Lewis Gomez in the City of New-York, at a reasonable Price.

January 7, 1750. Just imported from London, in the Brig Garland, Capt. Machet, and to be sold cheap by Benjamin Gomez at his Store, next Door to Mr. Isaac Gomez's, in the Smith's-Fly; An Assortment of East India and European Goods; Also London Single Refin'd Sugar.

November 5, 1750. On the first instant died Mr. Mordecai Gomez of the Hebrew nation, and of this city, Merchant, and was decently interred the following day, aged 62 years. During his life he was esteemed a fair Trader, and charitable to the poor; died with an unblemish'd character, has left a large family, by who he is deservedly lamented, as he is by all his acquaintances.

July 24, 1751. Just imported from Liverpool, and to be sold on board the Snow Nancy, William Beekman Master, Several White Servants; also sundry sorts of Earthen Ware in Casks and Crates, Cheshire Cheese, Loaf Sugar, Cutlery Ware, Pewter, Grindstones, Coals, and sundry other Goods too tedious to mention: by Abraham Van Horne, Daniel & Isaac Gomez or said Master.

New York, March 27 1767.

TEN POUNDS Reward

WHEREAS the House of Mrs. REBECCA HAYS, of this City, was, last ThursdayNight robbed of the following Pieces of Plate & Money, viz
1 Two Quart Silver Tankard, marked I. H. R.
1 Large Silver Punch Bowl, with two Handles.
3 Silver Porringers, marked M. M K.
1 Silver Sugar Castor, marked M. M. K
2 Pair of Round Silver Salts, with Feet, marked I, H. R.——And one odd ditto, marked in the same Manner.
1 Small Silver Salver, without any Mark.
6 Table Spoons, marked B, H. Maker's Name Myers.
1 Pair of Diamond Rings, with Drops.
1 Silver Coffee-Pot. no Mark, Maker's Name I, P, And a Silver Tea Pot.
1 £ 6 10 Jersey Bill, 35 Dollars, 25 Quarter Dollars, 12 Pieces of English Money, and three Pocket Pieces.
'Tis possible more of the Plate is marked, than what is mentioned above. Whoever takes up and secures any Person or Persons concerned in the above Robbery, so that they may be brought to Justice, shall have the above Reward, paid by me   MOSES M HAYS.

A 1767 Boston newspaper advertisement signed by Moses Michael Hays, a native-born merchant and maritime underwriter who eleven years later was elected grand master of the Massachusetts Grand Lodge of Masonry. When Hays was reelected in 1791, he appointed his friend Paul Revere to serve under him.

THE CALL OF THE FRONTIER

ALTHOUGH MOST Jews who came to America during the seventeenth and eighteenth centuries settled along the Atlantic seaboard, quite a few at one time or another ventured to remote areas of the country. As early as 1719, Lewis Moses Gomez began accumulating sizable tracts of land in Orange County, New York, to further his trade with the Indians. Some six miles north of Newburgh, Gomez built an outpost near a brook where Algonquin tribes would meet before and after hunting ex-

LEFT, *An eighteenth-century* esrog (*citrus fruit*) *case used in celebrating* Succoth (*the Jewish harvest festival*) *by the Gomezes, New York's premier colonial Sephardic family.* RIGHT, *Gomez family coat-of-arms.*
American Jewish Historical Society, Waltham, Massachusetts

peditions. Here he and his sons Daniel and David haggled with twenty to thirty Indians at a time over how much whiskey or how many trinkets constituted a fair price for a mink, a muskrat, or a sable. The massive walls of the Gomez outpost are still standing, a monument to their struggles and achievements in the New World.

The Gomezes were by no means the first Jewish Indian traders in America. Since the days of Peter Stuyvesant, Jews had been traveling up and down the Hudson and Delaware rivers bartering dry goods, hardware, and liquor for pelts and hides. By 1720, Jewish peddlers on the Pennsylvania frontier were selling furs and skins to Jacob Franks and other Jewish merchants, who in turn shipped them from New York and Philadelphia to London. Among Franks's earliest suppliers were his brothers-in-law Nathan and Isaac Levy. The first Jewish merchants to settle permanently in Philadelphia, the Levys bought grain and pelts from Joseph Simon, another early Jewish settler, who together with his nephew Levy Andrew Levy traded with farmers and Indians as far away as Illinois. For the Indians they furnished homemade liquor, silver trinkets, silk handkerchiefs, tomahawks, and axes. For the farmers they brought all kinds of agricultural equipment as well as the finest broadcloth, hardware, and housekeeping items. Profits were high, but so were the risks. In 1763, Levy was captured briefly during the Pontiac Indian uprising. In the same year Simon's pack trains were seized by Indians. In spite of incurring substantial losses that year, Simon and Levy took part in subsequent trading expeditions to such dangerous places as Detroit, Green Bay, and Kaskaskia. In the following account, the celebrated nineteenth-century American historian Francis Parkman describes what traders like Simon and Levy might have experienced on a journey from Fort Duquesne to the Great Lakes during these early years.

Their merchandise was sometimes carried in wagons as far as the site of Fort Duquesne. . . . From this point the goods were packed on the backs of horses, and thus distributed among the various Indian villages. More commonly, however, the whole journey was performed by means of trains, or, as they were called, brigades of packhorses. . . . The principal trader, the owner of the merchandise, would fix his headquarters at some large Indian town, whence he would dispatch his subordinates to the surrounding villages with a suitable supply of blankets and red cloth, guns and hatchets, liquor, tobacco, paint, beads, and hawks' bells. This wild traffic was liable to every species of disorder: and it is not to be wondered at that, in a region where law was unknown, the jealousies of rival traders would become a fruitful source of broils, robberies, and murders.

. . . A party of Indian wayfarers would often be met journeying through the forest, a chief, or a warrior, perhaps, with his squaws and family. The Indians would usually make their camp in the neighborhood of the white men; and at meal-time the warrior would seldom fail to seat himself by the traveller's fire, and gaze with solemn gravity at the viands before him. If, when the repast was over, a fragment of bread or a cup of coffee should be handed to him, he would receive these highly prized rarities with an ejaculation of gratitude. . . .

He who wished to visit the remoter tribes of the Mississippi valley . . . would find no easier course than to descend the Ohio in a canoe or bateau.

Iroquois country, c. 1650.

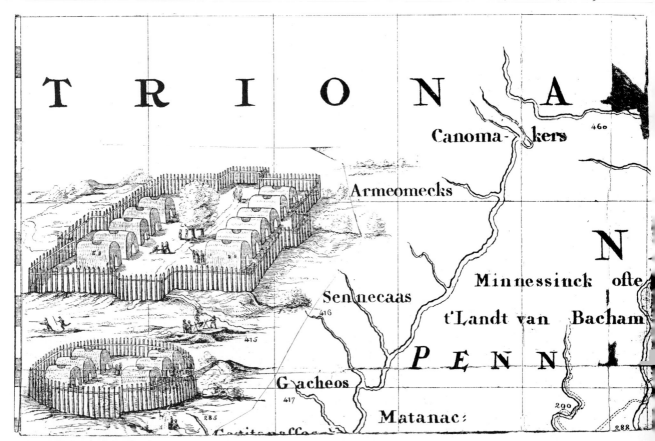

The oldest Jewish house in America. Originally an Indian trading post, it was built some six miles north of Newburgh, New York, by the Gomez family in 1720. The walls were so well constructed that even today they are as strong as when they were first built.

American Jewish Historical Society, Waltham, Massachusetts

He might float for more than eleven hundred miles down this liquid highway of the wilderness, and, except the deserted cabins of *Logstown*, a little below Fort Pitt, the remnant of a Shawanoe village at the mouth of the Scioto, and an occasional hamlet or solitary wigwam along the deeply wooded banks, he would discern no trace of human habitation through all this vast extent.

◄§ IN 1733, THE DIRECTORS of London's Bevis Marks Congregation shipped forty-two German and Spanish-Portuguese Jews to Georgia, a colony established a year earlier by James Oglethorpe for impoverished English Protestants and their persecuted co-religionists in Germany. Most of the Jews were themselves in poor circumstances. Some had but recently escaped from Portugal with little more than the clothes on their backs. Others, just as destitute, were émigrés from the ghettos of central Europe. As soon as they set foot in Savannah, a movement was started to get rid of them; however, since Georgia's charter excluded only "papists," it was not easy to do so lawfully. Meanwhile, a highly contagious disease broke out which a Jewish doctor, Samuel Nunez, succeeded in eradicating. To show his gratitude, Governor Oglethorpe provided Nunez and his Jewish shipmates with land grants.

In 1735, one of the original settlers, Mordecai Sheftall, noted in his diary that the Jews of Savannah had "agreed to open a Synagogue which was done emediately named K-K. Mikva Israel." Three years later, "a *mikva* was opened for the use of the congregation." These and other developments did not go unnoticed by John Martin Bolzius, a Lutheran pastor whose journal and letters to Germany contain frequent references to his Jewish neighbors.

The Spanish and Portuguese Jews are not so strict insofar as eating is concerned as the others are. They eat, for instance, the beef that comes from the warehouse or that is sold anywhere else. The German Jews, on the other hand, would rather starve than eat meat they do not slaughter themselves.

The German Jews have in Savannah the same liberties as the Englishman. They drill with a rifle, as all the soldiers do. They have no other profession besides farming or dealing in small trade. The latter comes easier to them than the former. They even have a doctor, who has the permission of the Trustees to cure them when they are sick.

The Jews use at their service, which they are holding in an old and miserable hut, with men and women separated, the same ceremonies which I have seen in Berlin. A boy speaking several languages and especially good in Hebrew is their reader and he is paid for his services. There are not more than two families who can speak Jewish-German.

They do not know if they will ever get permission from the Trustees to build a synagogue. It will be quite some time. As I mentioned before, the Spanish and Portuguese Jews are against the German Jews and they are going to protest the petition by the German Jews to build a synagogue.

◄§ WITH A DECLINE in the fortunes of the Georgia colony, many of the Jewish settlers there moved on to Charleston where by 1740 important commercial ties with Europe and the West Indies existed which the Jews of Charleston were instrumental in developing. In 1749, Kahal Kadosh (Holy Congregation) Beth Elohim came into being. The third old-est Jewish congregation in America, by 1800 Beth Elohim with 107 members was also the largest and wealthiest. One early member, Moses Lindo, was an expert judge and grader of indigo—a blue dye derived from the indigo plant and used in the cloth industry—who had traveled from London to Charleston in 1756 to see what could be done to improve and increase production.

In his capacity as "Surveyor and Inspector General of the Indico," Lindo succeeded in establishing and maintaining standards of excellence. Until Lindo arrived, annual exports of indigo seldom reached 350,000 pounds; however, with Lindo in charge, exports rose to over 1,000,000 pounds, making indigo the most profitable crop in the colony next to rice. Before Lindo's death in 1774 the industry had grown so large as to require ten thousand slaves as well as the services of such people as Abraham Seixas, an auctioneer and slave trader whose brother Gershom served for many years as *chazzen* of New York's Congregation Shearith Israel.

Processing indigo in South Carolina. Reproduced from an old print.

Abraham Seixas
All so gracious
Once again does offer
His service pure
For to secure
Money in the coffer.

He has for sale
Some negroes, male,
Will suit full well grooms.
He has likewise
Some of their wives
Can make clean, dirty rooms.

For planting, too,
He has a few
To sell, all for cash,
Of various price,
To work the rice
Or bring them to the lash.

The young ones true
If that will do,
May some be had of him.
To learn your trade
They may be made
Or bring them to your trim.
     South Carolina Gazette
     September 6, 1794

Abraham Seixas, a Charleston merchant whose brother Gershom was chazzen *for many years of New York's Congregation Shearith Israel.*
American Jewish Archives, Cincinnati, Ohio

IN COLONIAL South Carolina, a haven since the seventeenth century for Huguenots and other liberal-minded nonconformists, there were far fewer social barriers separating Jews from Gentiles than almost anywhere else in the New World. Thus, it was not unusual for Beth Elohim's *chazzen*, Isaac De Costa, in 1759 to be elected treasurer of Charleston's King Solomon Lodge No. 1, a Masonic organization which welcomed Jews into its ranks. Both De Costa and Moses Lindo mixed freely with wealthy landowners and their families, as did Francis Salvador, a plantation owner from England who became the first Jew to hold an important elective office in the New World. He was also the first Jew to die in the Revolutionary War.

The nephew of a director of the Dutch East India Company, young Salvador received an inheritance of £60,000, much of which he lost when the Dutch East India Company went bankrupt. It was at this point in his life that Salvador traveled to South Carolina where, many years before, his grandfather had bought over 100,000 acres of farming land. By becoming a planter, Salvador hoped to recoup his losses.

Arriving in Charleston in 1773, Salvador proceeded to what was then the western frontier of America where he acquired additional land be-

The interior of the oldest existing synagogue building in the South. Built by Charleston's Congregation Beth Elohim in 1840, it replaced an equally handsome structure destroyed by fire two years earlier.
Congregation Beth Elohim, Charleston, South Carolina

Charleston in the days when more Jews lived there than in any other city in America.
Mabel Brady Garvey Collection, Yale University Art Gallery

fore settling down with thirty slaves to cultivate the soil. Salvador soon became active in politics. When a Provincial Congress was organized in Charleston in 1775, Salvador was among those elected to represent his district. And when the Provincial Congress set up a republic in South Carolina, it was Salvador who signed and stamped the new currency. After open hostilities began, Salvador was among the first to take up arms. In the summer of 1776 he joined an expedition against a group of Cherokee loyalists. On a patrol one night a band of Cherokees suddenly opened fire. Salvador swayed in his saddle. The Indians closed in. A few hours later Salvador was found barely alive. "When I came up to him," his commander reported to John Rutledge, president of South Carolina, "he asked whether I had beaten the enemy. I told him 'Yes.' He said he was glad of it, shook me by the hand and bade me farewell. . . ."

Moses Nathan Ashur, an early Louisiana Jewish settler, and his son. From a painting by Jules Lion.
American Jewish Historical Society, Waltham, Massachusetts

❧ THROUGHOUT Jewish history there have been individuals who have yearned for the social novelty and "roominess" of the Gentile world, sometimes to the point of wanting to break away entirely from Jewish life. Perhaps this desire entered into the decision of Isaac Rodriguez Monsanto to settle permanently in Louisiana in the days when the nearest Jewish settlement was hundreds of miles away.

Born into an impoverished Sephardic family in Holland in 1729, as a young man Isaac traveled to Curaçao in the hope of prospering there. Hearing of even greater opportunities farther west, he moved on to New Orleans, where in 1758 he started a customer goods business. A few years later Isaac was living in a combination home–store–warehouse on Chartres Street with his sisters Angelica and Gracia, his brother Manuel, a mulatto slave from Martinique named Valentin, and "a little negro girl named Quetelle" for whom he had paid 1,400 French *livres*.

In 1762, the French ceded the territory of Louisiana to the Spanish, who quickly expelled the Monsantos and other Jewish merchants from New Orleans "on account of the nature of their business and the religion they profess." The new governor wanted Spanish merchants to dominate the economic life of the colony. Once they did so, the Monsantos were allowed to return, for Louisiana had already become an exception to the Spanish colonial policy of rigid exclusion of Jews.

As dealers in dry goods, cattle, and slaves, Isaac and Manuel traveled frequently up the Mississippi River from New Orleans to Baton Rouge and on to Pointe Coupee and Natchez, where a younger brother, Benjamin, and his wife Clara had settled. Living as they did in a free and fluid society, before long the Monsantos discovered themselves blending into their social surroundings, perhaps to the point of ceasing to think much about being Jewish. Both Angelica and Gracia married non-Jews, as did a younger sister, Eleanora. There is no record of Isaac or Manuel ever having married; however, another brother, Jacob, and a mulatto named Maimi whom Jacob freed in 1783 "in appreciation for her good service" had a daughter, Sophia. Both mother and daughter adopted the name Monsanto and lived for many years in a house of their own on Bienville Street.

Philadelphia's Arch Street Ferry, just a few blocks away from the big Norris House on Second Street, where by 1754 Barnard Gratz was working as a clerk for Jacob and Abigail Franks's son David at a salary of £21 a year.
Library of Congress

2
Merchants and Patriots

FROM SILESIA TO PHILADELPHIA

AMONG THE SCORES of Ashkenazim to find their way to colonial Pennsylvania were Barnard and Michael Gratz, merchant-adventurers whose lives are representative in many ways of both the promise and the fulfillment of the dream that brought other early settlers to these shores. Barnard, the first to arrive, was born in 1738 in a small town in Silesia where Jews had lived in poverty for generations. A restless youth, Barnard could find few reasons for remaining at home. Entry into a business, trade, or profession was severely limited by discriminatory laws. Crushing taxes made it next to impossible to earn a decent living. Even the right to marry was subject to approval by a local official. The effect on Barnard was to make him want to leave as soon as possible.

Having learned to look upon wealth as a key to happiness in a harsh and uncaring world, Barnard decided in the early 1750s to seek his fortune at the London countinghouse of a cousin, Solomon Henry, an exporter of manufactured goods to the East and West Indies and the American colonies. In London, much to Barnard's surprise, there were no important restrictions on Jews. Nor was a ghetto system enforced. Barnard worked hard at Solomon Henry's, familiarizing himself with the intricacies of the export-import trade. Driven by an ever restless spirit, around 1754 he decided to move on to the New World and settled in Philadelphia, at the time the largest and fastest growing city in North America.

Arriving at the onset of the French and Indian War, Barnard was impressed at the sight of ships and wharves jutting out into the Delaware River. A bustling metropolis, with a population of nearly twenty thousand, Philadelphia had much to recommend itself as a place for Barnard to settle down in. To be sure, houses were small, rents high, and furniture none too plentiful. Yet food was cheap and opportunities for advancement far greater than in England for people with a background in business.

After four years of working as a clerk in the Philadelphia countinghouse of Jacob and Abigail's son David Franks, Barnard was about to go

A merchant's countinghouse in colonial Philadelphia.
The New-York Historical Society, New York City

into business for himself when, upon learning of his younger brother Michael's return to London from a trading venture in the East Indies, he wrote a letter to his cousin Solomon Henry in London.

Philadelphia, November 20, 1758

Solomon Henry
London

Dear Cousin Solomon:

. . . I . . . heard my brother Michael is coming back from the East Indies, which am very sorry for, and I should be glad to know his reason for returning. I don't know what advice to give him that would be for the best of his interest, as I do not know . . . if he could content himself with living in the country, or else with living here at Mr. David Franks's in my place, as I intend to leave him next spring. . . . I believe I could soon get him my place, where he could learn the business of this country by staying with him two or three years, and might do a little business for himself as he has some money of his own.

This place requires honesty, industry, and good nature, and no pride, for he must do every thing pertaining to the business. So if you and he think he is capable of the last—I have no doubt of his honesty—and he has a mind not to be stubborn but to take advice after his arrival, I would advise him to come by the first vessel in the spring. I would assist him as far as in my power as a brother. That is not a great deal, as I am poor my self. But if he thinks himself wise enough and refuses to take advice . . . then . . . I would not advise him to come here, as it would give me much pain and uneasiness.

I regret I cannot remit you y'r money before next spring. Your kindness shall always be acknowledged by, dear sir.

Your aff'te cousin and most humble servant,
Barnard Gratz

Respects to Miss Hart. Will remit her money p'r next vessel.

Philadelphia merchant Michael Gratz, from a painting by Thomas Sully. Together with his brother Barnard, Michael shipped goods as far west as Illinois.

American Jewish Archives, Cincinnati, Ohio

⪧ IN THE following letter, Chaim Grätzer, an older brother in Silesia, offers Michael (Yechiel) some advice, along with a running account of the fortunes of their family.

Tworog, Sunday, Mishpatim 21 Sh'bat, 5519

Yechiel Gratz
London

Peace to my beloved brother Yechiel. May he live.

I have seen your few lines of Tuesday the 17th of Tebeth from London, and am heartened to hear that G-d has again helped you safely to London. But I am very much surprised that you have not written to me a separate letter. What have you profitted thereby? You know very well that I ask nothing of you and that I have no need for it, thank G-d. I believe that if this letter had not arrived you would not for my sake have expended as much as a few pennies for postage. "This is the law and this is its reward."

And in addition to this, you write that you are going again across the sea, to Philadelphia. From appearances you wish perhaps to become an English nabob. I certainly think it is your duty first to ask my opinion. And especially so because I have, thank G-d, no demands to make of you. Therefore I write you again: Don't you dare on any account to leave London without first informing me how much you have profitted and how much you are worth. After that I will write you what you have to do.

If you are able to bring home at least a thousand dollars in cash, then come to me. With the help of G-d, I will take care that you make a good match and have a living also. You well know that I have been at all times both brother and father to you, and I will continue, with the help of G-d, to promote your interests further. Therefore there is nothing else to do other than what I state here. I hope that the same thing will not happen to you as to the brothers of our Cousin Solomon. For they would not obey. . . .

Permit me to inform you that my son Koppel is engaged to the daughter of Abraham Prosk. He will receive as a marriage portion 100 Frederics d'Or and will be married after Rosh Hashonah. My daughter Friedel I have also engaged to be married to a poor young man, the son of Seligman of Zolz. He is also a learned man and has many good qualities. Before Pesach he is going to Hamburg and will continue his studies there for two years.

Our sister Leah will be married to our cousin Feibel. She has been compelled to change her nature entirely and must obey my wishes. I hope he will be able to make a living, but the trouble is he has nothing and I cannot give him much. But I believe his brothers will help him out with something. . . . If you have more than a thousand dollars to your fortune, you may bring something to our sister. If not, we will release you from your share of the dowry.

Mrs. Michael Gratz, whose father, Joseph Simon of Lancaster, Pennsylvania, was a pioneer fur trader who did business with the Gratzes. From a painting by Gilbert Stuart.
American Jewish Archives, Cincinnati, Ohio

*One of the most richly
ornamented pieces of American
classical furniture, this sideboard
was made for the Gratz family in
the mid-to-late 1820s, probably by
Joseph Barry, the only craftsman
in Philadelphia to advertise that
he made "burl work" or brass
inlay.*

Philadelphia Museum of Art. Bequest of Miss
Elizabeth Gratz.

Our brother Yonathan is in Streilitz. He is comfortable, is making a living and, thank G-d, enjoys much respect. Our sister Gitl is at present in
Welwish and is making an honest living but is not able to accumulate anything. My daughter Esther is in Lubinitz. She has till now neither added
to nor lost from her capital. What her parents gave her is still left, thank
G-d. She thinks of giving up the Kreutzborn distillery.

I hope with G-d's help, that when you come home, we will make a good
match for you. Perhaps with Rabbi Tost's daughter. This can be arranged.
You must write to me before you leave for home. Then I will write to you
and tell you what you will have to do. . . . Our brother, Reb Yonathan, will
shortly write you a letter also.

If you happen to come across a rich garment—that is to say, a garment
for a woman—then buy me one for my daughter the bride (may she live)
and see to it that it is sent off to Breslau. And also one watch for me up to
22 or 24 Reich Marks. See to it that it is safely shipped. Your money I will
send by bill of exchange to Breslau. And see that you come to my house
with little expense. Hope to see you here well and soon. I remain.

Your Faithful Brother, Haqaton
Chaim Grätzer, of Tworog

⌐§ HERE IS Michael's reply to his brothers Chaim and Yonathan, both of
whom, as far as we know, remained in Silesia for the rest of their lives.

Peace to my beloved Reb Chaim and Reb Yonathan from whom I beg forgiveness for going beyond the ocean to Philadelphia. But as G-d is my witness I vow that everything I do is for the good of our family, even if it is unpleasant for me. With what I have now I cannot support a family; there I hope to make something of myself. I have already paid over my passage to the Captain so I must make the voyage. But I promise that if G-d will be good to me I will return at the first opportunity to visit the graves of my parents. I have always had that in mind; I beg your forgiveness for not doing it now. Had I received your letter six days earlier, I might have been able to do otherwise, as Reb Solomon can inform you. But now it is too late. I hope everything will turn out for the best with the help of G-d. Amen.

What you tell me of my betrothal to Reb Tost's daughter is agreeable if it could be postponed for some years. But if it cannot, I think we must give it up. About my sister Leah, I hope with G-d's blessing if a wedding takes place with her cousin Feibel, that he will not make the mistake of thinking he can depend on her brothers to provide a living for him and his wife. But should he be able to support his wife in honor, then there will be no delay on the part of myself and our brother Berel, may he live, in helping her with all her needs as far as we are able. It is a pleasure to me to hear our sister Gitl may have some money coming in, even if she has nothing to lay aside.

I am sure that our brother Berel will meet with success in Philadelphia. He is connected with a great merchant in London and is honest and a good worker.

I beg that you will pardon me for not writing more now. I am in a great hurry as I must prepare for the voyage.

From me, your humble brother
Yechiel

SHORTLY AFTER Michael's arrival in Philadelphia, Barnard opened a store on Water Street "opposite Mr. Buckridge Sim's, near the Queen's Head." It started out as a small operation with Barnard and Michael doing everything from unloading goods at the pier to making deliveries.

THE PENNSYLVANIA GAZETTE

August 2, 1759

JUST IMPORTED IN THE LAST SHIPS FROM LONDON AND TO BE SOLD AT THE LOWEST RATES, FOR READY MONEY, OR THREE MONTHS CREDIT, BY BARNARD GRATZ

White and crimson English damasks; blue and cloth-coloured satin; black mantua, half-ell wide; crimson and changeable India taffeties; Manchester velvet; white sarsenet; 7-8ths and yardwide Irish linens of different prices; cambricks in pieces or patches; printed calicos and cottons; dark ground, mens and womens worsted hose; fine white ditto; mens brown and white thread hose; knit worsted patterns for breeches and waistcoats; double and single silk caps; cotton ditto; garters, pins; best Whitechapel needles; cotton gowns; black crepe and bombazine; muslin aprons with borders; corded and figured demity; fustians [coarse cloths of cotton and linen], thicksets [fabrics from which men's working clothes are made], white jeans, silk handkerchiefs; sundry sorts of black and coloured gauze ditto; 10-nail, 11-nail, 3 qr., 7-8ths yd., and 3-8ths wide cotton and linen checks; black, blue, red, green and cloth-coloured calimancoes; white, red and black durants; black, blue, white, red and green tammies; honeycomb shag; mohair and silk and buttons; thread, sewing silk; shaloons and buckrams; nuns thread; bobbin, tape, nonsopretties; red, blue, brown and green camblets; camblettees; scarlet, black and blue everlastings; Russia dowlas and sheeting; ozenbrigs; pewter; handsaws; sheep shears, taylors shears; ivory and bond handled knives and forks; cuttoe and pistol-capt knives; long and short pipes and several other goods too tedious to mention.

❧ THE MAJORITY OF Jews who came to Philadelphia before the Revolutionary War made their living as buyers and sellers of merchandise; however, there were also those who went into other lines of work, like Michael Moses, a professional tallow chandler in partnership with David Franks; Barnard and Michael's cousin, Henry Marx, a manufacturer of starch "in the English and Polish" manner; and Henry's brother Levy, a gentlemen's tailor. Another relative of the Gratzes, Cousin Solomon Henry's brother Koppel, came to Philadelphia in 1757 with a "neat assortment of European and East India Goods," which he promptly offered for sale in a rented store near the High Street wharf. As a retailer Koppel did well; however, he worked so hard that he soon became seriously ill. Ordered by his doctors to return at once to England, Koppel traveled instead from New York to Philadelphia, "the better to order his affairs," and died there on March 20, 1761, leaving an estate "substantially composed of debts owing by Jews."

ALONG WITH OTHER colonial Jewish merchants, the Gratzes had a Caribbean Jewish connection. Theirs was the Miranda brothers, Sephardic merchants with a warehouse on the Dutch island of Curaçao and a countinghouse in nearby St. Eustacia. Both families exchanged not only favors but also friendly concern for one another's welfare from time to time. The "disagreeable news" referred to in the following letter was a shipwreck that befell Michael on his return to Philadelphia from a Caribbean trading expedition early in 1766.

Mr. Michael Gratz,

Dear friend, with pleasure we receive your favor of the 9th November, which with impatience, we were waiting for, having had the disagreeable news of your being cast away. But thanks to the Almighty for [your] escaping. . . .

We are certain that you will act for our benefit with one third of five per cent commission on the cargo Messrs. Bradford consigned us.

Mr. Penha and spouse, Mr. Montez and spouse return you many thanks for your favors and desire to make their compliments acceptable to you. And we remain, Sir.

> Your Very Humble Servants,
> Elias and Isaac Rodriguez Miranda

&§ WITH THE EXCEPTION of some Quakers who frowned upon slavery, it was not unusual for people in business in colonial Pennsylvania to own slaves—and complain about them, as in the following letters. The first, to Michael, is from a Jewish storekeeper and friend in Reading. The second, to Barnard, is from a local slave dealer.

Reading (with the help of God, may God protect it herein)
Sunday, 5 Ab, 5522 [July 25, 1762]

Peace to my beloved friend, the honorable Mr. Yechiel. May the Lord protect him, and may this letter find his entire household at peace.

Your letter came at a propitious moment, also the books and bills of exchange and one jar of anchovies which was very important and which my wife, may she live long, has already eaten. Of course, I helped her somewhat. So if I could obtain another jar of this kind, will you send it to me, because it is the best I ever tasted. . . .

If you come here for the coming Sabbath Nachmu—may it come at an auspicious moment—it would please me very much, because we are presently very lonesome on the Sabbath. And if you could stay here with us for eight days, it would be still better.

Also, I may again sell my nigger wench at a profit. So if a ship with niggers should arrive, or a ship with indentured Germans, you will let me know, because I cannot manage without a servant. The wench I now have has two virtues. First, she is drunk all day, when she can get it, and second, she is mean, so that my wife cannot say a word to her. She is afraid of her. . . . So if you should have occasion to hear of a good nigger, or of a good servant, you will inform me.

I am,

> Your affectionate friend, the humble Meir, son
> of Joseph from Yever, scholar of blessed memory

[Postscript in English] My spouse gives hear complements to you and very much oblige to you for your coucumers.

Mr. Bernhard Gratz, Merchant in
Philadelphia

Sir:

I took your negroe George, some time ago, home, thinking I might be
the better to sell him, who, after being with me a night, behaved himself in
such an insolent manner I immediately remanded back to the gaol.

About a week since, I put him up at public sale at Christopher Wit-
man's tavern, where there was a number of persons who inclined to purchase him. But he protested publickly that he would not be sold, and if
any one should purchase him, he would be the death of him, and words to
the like purpose, which deterred the people from bidding.

I then sent him back again with directions to the goaler to keep him at
hard labour, which he refuses to do, and goes on in such an insolent manner that's impossible to get a master for him here.

I therefore request you'll send for him on sight hereof, or send me a line
by Drinkhouse, or the first opportunity, what I shall do with him.

He's now almost naked, and if not furnished soon with some cloaths, I
fear he'll perish.

Pray let me hear from you and, in the mean time, I remain, with great
regard, sir,

> Your humble servant,
> George Nagel

N.B. He's now chained and handcuffed on account of his threats.

A WEDDING, A WAR

⤳ UNTIL THE Revolutionary War, no one in all of Pennsylvania was qualified to perform a Jewish marriage ceremony. Thus, when in 1769 Michael Gratz was about to marry the daughter of Joseph Simon, a devout
Jew, arrangements had to be made for Chazzen Gershom Seixas to
travel from New York to Simon's home in Lancaster where the wedding
took place. Surely Michael must have considered himself lucky, for eligi-
ble Jewish girls in colonial America were hard to find, particularly girls
as attractive and level-headed as Miriam Simon. The following letter,
written by Miriam to her brother-in-law Barnard a few months after her
wedding, reveals a warm and understanding side to her nature.

Philadelphia, August 26, 1769

Barnard Gratz,
London

My dear Brother:

I have the happiness of acquainting you that our family enjoys perfect
health. Dear little Rachel [Barnard's daughter] has escaped the small pox
and is hearty. She often talks of her "dear little Daddy" and wishes to see

him, as, indeed, we all do. But how could it be otherwise when a person whom we all love and esteem is at so great a distance from us.

Would it was spring. Then would we be in expectation of a new happiness [Miriam was to give birth to a son in April 1770]. But, alas, a long winter is before us, though I can assure you there is nothing wanting but your presence to make us completely happy. . . .

I hope you'll make yourself entirely easy about Rachel and be assured she'll be as well taken care of by us as she possibly can be. . . . Rachel gives her love to you and hopes that you won't forget her London doll. I hope after the receipt of this I shall be favored with a few lines from you. I could not expect it before as it was my place to write first. My dear Michael joins me in love for you. I must conclude, wishing you every felicity this world can afford. From

Your ever loving and affectionate sister,
Miriam Gratz

P.S. "You must make haste home." Rachel Gratz.

Newport, May 3, 1770

Mr. Michael Gratz,

Worthy Sir: I had the singular pleasure of receiving your agreeable favor of the 21st ult., per Anthony, imparting to me the very pleasing account of it having pleased the Almighty to deliver your spouse with a fine son and that both mother and babe was in a fair way of doing well, which news was very satisfactory to me and all my family; and on which joyful occasion I beg you and Mrs. Gratz to accept our best congratulations. May the Dispenser of all Blessings grant that you may see every complete joy of him that your hearts can wish for. . . . I am, with great esteem and regard, Dear Sir,

Your Friend and Humble Servant,
Jacob Rodriguez Rivera

AT THE CONCLUSION of the French and Indian War, the British ministry issued the Proclamation of 1763 in order to prevent colonists from entering the western lands ceded in that year to England by a defeated France. The British ministry acted in this way out of fear of a confrontation between the colonists and the Indians; however, for a people just beginning to spread out, the Proclamation was looked upon as prejudicial to their interests. It did not keep settlers out.

In 1764, Parliament passed the Sugar and Currency Acts which, the colonists felt, placed unfair restrictions on their commerce, particularly on sugar and molasses imported from the French West Indies. Colonial merchants had been paying from 25 to 40 percent less for French molasses than for British; however, the tax more than did away with the difference. There was a way out and many colonial merchants, including the Gratzes, took it: smuggling. The British responded by seizing ships and confiscating their cargoes.

And that was not all. In 1765, the Stamp Act was passed requiring tax stamps on most printed materials. A law that affected nearly every colonist, it met with great resistance. The Gratzes and other Philadelphia merchants reacted by signing a nonimportation agreement in 1765. A year later the Stamp Act was repealed, and the following year, 1767, the duty on molasses was lowered; however, the Townshend Acts passed in that same year placed burdensome duties on Indian goods sent from England to the colonies.

The Gratzes adjusted to these conditions by entering the western fur trade together with George Croghan, a seasoned fur trader, and William Murray, a former army officer. The smuggling of supplies through Newport and Baltimore, where surveillance was notoriously lax, was Michael's responsibility, while Bernard managed affairs on the frontier. The brothers did so well that within a few years they had outpaced their chief competitors.

In addition to the Indian trade, the Gratzes invested heavily in several colonizing ventures involving western lands. Allying themselves with Benjamin Franklin, Joseph Simon, and various members of the Franks family, the Gratzes started buying up land as far west as Illinois. In 1773, two huge tracts between the Mississippi and Illinois rivers were purchased from a tribe of Indians for $37,000; however, the Northwest Ordinance of 1787 invalidated these grants without any compensation to the participants.

IN 1770, PARLIAMENT repealed the Townshend Acts, thus removing a major source of irritation in the colonies. But then the Tea Act of 1773 was passed. The new act gave the East India Company the right to send tea in its own ships, open its own warehouses in America, and sell directly to the American shopkeeper. This, Parliament reasoned, would cut down on smuggling while providing the colonists with cheaper tea.

An excellent idea for everyone but American importers and wholesalers, it would appear. However, the American consumer so feared what Parliament might do next that he found himself siding increasingly with political radicals like Samuel Adams. Adams was determined to start a war. He did not have long to wait.

In December of 1773, a party of men jumped aboard three East India Company ships in the Boston harbor, ripped open the ships' chests, and dumped $75,000 worth of tea into the harbor. A year and a half later, the Second Continental Congress met in Philadelphia to appoint George Washington commander of the Continental Army.

Philadelphia, May 30, 1775

Barnard Gratz,
Pittsburgh

My Dear Barnard:

. . . I wrote you sundry times, which I hope have reached your hands safe, in particular the one last week wherein I mentioned about the Vir-

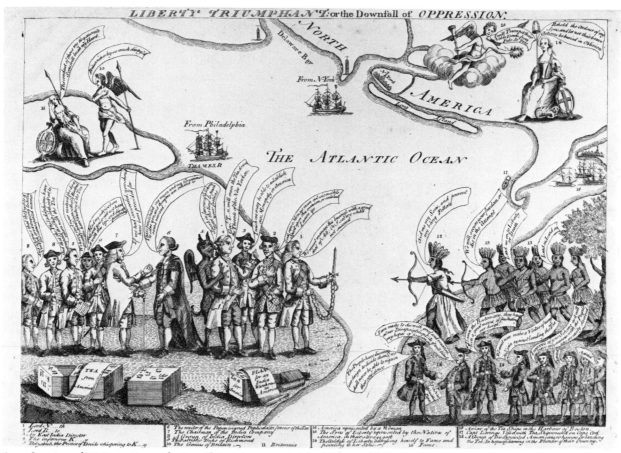

A 1778 *cartoon depicting a personification of America supported by the Sons of Liberty taking aim at British leaders of government and industry.*
Library Company of Philadelphia

ginia Assembly being called to meet the first Thursday in June, and that Mr. Randolph, the Speaker, who is a Delegate, left this place a few days ago for Williamsburg. So I doubt not that Mr. Simon will go down, who I hope will succeed, as I am told it is said here by one of the first members of that House, whose name is Mr. Patt. Henry, one of the delegates also, that if the Government lets the Assembly sit, all those accounts will be allowed and paid. God grant it may be so, else I cannot say what will be done. . . .

. . . Hoping this will find you both in perfect health as it leaves us at present, I am, Dear Barnard,

Your Ever Affectionate and Loving Brother,
Michael Gratz

[Postscript] . . . Governor Franklin was in town here . . . it seems nothing can be concluded on till the packet arrives, to hear from home if any troops are coming to this country.

❧ IN PHILADELPHIA in June of 1776, Thomas Jefferson wrote the Declaration of Independence on the second floor of a house on Market Street later converted into a store by Michael Gratz's sons, Simon and Hyman. In July of the same year Jonas Phillips, a Jewish merchant "in Market-street, near Mr. Dunlap's Printing office," bought a copy of the document from Dunlap and mailed it with the following remarks to Gimpel Samson, a business acquaintance in Amsterdam:

"The war will make the whole of England bankrupt. The Americans have an army of 100,000 strong men, and the English only 25,000 and some ships. The Americans have already made themselves like the States of Holland. The enclosed is a declaration of the whole country. How it will end who knows. Thank God the war does me no damage!"

The same sentiments might have been uttered by Michael when he was selected by Philadelphia's Committee of Safety to bring to the city "a quantity of Blankets and other Woolen Goods said to be proper for covering and Cloathing the Troops now raising for the Continental Service." As the war progressed, Barnard supplied the Continental Army with rifles (manufactured by Joseph Simon), ammunition, drums, blankets, and food, while Michael built and outfitted blockade runners on the Potomac River for the acquisition of European goods sorely needed at home. Overall, the Jewish share in privateering is estimated at 6 percent of the total, a figure far out of proportion to its tiny population.

Philadelphia, July 24, 1776

Barnard Gratz,
Pittsburgh

My Dear Barnard:

. . . Our dear family are all at Lancaster, safe moored for six months, though may God send peace that we may be able to bring them down again here. . . . No doubt you will stay now till after the treaty with the Indians is over, which I hope will be before Rosh Hashono, so that you can be with us for the Holidays. . . .

Skins are as yet 2/8 and 2/9 per w. sunr. 3/8 and 3/9; beaver, 13/ to 15/; raccoon, 2/10 to 3/ per a.w. Shipping furs, otter 10/ to 12/6 cats, 1/6 to 2/ foxes, 3/6 fishers, 22d to 2/. . . .

The Major [an unidentified deliverer of the letter] is in a hurry. I must conclude this time; and I remain, my Dear Barnard,

Your Ever-Affectionate Brother,
Michael Gratz

Barnard Gratz
Philadelphia

Dear Sir:

Colonel Atlee bespoke rifles from me for two companies when Colonel Tilonier was here. He said they must not be delivered until further orders. I have about 120 new rifles by me which I want to sell. The price is £6:10 each. The Council of Safety paid me the same. I will be much obliged to you if you will speak to Mr. Peters or to some of the Delegates and acquaint them of the number of rifles I have to dispose of. . . .

Yours Sincerely,
Joseph Simon

Lancaster, June 2, 1777

Michael Gratz
Fredericksburg

My Dear Michael:

I had the pleasure of receiving your several agreeable favors from Baltimore. It afforded me great satisfaction to hear that you were well and hearty, which I sincerely pray may continue; so with every other blessing which this world can afford.

I thank you, my Dear, for your good advice in advising me to be contented and happy in your absence. I assure you I shall endeavor to be as much so as possible, though you may well know it is impossible I should be truly so when I have so many anxious thoughts about you. You can remove them in a great degree by letting me hear from you as often as is convenient, and you may be assured I shall be as particular in writing as I can. I wait impatiently to hear from you, which I hope will be in a few days.

In regard to news, nothing new has developed worth communicating. All quiet. God knows how long it will continue so. . . . You desired me to let you know the prices of goods. It is a thing impossible. Everything is excessively high and changeable. Every day there is some alteration in the prices. . . .

Our little comforts are, thank God, well and give their love to you and hope to see you soon. I think I have wrote you a long letter and for fear of encroaching on your patience, I will conclude. Dear Michael

Ever your loving and affectionate Wife,
Miriam Gratz

HAYM SALOMON SAVES THE DAY

WHILE THE Gratzes were busy with their affairs, another Philadelphia Jew, Solomon Bush, joined the Pennsylvania Militia and "distinguished himself in the Public Service especially in the Winter of one thousand seven hundred and seventy-six, when the service was Critical & Hazardous." A year later, as General Howe advanced with superior British forces through the Jerseys toward Philadelphia, Solomon's brother Nathan "was dangerously Wounded in a skirmish between the Militia and the Advance of the British Army." "I am thank God getting better," Bush wrote to his friend Henry Lazarus in November of 1777. "My wishes are to be able to get Satisfaction and revenge the Rongs of my injured Country." Two years later Bush was made a lieutenant-colonel, the highest rank attained by an American Jew in a combat unit of the Continental Army.

Meanwhile, the British had entered Philadelphia. The Gratzes and other patriots had already left the city; however, Barnard's former employer, David Franks, stayed on. Ostensibly neutral, Franks's sympathies were clearly on the side of the British. Appointed by the Continental Congress to serve as a supply agent to American prisoners in British hands, Franks was jailed several times under suspicion of giving information to the enemy. Moreover, his daughter, the beautiful but flighty Rebecca, enjoyed nothing more than the company of young British officers.

At an elaborate affair given in honor of General Howe on May 18, 1778, at the Wharton estate in Southwark (just outside Philadelphia) Rebecca was chosen Queen of Beauty by a group of British officers dressed as knights in gold and scarlet. Wearing a white silk gown, a veil edged with silver lace, and a towering headdress filled with pearls and other precious stones, Rebecca watched all afternoon as handsome men in uniform dashed back and forth to impress her with their splendid pageantry. Later a banquet was held in a hall of many mirrors where Rebecca danced and laughed until dawn. In 1782 she married an English colonel, Henry Johnson, who subsequently became a general and a baronet. "No woman was ever blessed with a kinder, a better husband," Lady Rebecca told a visiting countryman, General Winfield Scott, years later, "but I ought to have been a patriot before my marriage."

A few months after the party at Southwark, Barnard Gratz reported to his brother Michael at Williamsburg that the British had left Philadelphia "and since gott beat in the Jerseys in a Battle they had with General Washington who commanded in person." As soon as Michael received the letter, he passed it on to Miriam at Lancaster, together with the "good news of our old city being again in our possession, to which place I expect to convey you at my return in a very short time."

With the Americans back again in Philadelphia, the harbor was cleared of obstacles and commerce with allies of the new nation resumed. A number of Jewish merchants who had fled British-occupied New York soon arrived. Among them was Haym Salomon, a penniless jack-of-all-trades who came to be regarded by the end of the war as the most competent bill broker in America. In the summer of 1778, Salomon petitioned the Continental Congress "to grant him any Employ in the way of his Business [as a sutler, i.e., one who follows an army for the purpose of selling soldiers provisions] whereby he may be enable to support himself and family." We hear nothing more of Salomon until 1780, when he began placing notices in local newspapers for "any kind of business in the brokerage." His office at the time was a coffeehouse on Front Street where he could be found "every day . . . between the hours of twelve and two."

In 1781, Robert Morris was appointed America's first Superintendent of Finance. Often in need of the services of a broker, more and more Morris came to rely on Salomon to turn foreign bills of exchange, which the United States was receiving in the form of loans, into hard cash. Salomon's commission never exceeded one-half of 1 percent, even though other Philadelphia brokers were charging 2 to 5 percent. To show his appreciation, Morris permitted Salomon to refer to himself as Broker to the Office of Finance, a title which helped bring in more busi-

A new synagogue for Philadelphia's Congregation Mikveh Israel. Designed in the Egyptian style by William Strickland, it was described by Rebecca Gratz shortly after its consecration in 1825 as "one of the most beautiful specimens of ancient architecture in the city."
Library Company of Philadelphia

ness. In fact, business was so good that in 1782, the year Congregation
Mikveh Israel raised enough money to build a synagogue on Cherry
Street, it was Haym Salomon, the largest contributor to the building
fund, who headed the procession from the old *shul* to the new building.

AS SOON AS the war was over, the Jews of Philadelphia began to reflect
on what they lacked. One thing in particular bothered Manuel Josephson, an emigrant from Germany who presented the following petition to
the board of directors of Philadelphia's Congregation Mikveh Israel in
1784.

This is the want of a proper *mikve* or batheing place, according to our Law
and institution, for the purification of married women at certain periods.
The necessity of having and using such place will readily appear from the
text (Leviticus 20:18) where a transgression of this ordinance is highly
criminal to both husband and wife. Nor does it rest with them only, but
the very children born from so unlawful cohabitation are deemed *bene
niddot* [children conceived during the menstrual period], which makes the
more heinous and detestable, in as much as it effects not only the parents,
but their posterity for generations to come. And should it be known in the
congregations abroad that we had been thus neglectful of so important a
matter, they would not only pronounce heavy anathemas against us, but
interdict and avoid intermarriages with us, equal as with a different nation
or sect, to our great shame and mortification.

Now, therefore, in full consideration of the foregoing, we have unanimously agreed that a proper *mikve* or batheing place for the sole use of our
congregation be forthwith built, and that no delay may be made in ac-
complishing so necessary and laudable a work.

FROM THE PAGES OF THE *PENNSYLVANIA PACKET*

PHILADELPHIA. *January 6, 1785.* Thursday last, expired after a lingering
illness, Mr. Haym Salomons, an eminent broker of this city; he was a native of Poland, and of the Hebrew nation. He was remarkable for his skill
and integrity in his profession, and for his generous and humane deport-
ment. His remains were on Friday last deposited in the burial ground of
the Synagogue, in this city.

PHILADELPHIA. *August 16, 1788.* A correspondent says that two Jews, one
of whom is a person of distinction, have lately come to this city from Jamaica, and who have not long ago been at Hebron, which is about 30
miles from Jerusalem, and which is their usual place of residence. Their
object is to collect subscriptions for some of their brethren, who have been

enslaved by the Turks for not producing a certain tribute at an appointed time. There are some who remember, that upon the failure of the payment of this tribute the Jews at Hebron were seized upon once as slaves by their cruel and insulting oppressors the Turks. It would be a laudable instance of generosity and magnanimity in the Christians to contribute according to their ability, as well as the Jews, for the purpose of relieving the oppressed. It has been said that mercy is twice blest; that it blesses those who receive and those who give.

PHILADELPHIA. *March 1, 1790.* Hebrew taught by Abraham Cohen, Son to the Rev'd Jacob Cohen—For particulars enquire at the above Rev'd Jacob Cohen's, Cherry Alley, between Third and Fourth Streets.

N.B. Spanish also taught as above.

82

An early-eighteenth-century view of New York showing the "Jews Burying Ground" at Chatham Street.
The New-York Historical Society, New York City

3
Congregational Affairs

OLD WAYS, NEW WORRIES

⤐ KEEPING CONGREGANTS on the narrow path of orthodoxy posed such a serious problem in eighteenth-century America that synagogue boards, called *juntas* in accordance with Sephardic custom, often had to go to great lengths to get Jews to come to services, observe the Sabbath, and adhere to the laws of *kashrut*. Sometimes threats were used; however, in a country with an ever-increasing appetite for freedom and diversity, threats alone were not enough to keep many Jews from doing as they pleased. The following selections from the minute books of Congregations Shearith Israel in New York (1757–1784) and Mikveh Israel in Philadelphia (1785–1792) highlight these and other problems.

1757. The Parnasim & Elders having received undoubted Testimony That severall of our Bretheren, that reside in the Country have and do dayly violate the principles of our holy religion, such as Trading on the Sabath, Eating of forbidden Meats & other Henious Crimes, and as our Holy law injoins us to reprove one Another agreeable to the Commandments in Liviticus *Hocheach tocheach et ameetecha* thou shalt surely reprove thy Neighbour and not suffer sin upon him . . . therefor whosoever for the future continues to act contrary to our Holy Law by breacking any of the principles command will not be deem'd a member of our Congregation, have none of the Mitzote of the Sinagoge Confered on him & when Dead will not be buried according to the manner of our brethren. But like Nehemiah who treated those of old that transgressed In the same manner he ordered the gates to be shut against Them, so will the Gates of our Community be shut intirely Against such offenders. . . .

1784. [To Hayman Levy, *parnas* (president) of the congregation, from Benjamin I. Jacobs] Gentlemen, the petitioner hereof Benjamin Jacobs, Being upon the point of marriage, and the Lady, Whom he is about to espouse, Being desirous to live as a Jewess; Joins with him in this petition, and Begs that she may be married according to the manners and customs of the Jews, as it is her desire, to live in the strict observance of all our Laws and customs, which if granted, will greatly oblige, both her and the Bearer, who waits at Mr. Cohens, to answer any questions, which the gentlemen, may think fit to ask him.

At a Meeting of the Parnass & Assistants, a petition was presented by Mr. Benjn I. Jacobs, to admit his being married to a Woman not belonging to our society, with intent to make her a Proselite, which Petition is refused in consequence of a Law to the contrary, dated the 6th day of Nisan 5523 [March 20, 1763].

1785. At a meeting held of the congregation [Mikveh Israel] on the 5th of Nison, 5545, or 16th March, 1785 . . . [a] letter was read setting forth that there is to be a burell of one B. M. Clava who was marrid to a *goy* [Gentile] by *goyim*, and as many to our sorry are in the same preditement, that some mode of buriall aught to be adapted from the comon way of good yehudim. Wher on it was debaited and agreed on, with out a desanding voice, that a *din towrah* [an authoritative decision] should be asked and oboydid by. When Messrs. Manuel Josephson, Moses D. Nathons, and Joseph W. Corples was chosen to give the *din* or wordeek in writig but as the corpse or *mes* was laying to be burried, there ansure is at present that B. M. Clava and all such persons in fewture is to be entiard with out washing and clothing, but put in the corphin as he now lays, and carried to the grave. Agreed unanimously.

October 13, 1788

Congregation Mikveh Israel
Philadelphia

To the anerable, the president, and the genthelman jauntay:
    Weer as I have pramis mie selleff in matteri mony whit one gall, the dogter of Mr. Barent Jacob, in the Norderen Libberthes in Philadelphia; and I would bie werry happay that jour anerable budday would order to Mr. Jacob Kohon as gasan of the congragashis of Mikvy Israel to give mie goupa and kadousin agins Dousday. Ther for, genttelman, I pray one ansver of jour shentel man to mourow . . . the 12 day of Tisri at 11 o'clok and, bo soo douing, your pertisnar will eiver pray.
                                    From jour omble sarwint,
                                    Salomon Raffeld

To the honorable, the president, and the gentlemen [of the] *junta:*
    Whereas I have promised myself in matrimony with a girl, the daughter of Mr. Barent Jacob, in the Northern Liberties [section] in Philadelphia, I would be very happy if your honorable body would order Mr. Jacob Cohen, as *chazzen* at the congregation of Mikveh Israel, to give me *chupah* [wedding canopy] and *kiddushin* [a legal and ritually proper Jewish

marriage] against [next] Tuesday. Therefore, gentlemen, I pray an answer from you gentlemen tomorrow . . . the 12th day of Tishri at eleven o'clock and, by so doing, your petitioner will ever pray.

From your humble servant,
Salomon Raffeld

September 3, 1792. . . . all and every person professing Judaism, and refuses to contribute a just and equitable proportion toward the support of the synagogue, shall be deemed as not belonging to our society, either in publick or private. Nor shall they be noticed in any concerns peculiar to the rites and ceremonies thereof, on any occasion whatever, and in case of death, of themselves or any of their family residing within their dwelling, they shall not be intitled to the aid or attendance usual on such occasions from any person belonging to the congregation. . . . And that no one may pretend ignorance of the aforesaid regulations, resolved, that the parnas order the same to be publickly read at synagogue on the first day of Rosh Ashana now next ensuing, after the morning service, before taking out the *sepharim*, that all persons may know the same and regulate themselves accordingly. "And all the people shall hear and fear."

85

CONGREGATIONAL

AFFAIRS

❧ THE FALLING AWAY of Jews from traditional religious practices in New York and Philadelphia was nothing compared to what was going on at this time in Petersburg, Virginia. The following extract is taken from two letters a Jewish wife and mother, Rebecca Samuel, wrote to her parents in Germany in 1791.

. . . When the Jews of Philadelphia or New York hear the name Virginia, they get nasty. And they are not wrong! It won't do for a Jew. In the first place it is an unhealthful district, and we are only human. God forbid, if anything should happen to us, where would we be thrown? There is no cemetery in the whole of Virginia. In Richmond, which is twenty-two miles from here, there is a Jewish community consisting of two *minyonim*, [quorums] and the two cannot muster a quorum when needed.

You cannot imagine what kind of Jews they have here. They were all German itinerants who made a living by begging in Germany. They came to America during the war, as soldiers, and now they can't recognize themselves.

. . . Anyone can do as he wants. There is no rabbi in all of America to excommunicate anyone. . . . Jew and Gentile are as one. There is no *galut* [exile] here. In New York and Philadelphia there is more *galut*. The reason is that there are too many German Gentiles and Jews there. The German Gentiles cannot forsake their anti-Jewish prejudice; and the German Jews cannot forsake their disgraceful conduct; and that's what makes the *galut*.

. . . Here Jewishness is pushed aside. There are here ten or twelve Jews and they are not worthy of being called Jews. We have a *shochet* [ritual slaughterer] who goes to market and buys *treyfe* [unkosher] meat and then brings it home. On Rosh Hashonah and on Yom Kippur the people worshipped here without one *sefer torah*, and not one of them wore the *tallis* [prayer shawl] or the *arba kanfot* [the small set of fringes worn on the body] except Hyman and my Sammy's godfather. . . .

. . . The way we live now is no life at all. We do not know what the Sabbath and the holidays are. On the Sabbath all the Jewish shops are open; and they do business on that day as they do throughout the whole week. . . .

All the people who hear that we are leaving give us their blessings. They say that it is sinful that such blessed children should be brought up here. . . . My children cannot learn anything here, nothing Jewish, nothing of general culture. My Schoene, God bless her is already three years old. I think it is time that she should learn something, and she has a good head to learn. I have taught her the bedtime prayers and grace after meals in just two lessons. I believe that no one among the Jews can do as well as she. . . .

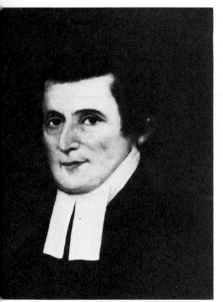

America's first native-born chazzen, Gershom Mendes Seixas. When the British occupied New York in 1776, Seixas preached a patriotic sermon and closed the synagogue. Thirteen years later he was one of thirteen clergymen to participate in George Washington's first inauguration.
American Jewish Archives, Cincinnati, Ohio

THE LIFE OF A COLONIAL *CHAZZEN*

⌁ GERSHOM Mendes Seixas, America's first native-born *chazzen*, was the son of an unsuccessful shopkeeper who barely made enough to feed and clothe a family of nine. Poor as he was, Gershom nonetheless was able to study under the tutelage of Joseph Pinto, an Amsterdam Jew "very well versed in the reading of the Pentateuch," who served as Congregation Shearith Israel's *chazzen* from 1758 to 1766. Two years later, Gershom applied "for the office of hazan." There being no other candidates, he was "unanimously, and without one Negative voted . . . to the said office."

The following year Gershom set out alone on horseback for Lancaster, Pennsylvania, to officiate at the marriage of Michael Gratz, the Philadelphia merchant, and Miriam Simon, the daughter of a wealthy Indian trader. "He has never been so far from home," Gershom's father wrote to the bride's father, an old friend, "and if you find anything amiss in his behavior, impute it favourably to his want of Experience, & Kindly admonish him for it."

When he returned to New York, Gershom settled down to his regular duties as *chazzen, mohel, shochet,* and *melamed* (cantor, circumcisor, ritual slaughterer, and teacher), which he found "verry Inconsiderable" and therefore requested in 1775 "an additional Sallery, the Sum [of] . . . One hundred and Forty pounds per Annum . . . otherwise beg leave to decline serving any longer than the present quarter." Having agreed to a basic salary of £100, with an additional bonus of £10 after six months and another £10 at the close of the year, Gershom de-

cided the time had come to marry. The bride was a Miss Elkaley Cohen, the orphaned daughter of a New York shopkeeper who brought with her a dowry of £200.

In the summer of the following year, when it looked as though New York would soon fall to the British, Gershom fled with his wife and infant son, Isaac, to Connecticut, where he remained until moving in 1780 to Philadelphia to serve as *chazzen* for those Jews who had fled from New York as well as for members of the local congregation, Mikveh Israel. Four years later Gershom was asked to return to New York and resume his old duties as *chazzen* of Shearith Israel.

Philadelphia, February 15th, 1784

The Honorable Parnass [President] and *Mahamad* [Board]
K. K. Mikve Israel

Gentlemen:

Being called to my former place of residence (and the place of my nativity), have to inform you that my quarter expires here on *Ros Hodes* Nisan [March 23], at which time have engaged to return to New York. That you may not lose the opportunity of providing yourselves with a suitable person for the office of hazen, beg leave to recommend a speedy application to those whom you think worthy. And I will on my part do every thing in my power for the benefit of the K. K. Mikve Israel, to whom I acknowledge myself greatly indebted for the many kind and generous favors that I have received during my stay amongst them, and shall ever make it my study to render every possible service in return.

May the Great God of Israel vouchsafe to hold you under His holy and divine protection. May you increase and prosper in peace and tranquility, most devoutly prays, gentlemen,

Your much obliged and very humble servitor,
Gershom Seixas

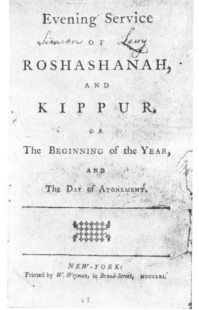

The first Jewish prayer book printed in America.

Philadelphia, 15th March, 1784

Mr. Hayman Levy [parnass Congregation Shearith Israel]

Dear and worthy Sir:

The unsettledness of the weather, almost makes me despair of being able to accomplish my contract with your congregation at the time appointed, which was to have been a week from tomorrow. . . . Several letters have passed between the parnass and junta and me. They condemn me for not having given them timely notice of my intention to quit them. Have said every thing I could to justify my conduct. The matter now rests entirely with you to say go or stay.

Should have wrote to you before, but was in such continual and violent pain upwards of a fortnight after my return home that I could not even speak without encreasing the pain.

J.R.BRADY
Architect.

בהכנ דקק בני ישורון תקפז לפק

The Synagogue of the Congregation B'nai Jeshurun......New York. A.M. 5587.

A synagogue that was once a Negro church. New York's Congregation B'nai Jeshurun on Elm Street near Canal, 1827.
Museum of the City of New York

With the greatest respect to Aunt Levy, in which my wife unites, and salutations to the rest of your worthy houshold and connexions, am, dear and worthy sir,

Your obliged and affect[iona]t[e] humble servitor,
Gershom Seixas

New York, 22nd March, 1784

The Honorable Parnass and Junto
of the K. K. Mikve Israel

Gentlemen:

Your letter of 14th inst. only reached us this morning. The time is so short that we have hardly sufficient to answer you with that precision we should otherwise do. We shall therefore answer the most material without going to particularities.

We are much surprised that you should complain of short notice, given you by Mr. Seixas of his *intention.* Those who have been obliged to take up their residence in Philadelphia while this place was in the power of the British always expected Mr. Seixas would return, and to your candor we submit, when we ask you, did you expect otherwise?

As to the gentleman who now officiates here, we make no doubt he will, when properly invited, pay you a visit. *Perhaps* the congregation of Mikve Israel may approve of him. . . .

With wishing you the enjoyment of many happy festivals, I am in behalf of the junto, gentlemen,

Your most obedient, humble servant,
Hayman Levy, parnas

BECAUSE OF Shearith Israel's limited resources, Gershom was expected in addition to his regular duties to supervise the behavior of the pre–*bar mitzvah* boys who sat directly behind him in the Mill Street *shul.* When a fellow congregant was offered £10 a year to "superintend the Children when in Synagogue," Gershom gladly relinquished this sum from his salary. Other problems, however, were not so easily solved. When it was discovered that the "funds of this congregation are inadequate to allow the *chazzen* his present salary," Gershom, by now the head of a family of ten, was asked to live on less. After pointing out that he couldn't, a ruling *junta* of wealthy businessmen relented, but only after getting Gershom to agree to furnish his own firewood.

Gershom fared better in the company of Gentiles. Chosen as an official delegate at the first inauguration of George Washington, and, some years later, as an incorporator of Columbia College and a trustee of the city's Humane Society, he was treated in Protestant circles more like a Jewish ambassador than a mere clergyman, and as such was "admired by all, esteemed alike in every grade of society . . . prosecuting uninterruptedly a line of conduct that obtained for him the love and respect of all sects."

NEWS FROM NEWPORT

⌇ AS EARLY AS 1660, ships from Newport were sailing to far-off Barbados with cargoes of horses and grain, and returning with molasses and rum. Even then Barbados had a sizable Sephardic community. When the Jews there learned that Roger Williams, the founder of Rhode Island, allowed everyone to practice his religion openly, it was only natural for some of them to travel to Newport.

The first contingent arrived in 1679. Mostly merchants, their Spanish and Portuguese names appear in various court records and petitions for the next ten years or so, but then all traces of them disappear, perhaps as a result of shifting patterns of trade, though there is no way of knowing for sure why or when they left.

Not until the 1750s did the Jews return to Newport. This time there was a stronger commitment to stay. Ships, shops, and warehouses were built, many by Aaron Lopez. A Portuguese-born Marrano, Lopez supplied his customers with everything from Bibles and bottled beer to looking glasses and violins. In addition, he was a manufacturer of shoes, clothing, and candles, a producer of cocoa and rum, and a slave trader. The owner of thirty ships, he was also Newport's largest taxpayer.

Much of the money for building the Touro Synagogue in 1763 came from Lopez. A major architectural achievement in its day, it was designed by Peter Harrison, a Quaker architect who also laid down the plans for King's Chapel in Boston. The following account of the dedication ceremonies is taken from the diary of Ezra Stiles, pastor at the time of Newport's Second Congregational Church and later president of Yale College.

December 2, 1763. In the afternoon was the dedication of the new synagogue in this town. It began by a handsome procession in which were carried the Books of the Law, to be deposited in the Ark. . . . There were present many gentlemen and ladies. The order and decorum, the harmony and solemnity of the music, together with a handsome assembly of people, in an ediface the most perfect of the temple kind perhaps in America, and splendidly illuminated, could not but raise in the mind a faint idea of the majesty and grandeur of the ancient Jewish worship mentioned in the scripture. . . . There may be eighty souls of Jews or fifteen families now in town. The synagogue has already cost fifteen hundred pounds sterling.

IT IS IMPOSSIBLE to overestimate the importance of the role men like Stiles played in breaking down social barriers between Christians and Jews in colonial America. A frequent visitor to Newport's Georgian-style synagogue, Stiles counted among his close friends the local *chazzen,* Isaac Touro, with whom he enjoyed sipping tea and discussing the Bible as well as the Talmud and the mystical Zohar. Stiles also struck up

*Inside Newport's famous Touro
Synagogue, built in 1763 and now a
national historical site.*
Library of Congress

friendships with a number of *maggidim* (itinerant preachers) who passed
through Newport in the course of their travels around the world. By far
the most intense friendship of all developed between Stiles and Rabbi
Chaim Isaac Carigal of Hebron, whose portrait Stiles kept near him
until his death. They first met on the eve of Purim three years before the
outbreak of the Revolutionary War. The following accounts are taken
again from the diary of Ezra Stiles.

March 8, 1773. This evening I went to the synagogue it being the eve of
Purim. The Chazan read through the Book of Esther. There I saw Rabbi
Carigal lately from the city of Hebron in the Holy Land. He was one of the
two persons that stood by the Chazan at the Taubauh or reading desk

while the Book of Esther was read. He was dressed in a red garment with the usual phylacteries and habiliments; he wore a high brown fur cap, had a long beard. He has the appearance of an ingenious and sensible man.

March 30, 1773. This afternoon the rabbi came to visit me. . . . We conversed largely on the Gemara, the two Talmuds (of which he preferred the Babylonish), the changes of the Hebrew language in different ages, etc., etc. . . . We talked upon the difference of the dialects of the Chaldee, Syriac, and rabbinical Hebrew, on the Targums, etc. Evening coming on he took leave in a polite and friendly manner.

April 6, 1773. In the afternoon I visited Rabbi Chaim Isaac Carigal. We conversed much and freely—he is learned and truly modest, far more so than I ever saw a Jew. . . .

April 8, 1773. This day is Passover with the Jews. I went to the synagogue. The Chocham Rabbi was there. . . . The rabbi's dress of apparel: common English shoes, black leather; silver flowered buckles; white stockings. His general habit was Turkish, a green silk vest or long under garment reaching down more than half way the legs or within three inches of the ankles. The ends of the sleeves of this vest appeared on the wrists in a foliage turn-up of three inches, and the opening little larger than that the hand might pass freely. A girdle or sash of different colors red and green girt the vest around his body. It appeared not to be open at [the] bottom but to come down like a petticoat, and no breeches could be discovered. This vest, however, had an opening above the girdle—and here he put in his handkerchief and snuff box and watch. . . . When he came into the synagogue he put over all the usual alb or white surplice, which was like that of other Jews except that its edge was striped with blue . . . and had more fringe. He had a white cravat round his neck . . . a long black beard, the upper lip partly shaven—his head shaved all over. On his head a high fur sable cap, exactly like a woman's muff, about nine or ten inches high. The aperture atop was closed with green cloth. He behaved modestly and reverently. Some part of the singing in the synagogue this day was exceeding fine and melodious.

April 23, 1773. I visited the rabbi. . . . We discoursed on many things. . . . I asked him whether Moses wrote all the Pentateuch, particularly the account of his own death . . . he answered yes, that he wrote of things future as present. . . . I asked him whether by the usual intercalation the Hebrew chronology was perfect—the Jewish year exactly solar? Yes. How long their chronology had been reduced to perfection and whether anciently there were no errors or deviations from solar time? He said it was perfect from the beginning, the principles of it laid down in the six days of creation and delivered down from the earliest antiquity. I wanted more closely to attend to this matter, as he spoke with the deliberate confidence of demonstration . . . but we had no time.

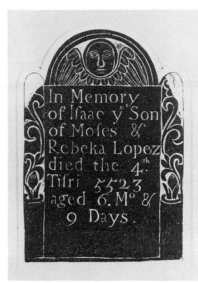

Newport, Rhode Island, tombstone in the days when Newport's Jewish community numbered several hundred souls.
Anne Williams and Susan Kelly. Courtesy of Museum of American Folk Art.

June 7, 1773. This afternoon . . . we had much conversation upon the antiquity of the Hebrew letters. . . . The rabbi told me that he had nothing written when he preached at the synagogue—but that he had sealed it first in his head and so delivered it. . . . He said that none but rabbis preached, and they usually preached on all the holidays but not every sabbath, and always without notes.

June 14, 1773. In the forenoon I went to visit the rabbi—discoursed on ventriloquism and the Witch of Endor and the reality of bringing up Samuel. He had not heard of ventriloquism before and still doubted it. . . . I turned him to the strong expression in his letter [to Stiles], "Your love has made such an indelible impression upon the inmost thoughts and affections of my heart that volumes are not sufficient to write the thousandth part of the eternal love wherewith I love thee"—and asked him how he could use so strong an expression of friendship. He in reply said he wished well to others besides his own nation, he loved all mankind, and turned me to Leviticus xix, 18—Thou shalt love thy neighbor as thyself.

June 28, 1773. This afternoon the rabbi visited me. We spent the afternoon very agreeably. He told me that there was one rabbi at the synagogue in Jamaica, another at Surinam, and a third at Eustatia or Curacao. . . . There are none on the continent of North America. . . . He wants now three or four months of being forty years old, so was born A.D. 1733, and was made a rabbi about A.D. 1753. He began to travel at the age of twenty and has visited Damascus, Alleppo, Grand Cairo, Baghdad, Ispahan, Smyrna, Constantinople, Salonica, Rome, Florence, Bologna, Venice, Vienna, Prague, Paris, London, etc. Of all cities he gives the preference to Venice and London.

Rabbi Chaim Isaac Carigal, a maggid *(itinerant preacher) from Hebron and a good friend of Ezra Stiles before he became president of Yale.*
Beinecke Rare Book and Manuscript Library, Yale University

July 15, 1773. Spent the afternoon with the rabbi, partly at the Redwood Library and partly at my house. I asked him whether the rabbis of this age thought themselves to have any particular reasons for expecting the Messiah immediately. He said not, but he thought it was high time for him to come. He added that if all nations were in war and universal tumult and confusion, then he should expect him immediately, but this not being more the case now than in every current age, etc. . . .

July 16, 1773. In company with the rabbi. He told me he rode over the River Jordan on horseback against Jericho which was near the river. He said it was a very shallow river and almost dry in summer. He had been at all the twelve or thirteen synagogues in the Holy Land, and gave me the following account which I wrote from his mouth. . . . 5 synagogues at Jerusalem, 2 at Saphat, 1 at Tiberias, 1 at Hebron, 1 at Gaza, 1 at Schchem, 1 at Acco—and 1 at Jaffa, only a chamber for worship occasionally, but not every Sabbath.

July 19, 1773. Finishing a Hebrew letter to the rabbi. In the afternoon I visited the rabbi and showed him my letter which I had not time to copy, it being four leaves or eight pages. He desired me to copy it and send it to him, and to correspond with [him], telling me he would always write to me from any part of the world wherever he should be. As he had told me he had rode over Jordan against Jericho, I observed to him that he had then seen the place where Joshua led Israel through Jordan on dry ground, and asked him if the stones Joshua put in the bottom of Jordan were still in being—adding that if they were they might easily be found, as the water was so shallow. He said he did not think of it when he passed Jordan, but that he believed the place of the passage was a little higher up. . . . Mr. Rivera showed me a marriage contract of his wife to her former husband. [We] conversed upon their customs as to matrimony. . . . I asked the rabbi whether there would be any marrying, any relations of husbands and wives in the Resurrection. He said yes. Whether Sarah would then be Abraham's wife? Yes. If a woman had had more husbands than one, whose wife would she be, particularly whose wife would Mrs. Rivera be . . . whether Mr. Rivera's or her former husband's in the Resurrection? Mr. and Mrs. Rivera joined me in this question. The rabbi was at a loss and could not determine. He said there were various opinions about it—God Almighty could only determine. He was contented to know that the Resurrection state would be happy and glorious. . . . He again took leave of me very affectionately, praying God to bless me. I told him I parted from him with great reluctance, and should ever retain an affection for him—that it was probable we might never see each other in the Land of the Living and wished we might after death meet together in the Garden of Eden and there rejoice with Abraham, Isaac and Jacob, and with the soul of the Messiah till the Resurrection. He wished me reciprocally and my family every blessing . . . said he loved me from the heart, had my name in his book, and should send it to Jerusalem, where I should be soon known as I was here.

July 21, 1773. This day Rabbi Haijm Isaac Carigal sailed for Surinam.

4

Native Sons and Daughters

MOVING IN NEW DIRECTIONS

GROWING UP as part of a new nation had an enormous effect on a generation of American-born Jews inspired by a still-living revolution. To be sure, certain states denied Jews the right to vote or hold office until well into the nineteenth century. Moreover, those who entered public life during the early years of the republic were by no means spared anti-Semitic attacks. Even so, in America there were more reasons for Jews to look upon themselves as fellow citizens than in any other nation at this time. Wherever there were jobs requiring certain kinds of skills which Jews had acquired by working in specialized fields, Jews were welcome. Those with a background in international trade became officers in their home ports or in the U.S. Navy; Indian traders became Indian agents; Jewish merchants who traveled frequently to foreign ports became American consular agents. The entry of Jews into civic affairs, while it did not come as early as their entry into government service, was not long delayed. In New York in 1797, Solomon Simson was elected president of the Tammany Society, a benevolent organization well on its way to becoming the city's principal political faction. Another New York Jew, Jacob Hays, served in the 1790s as a city marshal, crier for the Court of Sessions, and sergeant-at-arms of the Board of Aldermen.

New York City's High Constable, Jacob Hays. One of the most remarkable law enforcers of his day, Hays is said to have known every professional criminal in the East by sight and name. From a caricature by James A. Read in Yankee Doodle, *April 24, 1847.*

In 1802, however, his [Hays's] real life work began; Mayor Edward Livingston appointed him chief of the day police force and gave him the resounding title of High Constable of the City of New York. He occupied the office for almost half a century, and became one of the best-known men in the New York of his generation. In those early days of the American Republic the Fourth of July and Evacuation Day (the anniversary of the evacuation of the city by the British, formerly observed as a holiday) were celebrated with elaborate parades, and one of the High Constable's most cherished privileges was to march at the head of the procession with the mayor, as a sort of official bodyguard. On these momentous occasions Old Hays [as he was known throughout most of his career] shouldered a drawn sword and carried an ornate staff, while a flaming cockade decorated his hat and his diminutive person glittered with the badges and the insignia of his office.

The population of New York when Old Hays became High Constable was almost sixty-five thousand, but the police force was in an embryonic stage. The task of guarding the city during the daylight hours was entrusted to half a dozen city marshalls and two constables from each ward, but they were primarily attached to the courts and spent practically all of their time serving summonses, warrants, and other legal papers, so that for some thirty years Old Hays was the only peace officer to patrol the streets from dawn to dusk. So vigilant was he that he never had more than six hours' sleep at night. . . .

In the heydey of his career Old Hays was small, wiry, bald, and fussy, and walked with an amusing strut. Despite his posing and strutting . . . he was one of the most expert thief-takers New York has ever produced. He is said to have known by sight and name every professional criminal in the East at a time when the country fairly teemed with lawbreakers, and his fame was so widespread that he was often consulted by the police of England and the Continent. Whenever a major crime was committed the almost universal cry was "Set Old Hays after them!" He went unarmed except for his staff of office, but he was very courageous and possessed great physical strength, and he was always ready to attack criminals or rioters regardless of their numbers. Once while he was arresting Jack Reed, a notorious forger and cracksman, the latter attempted to stab him with a dirk. Old Hays gripped Reed by the wrist and twisted the knife from his hand, at the same time pressing the forger against a brick wall with such force that three of Reed's ribs were broken. Flinging the criminal over his shoulder, the High Constable fought off half a dozen would-be rescuers and lugged his man to jail. . . .

Several methods of detection which are still extensively used by the police were originated and developed by Old Hays. He was the first New York policeman to shadow a criminal, and the first to administer the third degree, although such refinements as the use of a rubber hose and brass knuckles were thought up by later civilizations. It was the High Constable's custom, when he thought a suspect whom he was questioning was lying, to crack the man on the knuckles or shinbone with his staff, meanwhile shouting angrily: "Good citizens will tell the truth!" Old Hays was also the first, so far as can be ascertained from existing records, to confront a suspected murderer with the body of his victim, a melodramatic idea which was subsequently adopted by the French police and became one of their favorite practices. . . .

During the first forty years of the nineteenth century New York was the scene of many riots and street brawls between the great gangs of the Bowery and the Five Points. Old Hays put down many of these disturbances single-handed, and employed a technique which for sheer efficiency and quickness of result has never been excelled anywhere in the United States. When he was informed that a riot or a street fight was in progress, he instantly repaired to the scene of the disturbance. He did not attempt to arrest the ringleaders immediately; instead, he rapidly circled

The first Jewish public official in Wisconsin, John Lawe. An agent for John Jacob Astor's American Fur Company, Lawe settled in Wisconsin in 1797 and became the first judge in the territory.

John Hays, frontier sheriff.
American Jewish Archives, Cincinnati, Ohio

*John Hays's log cabin courthouse,
Cahokia, Illinois.*
Illinois State Historical Library

*Cahokia, Illinois, as it looked a
hundred and fifty years ago.*

the jostling crowd and began knocking off hats with his staff, a comparatively easy task in those days because stovepipe headgear was generally worn even by the lowest ranks of society. Nine times out of ten a man whose hat has suddenly been jerked from his head will stop whatever he is doing to retrieve it, a trait of human nature of which the High Constable was perfectly aware. So, when a rioter stooped to pick up his hat, and consequently threw himself off balance, Old Hays gave him a shove that sent him sprawling on the pavement. Within a few moments what had been a potentially serious riot had been transformed into a ludicrous spectacle of a crowd of men scrambling about looking for their hats. Meanwhile Old Hays would have arrested the fomenters of the trouble and would be marching them off to jail. . . .

Old Hays's extraordinary activity finally enfeebled him, and after the organization of the Municipal Police in 1844 he confined his work largely to serving court papers. He died in 1850, in the seventy-eighth year of his age, full of honors, and was buried in Woodlawn Cemetery. At the next meeting of the Common Council the office of High Constable was abolished, and the artist Shegogue was commissioned to paint Old Hays' portrait, which was hung in the Governor's Room at City Hall, where it still offers inspiration to the few city officials who ever heard of him.

Herbert Asbury

❧ OLD HAYS was by no means the only pioneering member of his family. His cousin John became the first Jew to settle permanently in Illinois. Although isolated from other Jews for the greater part of his life, John remained a practicing Jew until the end of his days. Governor John Reynolds in his *Pioneer History of Illinois* provides the following account of Hays, beginning with his career as an Indian trader on the Canadian border.

It was toward the headwaters of the Red River that Hays and two Canadians were caught out in a snow-storm in the prairie and were compelled to lie under the snow for three days and nights. . . . No one who has not experienced the hardships of the Indian trade of the Northwest can realize it.

He returned safe from this storm and afterward settled in Cahokia where he kept a small assortment of goods. His boats, either with himself or agents, generally made a voyage once a year to Prairie du Chien with articles for the Indian trade, and returned sometimes the same fall and sometimes in the spring. With a due regard to economy he made money in this commerce.

He married a lady in Vincennes of excellent family and what is still better, of sound, good sense. They lived together in Cahokia and raised a respectable family. He then turned his attention to agriculture, purchasing land in the common-field of Cahokia and cultivating it to some considerable advantage.

He held the office of postmaster in Cahokia so long that "the memory of man" scarcely "runneth to contrary." This was no profit to him, but he held the office for the accommodation of his Creole neighbors, whose acquaintance with school-houses was extremely limited. He was appointed to the office of Sheriff of St. Clair County by Gov. St. Clair in 1798, and he continued to exercise the duties of this office down to 1818, when the State government was organized. I presume this was the longest term of office ever held in Illinois.

During a long life of industry and economy, he acquired a handsome property, and was in his advanced years very comfortably situated, having all the comforts of life that render the human family happy. He was not a member of any Christian church, but observed the precepts contained in the word with due respect and devotion. At his death his fortune descended to three daughters, his only children.

ᔰ ANOTHER PIONEER Jewish Indian trader, Abraham Mordecai, was the first native-born white man to settle in Montgomery County, Alabama. Mordecai also built Alabama's first cotton gin.

He traded extensively with the Indians, exchanging his goods for pink root, hickory-nut oil and peltries [fur-bearing skins] of all kinds. These he carried to New Orleans and Mobile in boats, and to Pensacola and Augusta on pack-horses. The hickory-nut oil was a luxury with French and Spanish epicures. It was manufactured by the Indians in a simple manner—by boiling the cracked nuts in water, and skimming off the oil as it floated on the surface. Mordecai bought cotton of the Indians in small quantities, ginned it, and carried it to Augusta on pack-horses, in bags much smaller than those of the present day. He was a dark-eyed Jew, and amorous in his disposition. Tourculla, Chief of the Coosawdas, hearing of his intrigues with a married squaw, approached his house with twelve warriors, knocked him down, thrashed him with poles until he lay insensible, cut off his ear, and left him to the care of his wife. They also broke up his boat and burned down his gin-house. Thus, a pretty squaw was the cause of the destruction of the first cotton gin in Alabama.

Pickett's History of Alabama

MEN AND WOMEN OF CULTURE

ᔰ ACCORDING TO popular legend, Washington Irving described Michael and Miriam Gratz's daughter Rebecca in such glowing terms to Sir Walter Scott that he named an important character in *Ivanhoe* after her. Perhaps it was so, because Rebecca happened to be one of the most attractive women of her day. For many years her spacious house on Philadelphia's tree-lined Chestnut Street served as a meeting place for such well-known figures as the American artist Thomas Sully, who saw in Rebecca "all that a princess of blood Royal might have coveted," and the English actress Fanny Kemble, who much admired Rebecca's ability

Benjamin Gratz
All, Library of Congress

*Rebecca Gratz at 25. From a
painting by Thomas Sully.*

to remain true to her faith without tormenting doubts or conflict. In the following letters to her brother Benjamin, who settled in Kentucky in 1819, and his Christian wife Maria, Rebecca provides us with a sense of what Jewish life in and around Philadelphia was like in the 1820s and '30s.

Rebecca Gratz in her old age.

February 27, 1825

To Benjamin

I am surprised you have no account of the consecration of the new Mikveh Israel synagogue building, except from the newspaper as it was a subject engaging universal attention.

. . . I have never witnessed a more impressive or solemn ceremony or one more calculated to elevate the mind to religious exercises. The *shool* is one of the most beautiful specimens of ancient architecture in the city . . . the decorations are neat yet tasteful—and the service commencing just before the Sabbath was performed by lamp light. Mr. Keys [minister of Congregation Mikveh Israel from 1824 to 1828] was assisted in the service by the *chazzen* from New York Mr. Peixotto, a venerable learned and pious man who gave great effect to the solemnity . . . the processions entered with the two Reverends in their robes followed by nine copies of the Sacred Rolls—they advanced slowly to the Tabah while a choir of five voices

Benjamin Gratz's second wife, Anne, in the library of their home in Lexington, Kentucky.

Rebecca Gratz's sister Fanny (ABOVE) shortly after her marriage to Reuben Etting (BELOW). The paintings are by James Peale.
All, Library of Congress

chanted the appointed psalms most delightfully . . . the whole audience was most profoundly attentive and tho few were so happy as to understand the language, those who did say they have never heard the Hebrew so well delivered as by Mr. Keys . . . all who were there acknowledge there has never been such church music performed in Phila. . . .

I think continually of you my dear brother when I enter that temple and I pray that I may again see you worshipping within its walls—I know your faith is unchangable and will endure even tho' you are alone in a land of strangers. May God be merciful to us all and keep us stedfast to our duties. I love your dear Maria, and admire the forbearance which leaves unmolested the religious opinions she knows are sacred in your estimation. May you both continue to worship according to the dictates of your conscience and your orisons be equally acceptable at the throne of grace. . . .

April 18, 1832

To Maria

I had my philosophy a little tried the other day by some good Christians, and as I dare not complain about it to anybody else (for I hate to set the subject in its true light at home) I must make you my confidante— You know I promised our friend Mrs. Furnass to apply for a little girl out of the Asylum for her. Well, there is a good little girl I have kept my eye on and she is ready for a place—and my application is rejected because it is for a Unitarian. "But ladies," said I, "there are many children under my special direction. You all know my creed. Suppose I should want one to bring up in my family?" "You may have one," said a church woman, "because the Jews do not think it a duty to convert." "But," said a Presbyterian, "I should not consent to her being put under the influence of a Unitarian." And so, my dear, after putting the question to a vote, I could do nothing. And when the meeting broke up I had the mischievous pleasure of telling one of the most blue of the board that I construed their silence into consent, for only one lady voted in the affirmative and they were all ashamed to vote no. . . . I got into a long discussion on the subject of religion with a lady after the meeting and though we have been more than twenty years acquainted I expect she will look shy on me for the rest of our lives. What a pity that the best and holiest gift of God, to his most favored creatures, should be perverted into a subject of strife—and that to seek to know and love the most High should not be the end and aim of all without a jealous or persecuting feeling towards each other.

September 2, 1832

To Maria

I received a heartrending letter a few days ago from our dear Sally Minis giving an account of that unfortunate affair of Philips. . . .

"He was consulting some of his friends at the races in April about naming a horse, when Mr. Stark passing by said, 'Name him Shylock,' and afterwards called him a 'D—d Jew.' Minis challenged him then. He apologized and the affair slumbered until some of Stark's friends induced him to retract his apology, and another challenge was sent and accepted. A difference about the hour of fighting arose between the seconds. . . . Although assured that the other party would not meet them then, they returned and publicly pronounced Minis a coward. The next morning they met accidentally at the City Hotel. Minis reproached Stark for his conduct. He drew a pistol and advanced. Minis did the same and fired instantly. Stark fell mortally wounded and Minis immediately expressed his determination to give himself up to the civil authorities and is now in close confinement where he must continue until January as his father is a judge in the inferior Court, and Mr. S's nearest relation is a judge in the Superior Court, and so a new election must take place before he can be tried." . . .

Henry Etting too has had a fight at the navy yard in Boston but no serious consequence is likely to result. Our sister had a few sleepless nights to endure on his account, as a mother's fears have so many objects, but the

Captain and other officers have sent testimonials of his good conduct in the affair that we have every reason to rejoice he has come off so well.

February 19, 1837

To Maria

. . . I have been to a party where I met Mr. Furness, and at his church where I heard an excellent sermon from Mr. Dewey. Mr. Furness told me he and I ought to be inimical to each other according to the usual system of mankind because in religion we were not very different, and yet not alike. I told him I claimed the privilege of not being inimical to any man's religion, yet being firmly attached to my own, and so I hope my dear Maria are you. . . .

⊷§ MORE JEWS LIVED in Charleston in the early years of the republic than in any other city in America; by 1800, one out of every fifteen Charlestonians was Jewish. Many were international merchants who encouraged their sons and daughters to excel in the professions and the arts, and these went on to become lawyers, legislators, doctors, editors, teachers, and artists. Penina Moise was one of them. The daughter of French-speaking refugees from the 1791 Negro Revolution in Haiti, where the Moises had been plantation owners, Penina combined a deep love of Judaism with a keen appreciation for secular culture. As a poet and teacher, she exercised considerable influence over a circle of friends and disciples. The following tribute to Penina was written by a devoted pupil a few years after her death at the age of eighty-three.

There died in 1880 a Jewish poetess, Miss Penina Moise, who for many years was the literary pivot of Hebrew Charleston, and whose influence extended far beyond the circle of her co-religionists. Blind, poor, getting her living in her old age by keeping a little school, she yet created a literary *salon*, to which the best minds of Charleston flocked. Her Friday afternoons were a centre of intellectual intercourse. To the romantic imagination of young girls whom she taught, sitting in her large rocking chair, in her plain calico gown, with her sightless eyes looking out from under the black coif which completely hid her hair, she presented herself as an incarnation of intellectual and social splendor—a queen of literary society. Madame de Stael squabbling with Napoleon Bonaparte, Madame Recamier reclining in limp garments on her tub-like couch with Chateaubriand reading his manuscripts to her, Madame du Deffand exchanging epigrams with Horace Walpole—these were but the prototypes of Penina.

Miss Moise was connected by blood and marriage with the best Hebrew families of Charleston, and many of her scholars were of her own kindred. Her pupils read aloud to her, and by her system of education girls of twelve were made familiar with George Eliot, Charlotte Brontë, Walter Scott and other English classics as well as numerous volumes of French female memoirs. Miss Moise had all of the gayety, the contentment and the joyous philosophy of the French temperament. Twenty-five years of blindness did not diminish her fondness for life's pleasures. She lived in books, and especially in the lives of noted French women found the enjoyment of the keenest sympathy. . . . Penina was in the finest sense the mother of her people. To her the girl-babies were brought to be blessed before their names were called aloud in the synagogue. Secrets of betrothal, marriage, business and illness were confided to her tender care, and her advice was asked upon all important occasions.

Charlotte Adams

SUBMISSION TO THE WILL OF GOD

God Supreme! to Thee I pray.
Let my lips be taught to say,
Whether good or ill may flow,
Hallelujah, be it so!

What Thy wisdom may dictate
Let Thy servant vindicate;
Though it may my hopes o'erthrow,
Hallelujah, be it so!

Friends may falsify my trust.
Kindred also prove unjust,
Wound my heart and chill its glow,—
Hallelujah, be it so!

Health and comfort may decline,
What at this should I repine?
Both to Thee, my God, I owe,
Hallelujah, be it so!

When by disappointment stung,
Hard it is for human tongue
Still to say, though tears may flow,
Hallelujah, be it so!

Yet from Mercy's aid shall spring
Strength of spirit still to sing
'Mid bereavement, pain, and woe.
Hallelujah, be it so!

Penina Moise

Detail from a Jewish wedding quilt. Frederick County, Maryland, c. 1840.
Collection of Joanna S. Rose. Courtesy of Museum of American Folk Art.

No DOCUMENTARY history of pioneer Jews would be complete without a record of the achievements of Isaac Harby, an early playwright and critic who lived and worked in Charleston when that city was the undisputed cultural capital of the South. The following account of Harby was written by Penina Moise's brother Abraham, a struggling lawyer, shortly after Harby's death in 1828. It is interesting both as a portrait of an important American Jewish figure of his day and as an example of the literary style and spirit of the antebellum South.

Isaac Harby was the eldest son of Solomon Harby, whose father was originally from Barbary, where he enjoyed a post of honor in the palace of the Emperor of Morocco, that of Royal Lapidary. He afterwards fled to England and married an Italian lady. Solomon Harby left England for Jamaica before he was twenty-one years of age, and settled in Charleston, South Carolina, where our author was born in the year 1788.

Young Harby received all the advantages of a liberal education. His preceptor, Dr. Best, was at that time known and distinguished as among the first classical teachers in our city; and such was the rapid progress of his pupil in the various departments of the school, that it was his frequent practice to act the part of under teacher to the rest of his class.

After this period he obtained without difficulty a situation as assistant teacher in the Charleston College. . . .

As a teacher he had few equals, and probably no superior in this State. His method was peculiar to himself. He paid little attention to rules, and none to former systems. He instilled knowledge more by verbal explanation and familiar conversation, not unlike the admirable plan of Socrates, than the ordinary modes of taxing the memory with the weight of long and tedious exercises.

About this time, he made choice of Miss Mordecai, daughter of the late Samuel Mordecai, of Savannah, to be his partner and future companion through life; and although the society of this lady was well calculated to wean him, for a time, from his literary pursuits, or check his aspiring ambition, yet to mingle with and partake of the pleasures of the domestic circle were not inducements sufficiently strong to divert him from his studies, or destroy that great zeal and anxiety he had always manifested for the rewards of a well earned fame. . . .

[During this period] he first undertook the editorial department of a periodical, published weekly, called the *Quiver*. This paper, though not of long duration, was conducted with considerable cleverness. Associated with a friend, he purchased the *Investigator*, then one of the journals of the city, and stood forth the eloquent champion of the republican cause. By altering its name to that of the *Southern Patriot*, and diversifying its columns with the effusions of his lively and felicitous pen, the offspring of his creation seemed at once to rise like a phoenix from its own ashes.

As a controversialist few were his superiors—the shafts of his satire were unerring. His essays generally were distinguished for eloquence, discrimination and taste, and his criticisms were admired by all who read them. . . . But as a dramatic critic he had, perhaps, no equal in the country. His general acquaintance with the works of the drama, particularly those of Shakespeare, rendered him at all times a correct and severe judge of the proper conceptions of the actor.

We come now to speak of our author, not merely as a newspaper essayest, but as a writer of a more formal character. His love of the drama having rendered him a votary to theatrical exhibitions, he was emboldened to venture on a field which might indeed exhibit some splendid trophies, though innumerable defeats. *Alexander Severus*, a tragedy in five acts, was from all appearances among the earliest efforts of his muse. In 1807 he

Isaac Harby. A gifted teacher, critic, and playwright, Harby was also a pioneer Jewish religious reformer who called for "order and decency in worship, harmony and beauty in chanting."
American Jewish Historical Society, Waltham, Massachusetts

produced *The Gordian Knot, or Causes and Effects.* This drama, though produced from a mere youth, certainly exhibits passages of considerable wit and humor. It did not, however, meet with complete success which a young and sanguine mind looked for and expected.

He made no other effort as a dramataic writer until 1819, when appeared *Alberti*, a play in five acts, the original object of which was the vindication of the character and conduct of Lorenzo D'Medici. The second representation of this play, being for the benefit of the author, was honored by the presence of the Chief Magistrate of the Union, Mr. Monroe, who was then on a tour through the States. Its characteristics were elegance of diction and true poetic spirit. It breathed in many parts elevated and patriotic sentiments, and it likewise had the high merit of a scrupulous chasteness, as well as a moral influence throughout.

SOON AFTER the premiere of *Alberti*, a movement for Jewish religious reform arose in Charleston. One of its leaders was Isaac Harby. Encouraged by recently inaugurated reforms in Germany, Harby questioned the value of whatever struck him as worn out and useless. The following selection is from a petition drafted by Harby and others in 1824 and addressed to the directors of Congregation Beth Elohim.

. . . By causing the *chazzan* or reader to repeat in English such part of the Hebrew prayers as may be deemed necessary, it is confidently believed that . . . the younger branches of the congregation . . . would become gradually better acquainted with the nature of our creed, the principal features of which distinguish the Jews from every other religious denomination, and the meaning, and the reason of our various forms and ceremonies.

With regard to such parts of the services as it is desired should undergc this change, your memorialists would strenuously recommend that . . . the principal parts, and if possible all that is read in Hebrew, should also be read in English (that being the language of the country). . . . Your memorialists would further submit to your honorable body whether, in the history of the civilized world, there can be found a single parallel of a people addressing the Creator in a language not understood by that people. . . .

Your memorialists would next call the particular attention of your honorable body to the absolute necessity of abridging the service generally. They have reflected seriously upon its present length, and are confident that this is one of the principal causes why so much of it is hastily and improperly hurried over. This must be evident to every reflecting mind when it is seen that . . . the service of Sabbath . . . continues until twelve o'clock, although usually commencing at nine. . . . Should the service be in future

Uriah Phillips Levy. From a painting by Thomas Sully. One of the first Jews to choose a lifetime career in the U.S. Navy, Levy was instrumental in chasing pirates out of the Caribbean and arresting illegal slave traffickers off the coast of Honduras. When Levy died in 1862, he was the highest-ranking officer in the Navy and the owner of Monticello, Jefferson's palatial Virginia home, which Levy saved from imminent ruin.
American Jewish Historical Society, Waltham, Massachusetts

conducted with due solemnity, and in a slow, distinct and impressive tone, its length would certainly occupy the attention of the congregation until two o'clock, if not later.

⪦ NO ONE DURING the early years of the republic epitomized the spirit of the adventurous Jew more than Mordecai Manuel Noah. Born in Philadelphia in 1785, Noah was the grandson and ward of Jonas Phillips, a wealthy merchant who apprenticed him at an early age to a carver and gilder. Unsuited for this kind of work, Noah went on to become a peddler of carved images in lower Canada and upstate New York. After his grandfather's death in 1803, Noah returned to Philadelphia where he joined a political society, the Democratic Young Men, and subsequently campaigned for the Jeffersonian candidate for governor, Simon Snyder. Snyder won the election and rewarded Noah by making him a major in the Pennsylvania militia, a title Noah later used to great advantage to further his career.

By now Noah had become a dramatist. His first play, *The Fortress of Sorrento*, did not attract much attention; however, he fared better with *Paul and Alexis, or The Orphans of the Rhine*, a Gothic melodrama about innocence, villainy, and heroism that appealed to a new nation inclined to see itself as an orphan of the Old World. The play was a great success in Charleston where Noah had become a columnist for the *Charleston Times* as well as a correspondent for the *Charleston City Gazette*. A staunch supporter of James Madison, who in 1812 captured South Carolina's presidential electors and then went on to win the presidency, Noah was subsequently appointed consul at Tunis. One of the first American Jews to hold an important diplomatic post, Noah set sail for Africa during the War of 1812 "to negotiate for the release of the crew of the brig *Edwin* captured by the Algerines." After the expenditure of a great deal of time and money resulting in the release of only two members of the crew (who, as fate would have it, turned out to be Englishmen), "Commodore Stephen Decatur appeared off the coast of Tunisia with his squadron."

The squadron lay off Cape Carthage, arranged in handsome order: the *Guerriere*, bearing the broad penant of the commodore, was in the centre, and the whole exhibiting a very agreeable and commanding sight. In less than an hour, I was alongside of the flagship and ascended on the quarter-deck. The marines were under arms and received the consul of the United States with the usual honours. Commodore Decatur and Capt. Downs both in uniform, were at the gangway, and most of the officers and crew pressed forward to view their fellow-citizen. After the customary salutations and a few inquiries, Commodore Decatur invited me into the cabin, where, after being seated, he went to his *escrutoire* [sic], and from among a package of letters he handed me one, saying that it was a despatch from the Secretary of State, and requested me to use no ceremony, but to read it. It had the seal of the United States, which I broke, and, to my great surprise, read as follows:

Department of State
April 25, 1815

Sir:

At the time of your appointment as consul at Tunis, it was not known that the religion which you profess would form an obstacle to the exercise of your consular functions. Recent information, however, on which entire reliance may be placed, proved that it would produce a very unfavorable effect. In consequence of which, the President has deemed it expedient to revoke your commission. On the receipt of this letter, therefore, you will consider yourself no longer in the public service. . . .

I am, very respectfully, sir
Your obedient servant,
James Monroe

A poster printed and distributed shortly after Mordecai M. Noah was "violently assaulted" by an angry reader of the New-York Enquirer, *a weekly newspaper Noah edited with the assistance of James Gordon Bennett.*
American Jewish Historical Society, Waltham, Massachusetts

AFTER RETURNING to America, Noah initiated a letter-writing campaign culminating in Secretary of State Monroe's assurance to Noah's influential uncle, Naphtali Phillips, "that the religion of Mr. Noah, so far as related to this government, formed no part of the motive to his recall." The State Department had learned a lesson. From now on, issues involving Jews would be dealt with more discreetly.

In 1817, Noah assumed the editorship of the *National Advocate*, a Tammany newspaper published in New York by his Uncle Naphtali. "Noah quickly succeeded at his new job," writes Jonathan Sarna in *Mordecai M. Noah: Jacksonian Jew*, an invaluable study of Noah and his times. "Copying a technique he had used in Charleston, he introduced humor and lighthearted articles into his newspaper. He appealed to women with articles on domestic economy and feminine virtues. He spiced political articles with *bons mots*, caricatures, and satires, including even the elite among his targets. And, he delighted in fierce controversy and scandalous revelations about his opponants."

Tammany Hall was quick to reward Noah by appointing him sheriff of New York in 1821. When he ran for the same office a year later, the *Evening Post* speculated on the "venomous satisfaction" a Jew would derive from bringing a Christian to the gallows. Noah reputedly replied, "Pretty Christians to require hanging at all." Noah lost the election. Two years later the *Advocate* fell into the hands of a Christian publisher who subsequently replaced Noah with a Christian editor.

Not one to remain idle, Noah soon persuaded a friend to purchase over 2,500 acres of choice real estate on Grand Island near Buffalo.

Noah's plan: to raise money for an asylum for the oppressed Jews of the world. Naming the area Ararat and himself "Judge and Governor," he then decreed a head tax of three shekels of silver "upon each Jew throughout the world." Privately, he admitted that he looked forward to "an immense profit." Others concurred, among them Rebecca Gratz's brother Benjamin. "His trick upon our nation to make money was too shallow to gull them," Gratz recalled long after Noah's scheme had been all but forgotten. "Filthy lucre was his object."

Years later Noah proposed that Palestine be purchased from the Turkish government with American aid and populated by Europe's persecuted Jews. For this his fellow Jews called him a madman.

PART TWO

THE CENTRAL EUROPEAN EXPERIENCE

1830–1910

FOR THE THOUSANDS *of German-speaking Jews who emigrated to America during the period preceding the Civil War, Jewish business establishments in New York and Philadelphia, some going back to colonial days, as well as newer operations in Richmond, Baltimore, and New Orleans, and later in Cincinnati, St. Louis, and San Francisco, were of tremendous importance as economic spearheads pointing toward a rapidly expanding frontier. Often supplied by Jewish manufacturers of clothing and wholesalers of dry goods in these cities, newcomers were encouraged to go out and find new markets for their merchandise. Following the general pattern of westward migration by covered wagon, riverboat, or on foot from one boom or bust town to the next, many Jews ventured where none had gone before. If businsess was good, they would return east and bring back Jewish brides. Others would follow the same pattern until a Jewish congregation might be formed, and then another and another, each congregation an extension of religious, social, and economic ties with older Jewish settlements back east.*

Those Jews who settled in the North and Far West before the Civil War built a manufacturing and merchandising network which formed the economic basis for sizable Jewish communities on the Atlantic seaboard, along the Great Lakes, on the Ohio, Missouri, and Mississippi rivers and along the Pacific coast. Out of these communities a distinctly Jewish American way of life evolved. What was achieved, which was as much a product of economic and social forces as of purely religious influences, in many ways prefigures Jewish communal life in America today.

By contrast, Jews who settled in the antebellum South frequently found themselves living in a largely Gentile world, often hundreds of miles away from the nearest Jewish community. So it was for the Jewish immigrant who started out as a peddler from New Orleans, Mobile, or

Chattanooga, hawking his wares from plantation to plantation, farm to farm, finally saving enough money to open a dry goods store in a town or village usually too small to provide enough to live on for more than a handful of merchants and their families. What resulted was the settlement of thousands of Jews over an immense territory with ultimately every Southern town of any consequence the home of at the very least a few Jewish families.

For those who went as far as the frontier where, in a free and open society, immigrant Jews tended to be looked upon by Gentiles as "fellow pioneers," a degree of Jewish involvement in civic affairs took place that was without precedent in modern Jewish history. By the 1890s scores of settlements in the West and Far West had benefited from the progressive leadership of Jewish journalists, Jewish doctors and lawyers, Jewish mayors, and, in later years, three Jewish governors. For a people kept down for centuries this was indeed cause for shepping naches *(feeling delight or satisfaction).*

Hamburg und San Francisco.

Hamburg-Amerikanische Packetfahrt-Actien-Gesellschaft.

Westindische Linie.

5

North of the Mason-Dixon Line

A NEW WAVE

We hold out to the people of other countries an invitation to come and settle among us as members of our rapidly growing family; and, for the blessings which we offer them, we require of them to look upon our country as their country, and to unite with us in the great task of preserving our institutions, and thereby perpetuating our liberties.

John Tyler, Message to Congress, June 1, 1841

Ye fellow-Jews and companions in misfortune, get used to gaze into the distant West, and become conversant with the idea. In free America the sun of freedom shines for us too.

Der Rosenberg-Kreutzberger Telegraph, November 28, 1848

A COMBINATION of factors on both sides of the Atlantic led to a rise in the Jewish population of America from a mere eight thousand in 1830 to almost twenty times that number in less than a generation. In Europe a wave of reactionary policies following the Napoleonic wars created havoc in the lives of millions of Jews. Though no longer required to live in ghettos, by 1820 Jews in the German-speaking lands of central Europe found themselves hampered on all sides by a host of discriminatory laws and customs. Simultaneously in America a steady westward expansion was opening up enormous opportunities for people eager to leave the adversities of Europe behind them.

In the South in a single decade three states were created—Louisiana (1812), Mississippi (1817), and Alabama (1819)—while in the North, Indiana (1816) and Illinois (1818) were soon followed by Missouri (1821), the first state to lie completely west of the Mississippi River. Then came Arkansas (1836) and Michigan (1837). This made twenty-six states in all—half of them old colonial commonwealths, the other half conceived and developed between the administrations of Washington and Jackson.

The opening of the Erie Canal in 1825 greatly accelerated the west-

Arrival of emigrants.

ward advance. According to an astonished Alexis de Tocqueville, it was proceeding at an average of seventeen miles a year as compared with two miles a year in over a century and a half of colonial occupation. And this was only the beginning.

The Jews who came to America during this period were primarily from small towns and villages in Bavaria, Prussian-controlled Poland, Bohemia, Austria, and Hungary. The sons and daughters of impoverished tailors and shoemakers, petty tinkers and traders, they were eager to leave grinding poverty and social injustice behind them for a land where they would be looked upon not as outsiders, as they had been in Europe, but as fellow countrymen. Frequently, large families came over, one or two members at a time. Spreading out over the country with the daring and often the ignorance of youth, Jews were to be found at every point of a rapidly advancing frontier.

The following accounts are taken from letters and memoirs written by pioneer Jews who came to America from Germany in the middle of the last century.

My Michael had learned the tinsmith trade according to his own wish, and he worked for a time as apprentice after having learned this trade. . . . In the meantime, he had planned with two young men, also Israelites, to emigrate to America. . . . The matter seemed quite feasible as there were then hard times in Germany, and his dear mother and I saw him, in our thoughts, wandering from city to city with his knapsack on his back. Therefore, we gladly yielded to his wishes, thinking to see him again in a few years . . . after he had made for me quite a stock of stovepipe, he entered upon his journey. . . . Parting was hard, but the hope of a reunion helped us to bear our sorrow. When we received his first letter, however, we began to relinquish hope of his return, for he wished that one of his brothers would come to him and wrote that it might probably be advantageous for us all to come later.

Jacob Greenebaum

My brothers, already in America, thought it would be best if I came to them while yet young. At last my mother gave her consent.

"It is time for you to go to America," my mother said. "I have secured a passport for you and a steamship ticket."

Her reason for this was prompted by a law at that time whereby every boy attaining the age of eighteen was subject to military service for seven years. The rich managed to have their boys escape military duty by bribing the military physician, but my mother did not have the money.

It was a great sacrifice for her, I being the youngest and only son at home. Still, I had no conception of the grief it would cost her. On the day of my departure Mother came to my bed, embraced me and cried that I was leaving her forever while all the time I ridiculed the idea of never seeing her again.

I left home on the twenty-second day of August, taking a steamer to

Hannah and Sarah Greenebaum in identical silk dresses. The sisters arrived in Philadelphia from Germany in 1847 to join their three older brothers, who had emigrated to America six years earlier and were already successful businessmen. They subsequently married Lewis Gerstle and Louis Sloss, partners in a Sacramento, California, grocery store. Later the two families moved to San Francisco, where they established one of the largest fur-trading operations in the West.
Reprinted from *Our City: The Jews of San Francisco*, by Irena Narell. Courtesy of Darwin Publications.

Mainz where my brother Wolf met us and took us on a train to Frankfurt where he lived. Here we took the steamer again, debarking at Rotterdam.

At that time it took from forty to sixty days to cross the Atlantic in sailing vessels. There were a few steamships plying from Liverpool to New York, taking twenty or more days to cross, but they were too costly for people of limited means.

Moses Berman

One day we received a letter from my brother, from Keokuk, Iowa, where my Uncle Gerstle had settled to run a small store. Ludwig wrote that two years earlier he had joined a group of young people who accompanied the mail coaches which ran from Fort Leavenworth, Kansas, across the Nebraska prairies, to Salt Lake City, Utah, and protected them from possible attacks by the Indians. He had returned to Iowa and was about to open a store; he wanted me to join him in America in order to become his partner.

At that time it was believed at home that all "Americans" were rich, for most of the emigrants who returned to their homeland for a visit were, or, appeared to be, wealthy. The sums of money sent by others to their poor relations in Germany helped to corroborate this evidence. From those who led a toilsome life in America, however, one rarely heard anything. . . .

Ernst Troy

Our two brothers in California told us that our oldest brother was coming home. Then, if my sister and I wished, we were to go to America with them. So it happened that in September our dear brother came to us. His choice of a wife, whom he wanted to take along, fell upon Lottchen Waldstein, our girlhood friend. He asked for her hand and was accepted. These were happy days for us all. Our good brother gave us and his bride lessons in English twice a week so that when we arrived in America we could make ourselves understood and would not be "green" as one says here. We departed from Posen on the 9th of May, 1855. My good sister would perhaps have remained at home if I had also wished it. There was, at this time, a very nice young man who wanted to marry her, but she would not stay alone so our plan was carried out.

Mrs. Joseph Solomon Newmark

⤳ IN READING the following German-Jewish newspaper accounts of emigrants leaving for America, it should be kept in mind that the importance placed on traditional religious considerations is in keeping with the fact that German-Jewish emigrants were mainly from small towns and villages where the old ways still prevailed. Nor is the assistance provided by wealthy co-religionists unusual in the light of the importance Jews have always placed on looking after their own.

WÜRZBURG. 1837. Letters from America bring information that last spring, during the heavy Jewish emigration, a ship whose passengers were mostly Israelites sailed to England. The majority of the passengers were in a most pitiful condition, from which, it is reported, the pious sentiment and benevolent interest of the noble Mrs. von Rothschild of London saved them. As soon as she received news of the wretched state in which many of her co-religionists found themselves, she arranged for assistance to be provided for them in every way possible. The persons thus saved could not find sufficient words to describe the humane and loving attitude of Mrs. von Rothschild.

Die Synagoge

HAMBURG. 1839. The first transport of Jewish emigrants, 86 persons strong, is to leave in the next few days on a ship for New York. They are Bavarians from the Würzburg region, mostly people with a skill or trade. Those who wish to eat kosher on the voyage pay a little extra for kosher meat and a separate stove. Provision has also been made for other ritual needs on board ship.

Allgemeine Zeitung des Judentums

SWABIA. *February 1840.* The emigration-fever has steadily increased among the Israelites of our district and seems about to reach its high point. In nearly every community there are numerous individuals who are preparing to leave the fatherland early next year and to seek their fortune on the other side of the ocean. This is particularly the case in Ichenhausen, the largest Israelitic community in Swabia with approximately 200 families. If I am correctly informed, there are in this place alone 60 persons contemplating the voyage.

Israelistische Annalen

MAINZ. 1845. Two hundred Bavarian Jews embarked here last week to seek a new fatherland in North America. They drew a very dismal picture of the situation of Jews in Bavaria, where nothing else is left but to suffer or emigrate. Of these emigrants one whose good humor did not desert him replied to the question of returning from America, "I will not return before North America has become Bavarian."

Allgemeine Zeitung des Judentums

⤷§ DESCRIPTIONS OF terrible shipboard conditions in contemporary accounts are anything but exaggerated. In Hamburg, Rotterdam, Amsterdam, Liverpool, and London, passengers were squeezed into sailing vessels which took as long as ten to twelve weeks to reach America. The food on board was unclean, the water often black and filled with worms. Fatal wrecks were far from uncommon. With as many as a thousand passengers traveling in steerage, frequent epidemics of cholera, yellow fever, and smallpox were unavoidable. Under such conditions it is hardly surprising that mortality figures often ran as high as 20 percent.

NEW YORK. *1851*. The dreadful condition in which many of the emigrant ships have lately arrived in this port should be brought to the immediate attention of our authorities. To those who have never crossed the Atlantic, to those who have never seen the sea lashed to fury by the raging of terrible storms, language must fail to convey an idea of the frightful sufferings endured by 700, 800 or 900 human beings (and often more) when the hatches are battened down on the putrid atmosphere, poisoned by their repeated breathings, and repoisoned by the exhalations arising from damp, filthy bedding and clothing, combined with the corrupt uxuviae of unwashed flesh, sweetened with the odor of that most disgusting, damnable and foetid fluid, "bilge water," and freshened with corruptions of the rotten provisions with which the starving immigrants keep body and soul together. The wonder is not that cholera, ship fever and yellow fever prevail on board such ships—that 30, 50 and 75 (as on a recent occasion) are thrown overboard from one vessel to feed the sharks of the Atlantic—that 50, 100 and 200 are landed at the fever hospital at Staten Island from one cargo—but the astonishment should be that one lives through the horrors to tell the tale.

The Asmonean

We arrived in New York in the middle of June, 1855. We remained there fourteen days until our ship arrived from Nicaragua, in which we continued our trip. It took ten days to reach Nicaragua. We landed in a little town where we stayed over night. The next day we had to cross the isthmus by land in order to reach the ship which was to bring us to San Francisco.

As the ship, the *North Light,* lay in the Pacific Ocean we sat on the deck and large fish flew about. My brother remarked that this was a bad sign, and this proved to be true. Before we started cholera broke out. There were fifty cases during our trip. It was terrible at night when we heard the corpses being thrown overboard.

Mrs. Joseph Solomon Newmark

THE SHOCK OF NEW YORK

IMAGINE YOURSELF a newcomer in America well before the outbreak of the Civil War. A German-speaking Jew with great expectations, you arrive in New York assuming all the dreams and hopes you brought with you will materialize right before your eyes, but instead of paradise you find chaos. Nowhere is there German order, German restraint. All you see is the strangeness of constant change. Only gradually do you begin to make sense out of what is going on, and when you do you like what you see even less than you did before. For New York strikes you as more like an overgrown village than a city. Only on Broadway as far up as Canal Street and in the business section east of Broadway are the begin-

nings of a metropolis perceptible. Elsewhere New York appears filled
with small, insignificant-looking people hurrying in and out of small
houses, small shops, small passageways. Even more disappointing, there
seems to be no Jewish community to speak of, only a hodge-podge of
German and Polish Jews.

So matters stood in 1846 for the future leader of Reform Judaism in
America, Isaac Mayer Wise.

New York . . . appeared to me like a large shop where every one buys or
sells, cheats or is cheated. I had never before seen a city so bare of all art
and of every trace of good taste; likewise I had never witnessed anywhere
such rushing, hurrying, chasing, running. . . . On that first day I longed to
be away. . . .

I had still a more depressing experience while inspecting a number of
houses. At Cohn's I found in a basement a number of young fellow-
countrymen of culture transformed into factory hands, cigar makers, and
peddlers, who, like a lot of political quidnuncs, uttered absolute and decided opinions about the Mexican War, which was then in progress. . . . I
had brought many letters with me. Two of them I delivered to the physicians B. and M. They both advised me to have nothing to do with the
Jews, although their practice was confined exclusively to Jews, and gave me
the fatherly advice to peddle or to learn a trade. I felt disgusted. . . .

There were seven Jewish congregations in New York. . . . The Portuguese congregation was the oldest and the oldest Portuguese a Polish
Jew. . . . The next oldest congregation was the English-Polish that had a
handsome synagogue on Elm Street, and used the Polish ritual as it ob-

New York "Old Clo's" peddler.
Museum of the City of New York

tained in London. On the very first morning I visited this synagogue, I longed for the sight of a Hebrew book, and asked the *shamas* whether I could obtain a volume of the *mishnah*. That individual laughed so mockingly that I readily perceived what a sign of "greenness" it was on my part to ask for an ancient Hebrew book in the New World. . . .

As for modern culture, things were little better. No Jew who had recently immigrated was fitted to occupy a public position creditably. Among the Portuguese Jews there was Mordecai Noah, who had achieved prominence through his literary and political activity. Beyond this, nothing worthy of note had been accomplished in that quarter. In the mercantile world . . . Chatham Square was a disgrace, Houston Street a vanity fair. On the Bowery on Division, Grand and other streets there were small stores owned by Jews, but on the whole Jews cut no figure. Thus matters stood in New York in 1846.

New York clothing store, 1875.

⤳ MOST JEWS who emigrated to America at this time started out as peddlers with packs on their backs filled with anything and everything they
could carry. For years native Americans had done this kind of work;
however, the rapid growth of New England industries following the
War of 1812 provided many erstwhile Yankee peddlers with easier ways
of making a living. The Jewish immigrant was quick to step in. Very little money was required—only the price of a peddler's license. As for
goods, they could be obtained on credit from Jews who had arrived earlier and were already running wholesale operations. No stranger to the
trade, the Jew in Europe had been forced into peddling by restrictive
laws. But now there was a difference: an expanding economy in a country with no tradition of keeping Jews down.

 Usually a peddler began his career in New York, Philadelphia, Baltimore, or New Orleans—the principal ports of arrival before the Civil
War. It was in New York that Isaac Mayer Wise had the following encounter with a peddler who turned out to be an old friend.

One afternoon I met on the street a man with a large, old straw hat
drawn far over his face. He was perspiring in his linen coat, and carried two
enormous tin boxes on his shoulders. He had a large clay pipe in his
mouth, a pair of golden spectacles on his nose, and dragged himself along
with painful effort. I looked at him closely and recognized my friend Stein.
Upon noticing my astonishment, he said, smilingly:

"Most of the German and Polish Jews in America look like this, and the
rest of them did till a very short time ago."

As he was going homeward I accompanied him to his house. A quarter
of an hour later he emerged completely metamorphosed. He looked genteel again. He informed his wife laughingly that I had met him in his peddler's costume. He now described to me graphically the misery and the
drudgery of the peddler's life.

Our people in this country, said he, may be divided into the following
classes: the basket peddler—as yet altogether dumb and homeless; the
trunk carrier who stammers some English and hopes for better times; the
pack carrier who carries from one hundred to one hundred and fifty
pounds upon his back and indulges the thought that he will become a
businessman some day; the wagon baron with a one or two horse team; the
jewelry count who carries his stock in a small trunk, and is considered a
rich man by some; the store prince who has a shop and sells goods in it.

"But what about the people of intelligence?" asked I.

"In America," said he, "a man must be either all head or all back.
Those who are all head remain in Europe; those who are in this country
must be all back, and forego all intellectual pursuits."

"But why?" I asked further.

"In order to become rich," said he. "The foreigner must either become
rich or go to the wall; he has no alternative. The end and aim of all striving
in this country is to become rich; everything else is secondary. Home,
friends, society, honor, religion, knowledge, yes, even pleasure and enjoy-

ment, are all of slight import compared with this. Money, much money, more money; this, it is, that moves the mind and controls the activities of the body."

He continued in this vein, and drew a picture that was most disagreeable to me.

"All spiritual treasures, then, are sacrificed to this chase for material gain," cried I. "If so, then tell me why these people form congregations and build synagogues?"

"Oh, they do this from inherited habit," rejoined Stein. "This one wishes to become *parnass*, and that one a trustee, in order to be able to give orders and make his importance felt. He saw this at home and imitates it here. There is no earnestness, no spirit, no idealism in the whole proceeding."

⌒§ THERE WERE a number of small storefront synagogues in New York by the 1840s. One of them was called the Indian Rubber *shul* because most of its members were peddlers whose principal stock in trade was suspenders made out of this material. The *shul's chazzen* was also a teacher, butcher, circumciser, *shofar* (ram's horn used on High Holidays) blower, reader, writer, and gravedigger. For women in confinement, he wrote amulets, listing all the angels and demons on them; for departed sinners, he recited appropriate prayers; with the living, he played cards; and for everyone he had a blessing for *chai pasch*, which came to a little over four cents. Often he had to accept bread, turnips, cabbage, and potatoes in payment, and when that wasn't enough to feed his family, he peddled. Most religious functionaries in America at this time were no better off, according to Dr. Max Lilienthal, a colleague of Isaac Mayer Wise, who wrote the following article for a Jewish newspaper in Germany in 1848.

NEW YORK. During this year many religious functionaries who came here could not obtain any position and had to grasp at other trades, such as peddling or various crafts. Thus one opened a shoemaker's shop; another is learning cigar-making, a third bookbinding. Others become clerks in offices. Positions that become vacant become so only owing to the fact that the Jewish congregations here soon get tired of their cantors and discharge them after the first year of their appointment. Cantors and teachers in Germany should pay special attention to the fact that here all positions are given as a rule for one year only and the appointee must submit to a new election each year. As it is easy to acquire enemies, the positions are extremely precarious. Of permanent appointments they know nothing. So it happened with Cantor Putzel. He was inducted in Easton, Pennsylvania two years ago, enjoyed general approval, married, and now with a wife and child has been discharged from his position and must open a dry goods business. He is a decent, fine accomplished man who nevertheless could not get along with the congregation. Accordingly, I entreat cantors and teachers not to be quick with their decisions to emigrate. If they hear of a position in America ... they might well consider that they may be exchanging a permanent position in their fatherland for a precarious, annual appointment here. It is extremely painful to me to hear accomplished men complain in my house that they have no recourse but to take the pack upon their backs.

Allgemeine Zeitung des Judentums

NEW ENGLAND THROUGH A PEDDLER'S EYES

ᔨ WHEN IN 1842 twenty-three-year-old Abraham Kohn of Fürth, Bavaria, put a pack on his back and set out from New York for Massachusetts, New England was little more than a Jewish no-man's-land. Not until 1840 was Connecticut's first congregation formed in New Haven. Rhode Island had hardly more to offer. When Henry Wadsworth Longfellow visited Newport in 1852, nothing was left of the old Jewish community but a synagogue and a graveyard. "How strange it seems," the poet observed, "These Hebrews in their graves ... at rest in all this moving up and down!" The first recorded Jewish religious services in Massachusetts were held in 1842 in a capmaker's home once inhabited by the family of Oliver Wendell Holmes. The first Jewish community in Maine was not established until the late 1840s, and in New Hampshire and Vermont not until well after the Civil War. It was into this alien world that Abraham Kohn ventured. The following selections are from a journal he kept of his day-to-day struggle for survival.

Pocket edition of a traveler's prayer book like the one brought to America by Abraham Kohn.

Is it liberty when, in order to do business in a single state, one has to buy a license for $100 and profane the holy Sabbath, observing Sunday instead? True, one does not hear the name "Jew," but only because one does not utter it. Can a man, in fact, be said to be "living" as he plods through the vast, remote country, uncertain even as to which farmer will provide him shelter for the coming night? O, that I had never seen this land, but had remained in Germany, apprenticed to a humble country craftsman!

Last week in the vicinity of Plymouth I met two peddlers, Lehman and Marx. Marx knew me from Fürth. That night we stayed together at a farmer's house. After supper we started singing. O, how I thought of my dear mother while I sang!

Today, Sunday, October 16th, we are here in North Bridgewater, and I am not so downcast as I was two weeks ago. Suppose, after all, I were a soldier in Bavaria—that would have been a bad lot. I will accept three years in America instead. But I could not stand it any longer.

As far as the language is concerned, I am getting along pretty well. But the Americans are a peculiar people. Although they sit together by the dozen in taverns, they turn their backs to each other. No one talks to any-

Boston's first synagogue, "a small wooden structure, tastefully decorated and pleasing in its appearance," was erected in 1851 on Warren Street with adjoining schoolrooms and a mikveh in the rear. The illustration is from J. S. Homans's History of Boston, *published in 1856.*

body else. Is this customary of a republic? I don't like it. Is this the fashion of the nineteenth century? I don't like it either. "Wait a little!" I can hear my brother talking. "There will be more things you won't like."

How glad I was to meet my two brothers in Boston on Saturday, the twenty-second! Now I am not alone in this strange country.

How much more could I write about this queer land. It likes comfort extremely. The German, by comparison, hardly knows the meaning of the word. The wife of an American farmer—for hours she can sit in her rocking chair shaking back and forth as she thinks of nothing but beautiful clothes and a fine hairdo. The farmer himself is able to sit down for a few hours every day to read his paper and smoke his cigar.

The whole country looks to me like an adolescent youth. That is America! Although she appears to know everything, her knowledge is, in truth, very elementary. American history is composed of Independence and Washington—that is all.

O youth of Bavaria, if you long for freedom, if you dream of life here, beware, for you shall rue the hour you embarked for a country and a life far different from what you dream of. This land, and this calling in particular, offers harsh, cold air, great masses of snow, and people who are credulous, filled with silly pride, and cold toward all who do not speak the language perfectly.

There is in addition that damn Dr. Miller who preaches the imminent end of the world. The majority of his hearers believe him. On April 20, 1843, the world is supposed to be consumed by fire, according to a prediction by the prophet Daniel. I should like to see this Dr. Miller preaching such nonsense in Germany.

In Hillsborough, New Hampshire they have dismissed the schoolmaster. Since the world is to end in three months, the children need no education. So goes it with the masses of a people which governs itself. These things can happen only in a country where each man is allowed to talk and write about anything whatsoever.

New Year's Day. The night before I recalled the gay New Year's Eve I spent in Fürth in 1841. God, I little thought that a year later I should be spending the night at a lonesome Massachusetts farmhouse. And God knows where I shall be a year from today.

We long to send a letter home which will bring joy and happiness, but, dear God, shall we lie like the Bavarians? This I should not like, yet they at home would be upset with the truth. It seems wisest to let them continue with golden hopes, and, for the time being, not to write at all. You alone, dear mother, may judge, should you read this journal at some future date, whether we have done right or wrong.

On Tuesday morning at ten I left Worcester, it being my turn to travel alone for seven weeks. A thousand thanks to God, I felt far stronger than when I first left my brothers in Boston. Now I have become more accustomed to the language, the business, and the American way of life.

I am satisfied with business, thank God. I hope it continues this way. I enjoy my meals and my slumber and pray twice each day. Thus, trusting in God's help, I quietly go my way.

On Sunday I attended the church service in Phillipston—a poor preacher but beautiful singing. The sermon dealt mostly with love of the Redeemer and displayed false and obscure ideas throughout. It was not worth comparison with the sermons of Dr. Löwi in Fürth. In the evening I read three different newspapers; such things could not be found in a German farmhouse.

On Sunday every farmer urges me to attend church, and this week in Williamsburg, at each house where I tried to sell my wares, I was told to go to church and pray to the "hanged" Jesus. The open field is my temple where I pray. Our Father in heaven will hear me there. "In every place

where thou shalt mention my name I shall come to thee and bless thee."
This comforts me and lends me strength and courage and endurance for
my sufferings.

On Saturday afternoon, May 20th, I saw a peddler pass by. "Hello sir,"
I hailed him. "How are you?" It turned out to be Samuel Zirndorfer from
Fürth. Alas, how the poor devil looked. Thus one man with eighty pounds
on his back meets another with fifty pounds on his back some 4,000 miles
away from their native town. If I had known of this a year ago, how different things might be now!

A year ago I left Fürth. How quickly this year has passed. But how
many sad and bitter hours has it brought me. Yet thou, Father of all, who
hast brought me across the ocean and directed my steps up till today, wilt
grant me thy further aid. With confidence in thy fatherly goodness, I continue my way of life. Thou alone knowest my goal. May I find contentment and a life of peace, united in well-being with my dear mother and
with my brothers and sisters.

WEST OF THE ALLEGHENIES

෴ OF THE HUNDRED THOUSAND or so German-speaking Jews who emigrated to America before the Civil War, many, like Jacob Seasongood of
Burgkundstadt, Bavaria, first came to New York, peddled for a while,
and then, hearing of greater opportunities farther west, moved on. Setting out in the summer of 1837 by way of the Erie Canal, Seasongood
sometimes carried as much as 100 pounds of merchandise on his back.
He traded mainly with people who lived on farms and had some money
to spend but little opportunity to travel to distant cities. At the time two
great fingers of population marked the limits of the occupied frontier.
One followed the Ohio Valley to the Mississippi River. The other advanced along the shoreline of the Great Lakes as far west as Michigan.
Taking the southern route, Seasongood came into contact with a number of Yankee, Irish, and German competitors with whom he enjoyed
matching wits as well as wares. Stopping for a while at Chillicothe, Seasongood met with considerable success as an auctioneer. Before long he
had saved enough money to purchase a horse and wagon and move on
to Cincinnati. There, in partnership with Philip Heidelbach, he opened
a clothing and dry goods store just a few blocks north of the Ohio River
which, in its peak years, had an estimated worth of half a million dollars.

As befitted the nation's sixth largest city, Cincinnati's waterfront was
by now almost always jammed with high-stacked, triple-decked steamers
awaiting their turn at the public landing. Already houses were staggering
up the slopes of the outlying hills, while stores near the Ohio River were
as spacious and well stocked as those in New York and London. Theaters, newspapers, publishing houses, libraries, picture galleries, even institutions of higher learning were not lacking. In 1836 a synagogue had

been dedicated, the first in the Midwest. Most of its members, like Seasongood, were young men from small towns and villages in Bavaria who had come to New York before peddling their way west. So many kept coming that in 1841 the synagogue was enlarged to accommodate 350 congregants.

The following account of these and other early events was written by Joseph Jonas, Cincinnati's first permanent Jewish resident.

From the period of the arrival of the first Israelite in Cincinnati [1817] to this date [1843], the Israelites have been much esteemed and highly respected by their fellow citizens, and a general interchange of civilities and friendships has taken place between them. Many persons of the Nazarene faith residing from 50 to 100 miles from the city, hearing there were Jews living in Cincinnati, came into town for the special purpose of viewing and conversing with some of "the children of Israel, the holy people of God," as they termed us.

The original founders of our congregation were principally from Great Britain, and their mode of worship after the Polish and German Jews. Being all young people not so prejudiced in favour of old customs, we introduced considerable chorus singing into our worship, in which we were joined by the sweet voices of the fair daughters of Zion, and our Friday evening service was as well attended for many years as the Sabbath morning.

At length, however, large emigrations of our German brethren settled amongst us. Again our old customs have conquered, and the sweet voices of our ladies are seldom heard. But we have so far prevailed as to continue to this day the Twenty-ninth Psalm, the *en ke-loheune* and *adon alom* [songs traditionally sung in the synagogue].

During the year 5589 [1829] Messrs. Morris Moses and David I. Johnson were appointed a special committee to procure subscriptions towards building a synagogue. During the month of July this year, the congregation purchased a suitable lot of ground on the east side of Broadway below Sixth Street, on which our present synagogue is erected.

Nothing of interest took place, except a gradual increase of the congregation, until 1834, when Messrs. Joseph Jonas, Elias Mayer, and Phineas

Cincinnati as it appeared to Jacob Seasongood, Philip Heidelbach, and other early German-Jewish arrivals.

Moses were appointed a committee for building a synagogue. With very insufficient funds we commenced the good work, and with liberal donations given through the influence of the committee and loans from the city banks, we were enabled to bring the holy work to its completion.

On the fourteenth day of Sivan, 5595, corresponding to the eleventh of June, 1835, the foundation stone was laid, with suitable enclosures and inscriptions. During this year we received the following donations from our brethren abroad: $100 from the late Harman Hendricks, Esq., of New York; $470 from our brethren in Philadelphia and Baltimore, whose names we have duly recorded. Five large brass chandeliers were received from the Holy Congregation Shearith Israel, New York, with the condition attached, "that in case the congregation in Cincinnati at any future period should decline to use them, then to return them to the trustees of this congregation."

During the months of May, June, and July [1836], we sold seats in our new synagogue, to the amount of $4,500, which enabled us to finish the interior of the building in a much superior style than we originally intended. The edifice, when finished was much admired. . . .

The ninth of September, 1836, corresponding to the twenty-seventh of Elul, 5596, was appointed for the consecration. The day having arrived, the crowd of our Christian friends was so great that we could not admit them all. We therefore selected the clergy and the families of those gentlemen who so liberally had given donations toward the building. The members of the congregation assembled in the basement rooms, a procession was formed, with the sepharim in front (under a handsome canopy), carried by Messrs. Joseph Jonas, *parnass*, Elias Mayer, *gabah*, and Phineas Moses, treasurer. Mr. David I. Johnson officiated on the occasion and chaunted the consecration service. He also led the choir of about twenty of the ladies and gentlemen of the congregation. Who did not enjoy supreme delight and heavenly pleasure, when the sweet voices of the daughters of Zion ascended on high in joyful praises to the great Architect of the universe on the glorious occasion of dedicating this first temple west of the Allegheny Mountains?

WITH THE FILLING of the hilly upcountry just north of the Ohio River, pioneers and their families began migrating to the level prairie country of northern Ohio, Indiana, and Illinois, while others advanced by way of the Erie Canal to Detroit (a city of ten thousand by 1836) and from there moved inland along the river valleys and over the uplands. Once the best lands had disappeared, a new army of settlers began journeying to Iowa, Wisconsin, and Minnesota. Towns grew rapidly; however, many disappeared just as quickly. A constant starting over, an eternal looking to the future characterized American life at this time, and Jews were no exception.

In 1845, the year Manifest Destiny became the byword for those who hoped to extend the United States across the continent, Wilhelm Krauss, a Jewish peddler operating out of Cincinnati, put everything he owned in a covered wagon and headed west with his wife, Minnie, at his side. The Krausses kept going until they came to the site of an abandoned army post on the Des Moines River and decided to try their luck there at selling dry goods to emigrants headed even farther west. Operating out of a log cabin, they soon sold everything they had brought with them. A few months later they were joined by Minnie's brother, who brought a fresh load of merchandise from Cincinnati. In no time he had to return east for more goods.

Like other frontier merchants, Wilhelm Krauss played an important role in bringing civilization to the frontier. One of the founders of the first public school in the area, he also contributed to the building funds of the city's pioneer churches. Methodist, Presbyterian, Baptist, Universalist, Catholic—Krauss aided all of them liberally. In 1849 he was among those who worked to bring about legislation for the establishment of the capital at Des Moines. Fifty years later Krauss could still take pride in "the great progress we were making, even in those early days."

An Ohio peddler during the days when Jews came to New York from Germany and then made their way west via the Erie Canal.
American Jewish Archives, Cincinnati, Ohio. Courtesy of Richard W. Welch and *Graphic Antiquity.*

IN THE 1850s Cincinnati became the center of a rapidly expanding Jewish manufacturing and merchandising network including, by 1859, a Jewish-owned clothing industry employing more workers (14,580) than any other industry in the city. With 134 factories producing goods valued at $15 million, Cincinnati was now the largest producer of ready-

Jewish peddlers who succeeded in business often opened small clothing stores like the one pictured here in an early photograph of downtown Columbus, Ohio.
Ohio Historical Society

made men's clothing in the United States. While most Jewish merchants in the Midwest, like the Krausses, bought their merchandise from Jewish suppliers in Cincinnati or, a bit later, in St. Louis, Chicago, or Milwaukee, others, like Little Jake Seligman of Pontiac, Michigan, traveled by rail and riverboat once or twice a year to "the great wholesale factories" back east. For Little Jake such trips formed the basis for a distinctly "New York" approach to advertising:

The approach to advertising which Little Jake Seligman introduced to Pontiac, Michigan compared to that of circuses and side shows which come to town. It was often personal, flamboyant, provocative, and stimulating. Hitherto most merchants had been content to list in a simple advertisement their names and their businesses. Little Lake used humor, taunts, braggadocio. He could be laughed at; but at the same time he had to be regarded as a serious threat to his competitors.

As his business grew, he took trips to the East twice a year, in the spring and fall, to make his own purchases from the great wholesale factories of New York, Boston and Rochester. Each trip was announced in his advertisements and in the personals column; and his return to Pontiac each time was trumpeted to the public through the columns of the newspaper. He liked to buy space in the "Local Notices" column, where he could insert items on the results of his trips in this fashion:

LITTLE JAKE has got home from the eastern cities, and has related his experience in the market. He struck the market just right and bought at such prices as warrant him in making the assertion that he can sell goods in this market cheaper than they have been sold at any time since 1860. New York at the time was almost deserted of buyers on account of the terrible condition of the streets and the recent railroad disaster, giving our clothing King his own way; competing houses were determined to sell to him at some price; and his western customers get the benefit of the condition of affairs.

If the reader missed the notice on the first insertion, he had further opportunity to see it as it was repeated from week to week. As the leading advertiser, he exacted a dividend from the editor in the form of free publicity. When he left on a buying trip to the East, it was announced in the personals column; while he was away, his absence was noted; and his return was announced in advance and again after the event.

In his large display advertisements he stressed certain particulars over and over again. "The One Price Clothier" was a basic claim. In his store, he insisted, there were no phony prices, everybody paid the same amount for the same item—no bargaining, or, as he advertised, "No Jewing."

John Cumming, *Little Jake of Saginaw*

◦◦§ IN THE 1830s a rapidly advancing wave of settlers pushed as far west as the Great Plains and then suddenly stopped. Beyond this point rivers were not easily navigable, nor was the new and unknown problem of prairie sod conducive to settlement for a people used to timberlands. An almost total absence of trees led many pioneers to think that much of the land west of the Mississippi was worthless. ("East of the Mississippi," writes one historian, "civilization stood on three legs—land, water, and timber; west of the Mississippi not one but two of these legs were withdrawn—water and timber—leaving civilization with one leg—land.") In addition, the prairie Indian was a formidable foe. He was an expert horseman, and his bow and arrows posed a serious threat, even after the invention of the Colt six-shooter.

In 1851 Simon Lazarus (RIGHT) came to Columbus, Ohio, from a small town in Prussia and opened a retail clothing store on South High Street. After earning a reputation as "one of the substantial businessmen of Columbus," Simon left the business to his sons Fred and Ralph, who changed its name in 1879 to S. Lazarus' Sons & Co. Today there are still Lazaruses in Columbus carrying on the family tradition.
Both, Ohio Historical Society

Isaac Rosenfeld, Jr., who came to St. Louis from Bavaria in 1849 and, after a successful career in wholesale dry goods, founded the State Savings Institution, which by 1860 had the largest money transactions of any bank in the western country.

"J. L. Isaacs—Home Decorations. Shown is a faithful illustration of the beautiful structure erected by J. L. Isaacs on the south side of Olive, between Twelfth and Thirteenth streets, in the year 1876. This building is one of the most ornate and attractive features in that part of the city. In its every appointment it is the finest west of New York devoted to the business for which it is used, and its interior decoration is perhaps the most elaborate in the world." From A Tour of St. Louis (1878), one of many books and pamphlets published at this time to encourage the growth of cities and towns in the West.

Though the farmer had been stopped for the time being, bands of hunters and Indian traders had long since traveled up and down the Mississippi and Missouri rivers in search of valuable furs and buffalo robes. St. Louis was where they obtained their Indian goods, sometimes from Jewish merchants. One of the first to settle there was Jacob Philipson. Born in Poland, Philipson arrived in 1808 from Philadelphia, and opened a general merchandise store opposite the post office where he offered for sale guns, beads, trinkets, blankets, knives, and alcohol, in addition to "a few German and English Bibles, testaments, hymn books, etc." By now St. Louis had all of fifteen hundred inhabitants—one fifth white American, one third black. Jacob's brother Joseph came out in 1810 and purchased Habb's Brewery, the first of its kind west of the Mississippi. Ten years later another brother, Simon, was operating a sawmill nearby.

Among other early Jewish arrivals were Wolf and Emmanuel Block, merchants from Baltimore, and their brother Eliezer, a lawyer who practiced before the bar with Thomas Hart Benton in 1821, the year Missouri was admitted to the Union under the Missouri Compromise. When we consider that there were no Jewish women within hundreds of miles until well into the next decade, it is not surprising that the Philipsons, the Blocks, and practically every other Jewish bachelor who came to Missouri during these early years married out of the faith, and that their children were invariably lost to Judaism.

Not until 1836 were there enough Jews in St. Louis to form a *minyan* (quorum of 10 necessary for holding religious services). In that year the first Yom Kippur services in the Mississippi Valley were held in a rented room above Max's Grocery and Restaurant on the corner of Second and Spruce streets, with a *Sepher Torah* (a parchment scroll containing the first five books of the Old Testament) and prayer books from Philadelphia provided by a Mr. Baumeister at his own expense. When *chazzen* Isaac Leeser of Philadelphia paid a visit to St. Louis fifteen years later, there were three congregations: the original, or Polish; the German; and the Bohemian. To Leeser's way of thinking this was unfortunate; however, to the Jews of St. Louis such divisions were far preferable to the friction that would have resulted by uniting Jews who did not yet share a common American heritage.

We regret to state that the Israelites of this flourishing city require a thorough reorganization, but little having as yet been done for religious instruction, except teaching a little Hebrew by the Rev. Edward Miers of the Fifth Street Congregation at such hours when his other duties give him leisure and opportunity. But the necessity that something ought to be done is felt very strongly. . . . We spoke everywhere in the simplest manner and merely touched on such topics as must be evident to the commonest understanding; and in the address to which we now allude, we only placed before the people the absurdity of keeping up three organizations, when the Polish, German and Bohemian customs hardly differ, except in the amount of poetical prayers to be recited on certain days . . . and hence the evident impropriety to keep aloof from each other, by which all good works are checked, and estrangement of feelings quite uselessly kept up. We trust that the approbation given to our remarks, which extended nearly for an hour, have had more than a passing effect. . . .

It is not more than about twelve years since our people resorted hither in considerable numbers; and still we found that several had accumulated a considerable amount of wealth in view of their former circumstances. . . .

❧ IN 1854 Julius Ullmann, a German-Jewish immigrant, gave up his liquor operation in St. Louis to see what advantages St. Paul had as a place for starting a new business. Finding all the streets obstructed with building materials, Ullmann wrote to his wife, Amelia, to "start as soon as possible, that we may begin our home life in this young Northwest." Ame-

St. Louis steamboats around the time Amelia Ullmann traveled with a small child by steamboat from St. Louis to St. Paul.
Library of Congress

lia's long and perilous voyage across the ocean two years earlier had filled her "with more confidence than as a girl in a quiet Rhine town I had thought myself capable of possessing." It was in just such a frame of mind that she set out from St. Louis in 1855 with a baby in her arms for a "strange land and a new life." The following selection is an extract from Amelia's recollections of her journey north.

The boat landed wherever there appeared to be the least excuse and even, at times, where there were none. There were no towns; a settlement of three or four houses was a "city." For many places, these boats were the only means of communication with the outside world. Arrival at one of the larger towns on route was an event of particular importance. From the distance we saw first the spires of the churches and then watched the spots and lines develop into houses and streets. Late in the evening we steamed up to the landing at Davenport. The lights of the streets and the houses and the busy landing so favorably impressed me that I felt that I would not be unwilling to make the bright new town the end of my journey.

The little settlements became fewer and fewer the further northward we went. Cultivated fields that were not uncommon in the lower parts of the journey disappeared; even the settler's hut was no longer visible to modify the wild aspect of the scenery. A forest primeval no woodman's axe had ever disturbed rolled down over the bluffs to the river's edge. Vines grew luxuriant, binding together giant trees. Through the thick underbrush wild animals alone could make their way. The air was full of birds and insects. Sometimes a deer broke through the tangle of vegetation and slaked his thirst at the edge of the river, or the shriek of a wildcat came from the depths of the woods.

The savagery of the scene and the length and tediousness of the journey had a depressing effect on me. Eight days, which was the scheduled time for the trip, had already passed, and we were still far from St. Paul. So long as we moved, even if at only a snail's pace, I was content, feeling that sometime at least we would eventually come to the end. But when day after day the boat ran upon bars and we were forced to remain stationary, my patience became exhausted and I would think with sorrowful longing upon the home that I had left behind. The sense of duty to my husband or the cry of the babe that lay in my arms, however, brought back my wandering fancies and stifled the feelings of homesickness.

We steamed slowly on northward, past Prairie du Chien, La Crosse, Fond du Lac, Red Wing, all then settlements of only a few houses scattered along the river bank. The journey had dragged along into the fifteenth day when the captain said that by evening we would arrive in St. Paul. Slowly the boat threaded its way past the shoals and bars. As the shades of evening fell, in the distance we could faintly see the lights of the landing of St. Paul. . . .

"This is the principal part of the city," said my husband with a wave of his hand. I saw one or two good-sized brick buildings and a collection of rough, unpainted, frame shanties, any one of the greater part of which could have been conveniently put into the parlor of an ordinary dwelling

On the way to St. Paul.

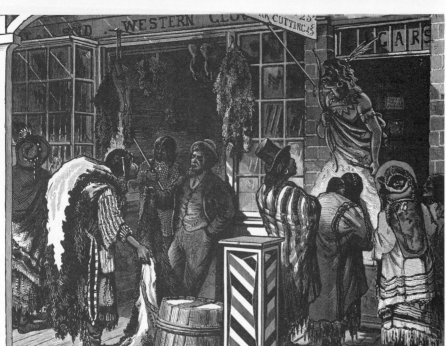

*Indians trading at a frontier town.
"The squaws, who do all the hard
work, are loaded with skins of various
animals, while the warriors, who
consider every kind of labor
degrading to a man, condescend only
to do the bargaining."*
—Harper's Weekly, July 3, 1875

house. The doors and windows were all closed. There were only a few persons upon the street and most of these were tall, erect, wild-looking creatures wrapped up in colored blankets. The impression was not at all favorable. . . .

"The principal business part of the city," I repeated. "Where? There appears to be no business and no people except those wild creatures."

"But today is Sunday. Wait until tomorrow and you will see life enough," was the reply. . . .

The American House, one of the principal hotels, was filled with guests. The only room the proprietor could place at our disposal was the little one my husband had been occupying but had found too small for his own convenience. The bill of fare was bacon, potatoes, biscuits, tea for breakfast and supper. Soup and a pie made from dried fruit distinguished the midday meal from the other two. Fresh meat, fruit, vegetables were too great luxuries for a hotel table. The river being low and lumber difficult to obtain, no houses were built. My husband found it even impossible to secure a storeroom. Days passed and grew into weeks and months, and the hotel continued crowded to its utmost capacity. Frequently, we were solicited for the loan of an old sofa in our room to make a bed for some weary arrival.

Only a conscientious housewife, only a devoted mother who lived in St. Paul in those days knows what I was forced to endure. The market house was a place where butchers endeavored to dispose of poor quality meat at a high price. The owner of the only cow in town agreed to furnish me weekly with milk and butter which she failed to do even for the first week. Every drop of water had to be carried from a well, and to get this it was necessary to crowd in among drivers and rough men from the prairies.

The means of amusement were few. There were no theatres; and, except the entertainments given at some of the churches, there were no attempts at amateur performances of plays or operas. People came often together at church meetings or the circles that were formed among the members. Men appeared to find some pleasure in conversing in the barrooms of the hotels or in attendance upon the sessions of the lodges, for already there were branches in St. Paul. In the dearth of public entertainment, we developed a reading circle that eagerly devoured all the books that could be obtained. Letters and newspapers, brought twice a week by mail sledge from Dubuque, were eagerly read and discussed.

ON THE SIDE OF THE UNION

ക THOUGH JEWS formed but a small portion of the population of the North in Lincoln's time, over six thousand Jewish soldiers rallied to the defense of the Union. One of the first to do so was Julius Ochs, the father of Adolph Ochs, publisher for many years of *The New York Times.* A jewelry merchant from Bavaria, Ochs in 1860 traveled to what was then the Northwest. "It was a severe winter," Ochs recalled years later, "and I crossed the Mississippi many times on the ice. I traveled by sleigh from Burlington, Iowa, to Des Moines, and was very nearly frozen to death." When the war broke out in the spring of the following year, Ochs was in Nashville.

At the hotel where I lodged, the sole topic of conversation was Secession or Anti-Secession. Tennessee was in the balance. I expressed my opinion very freely for the Union. On April 12, 1861, the news was flashed over the wires that Fort Sumter was taken. Instantly the whole political atmosphere at Nashville underwent a change. The rebels became defiant and it was dangerous for a Union sympathizer to express himself. I was advised to leave the city because of my Union sympathy. Some of my friends procured a carriage and I was hastily driven away.

I proceeded north with all possible speed. When I reached Cincinnati the excitement was at fever heat. Lincoln had just issued his proclamation calling for 75,000 volunteers for three months' enlistment. Companies were being drilled in every ward of the city. I enlisted immediately in the company of my home ward and had the honor of being immediately elected Captain. I received my Commission from Ohio's war Governor Dennison. Colonel A. E. Jones was the commanding officer of all the Cincinnati troops. He learned that I had been versed in military tactics and he did me the great honor of appointing me to his staff as Adjutant General.

. . . It was a sacrifice for me to leave my affairs to enter the army but I felt the call of country and responded, disregarding my financial interests, which suffered seriously in consequence. I had a wife and two children to support, with no immediate income, and my plight was quite serious. Rent

Enlisting Irish and German emigrants on the Battery at New York. From The Illustrated London News, *September 17, 1864.*
The New-York Historical Society, New York City

was falling due, money was needed for the necessities of life, and none was immediately at hand. I was compelled to dispose of my personal belongings and was dependent on the confidence of my landlord for our house. . . .

At this period General Fremont was organizing an army in Missouri and much artillery and ammunition was being shipped via Cincinnati over the Ohio and Mobile Railroad. Fearing that the bridges might be burned, General Mitchell sought troops to guard them. He asked Colonel Jones to recommend a good reliable officer whom he would commission to make up two companies to perform that service. Colonel Jones recommended me. He commanded me to organize two companies for guard and provost duty. I received major's pay and two horses, for I was in command of both companies. . . .

Precisely one month after I was mustered in, a fourth child, a son was born to us, October 27, 1861, and I named him George Washington, because I was then in the army of the United States.

Julius Ochs, father of the publisher of The New York Times, *shown here as an officer in the Federal Army during the Civil War.*

ANOTHER Jewish immigrant, Louis Gratz, was peddling Yankee notions with a friend in Pennsylvania when "suddenly the war broke out." Two years later Gratz was rewarded for his courageous conduct and presence of mind at Chickamauga by being placed on the personal staff of General Samuel Powhatan Carter. In the following selection from a letter to relatives in Poland, Gratz describes a world in which he was treated with "utmost consideration."

Business came to a standstill; all the public works were stopped, and after the call of the President to defend the country with arms, all the young folks flocked to the colors. Carried away by the general enthusiasm,

*The Menken brothers of Cincinnati in their
Civil War uniforms. Though only 150,000
Jews resided in America at this time, over
7,500 fought on both sides.*
American Jewish Archives, Cincinnati, Ohio

I became a soldier. I studied English with great zeal until I could talk fairly fluently. Since I had the good will of my superiors, I became a noncommissioned officer in a few weeks. However, the way to a higher position was barred to me, because I had to write and read English perfectly to get such an appointment. I started again, sometimes studying through the better part of the night, and all this without any help, since I did not have enough money to hire a tutor. Now I am able to speak, read, and write English well. In the meantime, our enlistment term, fixed for a period of four months, expired. Everybody had believed that this war would last only four months. We had been sworn in for this period only and were discharged on its expiration. However, the war was far from being finished, and therefore the President issued a second proclamation asking for soldiers for a period of three years.

Through the intervention of several high-ranking personalities, who had become interested in me, and possibly also because of the fact that I had shown courage several times during my first enlistment, I was introduced to Secretary of War Cameron and was examined by him. I had used my time profitably to study military tactics whenever I had a moment, and so I became a first lieutenant in the cavalry of the United States. The name of my regiment is the Lochiel Light Cavalry. . . . I have been given the promise of a captaincy as soon as possible, and therefore I am doing my best to make myself worthy of the commission.

We are now with our regiment in Washington; in a few days we will leave for the theater of war. Formerly a peddler, barely able to make a living, I have now become a respected man in a respected position, one filled by very few Jews. . . . Before this no one paid any attention to me here; now I move in the best and richest circles and am treated with utmost consideration by Jews and Christians.

◄§ NOTWITHSTANDING such conditions, Jews of the North became keenly aware of their vulnerability when General Grant issued an order in 1862 for the expulsion of the Jews "as a class" from the military district he commanded. Grant justified the order by insisting that Treasury regulations against speculating in cotton were being violated mostly by Jews. In fact, such activities were being carried out mainly by non-Jewish army officers, Treasury agents, and small-time speculators including, according to rumor, Jesse Grant, the general's father.

Hdqrs. 13th A.C. Dept of the Tenn.
Holly Springs, December 17, 1862

GENERAL ORDERS: NO. 11

The Jews, as a class violating every regulation of trade established by the Treasury Department and also department orders, are hereby expelled from the department within twenty-four hours from the receipt of this order.

Post commanders will see that all of this class of people be furnished passes and required to leave, and any one returning after such notification will be arrested and held in confinement until an opportunity occurs of sending them out as prisoners, unless furnished with a permit from headquarters.

No passes will be given these people to visit headquarters for the purpose of making personal application for trade permits.

By order of Maj. Gen. U. S. Grant:

Jno. A. Rawlins,
Assistant Adjutant General.

WHEN LINCOLN learned of Grant's order, he directed General-in-Chief of the Army Henry W. Halleck to telegraph instructions for its cancellation. It was but one of many acts of rectitude that moved Jews throughout the North to show their love for their martyred President in the spring of 1865 by placing black draperies on the altars of synagogues and substituting Yom Kippur hymns for Passover melodies. On April 19, the day of Lincoln's funeral, rabbis spoke of him as their patriarch holding fast to the promise of a blessed nation, their Moses "ever thoughtful of the duty to bring his people back to enjoy the whole land." For many it was as though a fellow Jew, "bone of our bone and flesh from our flesh," had died.

6
The Antebellum South

FREEDOM AND SLAVERY

NEGROES, NEGROES.

The undersigned has just arrived in Lumpkin from Virginia, with a likely lot of negroes, about 40 in number, embracing every shade and variety. He has seamstresses, chamber maids, field hands, and doubts not that he is able to fill the bill of any who may want to buy. He has sold over two hundred negroes in this section, mostly in this county, and flatters himself that he has so far given satisfaction to his purchasers. Being a regular trader to this market he has nothing to gain by misrepresentation, and will, therefore, warrant every negro sold to come up to the bill, squarely and completely. Give him a call at his Mart.

J. F. MOSES.
Lumpkin, Ga., Nov. 14th, 1859.

◄§ SOIL EXHAUSTION and the decline of tobacco as a profitable staple—coupled with the removal of the Indians from the old Southwest—led to the mass movement of pioneers in the 1820s and '30s into western Georgia, Alabama, Mississippi, and northern Florida where a new staple crop, cotton, promised quick profits. Almost overnight thriving communities came into being along the Yazoo, Alabama, and Mississippi rivers which Jewish entrepreneurs like Henry Lehman, a twenty-three-year-old cattle dealer's son from Rimpar, Bavaria, were quick to travel to.

Landing in Mobile, Alabama, in 1844, Lehman promptly set out with a wagonload of merchandise for sale to farmers, plantation owners, and their families. Moving north along the Alabama River, within a year Lehman had accumulated enough savings to open a general merchandise store in Montgomery. A prospering town linked by waterways to Mobile and New Orleans, it was already an important storage center and trading point for cotton. With a population of six thousand—four thousand whites and two thousand slaves—Montgomery was fast becoming a Southern metropolis. "There is money to be made here," Henry wrote back to his family in Rimpar.

In 1847 a younger brother, Emanuel, joined him. A year later a sign went up on a new store, a two-story wooden structure at Court Square, bearing the legend: "H. Lehman & Bro." A third brother, Mayer, arrived in 1850. As soon as the three brothers were united, "H. Lehman & Bro." was changed to "Lehman Brothers." Their store, which stood in the heart of town directly opposite Montgomery's main slave-auctioning block, was well stocked with everything from sheetings, shirting, and yarn to cotton rope and ball thread. Almost as a matter of course, the Lehmans began trading merchandise for cotton and shipping it to New Orleans, where payments often took the form of four-month drafts on New York banks. Since New York was already a major economic center for the South, it was only natural for Emanuel, who by now had assumed most of the financial responsibilities for the business, to visit New York frequently to sell drafts, pay bills, and buy merchandise directly from Northern manufacturers. When in 1858 the brothers decided to open a permanent New York office, Emanuel headed north for good and set up a brokerage house at 119 Liberty Street, just a few blocks away from the Kuhns, the Loebs, and the Seligmans.

The rise of Lazarus Straus and his sons Isidor, Nathan, and Oscar also started in the antebellum South. Bavarian Jews, the Strauses settled in Talbotton, Georgia, where Lazarus operated a general merchandise store for many years. After the war the family moved north. Isidor and Nathan soon became sole owners of Macy's Department Store, while Oscar, who served as Theodore Roosevelt's Secretary of Commerce and Labor, became the first Jew in America to hold a cabinet position. Looking back, Oscar recalled the South of his youth as a place where Jews felt welcome but never quite at home.

In our town, as in all Southern communities, the better families were kind, especially to their household slaves, whom they regarded as members of the family requiring guardianship and protection, in a degree as if they were children. And the slaves addressed their masters by their first names [but always preceded by Mr.] and their mistresses as "miss." My mother, for instance, was Miss Sara. I recall one of our servants pleading with my mother: "Miss Sara, won't you buy me? I want to stay here. I love you and the white folks here, and I am afraid my master will hire me out and sell me to someone else." At that time we hired our servants from their masters, whom we paid an agreed price. But, as the result of such constant pleadings, my father purchased household slaves one by one from their masters, although neither he nor my mother believed in slavery. . . .

As a boy growing up in the South, I never questioned the rights or wrongs of slavery. Its existence I regarded as a matter of course, as most other customs or institutions. The grown people of the South, whatever they thought about it, would not, except in rare instances, speak against it, and even then in the most private and guarded manner. To do otherwise would subject one to social ostracism. We heard it defended in the pulpit and justified on biblical grounds by leading ministers. With my father it was different. I frequently heard him discuss the subject with the ministers who came to our house, and he would point out to them that the Bible must be read with discrimination and in relation to the period to which the chapters refer; and it must not be forgotten that it is the history of a people covering more than a thousand years, and that even then there had been no such thing as perpetual bondage, as all slaves were declared free in the year of jubilee.

Looking backward and making comparisons between my observations as a boy in the South and later in the North, I find there was much more freedom of expression in the North than in the South. Few people in the South would venture to express themselves against the current of dominant opinion upon matters of sectional importance. The institution of slavery with all that it implied seemed to have had the effect of enslaving, or, to use a milder term, checking, freedom of expression on the part of the master class only in lesser degree than among the slaves themselves.

Baer Bros., Pine Bluff, Arkansas.
American Jewish Historical Society, Waltham, Massachusetts

June 1859. The Rev. L. G. Sternheimer of Columbus, Georgia, may be safely recommended to our fellow-Israelites residing in his vicinity, in Alabama and Georgia, as a competent *mohel.* He has officiated in that capacity at Memphis (Tenn.), Georgia, Mississippi, and Arkansas, and can, therefore, bring satisfactory reference to those who may require it.

The Occident Advertiser

December 6, 1860. Tallahassee, the capital of Florida, is a nice little town of about 3,500 inhabitants. The number of our brethren in faith that dwell here is fifteen—four families and the rest single men. Those that are merchants (only three in number) have the largest and the best stocks in the city. Those that are harness makers are the best workmen in the U.S.; they therefore are the most patronized; and those that are book-keepers (there are two) are well known as gentlemen of integrity and honesty. In short our brethren here are healthy and wealthy, and are greatly respected by their neighbors for their uprightness and honesty.

Israelites are also to be found at Apalachicola, St. Augustine, Aspaloga, Jacksonville, Lake City, Madison Court House, Pensacola, Quincy, Monticella, Riddlerville, Fernandio, Tampa Bay, Hawkinsville, Chattahoochee, and Fort Gaines, Georgia.

The Israelite

❧ BECAUSE MOST roads in the antebellum South were in poor condition, it was not unusual for itinerant merchants to sell goods to farmers and their families from floating country stores—i.e., flatboats fitted with shelves, counters, and seats. A wide variety of goods was always on hand: dry goods, china, shoes, bonnets, fine clothing, and tinware, in addition to every sort of article or tool a farmer might need. Sometimes customers paid in cash, though more often they relied on barter, trading pork, flour, and vegetables for whatever they needed that they couldn't provide for themselves. After selling and bartering as much as he could in one place, the floating storekeeper either moved on or stopped for a while to socialize.

Early in 1850 brother Isaac had purchased a trading boat and filled it with a stock of merchandise. The first place we stopped was at Captain Henderson's plantation near Warrenton, Mississippi. The captain came aboard and bought a quart of brandy, he said, for a sick negress. He got gloriously drunk and did not pay for the liquor, but as soon as it got dark, shot at us. We returned the compliment and dropped down a mile or so to the edge of the wood. The next place I remember stopping was the side of the Red River, Captain Leather's home. That night there was a party given at their house. I was invited and danced with the captain's younger sister and made quite a mash; I was fairly good-looking if I do say so myself.

Early in 1851 Valentine Cohn and I made a skiff trip, filling some trunks with an assortment of dry goods and notions. The river being very

Mississippi River peddler shortly after the Civil War: "As soon as the boatman-storekeeper caught sight of a settlement, he would blow a horn. Customers would then hurry to the riverbank to inspect a wide variety of merchandise—dry goods, china, shoes, bonnets, fine clothing, tinware, jewelry—every sort of article that a farmer and his family might need."
—Harper's Weekly, 1871

high, we put our skiff in the Willow Bayou on the Tallabeena Plantation. From the bayou we went into Brushy, Roundway, Joe's Bayou, Little and Big Tensas and some other little bayous, landing at last at Miller's Landing, now Delhi, Louisiana, where we closed out and returned home. We had a spendid time, both commercial and social. People before the Civil War were entirely different from what they are now. You were welcome at all times and treated with cordiality at every place if you looked any way respectable, tho you may never have seen the parties before.

In the fall of 1850 brother Isaac started in business at Richmond, Louisiana. I was doing very well, but it was so difficult to get goods there owing to the bad roads that I moved to Milliken's Bend the following spring. Brother Jacob, who lived at Vicksburg keeping a boardinghouse, sold out and joined his fortune with mine. We chartered a ferryboat to take our goods, household furniture, children, and dog. I had rented a very nice store and a double log house, a very comfortable dwelling belonging to the Canal Bank of New Orleans. I had a bedroom in the rear of the store.

We had an uphill business when we started there. A great deal of prejudice prevailed towards foreigners. But after living there a short time, we gained the confidence of the people, and by keeping a complete assortment of such articles that people needed daily, we got their trade, selling many things the other stores considered too trifling. The other stores came to us to fill the orders of their customers, charging a big profit. The people soon caught on and traded directly with us. It was not many years before we handled as fine goods as were sold anywhere—ladies' handkerchiefs as high as $10 each, embroidery and lace as high as $2.50 to $5.00 per yard. By 1860 we had put the other merchants out of business. . . .

The second year of our residence at Milliken's Bend we bought a house that had been used for a tavern, which we converted into a store, using a part for our residence and adding a warehouse by the side of it. About the same time I was appointed postmaster and notary public. . . .

In 1859 Milliken's Bend was incorporated. In the election for officers, I ran for mayor against George Sebastian, a brother-in-law of Captain James M. White in the wholesale grocery business in New Orleans. There were sixty-one votes cast. I received thirty votes. I would have been elected if the man running on my ticket as marshall had not voted my opponent's ticket. They made him believe he would be made marshall. I cursed that fellow, and you may be sure he never forgot. . . .

Milliken's Bend was a very nice little place—sociable, no snobbery either among the citizens or among the rich planters in the whole parish; simplicity was the rule. When some of the poorer people got sick, the rich would send them delicacies, and send them their carriages to ride out when convalescent. The world has sadly retrograded. If one nowadays has a few dollars more than one's neighbor, he forgets that his grandparents were paupers. I know whercof I speak.

Philip Sartorius

THE LURE OF NEW ORLEANS

JUDAH TOURO, one of the first native-born Jews to settle in New Orleans, was the son of the longtime *chazzen* of the synagogue in Newport, Rhode Island, which now bears the family name. Born at Newport on the eve of the Battle of Bunker Hill, Touro set sail for New Orleans from Boston in 1801 in anticipation of the Louisiana Purchase, which brought prosperity to New Orleans and eventually to Touro, who became the first American Jewish philanthropist to be recognized as such. The following tribute to Touro and Amos Laurence, a Boston blueblood, was delivered at a dinner at Faneuil Hall in 1839 in appreciation of their matching gifts of $10,000 apiece for the completion of the Bunker Hill monument.

View of the French Quarter, New Orleans, 1858.
Library of Congress

Amos and Judah—venerated names,
Patriarch and Prophet press their equal claims,
Like generous coursers running "neck in neck,"
Each aids the work by giving it a check.
Christian and Jew, they carry out one plan
For though of different faith, each is in heart a man.

1842. In the city of New Orleans there live 700 Jewish families. Among these you find no more than four households in which forbidden food is avoided, only two in which the Sabbath rest is observed. More than two-thirds of the congregation's members do not have their sons circumcised. . . . This of a rabbi! This stigma in the ranks of the Jewish ministry eats whatever comes before his maw, never keeps the feast of Passover, indeed, has had none of his boys circumcised. In addition to his post of rabbi, Mr. Markes—that is his name—holds a job as an actor at the American Theatre and that of chief of one of the fire-engines. At Purim the book of Esther could not be read, since, so the President of the Congregation informed the *minyan*, the rabbi/reader was preoccupied with his duties as fire chief. When challenged by a pious member of the congregation, the rabbi, beside himself with wrath, pounded the pulpit and shouted: "By Jesus Christ, I have a right to pray!" After his death the rabbi's widow, a Catholic, was restrained only with difficulty from putting a crucifix in his grave.

Allgemeine Zeitung des Judentums

1850. . . . The reader can hardly form a conception of how great the difficulty was to organize a congregation on a proper footing in that great mart of commerce New Orleans. . . . The Christian population itself was but little given to religious observances, and, formerly, a degree of freedom in living was indulged in but little promotive of the growth of piety. Those who are conversant with the decay of religious observance will therefore not wonder that the Jews in New Orleans were no better than their Christian neighbors and that, moreover, owing to the paucity of Jewish young women, many intermarriages produced a great estrangement to our faith, and the children of the mixed marriages are, in many instances, entirely lost to Israel. . . .

At least there are now three organized bodies in New Orleans, and there are people and means enough to make them all flourishing and respectable. . . . The Portuguese *kahal* has been fortunate in obtaining the first permanent place of worship, but the two others will not be long behind in the race, especially as the German, worshipping in Rampart Street, has resolved to erect a suitable house, large enough to contain the numerous worshippers belonging to the same. The Lafayette congregation, however, was but lately organized, and of course it will require some time to give it a proper firmness and consistence, before it would be advisable to erect a synagogue. . . .

Isaac Leeser

Florida's first United States Senator, David Levy Yulee.
National Archives

DIVISIVENESS AND WAR

⌇ DAVID LEVY YULEE, America's first Jewish congressman, was the son of an immigrant merchant who dreamed of establishing a colony of European Jews in Florida in the 1820s. Called a Hebrew visionary by some, Yulee's father worked hard to achieve his dream. Nonetheless, he attracted fewer than fifty Jews to sixty thousand acres of land in what is now the northeastern part of the state. It was here, as the son of a successful sugar planter, that Yulee became immersed in the life of the South. After a promising career as a lawyer, Yulee was chosen as congressional Representative-at-large for the Territory of Florida. In Florida no one had paid much attention to Yulee's Jewish background; however, in Washington there were people like Congressman John Quincy Adams to contend with. Adams seemed never to tire of referring to Yulee as the "Jew Delegate" or the "alien Jew Delegate from Florida."

Other political luminaries took a more enlightened view. In 1845, Yulee obtained ex-Governor Wickliffe of Kentucky's consent to marry his daughter. In the same year Yulee was elected to the United States

Senate from the new State of Florida. After a long and distinguished political career in Washington, Yulee stood up on the floor of the Senate and announced Florida's secession from the Union. It was a moving address which pleased Yulee's friends while providing others with an opportunity to underscore his Jewish background. "I remember him in the House," Senator Andrew Johnson of Tennessee, the only Southern senator to support the Union, recalled with rancor. "The contemptible little Jew—standing there and begging us to let Florida in as a State. Well, we let her in . . . and now that despicable little beggar stands up in the Senate and talks about *her* rights."

IN 1852, a grateful Louisiana constituency sent Judah P. Benjamin, a Caribbean-born grocer's son, to the United States Senate. An outstanding orator in an age of orators, Benjamin was considered among the most eloquent defenders of the Southern cause. "You may set our cities in flame," he declared from the floor of the Senate in 1860, "but you can never subjugate us; you never can convert the free sons of the soil into vassals, paying tribute to your power; and you never, never can degrade them to the level of an inferior and servile race. Never! Never!" Two years later, as Confederate Secretary of State, Benjamin was attacked vehemently for advocating a plan for using slaves as soldiers in exchange for their eventual freedom. "The trouble with him," General Robert E. Lee observed ruefully, "is that his first thought is not to be polite, but right." A serious shortcoming, especially for a Jew. Throughout the war, Benjamin was a popular target of attack. Blamed for "all the distresses of the people," on more than one occasion he was referred to as the "Judas Iscariot Benjamin" of the Confederacy.

BECAUSE of their vulnerability as "outsiders," most Jews in the antebellum South conformed outwardly to prevailing views; however, there were also those who risked their lives by expressing abolitionist sentiments. One such was David Einhorn, a Baltimore rabbi who did so until he was forced to flee with his family to Philadelphia. The following selection, from a sermon Einhorn delivered there in 1864 in opposition to the use of the Bible as a justification for slavery, is an eloquent testimony to one man's refusal to become a slave to the letter of the law.

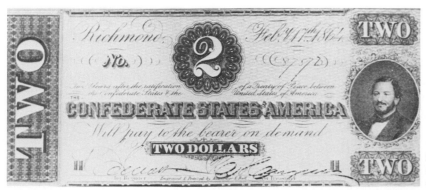

Secretary of State Judah P. Benjamin on a Confederate two-dollar bill.
American Jewish Archives, Cincinnati, Ohio

Remnants of grandeur: Judah P. Benjamin's Louisiana plantation house overlooking the Mississippi River.
American Jewish Archives, Cincinnati, Ohio

Is it anything else but rebellion against God to enslave beings created in His image and to degrade them to a state of beasts having no will of their own? Is it anything else but an act of ruthless and wicked violence to reduce defenceless human beings to a condition of merchandise, and relentlessly to tear them away from the hearts of husbands, wives, parents and children? We are told that this crime rests upon a historical right! But pray, can ancient custom indeed convert an atrocious wrong into right? Does a disease, perchance, cease to be an evil on account of its long duration? Is not the assertion that whatever our ancestors regarded as good, true and admissible, must be so also for us however much reason and conscience may militate against it—is not that assertion an insult to all mental and moral progress of humanity? . . . Was not the enslavement of Israel in Egypt equally a historic right for Pharaoh and his mercenaries, and did God's judgment not burst upon Israel's oppressors just at the time when this reputed right had been transmitted through centuries? No! Justice and truth may be perverted for a long space and time, but not forever. . . .

But it is still further asserted: slavery is an institution sanctioned by the Bible, hence war against it is war against, and not for God! . . . .

There is an ancient maxim in Judaism: "The law was not given for angels"; the law of God was intended for human beings, and is, therefore, a law of education, affording to the human mind the most powerful impulse for development, and, in this spirit, expanding itself more widely and beautifully from its very innermost nature. It is only the slaves of the letter that deny this capability of development—it is only they that convert the letter of the Bible into a slave-whip.

⤳ THE FOLLOWING ACCOUNT is by Major Raphael Moses. A fifth-generation descendant of Dr. Samuel Nunez of Georgia, Moses joined the Confederate Army along with his three sons.

Georgia was the chief source of supply, and the speculations of the men who were buying food for the army in Georgia became so intolerable that the farmers refused to sell. It occurred to me that if I could go to Georgia and speak to the people who had sons, brothers, relatives, and friends who were suffering for lack of supplies, I could get supplies. . . .

I suggested to General Longstreet to give me a furlough for this purpose. He consented at once, but it required the approval of Gen. Robert E. Lee. I carried my furlough, signed by General Longstreet, to General Lee's headquarters which were nearby. There was never any difficulty about approaching General Lee; he had very little red-tape routine. He was writing in his tent when I entered. He looked up with a friendly smile and said: "Major, what will you have?" I handed him my furlough; he read it and said: "Major, I would approve of it, but I really can't spare you." I then explained to him my plans. He hesitated a minute or two and then said: "Well, Major, if you think you can do anything for my poor boys, go, and may God crown your efforts with success." He approved my furlough and I started for Georgia.

The first meeting I called was at Columbus, in Temperance Hall. There were about thirty persons present. I thanked them for their presence and stated when I last spoke in this hall it was to urge the people to send their sons and brothers to confront the hazards of war and to redress their country's wrongs, the house was full from pit to gallery with patriotic citizens ready for the sacrifices asked. Now I come from those near and dear to the people here, to appeal to them for bread for the starving army, and I am confronted with empty benches. I must try more fruitful fields; an appeal to the few who are here could promise no good results. I thanked those present for their attendance and closed the meeting. I went from there to southwest Georgia and was met with a very different spirit and had a very successful trip. . . .

. . . My son, Lea . . . entered as a private soldier. . . . Albert, another son of mine . . . was killed at the Battle of Seven Pines near Richmond in 1862. I was near the battlefield . . . and the best information that I could get was that he was slightly wounded in the leg. . . . As I passed the treasury office in Richmond, Col. Clayton called out to me that a young man by my name had been carried in by an ambulance, and that he was shot in the head. I never for a moment thought of its being Albert, as my wife's brother, Perry Moses, had a son in the same battle . . . and I thought I knew that Albert's wound was a slight one in the leg. But as I was interested in the fate of my nephew, I went to the hospital . . . and inquired for the ward in which the wounded had been carried that day. . . . I saw some ladies standing by a cot and heard one of them say: "What a handsome young man!" I crossed over to the cot, and my shock was beyond my power of expression when I saw my son Albert lying unconscious with a wound in his head. I removed him in an ambulance to Perry's house, where he remained unconscious, never recognizing me. He died that night from loss of blood when the surgeon tried to relieve the pressure of the brain, and it was in this manner passed away a bright, promising youth of nineteen.

AFTER THE WAR a steady stream of Jewish peddlers from central and eastern Europe came south to do business with poor white farmers and Negro sharecroppers. Soon every town of any consequence in the South had one or more Jewish-owned stores carrying merchandise often unobtainable anywhere else in town. Because there were so few opportunities for economic growth in a land devastated by war, only the shrewdest and smartest prospered. As for the ordinary Jew, he was lucky to make just enough to keep himself and his family going.

The following selection from *Kentucky*, by the American Yiddish poet I. J. Schwartz, recounts the experiences of an East European Jew who went south to peddle shortly after the Civil War.

Harper's Weekly

FREEDOM AND PARDON FROM GOVERNOR MOSES

Franklin J. Moses, Jr., the "Robber Governor" of South Carolina during Reconstruction, as depicted by Thomas Nast in an 1873 cartoon for Harper's Weekly. *The half-Jewish son of a distinguished South Carolina chief justice, Governor Moses made no secret of receiving money for pardons and official appointments. After his term of office expired, Moses spent much of his time in jail for passing bogus checks to friend and foe alike.*

AFTER THE CIVIL WAR

Wide, free, open lay the land
Extending to the far horizon.
The sand-red road stretched far and strange
Deserted, dotted with low plants,
With unknown broad-leaved herbs. Free distances
Through which the plow had not yet passed,
Raw and deserted, with thick juicy grass
And here and there a damp, wild grove
Where tree grows into tree, root into root.
And all that heat and strangeness threw
A taste, unknown and tropical,
Of blossom and decay. Above arched wavy-pink
The dusky southland evening sky,
And all the landscape filled with light,
Red trees, red plains, all absolutely still.

From the deep blue of the evening sky,
Face turning to the burning west,
The wanderer came down the road,
His pack upon his shoulders.
The tall and boney figure bowed,
Tramping, tramping, in the soft red sand,
From head to foot—from bowler hat
To the hard and dried-up boots—
Baked in the milk-white dust.
The pointed yellow sunburnt beard,
The strained and bloodshot eyes
With every sorrow in their rosy depths,
Tramping, tramping, in the soft red sand.

The Jew came to the unknown from afar,
With sore feet, with a grieving heart,
Pack on shoulders, stick in hand,
Into the new, the free gigantic land.

Blue, wondrous, the night set in—
All colors melting, violet, blue, and red,
Until one hue embraced the world:
A deep thick blue. Only, in the west,
Upon the black and distant hills,
One deep red stripe still burned.
The first stars twinkled close and red,
And with the onset of the southern night
There lifted up a freshness as the land
Exhaled its juices, flowing warm and earthy scents,
Filling the cool blue air till it became
Like water to the thirsty, wine to those who ache.
So he went on and on and on,
Till at the road's bend, unexpectedly,
The settlement was there before his eyes.
From the blue stillness of the woods and fields
Noise, song, and fire struck him suddenly.
The people from the huts out, with kith and kin,
Around the fires in the middle of the street,
Whistling, banging on tin plates and brass,
Playing on banjos, singing, dancing
Strange wild half-naked dances.
Red from the red sheen of the fires and wild,
Black faces shone with red and heavy eyes.
The homemade brew went hot from mouth to mouth
And heavy Negro women with large red earrings
Rolled hoarse and hot and slapped their hips with joy.
Naked children, heads of pure black wool,
Jumped over fires like untamed forest monkeys,
Dust clouds rising to the reddening black sky,
As black dogs barked and fat cats ran around.

The Jew went through the red-black haze
The heavy pack upon his back,
Strangely familiar as it seemed to him,
Known from some past time. It was as if
He lived and did this many years ago.
He went through red dust as the strange dogs barked
And children shouted after him and women laughed
And red eyes followed him—till he went past,
Into the black fields where farm houses stretched.
He took the pack down off his back,
And knocked on the nearest door.

Noises carried from inside the house:
The heavy bolt unlocked itself,
The door was opened cautiously,
And in the black void of the door
There was a tall white figure of a man,

*Kentucky Jewish peddler Felix Moses,
better known as "Old Mose" of
"Stringtown on the Pike." Moses
made a living for many years after the
Civil War by buying up hides, wool,
rags, and ginseng from farmers in
Kenton and Campbell counties.*
American Jewish Archives, Cincinnati, Ohio

Black barrel of a rifle pointing out.
And then a voice hissed, hoarse and sleepy,
"Who are you?" and the pack-man said,
"A Jew, who seeks a place to rest his head.
I am exhausted from the heavy road."
"How did you come?" "I have my store with me.
Night fell. I'm tired. My feet hurt. Let me in.
Your wife can have a gift here, from the pack."
The rifle rose. The voice said, softer, "Wait."
Soon enough the figure came out to the Jew,
Bringing a burning lantern to his eyes,
Examined him from head to toe, and threw out, "Come."
He led him to a haystack in the barn
And said, with feeling, "Don't smoke here.
The whole place could go up in flames
Together with the cattle and your pack.
Remember that." Then he slunk out
And locked the gate behind him.

From *Kentucky* by I. J. Schwartz,
translated from the Yiddish by Richard Helfer

The Lemanns of Donaldsonville, Louisiana, and their Mammy, 1909.
Bernard Lemann

7
Farther West

TEXAS

❧ SOON AFTER WINNING independence from Spain in 1821, Mexico began encouraging colonization in Texas. During the next fifteen years over twenty thousand settlers poured in. Among them were a handful of Jews, including David L. Kokernot. Born in Amsterdam in 1805, Kokernot came to New Orleans with his father in 1817 and, in the same year, was apprenticed to a pilot on the Mississippi River. After a career as a merchant seaman which took him to Europe and the West Indies, Kokernot invested a few thousand dollars in merchandise and, in 1832, traveled by schooner with his wife and children from New Orleans to the town of Anahuac on Galveston Bay, where he opened a store in the vicinity of a large Mexican garrison. Two years later, on a trip to the pueblo of Nacogdoches, Kokernot met Sam Houston.

Sam Houston was dressed in a complete Indian costume made of buckskin and ornamented with a profuse variety of beads, and his massive head was covered with a fine broad beaver hat. When he arose I stopped and looked at him with both surprise and admiration and bid him good morning. . . .

"Now, my friend," said the General, "tell me the news."

I replied the news was war; that it was rumored that Santa Anna was gathering troops to send into Texas to disarm the inhabitants. "But," said I, "we are determined not to surrender our arms."

"Well, my friend," said he, "how will you act in that case?"

I replied: "We will fight them to the last, or die in the attempt."

"That is right," said he; "they shall never drive us out so long as we can fight them."

As he made this remark his eyes sparkled with lightning; a bottle of wine was ordered on the strength of it.

"Now," said he, "the people ought to organize and get ready to meet him."

I told him I was of the same opinion.

"Who will command the army?" he asked.

I replied: "My dear sir, if I had the authority to make the appointment, you are the man; for you are the finest looking man I ever laid eyes on."

He immediately replied, "Well, my dear sir, if I get the appointment of commander I will give you a commission."

Then he pulled out a small pocketbook and asked my name, which he wrote in his book, and then wrote his own name and handed it to me. After talking a while longer we shook hands and bade each other farewell. From that day I loved Sam Houston. He proved a friend indeed in times of need, as many letters in my possession will show.

Ernst Kohlberg, a German Jew who came to El Paso in 1886 and established one of the first cigar factories in the Southwest. Kohlberg was also a founder of the El Paso Railway Company, a director of the Rio Grande Valley Bank and Trust Company, and a member of the El Paso City Council.

⟡ ANOTHER EARLY Texas Jewish settler, Moses Albert Levy, served as a surgeon in Sam Houston's army, and in December 1835 took an active part in the storming of the Alamo, which resulted in the Texas forces capturing the fort from the Mexicans. In the following letter to his sister back east, Levy describes what was probably the most exciting experience of his life.

San Antonio de Bexar, Dec. 20th, 1835

Dearest Sister:

. . . The Americans with a view to besieging the town and fort which is the largest and strongest in all Texas, assembled themselves before its walls by slow degrees, but never at any one time amounting to more than seven hundred men. . . . When we reached the American camp after suffering a thousand deaths in traveling through and sleeping in the cold bleak prairies night after night without a tree or shrub to shelter us from the cold rain and wind, we found the greatest state of confusion and dissatisfaction. The men had left their families and homes with a view to driving the enemy out of their country at once, and then returning home . . . but instead of this their miserable general thought proper to starve out the enemy and prevented the Americans from immediately storming the place. The length of time this took tired out the patience of the soldiers who were all volunteers and some almost naked. . . . Finally affairs became so bad that the army broke up in confusion, and desperate would have been the consequences for we would all have been cut by the enemy when I, *insignificant I*, and another individual . . . beat up for volunteers who would join us two in storming the town and fort that very night. . . . Our

The storming of the Alamo.

company, called the Grays, immediately and to a man signed their names, and mounting one of the baggage wagons (for we, as I have observed, were just ready for a hasty retreat) I harangued them for a few minutes and thus succeeded in getting three hundred men. We laid our plans, appointed our leaders, and about daylight marched up to the enemy's halls, got into some strong houses in town and after a regular storm of five days and nights duration, during the whole of which the enemy kept up an incessant firing, we forced them to surrender, thus achieving a victory perfectly unparalleled in history, a victory obtained by 225 disorganized and undisciplined men armed with muskets and bayonets in a well fortified fort with 30 pieces of cannon of different sizes. Our men fought like devils, (even I fought). I worked in the ditches, I dressed the sick and wounded, I cheered the men, I assisted the officers in their counsels. For five days and nights I did not sleep that many hours, running about without a coat or hat, dirty and ragged, but thank God escaped uninjured. . . . I have crossed a street when more than two hundred muskets were shot at me, our men begging me not to expose myself as I was a double man, being both soldier and surgeon. . . .

Pioneer cattleman Mayer Halff of San Antonio, Texas. Halff and his brother Solomon in their peak years owned countless Leghorns and over one million acres of land. Among the first to realize that the days of Texas Longhorn cattle were over, Mayer's son Henry by the turn of the century became the largest breeder of Herefords in the Southwest.
Alex Halff

꿸 WHEN THE Republic of Texas was established in 1836, all newcomers who were heads of families were promised 1,200 acres of land free of charge, and all single men 640 acres. Five years later, a law was passed empowering the president of Texas, Sam Houston, to enter into contracts for the colonization of much larger tracts of virgin lands. Soon afterward Henri Castro, a wealthy French Jew, was given authority to establish a colony in southwest Texas between the Nueces and Rio Grande rivers. At his own expense Castro recruited 485 families and 457 single men, some with Jewish names, from France and Germany. Through his efforts, a frontier town called Castroville was established sixty miles southwest of San Antonio. Here Castro had buildings constructed and started raising crops, a bold step as the location was open to attack by Indians from the north and Mexicans from the west. Though Castro lost all his money in his ventures, he continued to direct affairs for the people of Castroville until his death in 1861. The town still stands, a monument to his pioneering spirit.

IN THE EARLY 1850s Isaac Sanger, a German-Jewish immigrant, traveled from New York to Texas to cash in on the cattle boom. In no time Isaac was operating a store in McKinney, a tiny settlement four weeks by wagon from Houston. After a younger brother, Lehman, arrived to take charge of the McKinney operation, Isaac opened another store at Weatherford.

At first all kinds of attempts were made by competitors to drive Isaac out of Weatherford. One day he received written notice to leave town or suffer "dire punishment." A few days later a skull and crossbones were painted on the door of his store. Not one to be intimidated, Isaac gained the support of his fellow pioneers by contributing generously to appeals on behalf of a number of fledgling churches in the area.

After serving in the Confederate Army, with his brothers Lehman and Philip, Isaac in partnership with Lehman opened a store in Millican, a frontier town frequented by soldiers from a nearby garrison. "The goods for which there was the greatest demand," Lehman recalled, "were shotguns, revolvers and musical instruments. . . . Our goods were sold generally for gold, very little currency being in circulation."

At the time the economy of Texas rested largely on barter. It was therefore not unusual for women to come to the Sanger brothers' store with eggs, butter, or whatever else they had to trade, while men would bring in hides, wool, or vegetables. Barter provided the Sangers with a variety of ways for acting as middlemen. To give but one example, they would exchange a gun for wool brought in by a rancher and then transport the wool to New Orleans and sell it to a wholesaler for cash, thus making a double sale.

Taking advantage of such opportunities, the Sangers accumulated sizable amounts of liquid assets which, in the late 1860s and early 1870s, they used to open a chain of general merchandise stores at strategic points along the Houston and Texas Railroad, with a different family member taking charge of each new venture.

As soon as Dallas began showing signs of becoming a major center of commerce and trade, the Sangers started consolidating their operations there. Except for a store in Waco, all other establishments were closed. The Sangers had no reason to regret this move, for as Dallas boomed so did "Sanger Brothers," until by the turn of the century it had a wholesale business second in importance only to that of Marshall Field's in Chicago.

The original Neiman-Marcus store. Founded in Dallas in 1907, Neiman-Marcus flourished from its inception by satisfying the whims of a wealthy clientele.
Neiman-Marcus, Inc.

Sam Dreben, shown here in a sombrero with Mexican revolutionaries. Dreben was a Russian-born Jew who gained renown as a First World War hero and a soldier of fortune in Mexico and Central America. "He was the finest soldier," General Pershing said, "and one of the bravest men I have ever known." When Dreben died, the Texas Legislature adjourned for a day in his honor.
El Paso Public Library

A RABBI WHO came to Texas at this time had to be resourceful in order to survive. So Abraham Blum learned soon after assuming his duties as spiritual leader of Galveston's Temple B'nai Israel in 1871. In addition to heading the congregation's Hebrew School, Blum served as president of the local school board, while his wife, a Sephardi from New Orleans, was in charge of the higher branches of learning in two female schools. A member of the Masons, the Odd Fellows, and the B'nai B'rith, Blum was also a doctor, having received a degree from the Medical College of Galveston in 1872. A few years later he delivered the opening prayer before the Texas House of Representatives in Austin. The following article from *The* [San Francisco] *Jewish Progress* was probably written by the Blums.

June 10, 1878. I suppose a good many people in your city think that Texas is an entirely wild country, for they hear of so many rough things happening along the Mexican border. But let me tell you that here in this Island City, on the beautiful Gulf of Mexico, everything looks as pleasant as in any other city twice or thrice its size. The Israelites form but a very small proportion of the 40,000 inhabitants, as we number only about 200 families; but among these children of Israel a spirit of progress and business ardor reigns so largely, that, were they to leave, Galveston would soon become provincial.

When you pass down Strand Street, you will read signs of such houses as L. & H. Blum, Block & Co., Max & Kempner (who also own the largest hotel in the Southern States), Bernstein & Co., M. Koppert, Banker, J. Dyer, President of Marine Insurance Co., G. Ranger & Co., J. Rosenfield—in fact the entire retail dry goods trade is in the hands of the Jews. We have three Jewish lawyers. Even Jews, Levy Bros. & Co., keep the largest livery stable and deal in coffins and shrouds. So much for the mercantile portion.

Know that we have a B'nai B'rith Lodge of 85 members, a Benevolent Society, a Synagogue built in 1871, with about 87 members and a fine Sunday School which numbers 120 pupils. The synagogue has been in charge of Rev. A. Blum since its consecration, and the Hebrew and Sunday schools are flourishing under his management. Last Sunday the closing exercises took place. The children were placed on this occasion in front of the Ark and questioned on the whole 24 Books of the Bible, then in Jewish history down to the period of Moses Mendelssohn. . . .

North of Texas: Adolph and Sam Frankel in Cushing, Oklahoma.
From *West of Hester Street,* by Allen and Cynthia Mondell. Courtesy of the family of Adolph and Sam Frankel.

FROM THE MINUTES OF THE HEBREW BENEVOLENT ASSOCIATION, JEFFERSON, TEXAS

Regular meeting held January 5, 1873 at 3 P.M. E. Eberstadt, President, presiding. The minutes of the previous meeting was then read and adopted. The following communications were then read and ordered spread on the minutes:

New Orleans. Novr 25, 1872

E. Eberstadt, Esq.

Dear Sir:

Yours of the 14th, inst only reached me today, and I am pleased to inform you that your action in ordering the body of the child in question in the Jewish Cemetery was in full accord with the Jewish custom and law. . . . There is, however, one point incident to this matter which ought to have been omitted, I mean the circumcision of the body prior to burial.

This revolting custom is founded on superstition and is better honored in its breach than its observance.

Moreover, circumcision applies to the living and not to the dead and hence should never be performed on a corpse.

You will pardon me for gratuitously adding my opinion on this point. It is not done for the purpose of finding fault, but springs from the sincere motive of disseminating correct notions and enlightened views concerning our religious views and practices.

I have the honor to be,

J. K. Gutheim

Cincinnati, Novr 28, 1872

Mr. E. Eberstadt

Dear Sir:

According to the Talmud and the Orthodox rule, the child of a Jewish mother is a Jew to all intents and purposes, hence may be buried, or rather ought to be buried according to Jewish rites and on Jewish burial grounds. I must tell you that the above rule is not mine, but in regard to burial the Talmud says, "Also the dead of heathens may be buried with the dead of

Eva Rosenwasser and her grandson Charles Landau in Ballinger, Texas, c. 1908. Eva and her husband, Morris, ran a dry-goods store in Ballinger for many years.
From *West of Hester Street*, by Allen and Cynthia Mondell. Courtesy of Fannie Levy Loeb.

Israel, to serve the cause of peace," hence in this case there can certainly be no objection.

Yours,
Isaac M. Wise

CURBSTONE CHAT

Sept. 19, 1893. City Treasurer Fassett remarks Yom Kipper is one day Phil Young, Si Ryan, Theo Eggers and Jersy McPike can't ring themselves in on. They can pose as sons of the Emerald Isle, Americans on the 4th of July and Mexicans on Cinco de Mayo and Frenchmen on the celebration of the fall of the bastile, but when Yom Kipper comes around they are out in the cold. They can't fast worth a little bit and know that it would be useless to try and atone for their sins in one day.

El Paso Evening Tribune

⊷§ THE FOLLOWING letter to a friend in San Antonio is from a young Jewish immigrant in Houston whose hero was Robert Ingersoll, a political orator who sought to rescue religion from "the aspersions of the pulpit."

Houston, Texas, Feb 10th, 1896

Mr. David Abrams
S. Antonio, Tex.

Kind friend:

Your letter received at noon to day and I hasten to answer.

The most important news in your letter is that you have left Wolfson's.

Now listen, it is not without consideration for your own good that I write you the following.

You come to this city by next train, and I have all the confidence that you will be more than pleased with this city.

You can believe me, S.A. [San Antonio] is asleep while Houston is a wide awake business city.

Besides what is the use of killing two weeks for nothing in S.A. You can do this in this city with more pleasure.

I shall receive you with open arms, and shall hope that your favorable answer will come in your own good and noble person.

Had a splendid time Sunday. At night I went to hear Ingersoll. All I can say is that he is the best speaker I ever heard and I suppose ever will hear. There is only one "Ingersoll." . . .

You know what is best for you, but let not my plea pass your ears. . . .

Besides, it is no fortune lost in coming to this city, in place to kill time in S.A.

My room is yours.

My friends are yours.

Max feels proud that you mentioned his name in your letter.

I'm very pleased with my position. You must excuse my hasty writing, as I worked steady today. I am in Gent's Furnishings. . . .

Sam Greenberg

BEYOND THE WIDE MISSOURI

ABOUT THE TIME settlers in wagon trains began lumbering overland across Kansas to the lush meadows of Oregon and the inland valleys of California, Jewish immigrants started settling in western Missouri. In 1840, "Messrs. Cahn & Block" opened a trading post in Westport, a favorite jumping-off point for immigrants heading farther west. By 1846, at least four Jewish merchants were outfitting wagon trains in Westport. Before long Jews were doing business in several nearby towns.

Soon after the establishment of the Territory of Kansas in 1854, Kan-

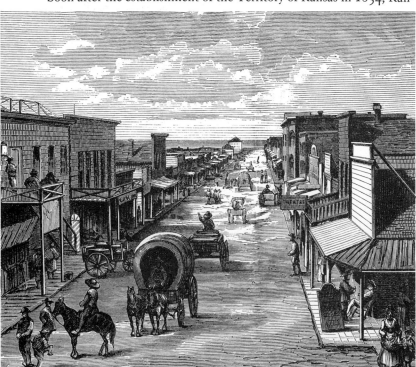

Wichita, Kansas, c. 1870.

The first locomotive that came to
Kansas City—the Louis
Hammerslough.
Missouri Valley Room, Kansas City (Missouri)
Public Library

sas City became an important supply center. Herman Ganz, the first
Jew to settle there, arrived by boat from Louisville in 1856. "When I
looked out of my cabin window to the west bluffs," he recalled fifty
years later, "they gave little promise of becoming the site of a great city.
Kansas City had barely two thousand people at the time." Starting out
as a peddler with a wagon, Herman later became a successful storekeeper.

Kansas City's second Jewish settler, Louis Hammerslough, achieved
success on a far grander scale. A native of Hannover, Louis journeyed
from Germany to Baltimore in 1854 to join his brothers, clothing manufacturers. Two years later he accompanied an older brother to Springfield, Illinois, where they opened a clothing store a few blocks away from

Liebman Liquors, future site of the
Kansas City Star, *c. 1905.*

Abe Lincoln's law office. In 1858, Louis was ready to start a business of his own. Moving to Kansas City, he had the good fortune to obtain the charge of outfitting the Illinois militia during the Civil War. After the war Louis financed the building of a railroad clear across the state. The first train to reach Kansas City was pulled by a locomotive named for him.

IN 1853, CONGRESS authorized President Franklin Pierce to negotiate with the Indians west of Missouri and Iowa with a view to extinguishing their titles to as much of their lands as possible. The following year, the Omahas ceded all they laid claim to west of the Missouri River except for a small area set aside for a reservation. Another large tract was opened in 1857, when the Pawnees ceded all but 450 square miles of lands claimed by them in what in 1854 had become the Territory of Nebraska. Meanwhile, promoters and jobbers were losing no time in encouraging the formation of boom towns along the waterways of the eastern half of the territory. By far the most successful was the city of Omaha. Within a year after the Territory of Nebraska was organized, Omaha boasted twenty houses and two dirt-floor hotels in addition to several saloons and stores.

Around this time Aaron Cahn, his wife, and his brother-in-law Meyer Hellman traveled by rail and riverboat from Cleveland to Omaha, freighting with them the makings of a simple 22 by 80 frame house. Much of the lumber had been sawed in Cleveland, where the Cahns

Elizabeth Friedlander, a princess of the Colville Indian tribe of Washington, and wife of Louis, a peddler.
American Jewish Archives, Cincinnati, Ohio

Indian trader Julius Mayer with Chiefs Red Cloud, Sitting Bull, Swift Bear, and Spotted Tail. After living for weeks at a time among the Pawnees, Julius was adopted into their tribe and renamed Box-ka-re-sha-has-ta-ka—Curly-headed white chief with one tongue.
Nebraska State Historical Society

Volunteer Fire Department in front of Myer Hellman's clothing store, Omaha, c. 1865. Of fifteen clothing establishments doing business in Omaha in 1870, about half were owned and operated by Jews.
National Council of Jewish Women, Omaha Section

J. L. Brandeis and Sons, pioneer storekeepers who helped put Omaha on the map.
The Bostwick-Frohardt Photography Collection, owned by KMTV and on permanent loan to Western Heritage Museum, Omaha

Fall opening, J. L. Brandeis and Sons of Omaha, 1910.
The Bostwick-Frohardt Photography Collection, owned by KMTV and on permanent loan to Western Heritage Museum, Omaha

A member of Omaha's Brandeis family.

had settled after emigrating to America from Germany in 1850. Omaha's population when they arrived was about six hundred. (Not until gold was discovered in Colorado a few years later did the city become an important outfitting and freighting center for those headed farther west.) The only Jews in Omaha for seven years, Hellman and the Cahns started a clothing store which soon became the largest mercantile establishment in Nebraska. Their customers included Mormons and other homesteaders headed west along the Platte River, in addition to Indians. Cahn was on such friendly terms with the latter that he was adopted into the Omaha and Pawnee tribes. The following account is based on the recollections of Aaron Cahn's sons Martin and Albert, who often heard their father speak of his early adventures on the Nebraska frontier.

There was a saloon on the south side of Farnum Street between Eleventh and Twelfth Street the owner of which had been called to the war [between the States] which was getting well under way at that time.

He left everything behind him, including a lot of debts which he could not meet, and so he turned over to Mr. Aaron Cahn, who was then in partnership with his brother-in-law, M. Hellman, in the clothing business, all of the stock of wines, liquors, cigars and saloon fixtures then in his place, in settlement of the debt he then owned the clothing firm. It was that or nothing.

Mr. Cahn did not particularly enjoy the prospect; how to get his money out of it was the problem. He began by getting someone to clean up and scrub out the place and make it presentable, but found that the owner of the building wanted it himself, and it was necessary to get another location.

He climbed up on a stepladder one morning in the saloon in order to adjust the oil lamp hanging from the ceiling and fell off, injuring his hip very severely. This made him more anxious than ever to get rid of the saloon.

Coming down town a few days afterwards and limping painfully from his accident, he met J. Sterling Morton, acting governor, who stopped to inquire what was the matter with Aaron. Every man was called by his first name in those days and after Sterling had been duly informed of the accident and the cause of it, together with the problem which confronted the present owner of the saloon, Mr. Morton was asked, "What in the world will I do with it?"

At that time there was often much difficulty in getting a quorum of the territorial legislature. It was frequently necessary for the sergeant-at-arms to come down town from the Capitol building and go through the various saloons of the city rounding up the missing members and trying to get them to come up to the legislative session.

Hearing of this situation, someone said, "Why not move the saloon up to the Capitol building and put it in the basement where there is plenty of room and where the quorum question will be permanently solved?"

That was what actually occurred.

In due time the saloon was moved up and although there was some opposition to its location there, it had a strong working majority in its favor among its members as well as an enthusiastic following among the spectators and lobbyists.

A rather primitive bar was established and a young man, Mr. Hartman, who afterwards became one of our leading citizens, is said to have acted as barkeeper and to have dispensed the liquid refreshments and have taken in the proceeds with what assistance Mr. Cahn could give him. . . .

It was not Mr. Cahn's intention to run a saloon permanently. Nevertheless it was a great success in every way. But as soon as the debt was paid and owing to the growing opposition of rival concerns . . . the saloon was discontinued.

Frank Burkley

Omaha City, Nebraska, November 1, 1867

Dear Sister Fannie,

I have no excuse to make for my long silence so I will plead guilty and hope you will forgive me this time. And I shall be more punctual in the future. As you see I am way out west now. As yet I am doing nothing and it is hard to tell how long I may not lay idle. I came out here with the intention of renting a store for father but everything is so very high here that I can hardly tell if we shall ever live out here. A store like your husband has could not be rented here for less than $300 a month and a house like we live in would cost $100 a month. Wood is $15 a cord, coal $60 to $70 a bushel, and almost all other things in proportion. So you can see how it would be for a large family like ours to live here. But if Mr. Simon could have his store here, he could do well without a doubt. Omaha is destined to be a large city. Five years ago it was all prairie here. Now it is a flourishing city containing 15,000 inhabitants and doing twice the business of any city of its size in America. We have 25 hotels, 200 saloons, 15 cigar stores, 6 fine millinery stores, 6 wholesale grocers and all other business houses that they have anywhere. But I must bring my letter to a close. I may be able to write you more next time. Give my best regards to your husband. Write soon—and all the news.

I am as ever

Your true brother,
Adolphus [Gladstone]

ᴈᏻ OF THE THOUSANDS of political refugees who fled to America in the wake of the European political upheavals of 1848, many like August Bondi took part in the pre–Civil War anti-slavery movement. As a boy of fifteen, Bondi participated in the 1848 revolutionary movement in Vienna. Three years later he gave up a job as a teacher in a German-speaking settlement near St. Louis to go to Texas, where he worked as a bartender for a time in Houston—"the muddiest town I have ever seen"—before turning to farming and storekeeping in the Territory of Kansas. In 1856, Bondi joined a military company organized in Kansas by John Brown and subsequently fought with Brown and his sons against pro-slavery forces in the "battles" of Black Jack and Osawatomie. After serving in the Civil War, Bondi held various public offices in Salina, Kansas. The following excerpt is taken from the *Autobiography of August Bondi.*

August Bondi in 1861, shortly after joining the Fifth Kansas Cavalry.

About August 20th [1856], old John Brown reached Osawatomie with a spick-and-span four-mule team, the wagon loaded with provisions. . . . Old Brown told me and some of the neighbors, who had come to greet him, that he intended to invade the pro-slavery settlements of Linn and Bourbon counties. . . . As he saw that I was not mounted, he ordered some of his men to capture all of Dutch Henry's horses; and when they were brought in, I received a four-year-old fine bay horse for my mount. . . .

The Capt. Cline Company joined us and we moved from Osawatomie about August 24th. . . . When [we were] camped for dinner rest, Capt. Brown made a talk to us of his company. He wished us all to understand that we must not molest women nor children, nor take nor capture anything useless to us or Free State people; further, never destroy any kind of property wantonly nor burn any buildings, as Free State people could use them after the pro-slavery people had been driven out; never consider captured horses or cattle as anything else than common property of the Free State army, the horses for military use, the cattle for food for our soldiers and settlers. He also ordered that we should keep some distance in camp from the Cline company as they were too riotous. Whenever he could he would hire our meals, as he had ample means to pay for them. He then made arrangement with Capt. Cline that the two companies should daily exchange places on the march. . . .

We camped the first evening near a small Quaker settlement of three families, near Sugar Creek, Linn County. Capt. Brown had them prepare supper and breakfast for us. We there received information that a large pro-slavery force of about 500, among them the Bourbon County Rangers, with a red flag ornamented with skull and crossbones, were raiding the Free State settlers of Linn and Bourbon counties. . . . By ten o'clock A.M. we came on the fresh tracks of the pro-slavery raiders and quickened our pace. By noon we received information of their camping on South Middle Creek and hastened to surprise them. . . . On the last hills, overlooking the valley two miles wide, the pro-slavery camp was in full view; [though] outnumbering us five or six to one, immediately upon sighting us galloping down the hill, [they] turned and fled, leaving the camp teams, many horses, provisions, tents, and their red flag with the skull and crossbones; yea, some who had been enjoying a noon siesta left their clothes, hats, shoes, and boots. I found a pair of boots which were just the fit, and as mine were in favor of keeping my feet aired, I was not long in changing. . . . Capt. Cline saw Capt. Brown about the division of the spoils; he claimed the larger share because his men were in advance. Capt. Brown remarked: "My men do not fight for plunder; keep it all," and so Cline kept almost the whole spoils. This was the Battle of South Middle Creek. . . .

➳ SIGMUND SCHLESINGER was born in Hungary in 1848 and came to New York during the Civil War. Eager for adventure, Sigmund kept right on going until he came to the very edge of the Kansas frontier, where he joined a company of Indian scouts. Sigmund never forgot his first day on a horse—"I was not used to the saddle. My equipment was always where it should not have been. My horse would not stay with the column but forged ahead. My bridle arm became stiff and lame. Every bone in my body began to ache." Sigmund's awkwardness did not go unnoticed; however, a chance to prove himself came when his company was attacked by a large band of Cheyenne and Sioux under the leadership of Chief Roman Nose. The siege lasted four days. When it was over, five scouts had been killed and seventeen others badly wounded. As for Sigmund, his days as a raw recruit were over. Now everybody marveled at "that brave and active young Israelite, a gallant soldier among brave men." During his career as an Indian fighter, Sigmund kept a journal, jotting down whatever struck him as worth preserving for posterity.

Wednesday 16. Seen signal Fire on a Hill 3 miles off in evening late.

Thursday 17. About 12 Indians carched on us. Stampeedet 7 Horses. 10 Minuts after, about 600 Indians attacket us. Killt Beecher, Culver & Wilson. Wounded 19 Man & Killt all the Horses. We was without Grubb & Water all day. Dug Holes in the sand whith our Hands.

Friday, September 18, 1868. In the night I dug my hole deeper, cut of meat oof of the Horses & hung it up on Bushes. Indians made a charge on us at Day brake but retreated. Kept Shooting nearly all day. They Put up a White Flag. Left us at 9 o'clock in the evening. Raind all night.

Saturday 19. The Indians came back again. Kept sharp shooting all day. 2 Boys started for Fort Wallace. Raind all night.

Sunday 20. Dr. Moore died last night. Raining part of the Day, snow about 1 inches thick. Indians kept sharp shooting.

Monday, September 21, 1868. Scalpt 3 Indians which were found about 15 Feet from my hole consealt in Grass.

Tuesday 22. Killt a Coyote & eat him all up.

➳ FROM 1866 TO 1886, the Texas cattle trade brought between five and seven million head of longhorns to the Kansas markets, where they were then shipped onward by rail to the Eastern markets. Abilene was the first center of the Kansas trade; however, by 1871 Ellsworth had already usurped much of Abilene's cattle business. A few years later Ellsworth was in turn surpassed by Wichita and Dodge City.

The few Jews to come to such places were aspiring entrepreneurs who went west with the railroad.

I was born in Posen and landed in New York City with one dollar in my pocket the day after the assassination of President Lincoln. Everywhere I looked that day flags were displayed at half mast and everywhere I observed crepe on every sleeve. My lone dollar went for a meal and a toothpick on which I was to whet a future appetite.

I located a cousin in New York City and remained with him until July when I went west to Shelbina, Missouri. It was here that I secured sufficient backing to start a butcher shop of my own and make a success of it from the start, but later I branched out into the buying and selling of cattle and this proved to be my undoing.

A man whom I had trusted took my stock to market at Chicago and sold the cattle but made no return of the money. This dishonesty of a trusted friend caused me to leave Shelbina and again head west, this time for Junction City, Kansas. This was in the year 1867.

I went to work in Junction City, Kansas on the assurance of $5 a day and my board, but all I got was my board. This was a butcher establishment and I quit after I found out that my employer was turning over to me for butchering stolen cattle. About this time I became acquainted with Jacob Goldsmith who was to become my brother-in-law. At this same period great herds of cattle were being driven out of Texas to the railroads for shipment. The Texans when they arrived were greatly in need of clothing. Learning of this, Jacob Goldsmith and Edward Rosenwald, who were then partners, loaded three wagons with men's furnishings and set out for Ellsworth, but owing to floods got only as far as Abilene, Kansas where they sent word for me to join them. A corn shed was rented and the stock laid out on the crates in which the clothing had been shipped. We sold between $600 and $1000 worth of goods each day. This was a start; we built a store building, one of the first to be erected at Abiline.

David Gottlieb

HAYS, KANSAS. c. 1870. In my mind's eye, I can see Old North Main Street in all its former glory: from east to west from Chestnut street were the Capless and Ryan Outfitting Store, the "Leavenworth Restaurant," Dalton's Saloon and Faro House, "Hound Kelley's Saloon," the office of M. E. Joyce, our first justice of the Peace, a jewelry store, Mrs. Gowdy's little sod hut, Ed Godard's saloon and Dance Hall, Tommy Drumm's saloon, Kate Coffee's saloon, Mose Walter's Saloon, R. W. Evans' Grocery Store and Post Office, Sol Cohen's Clothing Store, Paddy Welch's Saloon and gambling house, the Perry Hotel, M. J. R. Treat's Candy and Peanut Stand, Cy Godard's Saloon and Dance Hall and in the corner "Nigger White's" barber shop. . . . Most of the buildings were of flimsy construction and were taken down and put up again wherever the railroad made its next stop. Tents and dugouts were also numerous and while all was "hustle and bustle and go" and thousands of feet tramped the streets they were still paved with buffalo sod.

Josephine Middlekauf

ON TO CALIFORNIA

꿏⟩ AS EARLY AS 1796, Yankee sea captains had reached the northern Pacific coast; however, it was not until gold was discovered near Sacramento in 1848 that a wild rush to California began unlike anything the world had ever known before. Jews were no exception. Mostly immigrants from Germany, Poland, and France who came by ship from New York or New Orleans, some started out as prospectors, though the majority went directly into peddling. With mining camps springing up literally overnight, many Jews prospered by exchanging much needed merchandise for gold dust, and gold dust for more merchandise.

In their early stages, mining camps were mainly tent towns with a few wooden buildings here and there. The main street, if there was one, was covered with mud or dust, depending on the time of year. Sanitation facilities were nonexistent, epidemics of malaria and cholera not uncommon. Nothing looked permanent, nothing was, for once the supply of gold gave out a camp disappeared. Until then, it was the place to go for food, tools, clothes (usually furnished by "Jew clothing-men . . .

Nevada City, California, around the time Bernhard Marks went west to make his fortune as a prospector.
California State Library

in front of wretched looking tenements"), and entertainment in the form of hurdy-gurdy girls and gambling.

Among the first American Jews on the scene were Rebecca Gratz's nephew Edmund Moses ("He has the gold mania," Rebecca confided to a friend, "and means to adventure there") and Bernhard Marks. A book-keeper from New Bedford, Massachusetts, who came to California when he was nineteen, Bernhard described his adventures as a prospector in the following extract from a number of letters to a cousin in Philadelphia written between 1853 and 1857.

We were to start the following Monday morning at daybreak, and in the meantime, my companion was to have everything in readiness, including a mule to carry out provisions, etc. At about four in the morning I arrived at his cabin. He had everything nearly packed and requested me to saddle the mule. I looked in the direction in which he pointed, but could see nothing except a small mass of bone awkwardly put together, over which was thrown a well worn out hide. This, he gravely asserted, was a mule. I afterwards discovered that small mules, besides resembling small women in obstinacy, could like them endure more hardship than large ones. I requested to see the contents of the load, as we were to be gone several weeks and might not fall in with a human being for weeks together, but I was answered that not only was our comfort secured but that instead of experiencing the hardships incident to a trip of the kind in '49 we could fare sumptuously.

My companion had emigrated to this country in '49 and was subsequently a forty-niner. The forty-niners constitute a distinct class. A forty-niner knows, or supposes he knows, everything that is worth knowing and some things that are not. He has seen the greatest sights, gone through the most imminent dangers, heard and told the biggest stories and killed the biggest bears of any other human. Nothing is too extravagant for him to believe for he has seen greater things himself. According to his opinion, everybody that comes to California is grass green, and if he had only been here in '49 he could have shown him the Elephant. I could easily see that it was my companion's intention to make me fare as hard as possible. I determined, however, not to utter a word of complaint, as that would be just what he wanted, but to talk as though I found everything easier than I expected.

We traveled all day without meeting with anything worthy of notice. We had now got pretty well into the mountains. In the evening we camped. I had now an opportunity for the first time of seeing our outfit. First was what was called a "portable house," sufficiently large to accommodate two men comfortably provided they concentrated themselves into a bulk of 3 cubic feet. Also a pair of blankets apiece, coffee, sugar, crackers, smoked ham, worm pie (he called it cheese), matches, hatchet, two tin cups, a small camp kettle, a prospecting pan, a light pick, shovels, powder, ball, caps, Bible (my companion was a southern Methodist), a flask of brandy (supply for one only), and a compass. Besides which we had each a pair of colt's 8 inch navy revolvers and our hunting knives. Thus equipped, we considered ourselves a very fair match for double our number of grizzlies.

After cutting some wood with our hatchet, we kindled a fire and, putting on our kettle which we had taken the precaution to fill at a spring during the afternoon, coffee was soon made. A cupfull of it and some dry crackers made me a delicious supper. Extinguishing our fire so as not to attract attention, we prepared ourselves for our night's rest. We concluded to sleep and watch by turns, I to watch first. So overpowered was I by fatigue that I fell asleep in less than half an hour after my companion.

. . . We had sunk a shaft one hundred and eighty feet deep, seventy feet through hard rock, and started a drift or tunnel from the bottom to a distant part of our mine. In doing so, we wished to run to a certain spot which we had reason to believe to be extremely rich. About the title to which, there was, and is a dispute between my company, "The Golden Gate," and another on the opposite side of the hill called the "Humbug Tunnelling Co." They were running a drift to get there first as, according to our peculiar mining laws, the first to get possession could hold by priority. As they were making their way there very leisurely, we desired to get there first by running all night as well as day. It would not do to allow any hired hands to work in it, as we wished to keep our destination a profound secret. The whole work then devolved on us proprietors. We worked one at a time—that is, one stands up and works with all his might as long as he can stand it, generally from 8 to 10 minutes; he then lays down and the next goes through the same operation by which time the other is recruited. In this way many thousand feet are dug through the hills of California.

We had just reached ground which paid over four dollars to the bucket, or as our machinery is arranged, about four thousand dollars every eleven working days when, owing to some water which came through an old shaft, the whole concern caved. Fortunately, no one was hurt, but such bad air and violent exertion soon wet us to the skin. And although I took the precaution to have a pair of heavy blankets ready to wrap myself in when leaving the diggings, I still caught a very bad cold from which resulted a three month's spell of sickness. Though I am now as well and robust as ever, I intend never again to exert myself so violently or expose my health to such an extent.

June 10, 1864. The State of California has quite a number of Jews who are agriculturalists. As far north as Carson, Nevada, the Jew has changed thousands of acres of wild sage brush land into promising farms which yield their owners over $1000 a year for hay alone. At Sonoma there is a large vineyard belonging to Louis Tichnor. In Los Angeles we have quite a number of our people who own very extensive vineyards. At San Diego we find our people engaged in various agricultural pursuits. Along the San Joaquin, in Sonoma and San Jose valleys and over in Contra Costa we have a number of Jews whose business is to farm and raise stock.

The American Israelite

The first congregationally owned synagogue on the Pacific coast. Originally a Methodist Episcopal church, the building was sold to Sacramento's Congregation B'nai Israel in 1852 for a little over $2,000. In November of the same year it was destroyed by fire, one of many that swept through what was then largely a tent town.
Pacific Center for Western Historical Studies, University of the Pacific, Stockton, California

LEVI STRAUSS, *ET AL.*

LESS THAN five years after the discovery of gold in California, San Francisco had mushroomed from a sleepy adobe village into an instant city of 35,000 inhabitants, 399 saloons, a dozen newspapers, five theaters, two libraries, and 117 dry goods stores—many owned by Jews like Levi Strauss.

Menorah executed by Charles Brown, pioneer San Francisco hardware merchant, 1865.
Judah L. Magnes Museum

Born in the little town of Buttenheim, Bavaria, in 1829, Strauss was seventeen when he arrived penniless in New York with no knowledge of English and no trade. Willing to try his luck at anything, Strauss traveled to Lexington, Kentucky, to peddle goods provided by his older brothers in New York. In six years he had saved enough money to go on to California.

The journey by boat took three months and cost nearly $400, but it was worth every penny to Strauss the moment he laid eyes on the enclosed bay filled with ships, and beyond it a wood and canvas boom town of shanties and tents. All kinds of excitement filled the air; everywhere people were running about. Wasting no time, Strauss started out in a little dry goods shop perched on a makeshift appendage to the Sacramento Street wharf.

Expenses were high—$100 for a business license and at least as much a month for rent and grub. Only for those who knew how to buy cheap and sell fast was there a future here. Trade in those days was done by standing at the door of your store and inviting in sailors and miners and then soaking them for all they were worth. Leaving this part of the business to a brother-in-law, Strauss proceeded to peddle goods from trunks on the back of a hired wagon in nearby gold towns with such odd names as Fiddletown, Michigan Bluff, Murphys, and Chinese Camp.

In 1857, a Hebrew Young Men's Literary Association was meeting in San Francisco every other week to hold debates on history, politics, economics, religion, and practical philosophy. It is unlikely that Strauss ever attended a meeting, for during this period of his life it took all of his strength and ingenuity just to keep going. "Nowhere is fortune so fickle," an astute observer noted. "Nowhere do so many, all in a day, go from wealth to want."

Others went under, but not Strauss. Benefiting from opportunities for expansion created by the Civil War, Strauss soon headed a thriving $3 million a year dry goods, clothing, and household furnishings store in a brand new four-story building on Battery Street. Already he was well on his way to becoming a leading manufacturer of clothing "specially adapted for the use of farmers, mechanics, miners and working men in general." In 1880 alone, 100,000 Levi Strauss overalls and jackets were turned out, with a printed oilcloth guarantee attached to the seat of each pair of pants promising "a new pair free" if a rip occurred in the "exclusive XX special top weight all cotton denim material."

Strauss, who walked to work each day in a black split-tail coat and a glistening stovepipe hat, was by now but one of many wealthy San Francisco Jewish entrepreneurs. Among the most prominent were Benjamin

Davidson, a Rothschild agent; Louis Sloss and Lewis Gerstle, monopolizers of the West Coast seal trade; Mortiz Friedlander, wheat king of the West; Adolph Sutro, builder of the Sutro Tunnel to the Comstock Lode and later mayor of San Francisco; David Livingston, Isaac Magnin, and Solomon Gump, owners of the city's leading department stores; Philip N. Lilienthal and Ignatz Steinhard of the Anglo-California Bank; M. H. de Young, publisher of the *San Francisco Chronicle*; and Anthony Zellerbach, founder of one of the nation's largest paper and pulp businesses.

"As a class," Isaac M. Wise observed on a visit in 1877, "the San Francisco Israelites are more prominent than the Hebrews as a class in any other city I have visited." Wise's impressions are amplified in the following selection from Benjamin Lloyd's *Lights and Shades in San Francisco* (1876).

California merchant Lewis Gerstle and his Philadelphia bride, Hannah Greenebaum Gerstle, in 1858. Soon after their marriage the young couple traveled via Panama to Sacramento, where Gerstle operated a general merchandise store in partnership with Louis Sloss, who had married Hannah's sister Sarah.
Reprinted from *Our City: The Jews of San Francisco*, by Irena Narell. Courtesy of Darwin Publications.

In commercial matters they are leaders. In any business pursuit involving traffic, they are, as a class, more successful than those who reject their faith. There is more poverty among them than in New York; yet, taken as a whole, they own more real estate, and command more wealth, comparatively, than in any city in the United States. Ten members of the Temple Emanu-El—the principal synagogue in the city—have an aggregate wealth of forty-five million.

They are leaders in, and control, to a great extent, the principal mercantile businesses. The clothing trade—here as elsewhere—is monopolized by them, and the principal dry-goods houses, and crockery and jewelry establishments, belong to Jews. In the manufacturing industries they have control of the shoe and soap factories, and the woolen mills. . . .

Few of them have any political aspirations, and it is a rare occurrence to find them occupying any official position, either municipal or State. Yet they take a lively interest in politics, and seem to hold as decided opinions regarding political issues as the ordinary American-born citizen. It is noteworthy that there are less number of Jews arraigned before the criminal tribunals of the city than of any other class of citizens. In no instance has a Jew been before the courts of San Francisco to answer for the crime of murder. When they are subjects of prosecution it is generally a petty charge that is brought against them—some small theft or swindle, for the indulgence in which the lower-class Jews are characterized.

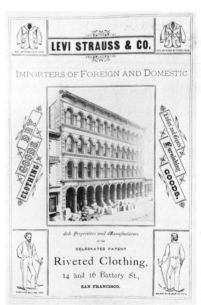

The Bancroft Library, University of California

SAN FRANCISCO'S pioneer Jewish community had more than its share of eccentrics. Perhaps the strangest of them all was Joshua Norton, "Emperor of California and Protector of Mexico." The following account of Norton is also taken from *Lights and Shades in San Francisco*.

. . . He was born in England, and from there went to the Cape of Good Hope, where he entered the military service as a member of the colonial riflemen. How long or how well he served in that capacity we are not informed.

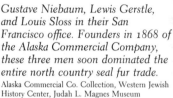

*Gustave Niebaum, Lewis Gerstle,
and Louis Sloss in their San
Francisco office. Founders in 1868 of
the Alaska Commercial Company,
these three men soon dominated the
entire north country seal fur trade.*
Alaska Commercial Co. Collection, Western Jewish
History Center, Judah L. Magnes Museum

In 1847 or '48 he came to San Francisco, and is remembered by the early pioneers as having been a shrewd, safe and prosperous man possessing more than ordinary intelligence, fertile of resource and enterprising. His business pursuits were varied. At one time he was buying partner for three or four mercantile houses in the interior of the State, and in this capacity manifested great business ability. Then he engaged in the real estate business, in which he continued with apparent prosperity a number of years. . . .

It appears that his business career culminated in a grand effort to get a "corner" on rice, which staple was, some ten or twelve years ago, a favorite article for speculation. He purchased all that was in the city and (as rumor has it) all that he could ascertain was in transit, paying large prices with a view of controlling the future market; [however] . . . the market was so "flat" that he could not meet his contract, and a protracted law suit followed, during which the mania that he was "Emperor" first became manifest. . . .

His hallucination is that he is Emperor of California and Protector of Mexico. . . . San Francisco, his favorite city, he calls the "Queen of the Pacific," and the world pays tribute to her. The municipal authorities receive his praise or condemnation as their administration pleases or offends him. By proclamation (sometimes to humor his whim published in the city press) he communicates to his subjects his ideas of progress and justice, and never fails to attach his signature with the imperial seal, "Norton I. Emperor of California and Protector of Mexico. *Dei Gratia.*" . . .

Emperor Norton may be known by his dress, as he pays no attention whatever to the varying fashions. His coat is navy blue, cut in the military style, and lavishly trimmed with brass buttons. On the shoulders are heavy

A San Francisco rig owned by Anthony Zellerbach, a Bavarian Jew who traveled to California from Philadelphia in 1856. After failing as a banker, a miner, and a storekeeper, Zellerbach entered the paper business. Paper was scarce and fetched good prices. By 1887 his House of Paper was worth $20,000. Anthony's son, Isadore, propelled the firm to its present position as the world's second-largest pulp and paper concern.
Crown Zellerbach Corp.

LEFT, *Levy Brothers' Pescadero and San Mateo Stage Co.*
San Mateo County Historical Museum

BELOW, *Sweatshops were not an Eastern monopoly: San Francisco's California Standard Sack Co., 36 Clay Street.*
The Bancroft Library, University of California

epaulettes usually tarnished from exposure to weather, though sometimes brilliantly polished. His hat, the regular Jehu style, is trimmed with some brass ornament, from which extends two or three waving cock-plumes. His boots are notorious for their size, and are less frequently polished than otherwise. . . .

Of evenings he may be found at the theatre or in the lecture room, a cool observer and attentive listener. His face is a free ticket for him to all places of amusement and public gatherings, and oftentimes he makes quite extended journeys by rail and other public conveyances without expending a dollar. . . .

His living is very inexpensive. He occupies a cheap room, is temperate in his habits, boards at cheap restaurants, which, with many privileges granted him that others have to pay for, reduces his expenditures to a very small sum. When he wants money he will draw a check on any of the city banks, take it to an acquaintance who humors his delusion, and get it cashed. . . . Some of the merchant Jews contribute to his support, and he is much better cared for than many who labor hard every day for a livelihood. Thus does his affliction secure him a comfortable living, happy today, without care for the morrow, and free from all the annoyances that to many renders life a burdensome existence.

Joshua Norton, "Emperor of California and Protector of Mexico."
The Bancroft Library, University of California

WHEREAS San Francisco had grown into a full-fledged city in a few years, Los Angeles remained a dusty little cowtown until well after the Civil War. When Harris Newmark arrived via Nicaragua in 1853, there were no more than a few thousand settlers living in an assortment of flat-roofed houses spread out helter-skelter from the town's center into the flatlands beyond. What follows are Newmark's recollections of those early days, taken from his memoirs.

After heavy winter rains mud was from six inches to two feet deep, while during the summer dust piled up to about the same extent. Few city ordinances were obeyed; for notwithstanding that a regulation of the City Council called on every citizen to sweep in front of his house to a certain point on Saturday evenings, not the slightest attention was paid to it. Into the roadway was thrown all the rubbish: if a man bought a new suit of clothes, a pair of boots, a hat or a shirt, to replace a corresponding part of his apparel that had outlived its usefulness, he would think nothing, on attiring himself in the new purchase, of tossing the discarded article into the street where it would remain until some passing Indian, or other vagabond, took possession of it. So wretched indeed were the conditions, that I have seen dead animals left on the highways for days at a time. . . .

The principal industry throughout Los Angeles County, and indeed throughout Southern California, up to the sixties, was the raising of cattle and horses—an undertaking favored by a people particularly fond of leisure and knowing little of the latent possibilities in the land; so that this entire area of magnificent soil supported herds which provided the whole population in turn, directly or indirectly, with a livelihood. The live stock subsisted upon grass growing wild all over the county, and the prosperity of Southern California therefore depended entirely upon the season's rainfall. . . . If the rainfall was sufficient to produce feed, dealers came from the North and purchased our stock, and everybody thrived; if, on the other hand, the season was dry, cattle and horses died and the public's pocketbook shrank to very unpretentious dimensions. . . .

Business conditions in the fifties were necessarily very different from what they are to-day. There was no bank in Los Angeles for some years. . . . People generally hoarded their cash in deep, narrow buckskin bags, hiding it behind merchandise on the shelves until the departure of a steamer for San Francisco, or turning it into such vouchers as were negotiable and could be obtained here. . . .

ABOUT THIS TIME Isaias W. Hellman, the future organizer of the Farmers and Merchants Bank of Los Angeles and later president of the Wells Fargo Bank, was operating a small dry goods store on the corner of Main

Downey's Old Block (occupied now by the Federal Building), showing stores owned and operated by pioneer Los Angeles Jews Leopold Harris, Charles Jacoby, Maurice Kremer, and Solomon Lazard. Lazard in 1867 built one of Los Angeles's first brick stores, the "City of Paris," and was one of the organizers of the city's first water company.
Security Pacific National Bank Photograph Collection/Los Angeles Public Library

and Commercial streets. The following account by Jackson A. Graves describes how Hellman got into banking.

[In his store Hellman] had a large old-fashioned Tilden & McFarland safe. Miners would come in, with those long buckskin purses, in vogue in early days, and would deposit their gold dust with him. He had at times $200,000 in gold dust in that safe. . . . His safe was in a building that a child could have broken into and yet it was never robbed. . . . Merchants would also deposit gold with him, where they had no safes.

These miners would get gloriously drunk and gamble. When out of funds, they would come back to him, get out the purses deposited in their respective names, take out gold dust, tie the purse up again and put it back. [Once] a great big double-jointed Irishman who had been on a glorious drunk . . . came to get the remnant of his deposit. His purse was nearly empty. . . . He looked at it and, with an oath, he said: "You—you have stolen my gold." Fortunately, a companion, who had stayed sober . . . had been with him every time he opened his sack. He put his hand on Pat's arm and said: "Pat, that will not do. . . . You took this gold out yourself, and you must apologize to Mr. Hellman," which he did.

Mr. Hellman told me that it was against his commercial instincts to have so much gold not earning anything, and that, after this incident with the Irishman, he said to himself, "What is to prevent one of those fellows from cracking me over the head, sticking a knife into my ribs, or shooting me," and, as he was a man of peace, he cudgeled his brains what to do. [One] Saturday he got hold of a good friend who was running a newspaper, and between them they fixed up some passbooks and some deposit slips marked "I. W. Hellman, Banker." The next miner who came along with gold dust was told he could not leave it there, "but," said Mr. Hellman, "I will buy your gold dust, at current rates . . . I am running a bank. Here, see this book. After I buy your gold you can deposit the money with me, take this book and check it out as you please. All checks drawn on me, while your money lasts, will be paid." The scheme took and, strange to say, the miners spent much less money after they began to make bank deposits than they did before. . . .

At that time, all the merchants were paying their bills in San Francisco, where all purchases were made, shipping their money by express. The express company made a flat charge of one dollar for every package, no matter how little or how much it contained, and then a stiff percentage on the value of the gold shipped. Hellman persuaded the merchants, one by one, to open accounts with him, and [then] sold them exchange on San Francisco with which to pay their debts. Hellman had to ship gold to San Francisco to keep up his bank balances there, but by shipping large quantities he saved the dollar charge on the many small packages, so that the business paid him from the start.

8

Bridging the Gap:
Between Texas and California

⤷ IN THE MID-NINETEENTH CENTURY a vast expanse of land stretching from the Great Plains to beyond the Rocky Mountains was inhabited by various Indian tribes—the Sioux, Blackfoot, and Crow in the Dakotas, Montana, and Wyoming; the Pawnee, Cheyenne, and Ute in Kansas and Nebraska, Colorado, and Utah; the Commanche and Apache in New Mexico and Arizona. With the exception of a few Mormon communities around the Great Salt Lake and a sprinkling of trading outposts along the banks of the upper Rio Grande, the white man was hardly anywhere to be seen. Within thirty years all this had changed.

First came mining camps in the mountains and cattle kingdoms on the grasslands. Then came towns and villages and farms, hastened into existence by the colonizing efforts of the railroads. The Northern Pacific, with 40 million acres to dispose of, encouraged emigrants from Europe and the eastern half of the country to come. Other railroads worked just as hard to move settlers in until a solid band of states stretched clear across the continent. By 1890 the frontier was no more.

Many of the first Jews to come to this part of the country were immigrants from Russian- and Prussian-controlled Poland, who settled initially in the East and then moved on by rail and covered wagon to take advantage of greater opportunities in what was then called "the new country." In 1877, during a visit to America, these Jews were described as follows by the Polish Nobel laureate and author of *Quo Vadis*, Henry Sienkewicz.

Because of their acuteness, knowledge of the German language, and business initiative, our Polish Jews fare . . . rather well in the United States and do not suffer the hardships of our peasants. At the recently discovered gold mines where adventurers quickly congregate, where the knife, the revolver, and the terrifying lynch law still prevail, where an American merchant hesitates to open shop out of fear both for his merchandise and his life, the first stores are generally established by our Jews. By their courtesy, kind words, and, above all, extension of credit, they win the favor of the most dangerous adventurers. . . . And once having the revolvers of these desperadoes on their side, the storekeepers conduct their affairs with complete safety. Profits are enormous in such localities because the miners pay

"Painting the Town Red," drawn by R. F. Zogbaum for Harper's Weekly, 1886. Note the Rosenthal, Levy Solomon, and Laubenheim signs.

for their goods with unweighed gold dust instead of with money. I saw our Jews operating stores under the conditions I have just described at Deadwood, Dakota; Darwin, California; and Virginia City, Nevada. Perhaps within a few years their proprietors will become millionaires. . . . In Polish villages there are hundreds of Jewish families who do not possess the means of livelihood and are engaged only in the harmful, unproductive tasks of middlemen. In the United States where willing hands and an enterprising head can make one wealthy, where many branches of commerce have not yet been developed, wide possibilities for prosperity and profits would open to them.

NEW MEXICO SUPPLIERS

ON MAY 13, 1846, President James K. Polk sent a message to Congress formally announcing that a state of war existed between the United States and Mexico. Three weeks later General Stephen Kearny, the commander of an army unit entrusted with the task of conquering the northern Mexican provinces, received word that a caravan of goods, including two wagonloads of ammunition, was being transported through New Mexico by Albert Speyer, a Prussian Jew who, with other traders, had left Missouri early in May to dispose of merchandise at war prices. Despite forced marches, Kearny's men failed to catch up with Speyer, who subsequently sold the bulk of his goods in Mexico at a handsome profit.

In the winter of the following year another Prussian Jew, Solomon Jacob Spiegelberg, accompanied a detachment of American troops from Santa Fe to Chihuahua. A suttler or a soldier, perhaps both, Spiegelberg subsequently went east and purchased a large stock of merchandise before returning to Santa Fe. Four brothers followed. Before long all were speaking Spanish as fluently as English from behind the counters of stores they soon established throughout the territory.

In describing the structure of such operations, Rabbi Floyd S. Fierman points out that "success was facilitated by tandem effort and, in many cases, by joint capital. Cousins, brothers-in-law and, above all, younger brothers were welcomed into the founder's enterprise. . . . Later, as a business prospered, it was of great help for one member of the partnership to work as a resident buyer in New York, while the others remained in the selling market out west: The New York buyer could quickly find government advertisements for goods destined for

New Mexico money issued by the Spiegelberg family in 1863. "At times during the Civil War there was a great scarcity of small silver coins, and in order to remedy this inconvenience to business the Federal government granted the privilege to reliable, trustworthy merchants and bankers to issue scrip."
—Flora Spiegelberg
American Jewish Historical Society, Waltham, Massachusetts

Five for one, one for all. The Spiegelberg brothers—Willi, Emanuel, Solomon, Levi, and Lehman—owners of one of Santa Fe's largest retail and wholesale dry-goods stores. Jewish families on the southwestern frontier also went into banking, freighting, mail delivery, mining, insurance, real estate, and hotel- and saloon-keeping.
Special Collections, The University of New Mexico

Phoebus Freudenthal, a major owner of real estate in Las Cruces and one of New Mexico's most substantial and influential pioneers.

western garrisons, or notice of Indian Bureau requests for bids to supply their wards with provisions. This was sound business practice, for who could be more trustworthy in such an important role, either in the home store or in the eastern marketplace, than a family member?"

Among the many Jews who came to this part of the country, one of them, Sam Dittenhoefer, achieved the status of a Jewish folk hero for outwitting Billy the Kid. The year was 1877 and Dittenhoefer was delivering 25,000 silver dollars from Mexico to the Spiegelbergs' main store in Santa Fe. As a precautionary measure, Dittenhoefer had the silver packed in six flour barrels with double heads and bottoms. The spaces in between were filled with flour and the coins wrapped in paper to keep them from jingling. Sure enough, before long Dittenhoefer ran into Billy the Kid. "I've a good mind to help myself to a few pounds of this flour," the outlaw remarked before riding off without looking any further.

Known as Navajo Sam, Dittenhoefer was a great friend of the Indians. So was Solomon Bibo, a Polish Jew who in 1884 obtained a thirty-year title to the entire 95,792 acres of the Acoma reservation in exchange for an annual fee of $40. Subsequently, Bibo married the chief's daughter and served as governor of the tribe. In the following account, Solomon's brother Nathan describes how he and a third brother, Simon, delivered 100,000 pounds of corn to an army camp in the White Mountains.

. . . The first thing I did was to send a number of men with my brother Simon to follow the Indian trails as far as possible and locate a possible

The Bibo store in Bernalillo, New Mexico.

Solomon Bibo, Jewish governor of the Acoma Indians of New Mexico, receiving the papers for a railroad right of way through Acoma territory, 1885.
Carl Bibo

way for the heavy teams. He returned after one month's time and reported a fair road up to the White Mountain range. . . . My brother [then] went to see Lieut. Colonel Green who . . . assured my brother he would put all available men to work during the summer months to cut the trees and prepare as much as possible the road . . . selected by my brother. . . . Between the Little Colorado River and Camp Apache was still noted on the map as "Terra incognita," and I now claim the honor for my dead brothers, Simon and Sam Bibo of having opened this road for the first time in its history for commercial purposes and inter-commercial traffic between New Mexico and northern Arizona.

I was obliged to buy up along the Rio Grande all the available last season's corn to commence filling my contract for delivery as soon as the season would permit. . . . So I traveled up and down the river and procured the first shipment of 100,000 pounds. . . . My brother Simon had three large wagons loaded with provisions and camp outfit for 12 men, who with plows, scrapers, spades, pickaxes, shovels and all other necessary material, had to prepare the road for the advancing ox teams and also a number of mule teams. One of the wagons my brother had loaded with heavy pine timbers and boards to build bridges across deep creeks until all the teams had safely crossed . . . as for a stretch of 65 or 70 miles no heavy timber could be procured.

My brother advanced slowly . . . to Mineral Springs at the foot of the northern slope of the White Mountain range. Winding up the mountain slope from that point, and blazing their way along the forest of pine trees, the summit was reached after about eight days of hard work. . . . When the wagons arrived there was great rejoicing in the camp, not alone of the officers and the men, but also the Apache Indians, who were a half starved and hungry looking crowd, my brother told me. All of them treated him royally and brought him presents for me also, and the Indians, about 300 or 400 of them, made a spectacular dance for him. . . .

SETTLING DOWN IN THE CITIES

IN THE DAYS when Indian fights, drunken brawls, and cold-blooded murders were everyday occurrences in New Mexico, Jewish settlers went to Europe in search of cultivated Jewish brides. This is what Willi Spiegelberg did in 1870 when he traveled from Santa Fe to Germany and married Flora Langerman. Flora never forgot her arrival a few months later in the frontier town of Las Animas:

The train arrived at sunset and I was fearfully tired for there were no Pullmans or any riding comforts at the time. The hotel was a small, two-story ramshackle frame building surrounded by shacks that looked like large packing cases for the town was still in its infancy, being but one year old. As we stepped up to register, some two hundred cowboys who had just returned from a round-up and were naturally armed to the teeth rose as one man and, doffing their sombreros, bellowed their greetings and cheered me until the very rafters shook. "Hello, lady, glad to see you," they shouted, and they really meant it for I was the first woman they had laid eyes on in months.

IT TOOK SOME TIME for Flora to get used to her new life, but once she did her reputation for charm and hospitality grew rapidly. Among her closest friends were the local archbishop, the commanding general of a nearby army garrison, and the territorial governor, General Lew Wallace, who took a number of Flora's suggestions into consideration concerning Jewish customs before sending *Ben Hur* off to his publisher. At the time there were no nonsectarian schools in Santa Fe, so in 1879 Flora purchased a small adobe house and hired a teacher to instruct twelve Jewish and Protestant pupils. A few years later she collected $1,000 from local merchants and had a three-room schoolhouse built where she often helped out by teaching gardening, nature study, and sewing. This was just after Willi had been elected mayor of Santa Fe. To celebrate the occasion, Santa Fe's first gas lamp was installed in front of their Palace Avenue residence. A year later another New Mexico Jewish merchant, Charles Ilfeld, added even more class to the town by opening a western version of Wannamakers "at a point on San Francisco Street which makes it the most prominent house on the street."

ARTHUR SELIGMAN, ESQ.
SANTA FE

Arthur Seligman, New Mexico's first Jewish governor. Seligman's father, Bernard, a native of Germany, arrived in Santa Fe in 1856 and subsequently established the first bank in Santa Fe and financed the construction of what is now the Denver and Rio Grande Railroad to Santa Fe.
Special Collections, The University of New Mexico

LEFT, *Albuquerque, 1882. Because of its relative inaccessibility the town remained small, with only three to four thousand inhabitants until the first train reached it on April 15, 1880. By then the Rosenwald and Ilfeld families had arrived, soon to be followed by Herman Block, Mike Mandell, Sussman Lewinson, and D. S. Rosenwald. By 1883 there were enough Jews in town to establish a B'nai B'rith lodge.* RIGHT, *Railroad Avenue (now Central Avenue), in 1898.*

Henry N. Jaffa, first mayor of Albuquerque and first president of the local Jewish congregation. Like many other Jewish merchants, Jaffa, a native of Germany, had come to the Southwest in pre-railroad days and shared in the general prosperity that followed.

LEFT, *Laying the cornerstone of Temple Albert at Seventh and Gold in 1899, with the territorial governor of New Mexico, the mayor of Albuquerque, officers and members of the Masonic Grand Lodge of New Mexico, and the First Regimental Band of the New Mexico Territorial Militia looking on. The privilege of naming the temple was auctioned off to pioneer merchants Ivan and Alfred Grunsfeld, who named it in honor of their father.* RIGHT, *Temple Albert shortly after its completion.*

*The social event of the season, the Lewinson-Weinman wedding, with Judge N. C.
Collier of Albuquerque officiating.*
Special Collections, The University of New Mexico

*Wives and sisters: Mrs. Ivan
Grunsfeld and Mrs. Alfred Grunsfeld.*
Special Collections, The University of New Mexico

Oct. 14, 1880. . . . Its front is handsome and imposing. . . . Once inside
the visitor of this mammoth establishment beholds a store [with] . . . all
the fittings and facilities that could be needed.

The shelves and counters are handsome, and conveniently arranged. . . .
Pendant from the ceiling are four elegant chandeliers supplied with handsome lamps to be used until gas can be secured. In the rear of the store
there is a broad stairway leading to the second story, guarded by handsome
walnut bannisters at the foot of which are two handsomely carved and
heavy walnut posts. Upon each of these posts stands a graceful bronze figure of a woman who bears in the palm of the right hand a lamp which she
holds aloft. . . .

Messrs. Ilfeld & Co. have just received enormous supplies of general
merchandise and have on hand large quantities of dry goods, clothing,
gents furnishing goods, hats, caps, boots, shoes, native wines, tobacco,
cigars, staple and fancy groceries, wool and hides, country produce, hardware, platedware, glass and chinaware, saddlery and leather, musical instruments, patents medicines, drugs, miners supplies, etc., etc.

Old customers and new are invited to call and examine their goods in
the new quarters today, the opening day.

The Daily New Mexican

EAST OF CALIFORNIA

◆ᔑ DURING THE DAYS of Indian raids and mining booms, Arizona attracted a number of people like Mike Goldwater, a Polish-Jewish capmaker who in 1852 went west to make his fortune. After declaring bankruptcy twice, in Sonora in 1856 and in Los Angeles in 1860, Mike and his brother Joe loaded up a wagon with Yankee notions and headed east for La Paz, an Arizona mining camp between Fort Yuma and Needles, where they hoped their luck would change. It did, but not dramatically. From peddling goods along the gold fields of the Colorado River, the brothers went on to become *balegolem* (freighters) and storekeepers in the town of Ehrenberg, where Mike soon became known among the Mexicans as "Don Miguel." In 1872, the Goldwaters opened their first store in the newly founded village of Phoenix. They couldn't make a go of it; however, they had better luck in Prescott, the territorial capital, where in 1878 Mike and his son Morris put up a new brick building, one of the first in Arizona. Mike remained in Prescott for several years with his sons Morris, Baron (father of Barry), and a younger brother, Henry. (There were two other boys—Ben, a professional faro dealer, and Sam, a tobacco salesman.) Meanwhile, Joe joined up with a Mexican from Yuma with whom he operated a string of stores in Tombstone, Bisbee, and Benson. Well before the turn of the century Mike turned the Prescott operation over to his sons and retired to San Francisco while Joe went on to become a successful clothing manufacturer in Los Angeles.

The following newspaper accounts document the activities of the Goldwaters and other Arizona Jewish pioneers from the late 1860s to 1885, the year Mike was elected mayor of Prescott.

Barry's grandfather, "Big Mike" Goldwater.

Mike Goldwater's son Baron (bottom right) with friends shortly after joining his father and older brothers in the operation of their store in Prescott.
Arizona Historical Foundation, Hayden Library, Arizona State University

FROM NEW MEXICO. *March 25, 1871.* M. Wormser and J. Goldwater arrived home Saturday last from New Mexico where they have been for some time past buying and shipping grain to this Territory, to fill a contract they have with the Government. A party of immigrants came with them.... The grain purchased by Messrs. Wormser and Goldwater is being hauled to Camp Verde for about four cents per pound.

The Arizona Miner

June 22, 1872. On the morning of June 15, Joe and M. Goldwater and Dr. W. W. Jones parted from friends here and took the road leading to Ehrenberg, Dr. Jones and M. Goldwater in one buggy, and Joe Goldwater in another. They had reached the "divide" of Granite Mountain and had, indeed, proceeded nearly one-half mile beyond that dangerous place and were, no doubt, feeling that they had passed the Rubicon when, horror of horrors, bullet after bullet flew at them, from guns in the hands of treacherous Apaches. Doctor Jones and M. Goldwater were ahead and had a very narrow escape, as one bullet passed through the Doctor's shirt sleeve, and another passed through Goldwater's hat.

But poor Joe got the worst of it, having received two dangerous wounds, from bullets, in the back. Jones was for staying and fighting the savages, who numbered about forty, but upon reflecting how Joe Goldwater was suffering retreat was the word, and retreat they did, followed by the Indians. Skull Valley was soon reached. The party stopped at E. F. Bowers' place. Dr. Baily, Medical Director of the Department, sent down surgical instruments. The balls were probed for, the wounded man relieved and is now, we believe, in the hospital at Camp Date Creek where, it is hoped, he will speedily recover.

The Weekly Arizona Miner

PRESCOTT. *September 7, 1877.* M. Goldwater, one of our successful merchants, we learn from a telegram received by Morris, his son, arrived in San Francisco today, where he intends to remain four or five weeks, and be present during the Jewish New Year and participate in the festivities attendant thereto. He will also purchase a large stock of goods for the company's stores in Ehrenberg and Prescott.

The Weekly Arizona Miner

September 27, 1879 of the Christian Era corresponds with the 10th day of the Jewish month, Tishree, in the year 5640, the day of Atonement, or Yom-Kipoor ... the most sacred of all Jewish days of religious observance. Our Jewish friends will on that day close their places of business and devote themselves strictly to atoning for their sins of omission and commission during the past year.

The Arizona Miner

TUCSON. *December 29, 1881.* Phil Drachman has fitted up his new saloon in a costly manner. The counter is inlaid with rare pictures, and the whole place has an air of tone and elegance. It is named "Postoffice Exchange."

LEFT, *Downtown Phoenix when High Holy Day services and impromptu Sunday School classes were held over Melczer's Liquor Store on West Adams or over the Donofrio Store on Washington. The chief religious functionaries in these early days were Wolf Lukin, a Tempe grocer, and Harry Friedman, a saddle store owner who also officiated at marriages and funerals.* RIGHT, *The Jefferson Street warehouse of Michael Wormser, a Yiddish-speaking Jew who operated an agricultural empire in what is now Tempe and South Phoenix. A shrewd and thrifty businessman, Wormser furnished hundreds of Mexican sharecroppers with seed, animals, tools, land, and water to raise vegetables in the summer and wheat and barley in the winter. When Wormser's estate was appraised following his death in 1898, its total value came to over $275,000, tied up mainly in 7,200 acres of farmland.*
Both, Arizona Historical Foundation, Hayden Library, Arizona State University

LEFT, *William Zeckendorf's store, corner of Main and Pennington, Tucson, Arizona, c. 1880. The grandfather of the New York realtor of the same name, Zeckendorf, in addition to being a storekeeper, was a legislator, a miner, and a rancher.* RIGHT, *Herbert Drachman's Cigar Store, Tucson, where "you can get all the leading brands of chewing and smoking tobaccos, and all kinds of Imported and Domestic cigarettes."*
Both, Arizona Historical Society

Paul Jenicke, late of the Mint, presides behind the bar. The place will be opened to the public this afternoon. Location: the corner of Congress and Church Streets, near the printing office.

The Arizona Star

Invitation to an execution. Miss Ringgold may have been related to Johnny Ringo, the outlaw whose name originally was Ringgold and who was reputedly Jewish.

December 15, 1883. At about 7:30 in the evening five robbers rode into Bisbee, dismounted at the lumber yard just below Castenda's store, hitched their horses, and proceeded leisurely to their destination. Three entered Castenda's, two stayed outside.

Drawing their revolvers, they ordered those inside to throw up their hands. One of them then commanded the bookkeeper to open the safe. He replied that he did not have the combination.

Another of the robbers then pointed to Joe Goldwater and said, "There's the son of a bitch that can open it." Three revolvers were immediately leveled at his head and the order given.

"Open the safe you one-eyed sheeney."

Joe lost no time in complying.

Meanwhile a terrible scene of bloodshed was taking place in the street. One of the robbers outside ordered J. C. Tappenier, an assayer and inventor, to throw up his hands. Tappenier started to run and the top of his head was blown off.

D. T. Smith was across the street in a restaurant. Hearing the firing, he came over and said, "I'm deputy sheriff."

"You're the kind we're looking for," replied one of the robbers. Smith was killed instantly.

Mrs. Roberts, a boarding-house keeper, hearing the disturbance came to the door and was struck by a stray shot and killed.

The robbers escaped with $2700.

The Tombstone Republican

On the road between Willcox and San Carlos in the days when the Goldwaters and other Arizona Jewish pioneers made their living by freighting supplies to army camps and Indian reservations.
Arizona Historical Foundation, Hayden Library, Arizona State University

January 9, 1885. Mr. M. Goldwater will soon be Mayor of Prescott. The new Mayor and Council take office at a time when the city owes the water works and other improvements upwards of $70,000. In case the water works are good, they will find the city pretty well equipped and should do what they can by way of retrenching. . . . As Mayor Goldwater and his colleagues are successful business men and large taxpayers, the *Courier* believes they will run the city government in a wise and economical manner.

The Prescott Weekly Courier

⇜ᘓ SHORTLY AFTER the Civil War, Isadore Solomon and his wife, Anna, left the Polish *shtetl* of Krushwitz behind them for better things to come in America. After experiencing business failure after business failure in the East, the Solomons—by now a family of five—decided in 1876 to take the advice of Anna's brothers in New Mexico and try their luck there. Her brothers, Phoebus and Morris Freudenthal, were already operating general merchandise stores as far west as present-day Arizona, where, together with their kinsmen the Lesinskys, they established a successful copper mining operation at Clifton.

We sold everything we possessed except our three children and started on our journey for New Mexico. We had a very hard trip. . . . Traveling with those three babies was bad enough, but when we reached La Junta, the end of the railroad in those days, [we] had to travel by stage, packed in like sardines day and night for six days. [We] only stopped to change horses and get something to eat, like chili con carne and frijoles. When we got [to Las Cruces], I was tired out to death. We found [a house], the best one in town, but I could not help having tears come into my eyes when I saw the mud floors and the mud walls. But after a few days I had the house looking very nice and comfortable. . . . I lived in Las Cruces with the children for four months while my husband looked around for a location for our business. He finally found a place, and this is where we have been living now for thirty years.

When we were going to leave Las Cruces, we bought a two-seated wagon called a buck board, and a pair of horses. Into this we put a tent, some bedding, our cooking utensils, our provisions, our clothes, our children, and ourselves. We also brought a Mexican clerk along, but he came on horseback. It took us several days and nights to get there. How often I was frightened thinking I saw Indians. I did not expect to get here alive with our children.

Now we had to start the housekeeping, but we had no furniture, no cooking stove, and nothing else that belongs to the comfort of the human race. [So] we cooked outside on the ground. We had a stove and other very necessary things coming from Las Cruces, being sent by an ox team with two loads of goods for the store that we were going to put up. But the wagons broke down on the road, and we had to send someone to repair them. They got here after three months. Until then we had no bed to sleep

Anna and Isadore Solomon.
Carmen Freudenthal and Elsa Freudenthal Altshool

in, no stove to cook in, no table to eat off, no flour to bake bread. For three months I baked bread out of corn meal in a Dutch oven.

[Meanwhile], I took sick with chills and fever and my baby, Rose, also took sick. We had some very dark and sad times, but that did not hinder us from doing a good deal of business. We had a contract to deliver charcoal to the Clifton Mining Company, which belonged then to my Uncle J. Freudenthal and my cousins Charles and Henry Lesinsky. This took a great deal of hard work to oversee and manage. We also started building—at first a bedroom, then a store. When that store was finished I felt like the Queen of England.

   A TOWN MADE ALMOST entirely of mud when the Solomons arrived, Pueblo Viejo (as it was called then) soon became big enough to merit its first post office, and a new name. The Solomons pushed for Solomon-

*Members of the Freudenthal–
Solomon–Mashbir clan, Solomonville,
Arizona, c. 1905. Anna is the woman
in the center with the lace collar.*
Carmen Freudenthal and Elsa Freudenthal Altshool

ville, and won. A hefty boost to the town's significance came in 1883 when it became a county seat. That year Arizona's territorial governor, John C. Fremont, appointed Isadore Graham County treasurer. Two years later Isadore ran for the same office and was elected. Soon afterward a newspaper financed by Isadore and other local land promoters came into being.

Meanwhile, Anna in addition to giving birth to three more children (all of whom married Jews) opened a hotel next to their store, the Solomon Commercial Co., on the northwest corner of Bowie and Main streets. A two-story adobe building, for years the hotel was a popular gathering place for townspeople as well as for travelers between Tucson and El Paso, all of whom marveled at Anna's homestyle cooking and unpretentious ways.

*Mark Strouse, Virginia City,
Nevada's first Jewish Chief of Police.*

*Anna Solomon's brother Wolff
Freudenthal on a horse. Another
brother, Phoebus, settled in Las
Cruces and became one of New
Mexico's most substantial and
influential citizens.*
Carmen Freudenthal and Elsa Freudenthal Altshool

Not until 1893 did Solomonville acquire its first brick building, a new Solomon Commercial Co. store. In the corner of their new store the Solomons opened one of the first banks in that part of the country. "Right next to the window of the bank," writes a local historian, "was the credit window of the Solomon store. If a customer who owed money at the store tried to make a deposit with the bank, someone was sure to sing out, "You're at the wrong window! Pay your store bill first!""

In addition to supplying most of the credit required by local farmers and ranchers, the Solomons bought and sold a great deal of property in the area. For thirty-five years, Isadore and Anna prospered until, in Isadore's words, "they cut up that county and took the richest part to Clifton and made the county of Greenlee. What was left they took back to Safford, where the county seat is now." This was in 1918. As a result, the population of Solomonville (never much more than a thousand) shrank rapidly. The Solomons sold out around this time and moved to California where, in 1930, Isadore passed away, followed three years later by Anna.

Today, scores of descendants of the Solomon-Freudenthal-Lesinsky clan reside in towns and cities in New Mexico and Arizona—living testaments to the courage and fortitude of their pioneer ancestors.

ॐ ON THE WESTERN FRONTIER even the story of *Pesach* acquired a Western ring to it, especially in mining towns like Austin, Nevada, where the following account was written by Fred Hard, a local newspaper editor, in the days when "150 Israelites" lived there, "including three families."

Austin, Nevada, in the days when it boasted a Hebrew Benevolent Association with nearly sixty members.

American Jewish Historical Society, Waltham, Massachusetts

The Bancroft Library, University of California

LEFT, *Adolph Sutro (the man with the whiskers) was a German-Jewish immigrant who built a tunnel in 1879 to drain and ventilate Nevada's fabulous Comstock Lode at a cost of $6,500,000. In 1895, Sutro was elected mayor of San Francisco. His great library, which he donated to the city, included many Hebrew manuscripts. RIGHT, Nevada storefronts, 1930s.*

When Pharaoh was Khedeve of Egypt, he was building government buildings by contract, and the Israelites were working for him making brick by the day. Like all government contractors, he neither furnished a good article nor treated his employees with justice.

The Israelites struck for higher wages and eight hours a day, and organized a trade union and elected a man named Moses as President. Moses was in the clothing business; and because he didn't know anything about labor the Israelites thought he would make a good presiding officer of a labor organization.

When the Israelites struck, Old Pharaoh hired a new set of hands, and the Israelites concluded to go on a prospecting trip into Canaan District, where there was represented to be a big milk and honey ledge. Owing to the snow blockade on the Suez Canal the market was bare of yeast powders, and the mill that made the self-rising flour had shut down; and as the Israelites were afraid the claims would all be located if they didn't get there quick, they started off with a few sacks of flour and mixed bread in the flour sack and baked it on a hot rock.

After they had crossed the creek Pharaoh missed some picks and shovels, and thinking the Israelites had stolen them, he swore out a search-warrant and sent a sheriff's posse after them. The sheriff's party missed the ford and were drowned, and to this day the Israelites eat unleavened bread in commemoration of the event.

Wakar, Chief of the Utes, painted by Solomon N. Carvalho. A Sephardic artist and photographer from Charleston, Carvalho accompanied John C. Fremont on his 1853–54 expedition across the Rocky Mountains and into the Far West.
The Thomas Gilcrease Institute of American History and Art, Tulsa, Oklahoma

AUSTIN, NEVADA. *March 18, 1864.* There are here about 150 Israelites, including three families, and the progress they have made toward the advancement of the true principles of the Jewish faith is actually praiseworthy. . . . The Israelites of this town have a Hebrew Benevolent Association with nearly sixty members; this society is founded on the same basis and with the same laudable views as the First Hebrew Benevolent Society of San Francisco. . . . The society have procured a suitable burying ground, and such is the stride of advancement . . . that the Israelites have placed themselves by their meritorious actions on the highest scale of civilization, and as I know many of your subscribers read with pleasure any news from this portion of Nevada Territory, you shall be fully informed of anything worthy of the notice of an Israelite. . . .

The [San Francisco] *Hebrew*

AUSTIN, NEVADA. *September 24, 1882.* The present population of Austin is eleven. They may be subdivided into nine males and two females. There are eight adults, of whom seven are males, and three children. Of the children, two are boys and one is a girl. The mother of these children is not a born Jewess, but she joined the faith . . . and is, I believe, as sincere a Jewess—though a liberal-minded one—as though she had been born of Jewish parents. She is the wife of an American Hebrew. All of the other males are unmarried, although one of them has once been married. The father of these children sent, some four years ago, upon the birth of a boy, to San Francisco, Cal. (over 600 miles), for a mohel in order that his son might be admitted into the Abrahamic Covenant. When it is known that he pays no attention whatsoever to religious observances, and that this involved an expense of $250, this is worth noting as an evidence of the strong attachment of the Jew to his faith. Though he does not fast upon Kippur Day, yet he closes his store, which is more that I can say for others of the same faith in this town. At the last Passover he was the only one here who had matzos, although others who had lately come from the Old Country were not ashamed to eat leaven. They did not even have the excuse of poverty as a cloak for their violation of the Mosaic injunction.

Upon Rosh Hashanah all the stores owned by Jews (of which there are three) were in full blast. Minyan is out of the question. With the exception of one family at Lewis, about twenty miles distant, there are no other Hebrews in our county. Two Israelites are interred here, both of whom met violent deaths. One was killed by an accident in the mines, the other was murdered.

The American Hebrew

Samuel Newhouse, a Russian-born Jew who in the early years of this century financed the construction of New York's Flatiron Building with money he made as a Utah mining speculator.

Goldsmith & Co., Salt Lake City's leading clothiers.
Utah State Historical Society

"PIKE'S PEAK OR BUST" BOOMERS

❧ Colorado was still a wilderness when the discovery of gold near Pike's Peak in 1858 ushered in a turbulent era coinciding with the construction of railroads clear across the country. The played-out mines of California combined with the panic of 1857 set off an unprecedented rush of fortune seekers. By the spring of 1859 all kinds of conveyances were advancing along the Platte and South Platte rivers, along the Arkansas River and Fountain Creek, and across the arid plains of Kansas to such remote places as Gold Hill, Jackson's Diggings, and Gregory Gulch. In June of that year Horace Greeley, editor of the *New York Tribune,* came to inspect "this wild country" first hand. Right from the start Greeley was struck by the variety and mobility of the people he encountered:

Among any ten whom you successfully meet, there will be natives of New England, New York, Pennsylvania, Virginia or Georgia, Ohio or Indiana, Kentucky or Missouri, France, Germany, and perhaps Ireland. But, worse than this, you cannot enter a circle of a dozen persons of whom at least three will not have spent some years in California, two or three have made claims and built cabins in Kansas or Nebraska, and at least one spent a year or so in Texas. Boston, New York, Philadelphia, New Orleans, St. Louis, Cincinnati, have all contributed their quota toward peopling the new gold region. The next man you meet driving an oxteam, and white as a miller with dust, is probably an ex-banker or doctor, a broken merchant or manufacturer from the old states, who has scraped together candle-ends charitably or contemptuously allowed him by his creditors on settlement, and risked them on a last desperate cast of the dice by coming hither. Ex-editors, ex-printers, ex-clerks, ex-steamboat men, are here in abundance— all on the keen hunt of the gold which only a few will secure.

❧ Jews also took part in the hunt. Among the most colorful was Samuel J. Kline's father, a "Pike's Peak or Bust" boomer who then went on to Montana, New Mexico, the Black Hills of North Dakota, and Coeur d'Alene, Idaho, in search of a fortune he never found. As for Samuel, the trip he took with his mother from Leavenworth to Denver in 1865 was an experience he never forgot:

The trip from Leavenworth to Denver has always remained with me. The caravan or train consisted of eighty covered wagons, "prairie schooners," in the parlance of that day. The motive power of such caravans was furnished by mules or oxen; I believe ours was of the mule variety. The wagons were large, almost like the moving vans one sees these days. They were canvas covered and carried all manner of household and cooking utensils. I remember particularly that ours carried a stove and being cautioned against burning myself. We carried, too a full complement of bedding, mattresses, etc. . . .

Wolfe Londoner as a young man on the Kansas plains. Londoner later became one of Denver's most colorful mayors.

The Indians, Arapahoe and Cheyennes, were then hostile and at constant war with the whites; at times the Utes, too, but the latter were generally friendly and were frequently seen in the streets of Denver. There may have been other tribes but I remember these three only. About that time a family named Tiedemann, friends of ours who lived on a ranch a few miles from Denver, were massacred, scalped, and horribly mutilated by these savages. I recall with a shudder seeing their bodies laid out in an improvised morgue: father, mother, and children. I believe one of the family escaped and brought in the news. Occurrences of this kind were not uncommon. This particular one has remained in my memory because we knew the people.

One night stands out in my mind vividly as filled with fear and horror. We were living on the outskirts of Denver with a few houses scattered here and there, the nearest neighbor perhaps an eighth of a mile away. In the dead of night we were all aroused by the dread alarm: "The Indians are attacking the town." We hastily dressed, and father, mother, and we children (four of us) went downtown into the business district, where we were hurried into a dry goods store on Larimer Street, which was crowded with other women and children in more or less scanty attire. As I remember, it was a brick building, with iron doors or shutters, which were then in vogue. Meantime, the men were being armed with such weapons as were available, formed into companies, and preparing for the attack. This, however, did not materialize, as next day it was learned that the "Indians" on the warpath consisted of a crowd of drunken Mexican freighters who were making night hideous with war whoops and other outlandish noises. Someone, a man named Brenner, I believe, had ridden by and in his fright mistook them for Indians and had carried the alarm to Denver.

For some days the newspapers carried jokes and funny stories regarding the scare. In a humorous vein they told how a neighbor of ours, Charley Schayer, a little Jewish confectioner and baker, had loaded his gun, ramming the bullet down the barrel, then the powder and then the wad. Subsequently it had to be drilled out.

Russian-born roadbuilder and politician Otto Mears with Colorado Ute Chief Ouray, with whom Mears negotiated a treaty that led to the removal of Ouray's tribe to Utah.
Denver Public Library Western History Department

◆§ NO HISTORY OF Jews in America would be complete without noting the achievements of Otto Mears, a Russian Jew responsible for the construction of a 450-mile toll road system on the southwest Colorado frontier. Known as "the Pathfinder of the San Juan," Mears settled in 1865 in Conejes County, where he erected one of the first grist mills in the area and then constructed a wagon road on which to transport flour from the San Luis Valley to the Arkansas River. In 1872 Mears founded a newspaper, the *Saguache Chronicle*, to attract settlers to the region. A few years later he founded the *Silver World*, the newspaper that started the Lake City boom.

It was in Saguache that Mears became a government supplier of cattle, vegetables, and flour to a nearby Ute reservation. After the discovery of rich mineral deposits in the area, Mears in 1873 talked the Utes into ceding 4 million acres of land to the federal government for the interest on $0.5 million for the tribe and a salary of $1,000 a year for Ouray,

Jewish-owned stores in Irwin, Colorado, c. 1880.
Rocky Mountain Jewish Historical Society, Beck Archives, Center for Judaic Studies,
University of Denver

Stagecoach on one of Otto Mears's Colorado toll roads.
Library of Congress

their chief. Mears then facilitated the removal of the entire Ute nation
from Colorado to Utah by offering each Indian who signed a treaty $2
for his signature. For this Mears was ordered to Washington to stand
trial on charges of bribery; however, due to pressures exerted by Secretary of the Interior Kirkwood these charges were dropped. Subsequently,
Mears returned to Colorado to supervise the removal of the Indians. In
1882, Mears was elected to the state legislature by a grateful constituency who shared the same attitudes as Mears toward the native population.

On a trip through Colorado a few years earlier, Isaac Mayer Wise was
"pleasantly surprised by the prominent number of Hebrew politicians"
he encountered:

Here I met Fred Z. Solomon, the last treasurer of the Territory and the
first of the State of Colorado, a prominent merchant of Denver, president
of the Chamber of Commerce, who built the waterworks . . . was in the
Legislature, and stands very high socially.

In the United States Mint I found as its Superintendent, a highly respected position, Mr. Herman Silver. . . . Among the legislators of the
State I found the names of E. Pisko, I. Gotthelf and Otto Mears, men of
brains and influence. B. W. Wisebart was mayor of Central City. Simon
Block is alderman of Denver. L. Anfenger is deputy clerk of the County.

Dr. Samuel Cole, the president of the congregation, is the Health Officer of this city. And yet there are, perhaps, not more than 500 Hebrew

Wolfe and Joseph Londoner's branch store in Leadville. Among the leading merchants in Colorado, the Londoners' business amounted to nearly one million dollars a year.
Colorado Historical Society

Cohen's general store, Fairplay, Colorado, c. 1885.
Rocky Mountain Jewish Historical Society, Beck Archives, Center for Judaic Studies, University of Denver

souls in the whole state. . . . Jewish lawyers and physicians are almost everywhere.

One of the most distinguished physicians I met is Dr. John Elsner, in Denver, who is, besides his medical practice, also a prominent scientist, and has collected a very fine mineral cabinet.

꿱 MEYER GUGGENHEIM, a Swiss-born Jew, had already made a fortune in Philadelphia as an importer of machine-made lace from Switzerland when in 1879 he acquired an interest in two silver mines in Leadville, Colorado. Adroit trading netted him free and clear two claims which, in a single month, earned a profit of more than 800 percent on Guggenheim's initial investment. "I have made a thorough investigation," Guggenheim told a reporter shortly after visiting the mines, "and if what the geologists tell me is true, we could get three or four millions cash money out of them."

In 1882, Guggenheim talked one of his seven sons, Ben, into studying metallurgy at Columbia University. Two years later, another son, William, entered the University of Pennsylvania's metallurgy program. By now the other boys were learning all they could about the business end of mining. Quickly grasping what miners knew all along—that the lion's share of the profit went to the smelter—in the late 1880s the Guggenheims expanded what was already a multi-million-dollar operation by building the largest copper smelter in the world in Pueblo, Colorado. From there they went on in 1901 to gain a controlling interest in the American Smelting and Refining Company, a huge conglomerate including every principal copper smelter in the United States.

While on the whole no philanthropist, Guggenheim did make contributions from time to time to various Jewish charitable institutions. His sons, however, proved far more generous. Simon, a U.S. senator from Colorado, provided the state university with several buildings. In addition, he set up a world-famous foundation for dispensing fellowships to scholars, writers, artists, and scientists. Another son, Solomon, provided $12 million for the establishment of one of America's outstanding art museums. A third son, Daniel, set up a multi-million-dollar aeronautics foundation to "stir the air consciousness of the American people" several years before Lindbergh's lone flight across the Atlantic.

Max Stein, mounted policeman. Pueblo, Colorado, c. 1900.
Rocky Mountain Jewish Historical Society, Beck Archives, Center for Judaic Studies, University of Denver

Sol Jaffa and his family in their general merchandise store in Trinidad, Colorado. "With my brothers I came to the United States in the late 1860s from Cassel, Germany. In 1871 we formed the Jaffa Brothers General Merchandise Company in Trinidad. I was in business here until 1919, and thus witnessed the change of business houses from adobe huts to buildings of brick and stone."
—Sol Jaffa
American Jewish Archives, Cincinnati, Ohio

MONTANA ORIGINALS

ᴥᔓ GOLD BROUGHT Isador Strassburger to Montana soon after its discovery in Grasshopper Creek in 1862. A Polish Jew, Strassburger came to New York in 1857 and to Denver two years later. From there in 1863 he traveled by wagon train to Bannack and then on to Alder Gulch, where for months he lived and did business in a tent. Strassburger finally settled in Virginia City. In 1867, he married Rachel Cohen. The territorial governor (who had been instructed to come wearing a hat) was among the 150 guests who attended what was described in a local newspaper as "an old-fashioned Jewish ceremony." In the following account, Strassburger tells of an event that happened a few years earlier:

Had some experience with George Ives. It was on a Sunday. He came in on horseback, drunk in front of my store in Va. City, demanded a pair of gloves, when I could not comply with his request, he then drew a six shooter, levelled at me, and with an S. of a B. and other wild exclamations coaxed me for gloves. Being afraid to advance or retreat, I tried to assure him of his waywardness and with a few more invectives, he took an axe that I had as a show, and to my utter astonishment left me unharmed and departed. A few months later he went where "other good Injuns go," to the happy hunting ground, by way of the rope.

There were considerable hanging Bees in early times, but as I had witnessed such trifles in '59 and '60 in Denver, it did not amuse me any more.

ᴥᔓ "HOW HELENA GOT ITS NAME" is the subject of the following account taken from the March 1, 1890, issue of *Helena Illustrated*:

At this time [c. 1865] there were only three women living in this region, the wives of John Somerville, Abraham Mast and P. B. Anthony. John Somerville, who afterward lived near the head of Nelson Gulch, about six miles south from Helena, where he prosecuted mining, was made chairman of this meeting of citizens, and, it is said, proposed the name which the city now bears. Just how it happened that this name was chosen seems to be a matter of speculation. By some it is said that Somerville suggested it as being a Greek word, and took occasion to air his classical knowledge

HELENA, MONTANA

Bissinger & Co., Missoula, Montana.
Bissinger Collection, Western Jewish History Center,
Judah L. Magnes Museum

by defining it for the assembly, telling them that it meant "far in the interior." By others it is claimed that a small town in Minnesota, the home of some of the miners present, suggested the name that was adopted. Still others maintain, with great earnestness, that the many kind acts and personal popularity of Mrs. G. Goldberg, who had been well known by many in Virginia City, from which place a large part of the population had come, prompted the Hebrew population to vote with great unanimity to name the town after her, whose name was Helena.

Until the arrival of the first railroad in 1883, Montana was difficult to reach. One had to travel either over the mountains from California or across the plains from St. Louis. Moreover, travel within the territory was slow. In 1869 it took Samuel Pizer, a Jewish merchant, eight days by wagon to get from Fort Benton to Helena, a distance of less than two hundred miles. Yet already a Jewish community was beginning to take shape in Helena and, a few years later, in Butte. The 1868 City Directory of Helena lists the names of over fifty Jewish merchants, peddlers, cashiers, tailors, dressmakers, miners, barbers. Even a cook and a teamster are mentioned. Later entries include factory owners, cattlemen, and bankers. Every bit as diverse, Butte's pioneer Jewish population included two mayors, a newspaper editor, a *shochet*, a jailer, and quite a few prostitutes.

The following selections are from *Copper Camp—Stories of the World's Greatest Mining Town, Butte, Montana*, compiled in the 1930s by writers working for the WPA.

Jacob Ehrlich was a frock-coated, bewhiskered, and derby-hatted rabbi known to hundreds as "Cockelevitch." Rabbi Ehrlich was the kosher butcher of the old camp, to whom members of his faith brought their sabbath chickens. Those Cockelevitch unconcernedly butchered on the main street sidewalk in front of his store, usually before the eyes of a group of gaping youngsters. As a sideline, the rabbi did a thriving business in the unleavened bread called matzoth and in pickled herring. The variegated aroma which wafted from the establishment is well remembered by old time residents to whom the rabbi's activities were but another phase of a cosmopolitan camp.

Jew Jess, one of the cleverest pickpockets in the Northwest, was personable and smart as a whip. Times without number she had been arrested, but rarely convicted. Jess was a drug addict, and when "junked up" her crafty brain and nimble fingers were capable of anything.

The story is told of Jess being hailed before a police magistrate on the usual charge of petty larceny and vagrancy. The evidence on this occasion was rather vague. The man who accused her of rolling him was not able to prove the charges, and the judge was forced to dismiss her.

Apparently under the influence of a recently administered "shot," Jess, in gratitude, threw her arms around the broad shoulders of the surprised judge.

Embarrassed, his honor finally disengaged her and blushingly endeavored to rearrange his disheveled clothing. A few moments later he discovered that his watch, wallet, tie pin and lodge emblem were missing.

A police officer was sent to rearrest the girl, but not a trace of the missing articles could be found. Indignantly, she asserted her innocence, and without a single shred of evidence to connect her the chagrined judge was forced to release Jew Jess again. About a week later a messenger delivered a package containing the missing articles to the judge's chambers. There was no explanation.

Down on the line, Jess could usually be found sitting in the window of her tiny room knitting or sewing, the picture of domesticity—that is, when she wasn't otherwise occupied.

꿍 HERE ARE A FEW newspaper articles documenting the career of Moses Solomon, a Yiddish-speaking fur trader and Indian fighter who, late in life, became a symbol of a world that was no more.

FORT BENTON. *February 5, 1875.* Our usually quiet and peaceful burg was, on the night of the 12th inst. disturbed in its serenity through an attempt to murder. Mr. Moses Solomon, in company with Mr. Jeff Perkins, proceeded to the saloon of the latter to take a drink. All the other saloons were closed at the time and the folks abed. Perkins placed a bottle and some tumblers on the counter, reached under the counter, presented a revolver, and without a word fired at Solomon, the bullet striking him in the right breast. . . . Solomon retreated and endeavored to reach the door and had his hand on the knob when Perkins again fired, the ball striking Solomon in the hand. In the attempt to open the door, Perkins fired another shot, which luckily did not take effect. By this time, people were aroused, and Judge Mills, Mr. Conroy and Mr. Tillman knocked Perkins down and took the revolver from him. But for this interference, Perkins would undoubtedly have completed his work. Solomon was carried to his own house, and is now under treatment by Dr. W. E. Turner, U.S.A.

Benton Record

C. *1900.* Hale and hearty at 72 years of age, Mose has been "up against the real thing," as evidenced by nine separate gunshot wounds that have left their impression on his person. One shot went through his lungs, but Mose is none the worse for it. He has figured in many Indian encounters since 1864—all the way from Ft. Benton to Ft. Peck, and from Cypress Hill to the Missouri River. Now where he used to hunt buffalo and trade with the Indians he crosses the great Judith Basin through barbed wire lanes and growing fields. Mose has been overtaken by civilization. The Great Northern spans the Marias River in front of his house; the traffic of a great railway rumbles at his door.

Lewistown Democrat

9
Religious Adjustments

PROGRESS AND MODERNIZATION

Isaac Mayer Wise in 1854, the year he came to Cincinnati and founded The Israelite.
American Jewish Archives, Cincinnati, Ohio

WITH THE ARRIVAL in the 1840s and '50s of a number of university-trained rabbis from Bavaria, Prussia, and Bohemia, a movement for religious reform came into being in America. Its goal: to adjust age-old religious beliefs and customs to the "progressive" spirit of the times. The Talmud, for these rabbis, was as much an impediment to their faith in science, humanism, and the Enlightenment as was the auctioning off of honors or the belief in miracles. In 1854 a fiery proponent of Reform, Rabbi Isaac Mayer Wise, became the spiritual leader of Cincinnati's Reform congregation, Bene Jeshurun. In the same year Wise founded *The Israelite* (the title was changed after the Civil War to *The American Israelite*), a weekly English-language publication dedicated to doing away with whatever struck Wise as old-fashioned and impractical. A year later he established a German-language supplement, *Die Deborah*, for his female readers. Both publications were soon being read by Jews throughout America who shared Wise's views on the need for religious reform.

Lay your hand on your heart, be calm and honest, and ask yourselves whether you can justify your cause before God if coming generations of Israel will be lost to our sacred cause, because you imposed on them doctrines which caused them to reject the whole system? I could not. Or do you think a generation grown up in a free and enlightened country will not do so? I do not, and therefore I think it my sacred mission to teach an enlightened and pure Judaism to remove as much mysticism as possible from the system of our faith; to give as much rational evidence for it as I can bring forward, and if I am wrong I am honest, and God will not judge me too severely.

. . . When the Talmud comes into conflict with the demands of our age, which, if listened to, will bring distraction and ruin in its train, then I am fearless on the side of reform; and if thousands of learned or not learned doctors say "The Talmud is Divine" I must a thousand times pity them

OPPOSITE, Front page from an early issue of The Israelite.
American Jewish Archives, Cincinnati, Ohio

THE ISRAELITE.

A weekly Periodical. devoted to the Religion, History and Literature of the Israelites.

PUBLISHED BY

CHAS. F. SCHMIDT & CO.

OFFICE:

NO. 31, EAST THIRD STREET.

אור יהי

"LET THERE BE LIGHT"

EDITED BY

ISAAC MAYER WISE.

RESIDENCE:

NO. 141, EAST THIRD STREET.

Vol. I.　　　Cincinnati, O., July 21, 5614 A. M., 1854 A. C.　　　No. 2.

(Continued from our last.)

THE CONVERT.

Chapter II.

On the west side of the Geist street, in the city of Prague, stands a four story stone building, celebrated for having given shelter to more poor students than any other house of that city. Its walls witnessed the advance and retreat of the Swedes and of Frederic the Great. Martin Huss, if he should ever return from the eternal abode, whither the hirelings of fanaticism hurled him, could tell us tales of thrilling interest of the bricked roof of this very house; and the High Rabbi Leb, (as the man of the thousand fables is called there) saw that structure in its present form and appearance, the structure in fact is as durable a monument of the Middle Ages, as many of its inmates were.

On the second floor and in a room in the front of the house, two young men sat at a table, upon which laid heaps of books, ... In the center ... a ... green ... surrounded by ink, quills and paper. In every corner of the room was a pile of books, intermingled with numerous manuscripts. Every one of the chairs in the room was occupied either by a man, or some article of male costume. Half a dozen long pipes, and two humble canes formed the ornaments of the room and completed its furniture. One of the young men, about twenty-seven years of age, was elegantly dressed, a profusion of black curls hung over a high and classical forehead, a pair of resolute black eyes revealed a countenance characteristical of strong emotions and powerful intellect, not unmixed with pride, yet overstrewed by features of kindness, which manifested themselves occasionally by a smile creeping his lips, apparently against the will of our Doctor Moses Baum, who sat now silently opposite his friend, Samuel Cohn, the son of Rabbi Hayim. Samuel was a young man of about twenty-four years of age, his dress was simple, his hair hung loosely around a pale, contemplative, yet open countenance, which was enlivened by a pair of penetrating hazel eyes, his dark ... ... in the justice and ... ... a ... ... bespoke kindness and purity.

These two friends conversed on a topic, known to us already. Samuel Cohn, a student of theology, contested in strong terms the step of his friend Moses in having embraced Catholicism. Our Doctor

faith. He contended that the numerous obstacles put in his way by the laws of the land and the disadvantages to which he was exposed by the common prejudices of the people, could not be overcome as long as he professed to be a Jew, but now he had many and influential patrons, and hopes to obtain a professorship at the university. As a Jew, he observed, he was obliged to impose on the generosity of his poor parents, and would have been obliged to do so for some years to come; as a Catholic he was enabled to support them fully, and to do something for his brother and sister; he concluded his argument with the words "I could bear no longer to read the complaints of my father about our dull business, and the charges of my brother, that he must work to support me." Samuel Cohn who had not seen his friend since the day of his conversion, now solemnly and earnestly protested against the sufficiency of these arguments. He said that a young man of such brilliant ... ... of circumstances, a man of extensive learning was not bound to be a physician or to live in Austria. He supposed that it was in consequence of the early education of his friend, having learned in the prime of life to humble himself before the almighty power of money, he now disposed of his conviction, the happiness of his parents, and his obligations to the nation which gave birth to him and his ancestors — because he was offered better chances to become wealthy. But it was the duty of a philosopher, which our Doctor imagined himself to be, to divest himself of all the crude impressions of youth, and a corrupted education. The Doctor protested against this view of his friend, and advanced that ambition was at the bottom, his motive was to take an honorable position in society, and to see his relatives occupy the same.

Samuel Cohn was not satisfied by this. He said, "It was a misguided ambition to mount the elevation of honor upon the steps of remorse and self-contempt, which he was sure and sorry, would overreach his friend as soon as he would have obtained that position in society for which he sacrificed his convictions. Here our Doctor suddenly interrupted him, "I did not sacrifice my conviction; for religious societies claim no conviction of the individual. As a Jew the performance of a certain set of ceremonies was demanded of me, as a Catholic I am required to perform another set of rites, both upon it with

pearance of a young man. It was Solomon, the youngest brother of Samuel Cohn, who entered the room, bringing letters from home. Samuel unfolded the letter of his father, and read in a loud and impressive tone the old man's simple and touching description of the melancholy scene which he witnessed in the house of Moses Baum, when that family was apprized of the conversion of Doctor Baum. The Doctor's eyes filled with tears, and after Samuel had finished and laid the paper upon the table, a painful silence reigned in the room. The Doctor, without looking again on his friend, rose slowly from his seat, and left the room, without uttering a single word. Solomon took the vacant seat, and taking another letter from his pocket, he gave it to his brother with the remark, "Here is another letter for you, I did not open it, because the term *private* is written on the envelope." Samuel did not hear his brother, nor did he see the letter; he sat his forehead buried in his hands, his features manifested painful emotions, he apparently deliberated on some important subject. Solomon, after a pause, again called the attention of his brother to the letter, but it was again in vain. Samuel suddenly rose from his chair, and walking the room in rapid strides for awhile, suddenly stopped before his brother, and taking up a book, he said, "this is the biography of Solomon Maimon; he remained a Jew, notwithstanding the calamities which befell him on account of Judaism; because he was a philosopher, he understood Judaism. I must write a treatise on Jewish education. Our youth are taught to perform a set of ceremonies, that is they are trained to be Jews. Judaism itself is foreign to them. How could it be expected of them to love their religion, and be willing to make sacrifices on its behalf? His words are two edged daggers. 'Religious societies claim no conviction of the individual. You must perform a set of ceremonies, and that is religion in their morbid imagination! Why should one set of ceremonies be preferable to the other?' He, my poor and misguided friend, was a ceremonial Jew and now he is a ceremonial Catholic."

"Do so, as soon as you please," said Solomon, "but presently I advise you to read this letter; it is directed to you privately." Samuel took the letter, and opened it indifferently. "It is an unknown hand," said he, and laying down

"I wonder, why Rachel Baum writes you a private letter?"

"Rachel Baum!" Samuel suddenly exclaimed. The mention of this name was an electric shock upon the system of our young philosopher. He seized the letter, and having discovered her name under it, pressed it to his lips. The features of his countenance were changed, on a sudden, his eyes sparkled, a melancholy smile surrounded his lips, youthful ardor triumphed over the artificial character of the philosopher. Samuel stood silently for a good while with the letter pressed to his lips; and then commenced to read, it was the first letter he had ever received of her — and we must acquaint the reader with its contents.

"*My Beloved Samuel,*

Under the pretext of begging you to save my poor brother, I obtained permission of your father to write this letter in his study, as I have no place in the house of my beloved and mourning parents, where I dare venture writing to you. My father, persuaded by brother Zadok, insists upon giving my hand (but not my heart) to the son of our wealthy neighbour. I cannot live without your love. Hasten to my rescue. Samuel, save me if you can.

You are represented to my father as the cause of my brother's apostacy. My father is enraged at you. Pardon him, he was misinformed, he always loved you dearly. Take measures, to convince him of your innocence; it will be easy for you. Do not desert my brother, and forget not to take speedy measures on behalf of your

RACHEL."

Samuel stood for awhile immovable as a marble pillar. His brother gazed compassionately at him. Samuel appeared excited in the highest degree, but the next moment he exclaimed, and there is a world of sentiments in his words — "Rachel weeps, I must save her." "Yes save her," said Solomon, and then drawing forth a well filled purse from his pocket, he threw it upon the table with the remark, "Here is plenty of money for the journey, go and save her. And if you write a treatise or a book when you do not forget to devote a section on the danger of attaching too much importance to wealth, which betrays and sells honor, happiness, heart, love and human dignity. Go and save her, try how much sought knowledge, learning and discovery have opposed to gold and prejudice. I am anxious to learn the result."

that they do not look deeper into the matter, or that they lack the moral courage to speak the truth.

. . . Our poor philosophers maintain that it is wickedness to think differently from our forefathers, to remove the old and tottering wall of separation, to think on a more enlarged field than our old men did. How pitifully narrow, how little touched by the spirit of our age are those men if they are honest! We pity them, but "I and my house will serve the Lord." Progress is the will of the Lord; rapid progress is the spirit of ours, the youngest creature of Providence. . . .

If the service is too long so that one cannot read the whole of it and deliver his sermon, then shorten it, omit such prayers as *Piutim*, which are of later origin. In shortening your service you derive the following benefits: (a) That one minister can read the service and preach without fatigue, and you save the expense of paying two salaries; (b) You will not be fatigued and worried in the house of the Lord by a service which lasts two to three hours; (c) You will be able to maintain a proper decorum in the synagogue.

. . . This nation, America, uses the English language; therefore we invariably endeavor to speak English at home, in our schools, and in our synagogues. We feel no regret in abandoning a language in which we heard and felt the terms *Judenhass* and *Judenverfolgung* and *Judenverachtung* [hatred, persecution, and contempt of the Jews] for the language of a nation whose dictionary is not polluted by such terms. . . . As citizens we must not be distinct from the rest. In religion only are we Jews, and in all other respects we are American citizens.

Is it not an insolence that men say in their morning prayers, "Blessed art thou &c., that thou has not made me a woman." Is not this offensive to their mothers, wives, sisters and daughters? And if it should not be said, why is it printed in the prayer books? Is it not a rudeness of the meanest kind that a female is considered as nobody not only in the Synagogue, but even at the table and in the family circle? If it was a custom among us that a man with his wife and children should go to the Synagogue and occupy their seats together, the whole would be improved, decorum and devotion would be gained, and a ready attendance would be secured.

To the Editor of *The Israelite*:

. . . I fully approve your advocacy of Reform. Orthodoxy suited past times; but reform suits times of progress; be not discouraged; steadily advance, and sound the trumpet of reform constantly; the elevation of our position in society from day to day is caused by the system of religious reform. Orthodoxy would have kept us 500 years back in our position, whereas reform steadily advances our position—socially, morally and religiously.

Emanuel Linoberg, Tuolumne County,
California, November 13, 1857

*Cincinnati's Plum Street Temple in 1866.
At the time of its dedication, it was one of
the largest Jewish temples in the country.*
American Jewish Archives, Cincinnati, Ohio

ᵛᵍ§ IN 1873, Isaac Mayer Wise invited delegates of thirty-four synagogues
from the West and the South to Cincinnati to form the Union of
American Hebrew Congregations. Its main purpose was "to establish a
Hebrew Theological College to preserve Judaism intact." Two years
later Hebrew Union College (HUC) was founded, with Wise serving as
president until his death in 1900. In the beginning, students attended
the University of Cincinnati in the morning and HUC in the afternoon.
"It was no child's play for those of us who were in earnest," David Philipson, an early graduate recalled, "and most of my fellow students were
indeed earnest-minded. . . ." Philipson's account continues:

. . . 1883, the most important year in my life . . . that first ordination of
American-trained rabbis was looked forward to by Reform Jewry in this
country as an epochal event. . . . Most of the leading rabbis of the country
were present. . . . The convention of the Union of American Hebrew Congregations, whereof this rabbinical ordination was the peak, closed with a
great dinner at a famed hilltop resort, The Highland House. Knowing that
there would be delegates from various parts of the country present who
laid stress upon the observance of the dietary laws, the Cincinnati committee engaged a Jewish caterer to set the dinner. The great banqueting

hall was brilliantly lighted, the hundreds of guests were seated at the beautifully arranged tables, the invocation had been spoken by one of the visiting rabbis, when the waiters served the first course.

Terrific excitement ensued when two rabbis arose from their seats and rushed from the room. Shrimp had been placed before them as the opening course of the elaborate menu. . . . The hosts had, as they thought, provided for just such eventualities by engaging a Jewish caterer. But he failed in the emergency. The Highland House dinner came to be known as "the *trefa* [ritually defiled] banquet." This incident furnished the opening to the movement that culminated in the establishment of a rabbinical seminary of a conservative bent. . . .

&ς REFORM WAS NOT for everyone, certainly not for Wolff Freudenthal's father, a pioneer New Mexico merchant who "always clung to his religious convictions and kept up the ritual in the same way he always did in his home."

When he went to New Mexico he was in a predicament. He lived in a small village, Belen, where he could not get any kosher meat, nor much of anything else. Once in a great while he was able to get some fish and that was about the only change in his dreadfully monotonous diet. Thus he lived for two years and no wonder that he began to feel weak. . . . One day my father took courage to write to his father in Germany [for] permission to kill an animal and enjoy a piece of meat. So sure did he become that

Hebrew Union College of Cincinnati, established by Isaac Mayer Wise in 1875 to furnish competent rabbis for American Reform congregations.

grandfather would say yes and allow him to slaughter an animal that he went outside of his house to kill a chicken. At that moment two stones were thrown at him by robbers who tried to kill him and steal the goods in the store. Fortunately only the smaller stone hit him so that he fell to the ground and lost considerable blood, but was not seriously hurt. . . . The next day the long expected letter from Grandfather Koppel arrived and what did this good old man say?—Was my father's education all in vain? Will the God of Abraham, the God of Isaac and the God of Jacob permit a man who knows nothing about the ritual of slaughtering animals to commit such a crime merely to satisfy his stomach? Never could such an undertaking end well. No! Never! . . .

After that . . . the strength of my father's conviction was never again shaken. He followed the same strict laws to his last breath.

◄§ IN 1885, fifteen prominent Reform rabbis gathered in Pittsburgh and passed a resolution denying the modern-day relevance of many of the most basic tenets of traditional Judaism. Known as the Pittsburgh Platform, it guided the Reform movement for almost half a century:

. . . we . . . maintain only such ceremonies as elevate and sanctify our lives, but reject all such as are not adapted to the views and habits of modern civilization. . . .

We hold that all such Mosaic and rabbinical laws as regulate diet, priestly purity, and dress . . . are apt rather to obstruct than to further modern spiritual elevation. . . .

We recognize, in the modern era of universal culture of heart and intellect, the approaching of the realization of Israel's great messianic hope for the establishment of the kingdom of truth, justice and peace among men.

We consider ourselves no longer a nation, but a religious community, and therefore expect neither a return to Palestine, nor a sacrificial worship under the sons of Aaron, nor the restoration of the laws concerning the Jewish state. . . .

We reassert the doctrine of Judaism that the soul is immortal, founding this belief on the divine nature of the human spirit, which forever finds bliss in righteousness and misery in wickedness.

We reject as ideas not rooted in Judaism the beliefs both in bodily resurrection and in Gehenna and Eden . . . as abodes for everlasting punishment and reward.

◄§ THE SUPPORTERS OF the Pittsburgh Platform were also in favor of changing the Jewish day of rest from Saturday to Sunday. It was folly, they argued, to speak of a Sabbath transfer as a concession to Christianity. Rather, they saw conformity as a way to alleviate religious apathy. "The malady is upon us," Joseph Krauskopf, a Hebrew Union College graduate, proclaimed from his Kansas City pulpit in 1886. "The present Saturday farce is a disgrace, and works greater havoc in our ranks than ever a Sunday observance could possibly do." Though some of these rabbis got their congregations to go along with them, others, including

Krauskoph's predecessor, Elias Eppstein, realized the gravity of the problem of religious apathy in America and that it was not likely to go away.

To the Editor of *The Jewish Tribune*:

It cannot be denied that the Israelite is very apt to change his place of abode. Wherever there is a "boom" booming you will see Israelites taking advantage thereof, but in very few such cases do such newcomers create a "boom" in existing congregations. These Jehudim who move from over-crowded cities into new places have an object in view, to accomplish which requires all their time and energy: to make money, as the common expression has it—to gain wealth is the all absorbing idea. Such men will not belong to congregations for they have no time, as they say, at present. I once asked such a man to join the congregation in order to contribute his share toward supporting the same. He stared and was vexed with me. "On Rosh Hashonah and Yom Kippur I close my business and rent a seat in your temple for ten or fifteen dollars," was his reply. "Is that not more than my share?" There is no use arguing with such men. Their mind is not open to anything but business, and they look even upon religion in a busi-nesslike way. It is with such elements we have to contend with in the West—and I believe all over.

Elias Eppstein,
Kansas City, Missouri, April 30, 1880

A NEW KIND OF RABBI

⌇ A NEW COUNTRY where Jews were seen by and large as fellow citizens required a new kind of rabbi willing to suppose that the Diaspora was a blessing, not a curse. Nowhere was this conviction expressed more suc-cinctly than by Polish-born Rabbi Gustavus Poznanski, who declared at the dedication in Charleston in 1840 of Congregation Beth Elohim's new temple: "This country is our Palestine, this city our Jerusalem, this

Kansas City Torah ark decoration.
Karp Family Collection/Museum of American Folk Art

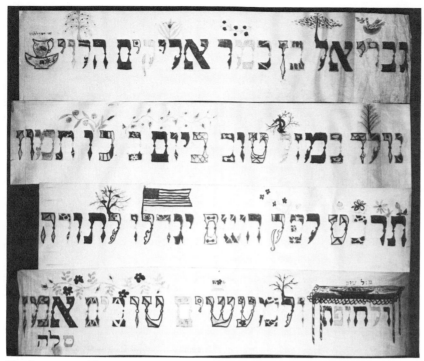

Torah wrapper, 1869.
The Jewish Museum

house of God our temple." It was a sentiment that German-born Rabbi Solomon Sonnenschein of St. Louis' prestigious Temple of the Gates of Truth combined forty years later with a vision of himself as a bridge between liberal Christianity and universal brotherhood.

The following selections from Rabbi Sonnenschein's letterbooks provides a glimpse into this as well as other aspects of the life of a representative Midwestern rabbi of the late nineteenth century.

April 26, 1882

Rev. J. L. Douthet
Mattoon, Illinois

. . .Wherever the disciples of Moses and the followers of Jesus cordially meet nowadays, it is no longer the special pleading of tolerance that prompts their mutual goodwill. This tolerance was good enough in the first hour of the dawning day, when timid doubts and misty confusion were yet lurking in the air. In this rather advanced religious and intellectual forenoon, in the broad and brisk flood of light, tolerance is too narrow an influence: the Jew recognizes in the Liberal Christian the fellow man who comes nearest to the Mosaic Prophecies than any other of the Gentile fraternity, and the Christian finds the Liberal Jew abreast with the vanguard of the Universal Church. We have both of us all the reason in the world to congratulate each other upon this happy success.

May 12, 1882

Mr. W. F. Cloud
Springfield, Illinois

You will make allowance for the brevity of my information as to the origin of written language. My time is especially at present so preoccupied with pastoral work of all kinds that I am forced to treat my correspondence rather miserly.

Ancient historians like Herodot, Pliny and Tacitus agree that the art and knowledge of writing, i.e. the invention of the primeval alphabet, originated among a Semitic race in either Africa or Asia. As to the time, place and nation: all dates are hidden in obscurity. . . . The Hebrew alphabet now in use is comparatively of later origin and was first introduced through the contact of the Babylonian exiles with Chaldaic scribes. Previous to that time the Hebrews had an alphabet of their own, which was kin to the Phoenician script.

Hoping this information will satisfy you. . . .

May 26th, 1882

Mr. Max Eichberg
Champaign, Illinois

In response to your inquiry of the 24th inst. I cheerfully state that Mrs. Cuthbert's "Young Ladies' Seminary" is highly spoken of and enjoys a first class reputation among its many patrons.

You may safely entrust the education of your daughter to this institution, and in order to secure the best of attention, while you will negotiate the matter you may refer to the fact that I had recommended the establishment.

May 30th, 1882

Mr. H. S. Ottenheimer, Secretary
Congregation Anshe Emeth, Peoria

Complying with my promise made upon your recent invitation, I have the honor to inform you now, Shevuoth being over, that I intend to visit your city and to preach in your midst, God willing, on Sabbath the tenth of June. Of course, events unforeseen in a large Congregation like mine— God bless them!—may in the eleventh hour interfere with my intentions. But I anticipate no difficulty. . . .

June 2nd, 1882

Mr. Lipman Levy, Secretary
Union of American Hebrew Congregations, Cincinnati

. . . I am at a loss how to act on your kind favor of yesterday. Of course, you simply were instrumental to the explicit desire of the Peoria Congregation. But the rather narrowminded precaution which these good people take in letting me know through you that they are too poor for paying the invited circuit preacher anything outside of the bare traveling expenses is so silly a measure that it somewhat chills the ardour of my willingness to go and preach before them. . . . As a matter of fact these good people of Peoria shall never feel the awkward position they have placed themselves in. I will preach to them: "wine and milk without money and without praise."

July 28th, 1882

Rev. Dr. I. M. Wise, Cincinnati

Two friends are disputing about the question: whether it is proper and decent to use the Sabbath School rooms of a Temple as a depot for receiving and distributing old clothes and second-hand furniture for the benefit of the Russian emigrants. One friend maintains the principle of charity, the other advocates the principle of cleanliness and decency. One says: there cannot be found a more proper use for school rooms during vacation than the one in question; the other replies: as long as there are premises in town equally adapted to the purpose, the sanctity of the Temple ought to be shielded. Being myself one of the disagreeing parties and desirous of settling the dispute in a conclusive manner, I suggested it to my friend to call on you as the Judge and Referee.

Dec. 17th, 1882

Mr. Henry Sinauer, Lexington, Mo.

My Dear Sir: It is customary to place Jewish tombstones at the graves of the respective lamented persons at the close of the first eleven months after the burial. But this is simply a custom and there is nothing in our religious code which is in the way of erecting a tombstone either before or after that date, as unavoidable circumstances may prompt it.

Dec. 24, 1882

Rev. Jacob Voorsanger, Houston

My Dear Colleague: I have an official communication from the Denver Congregation requesting me to recommend a first rate Minister for that Pulpit. The town is marvelously growing into metropolitan proportions and a gentleman with your talents and energies would be the right man in the right place there, with a spiritual influence of incalculable growth and results for good. But then, the Denver brethren would have to pay a higher compensation. . . . Kansas City too wants a man of real mettle. But there too prevails the low-ebbing of the salary. And still, for the proper choice they would not only be willing but able to widen the purse strings. . . .

RABBI SONNENSCHEIN was a poet as well as an accomplished letter writer. The following selection first appeared in *The Menorah*, a B'nai B'rith publication widely read in its day.

Through the blinds the shut-out rays
    Cast one single golden beam.
It is the sign of Heaven's grace,
    The seal of our happiest dream.
We know the cloud is bound to fade
    Before the conquering sun,
And when we stand at Death's own gate,
    Then—Life is but begun.

The doors ajar, and into Paradise
    We peep like children, standing on our toes.
How flushed the pulses, how glistening the eyes,
    With every second the shy impatience grows.
Ah! for *one* substantial taste from wisdom's tree,
    For *one* sweet leaf from Life's eternal plant;
May we not go nearer, that we better *see*
    And hear Heaven's beauty and the Angel's chant!
                S. H. Sonnenschein
                St. Louis, October 8th, 1887

⌇ IN THE OLD COUNTRY, a rabbi was a man of learning and piety who, more often than not, commanded the respect of his congregants. In America, where businessmen were the bosses, it was as easy for a rabbi to lose his temper as his job.

PORTLAND, OREGON, 1880. Friday morning at 9:30 the Rev. Rabbi May and Mr. Waldman of Beck & Waldman engaged in a malee in which the Rabbi shot twice at Waldman [wounding him in the leg] and Waldman put a pair of beautiful rings about the Rabbi's eyes. The affair caused intense excitement on account of the standing of the parties. Mr. Waldman is a well-known and highly respected citizen while Rabbi May has had charge of the Synagogue Beth Israel for the past four years. To get at the root of the matter our reporter visited both gentlemen and obtained statements from both in regard to the unfortunate affair.

Mr. Waldman who was found in his store said in effect that for a long time trouble had been brewing in the congregation over the doings of the Rabbi who was not only deficient mentally but also morally, and who would have long ago been kicked out of his charge but for the sympathy which was expressed for his family. A Sunday School had been started, and Mr. Waldman, appointed Secretary, was required to make an annual report of its workings. Mr. Waldman made said report about a week ago, and used this language:

"The progress of the school would have been more encouraging but for the ungentlemanly conduct of Rabbi May towards both scholars and teachers."

The Rabbi took great umbrage thereat, and last Monday shouted to Waldman as he went past his store, "You are a liar."

This was the last the Rabbi saw of Waldman until Friday when all of a sudden he felt someone grab him roughly and he received two terrible blows in the eyes. Not knowing who his assailant was, the Rabbi drew his pistol and, dazed and blinded, fired in the direction of the blows. Just as he fired he recognized Waldman, and as he was coming toward him in a threatening manner, he fired again. . . .

"I would have killed him if I could," said the Rabbi, "and would have done so to even my father or brother had they treated me as this man Waldman did."

The Daily Standard

Eureka, Nevada, August 20, 1875

To the Editor of *The American Israelite*:

We had one of those self-styled "Rabbis" up here last year—a sleek Pollack, utterly ignorant of the German language, and speaking but a miserable English. This man advertised as follows in our local paper: "The Rev. Dr. —— will deliver a lecture on the first day of Rosh Hashanah." The Christian public were respectfully invited. Of course such a thing being a novelty in our town, the place of Jewish worship, the Masonic Hall, was attended by several Christian ministers, lawyers and the editor of the *Eureka Sentinel*, in anticipation of listening to perhaps the first Jewish religious lecture they ever heard. I sincerely hope it may be the last; for such a rhapsody of unintelligible English, intermixed with Polish-German (Yiddish) and Hebrew sentences, never before assailed human understanding.

Well, sir, the Jews were utterly confounded with shame, and we were exceedingly glad when the Christian portion of our audience left the room—in disgust. The pretenders to the sacred title of "Rabbi" are generally also "Chazans," Shochets," and "Mohels," in fact, "Jack of all trades," and in nine cases out of ten perfect frauds in every one of these sacred callings.

Our last year's reverend fraud struck a perfect bonanza in our town. Mr. G. had four sons upon whom the rite of circumcision had never been performed, Mr. L. had one boy in the same fix, and Mr. K.—his first born was just a few days old, so that besides the handsome sum—far beyond his merits—which the man received from the Jewish community, he officiated as Mohel in the several cases named, and received in gold from Mr. G. $100, from Mr. L $25 and from Mr. K $25.

But this pious extortionist was not content, especially in the case of Mr. G's children, and exacted $25 more, which Mr. G. paid just to get rid of him. The job was a slovenly one, as the children suffered great pain for nearly two months after the operation and every one of these children—though not really injured—are more or less disfigured.

Such then are many of the guides and teachers in Israel. . . .

A Regular Reader

10
Emerging Communities

ON THE ROAD WITH ISAAC MAYER WISE

❧ DURING THE PERIOD of central European Jewish migration to America, a Jewish community often came into being with the establishment of a Hebrew Benevolent Society or *chevra* to take care of the sick, pay proper respect to the dead, and purchase and look after a Jewish cemetery. The first *chevras* during this period were organized by Bavarian Jews in the Northeast and Midwest. Later arrivals from Poland, Hungary, and Bohemia formed organizations of their own in New York, Cincinnati, Chicago, New Orleans, San Francisco, and other major centers of central European migration. While in settlements that stayed small, institutional Judaism rarely advanced much beyond the *chevra*, in rapidly expanding communities prayer meetings would be held regularly, congregations formed, and religious functionaries hired. Initially a *chazzen* was hired who also served as a *melamed, shochet, shamas,* and *mohel*. Once they could afford to or felt they wanted to, congregations would build synagogues (usually with Gothic or Moorish-Byzantine exteriors), establish Hebrew schools, and hire rabbis, generally from Germany, "in part," as Oscar Handlin points out in *Adventures in Freedom: Three Hundred Years of Jewish Life in America*, "because a majority of the immigrants were themselves Germans, in part because . . . German culture and learning then commanded the respect of all Americans, whether Jews or not."

In the following reports, Rabbi Isaac Mayer Wise provides us with a bird's-eye view of a few representative congregations in Indiana and Illinois during his early days as a traveling preacher and spokesman for Reform Judaism.

1857. Lafayette [Indiana] is quite a place. . . . The packing and produce business must be considerable. Here I saw, the first time, Israelites in the pork-packing business. Messrs. Eichbold & Bloom do a considerable business in this line and in grain. The rest of the Israelites are in the clothing, dry goods, jewelry, cigar, grocery provisions, and other businesses, and are not exactly rich, but well off, so that none is actually poor. The Israelites of

The Ehrman brothers and their wives, Portland, Oregon, 1892.
Oregon Historical Society

Denver marriage certificate, 1891. The officiating rabbi, William Friedman, was a Hebrew Union College graduate.
Rocky Mountain Jewish Historical Society, Beck Archives, Center for Judaic Studies, University of Denver

The Kaufman children. St. Louis, Missouri, c. 1905.
Congregation B'nai Israel, Little Rock, Arkansas/Charles H. Elias

this and a neighboring place, Delphi, about thirty families in all, are united in a congregation, have a *chazzen*, Mr. Shoenberg, a temporary synagogue, a burial ground, and are now about establishing a school. They live quite neighborly together, but in congregational matters they cannot boast much progress. They should have a better synagogue, against which the ladies can raise no objection, and should be less divided in opinion in regard to school and other congregational matters. I am sorry to say that the *chazzen* frequently finds no *minyan* in the synagogue on Sabbath. I therefore instructed him to count the ladies to *minyan*, not to suspend the divine service, as the act of confirming girls puts an end to the idea that females are not members of the synagogue, as well as males.

1857. What a handsome place is this Indianapolis! A city, a capital, in the centre of an extensive and fertile plain; yet every house is a fine country seat, and every person has a smile on his or her lips. Had old Jupiter known of the capital of Indiana, I am sure he would not have selected Olympus for his residence. . . . Our brethren of this city are a highly respectable class of people, and are as such held in high estimation by their fellow citizens. Most of them are young, intelligent and enterprising merchants, and the result of their activity and conduct is esteem and opulence. Our race is eminently represented in this western capital. There is much religious sense in them, especially in the ladies; yet they did not succeed hitherto in organizing a congregation, on account of their being but few in number (about thirty adults), and being too near to Cincinnati to feel seriously the want of an organization.

1856. Here I sit in Chicago, a miniature New York. If I say that there are just now between 3000 and 4000 houses to be built, fully two thirds of which are intended for stores, that it is hard work to cross the very streets at the places of junction, that notwithstanding the extensive hotels no rooms can be got a great many times, one has a faint picture of the city of Chicago, the youngest daughter of the great West.

In regard to benevolence and charity the Chicago Israelites are by no means behind their brethren anywhere. The Hebrew Benevolent Societies and the Ladies Benevolent Societies are as flourishing and well supported here as in all the larger congregations of our country. One of these societies has the avowed and laudable object in view to establish in this city a Jewish hospital. I have no doubt of their effecting the charitable purpose, for there is so much enterprise in this city that everything is carried out that is considered necessary and good.

The Hebrew School under the care of the Rev. Mr. Shneitacker is a flourishing and well attended school. This school is supported by the congregation and every child, rich and poor, finds an excellent opportunity to receive a thorough English education and instruction in Hebrew, Bible, etc., and also in the German language.

I have to mention but one unpleasant fact. The congregation stands divided in a German and Polish congregation, the former numbering about 90 members and the latter about 50 members. (There are about 1000 souls of our race in this city.) This is an unhappy situation, engendered, as we are told, by one outward and grumbling office seeker who, having been discharged in several congregations from his singing functions, attempted to establish here a Polish congregation, and succeeded unfortunately in his attempt. Why should American Jews not be united in all respects? "Have we not all one father, has not one God created us?"

EARLY L.A.

ON JULY 2, 1854, a motley group of peddlers, cattle dealers, dry goods merchants, and clothiers met in a tiny back room in Los Angeles to organize a Hebrew Benevolent Society "for procuring a piece of ground suitable for the purpose of a burying ground for the deceased of their own faith, and also to appropriate a portion of their time and means to the holy cause of benevolence." Eight years later a congregation was established and a full-time religious functionary hired in the person of Abraham Wolf Edelman. A Polish Jew who had worked previously as a dry goods salesman in San Francisco, Edelman proved to be an expert *shochet, mohel, melamed,* and *shamas* as well as an effective Jewish ambassador to the Masons, the Odd Fellows, the Independent Order of Chosen Friends, and the Pioneer Society of Los Angeles. Often called upon to say a few words on behalf of the Jewish community at civic functions and fund-raising affairs, Edelman soon learned to deliver beautifully polished speeches—a rarity in a town with a reputation for gambling, prostitution, and murder. The following items from the *Los Angeles Star* begin with Rabbi Edelman's first examination of Hebrew School pupils in 1868 and end four years later with the laying of a cornerstone for a new synagogue—perhaps the first in America with a five-pointed star in the center of the building.

Pioneer Los Angeles rabbi Abraham Edelman, c. 1870.
History Division, Los Angeles County Museum of Natural History

September 26, 1868. On Saturday last the first examination of the pupils of this [city's Hebrew] school was held in the Hall, Arcadia Block. There was a large attendance of the parents and guardians of the scholars, and many other ladies and gentlemen visited the school on the occasion. The exercises consisted of spelling and reading in the Hebrew language, translating Hebrew into English, and examinations on the history of the Hebrew nation, all of which was gone through with to the satisfaction of those present. The Rev. Mr. Eidelman [sic] is the teacher; he labors under great disadvantages in conducting his classes as the pupils cannot attend their studies with him until after dismissal from the other schools. Hence, the children always come to him fatigued and worn out, and very ill prepared for entering on a course of severe study. But notwithstanding this and other serious drawbacks and discouragements, he earnestly applies himself to the good work. . . .

Rabbi Edelman and members of his family in front of their South Flower Street home, Los Angeles, 1886.

June 4, 1870. A confirmation ceremony consisting of the Israelitish boys and girls of Los Angeles will take place on Sunday the 5th instant at the Teutonia hall (under the guidance of Rev. A. W. Edelman) at 9 o'clock A.M. Parents, guardians and the public at large are respectfully invited.

August 5, 1870. Rabbi Sneersohn has consented to deliver two lectures in this city, on the evenings of Thursday next, and the following Tuesday, the 11th and 16th of August. The subjects selected are full of interest, as nothing can be more desirable than information concerning the past and present condition of the Holy Land. The habits and manners of the modern Jew, Turk and Arab are also subjects of great interest, and will be made doubly so by the high descriptive powers of the learned lecturer. Those intending to be present should secure tickets immediately, as but a limited number will be issued, and many are already engaged.

October 12, 1870. The Hebrews, who during the feast of their New Year, and, that most solemn one of all their feasts, the Atonement, met in the Court House, for the want of a room in which all could join in the performance of their religious rites, cannot refrain from manifesting their obligations to Judge Sepulveda . . . [for permitting] them to meet in the County court-room, and there to worship the God of Abraham, Isaac and Jacob, in accordance with the dictates of their consciences and the usages of their fathers. . . .

February 9, 1872. Last night the ball given in aid of the Hebrew Congregation at Stearns' Hall was one of the most brilliant and fashionable balls that has ever been given in this city. The dresses of the ladies were splendid and in keeping with the most stylish patterns, and reflected credit, as well as beauty, on their fair owners. The tasty and becoming attire of the gentlemen indicated that Los Angeles in point of refinement is not behind any city on the coast.

August 19, 1872. On yesterday afternoon the corner-stone of the new synagogue of the Congregation B'nai B'rith was laid in the southeast corner of the building, with all the Hebrew ceremonies pertaining to this impressive and jubilant occasion. A large number of spectators were present, including the fair sex who formed a lovely *parterre* around the sacred edifice.

The Tabernacle will be the finest Church in Los Angeles when completed. It will be of gothic formation and adornment. The front of this fine building will be plastered and have two massive buttresses, surmounted by ornamental stone spires handsomely carved. The finial in the center of the building will be surmounted by a five pointed star set in a circle. . . .

The society having gathered punctually at 4 o'clock P.M. to lay the cornerstone, the meeting was called to order and the following oration was delivered by I. W. Hellman, Esq., President of the Society:

". . . I am happy to say that our society is at present in a flourishing condition; our membership is continually increasing and we hope soon to see the time when every Hebrew residing in the county of Los Angeles will belong to this congregation."

ఆ§ IN 1881, ISIDORE CHOYNSKI, *The American Israelite*'s West Coast correspondent, paid a visit to Los Angeles. An irascible wag, Choynski loved nothing more than writing about the foibles of modern Jewish life. In this respect Los Angeles did not disappoint him:

. . . In 1873 the Congregation B'nai B'rith had thirty-two paying members—the entire Jewish inhabitants belonged to the *schul*; today there are thirty names borne upon the roll of the synagogue, half of them deadheads. The Rev. A. W. Edelman, who has lived with and for the congregation these twenty years, is becoming disheartened at the doleful aspect of affairs. He acts in the capacity of preacher, reader, teacher, and *shochet* and receives $75 a month—when in the treasury—just one-half the amount they paid fifteen years ago with but a handful of Jews to defray congregational expenses. . . .

Calculating and indifferent to everything that pertains to Judaism . . . the moment death claims one of their numbers, then they turn their faces toward Jerusalem; then they ponder over the uncertainties of life and become Jews just long enough to inter their dead. Socially our Jews are capital fellows. They make every stranger welcome at their firesides, and, if that stranger happens to be a poker-sharp, he is doubly welcome, especially when some of the ladies, who are experts in the matter of "flushes and

WEEKLY GLEANER.

המאסף

VOLUME I.   SAN FRANCISCO: FRIDAY, JANUARY 16, 1857.   **NUMBER I.**

THE CAVE OF MACHPELAH; OR THE SEPULCHRES OF THE PATRIARCHS.

The Weekly Gleaner,

A PERIODICAL, DEVOTED TO
RELIGION, EDUCATION, BIBLICAL AND JEWISH ANTIQUITIES, LITERATURE AND GENERAL NEWS.

JULIUS ECKMAN, D.D.,
EDITOR AND PROPRIETOR.

Terms of Subscription.

Per Annum, payable in advance,............$5
Per Quarter,.........................$1 50
Per Copy,........ ....12c.

Advertisements inserted at the following rates :
One Square of five lines, one month,......$2 00
Every additional Square,...................1 00

Double the above rates for three months.

All communications to be addressed to "EDITOR OF THE GLEANER."

OFFICE 119 SACRAMENTO STREET.

Hebron and the Cave of Machpelah;

OR

The Sepulchre of the Patriarchs.

To the cultivated mind, the city of Hebron must ever remain one of the most interesting localities on earth. It was the home and the burying place of the patriarchs Abraham, Isaac, and Jacob, and their families, and after a lapse of thousands of years, is still looked upon with equal veneration by Moslem, Jew and Gentile. Here it was that Abraham fed his flocks, and after his return from Egypt, discoursed to his friends and neighbors of the wonderful things he had there seen. Here David was crowned, and here he fixed his residence for more than seven years, until Jerusalem was captured from the Jebusites. Here Absalom declared his rebellion and Adonijah assumed the reins of government, while his father David lay dying, in order to exclude Solomon, the favored son of Bathsheba. In this immediate vicinity was enacted the whole bloody drama of the wars in the times of the Judges. Here, finally, long before the age of the prophets, the Sun worshipers had performed their rites, and here, at last they found among them the tents of a mighty prince (Gen. xxiii, 6) who did not worship sun or star.

The venerable name of Hebron, the Mamre of the . . . . . Beth-el-Khalil the "House of the Beloved," so called by the Moslems, in honor of Abraham, the "Friend of God." The city is the highest inhabited spot in Palestine; being 2,700 feet above the level of the Mediterranean. It is mainly built on the eastern declivity of a deep narrow valley, called in Scripture "the Valley of Hebron" (Gen. xxvii, 14,) and running nearly north and south. It has no walls but to guard against the depredations to which unwalled cities in the East are liable, the main town is divided into three quarters, separated from each other by gates, which at night are kept closed. The Jews have a quarter, or Hatzere, to themselves. The streets are narrow, angular and gloomy, and the houses which are flat roofed, and of stone, and which were originally well built and lighted, are said to be much dilapidated. The roofs themselves are formed of domes; a style of architecture prevalent at Jerusalem, and in general throughout the East, where timber is scarce. The old town, of which the ruins are still visible, was situated farther up the hill. The population of modern Hebron is variously stated at from four to seven thousand; but the former estimate probably comes nearer the truth. It is composed of about 1,500 Mahometans who pay taxes, 200 who do not; and about 700 Jews. There is not a single Christian, it is asserted, in the place. Sandys, an English traveller, who visited these localities early in the 17th century, describes the valley of Hebron as "the most pregnant and pleasant valley that the eye ever beheld." Nature has certainly lavished her bounties upon it with no sparing hand, and it would seem that in spite of man and all the harm his petty malice can wreak upon her, she takes a serene and disdainful pride in rendering it a paradise for his habitation. The winter pasture ground of Abraham is still alive with flocks as when the patriarch watered his own at the wells of Beersheba. The birds still sing as sweetly, the white bright rose still dances as gracefully on the spray, the cyclamen still peeps out as coyly from under the snarled trees, and the sun still floods the landscape with as mild a light, as when he first rose upon this enchanting scene from behind the mountains of Moab.

The vineyards and olive trees of Hebron still yield abundantly. Sir Moses Montefiore mentions, that he got there a bunch of grapes, about a yard in length. They yield an excellent wine which is said to be the best in Palestine. They are planted on terraces on the hill slopes and are defended by rude stone towers which also serve as repositories for the husbandman's tools. Durbin saw venerable Arabs in flowing robes, walking about among the vineyards and superintending the pruners and vine dressers, while women half veiled, were washing at cisterns on the hill sides. These cisterns are a peculiar feature of the country. They are for collecting rain water, and may be found on every hill side and in every valley. There are two within the city limits, one of which may reasonably be supposed to be "the pool of Hebron" where David took summary vengeance on the murderers of his friend Ishbosheth. The larger of the two is, according to Dr. Robinson, 133 feet square, and nearly twenty two feet deep. It is built of massive masonry, and its foundations are probably as old as those of King Solomon's Temple. It is not consistent with the limits of the present article, to give even an outline of the varied fortunes that have attended the rise and fall of Hebron; once the metropolis of Judah and the mart of a busy and lucrative commerce its population, wealth and trade are now constantly decreasing. The last terrible blow it suffered was that inflicted in 1834, by Ibrahim Pacha, who took it by storm and gave it up to pillage, simply because its inhabitants resisted the Egyptian conscription, and wished to throw off the galling yoke of Mohammed Ali. The Jewish portion of it, notwithstanding, suffered severely on this occasion notwithstanding the pledge given them by Mohammed that they should not be harmed.

As seen from a distance, the town with its stone houses covered with white flat roofs, each of which is surmounted by a low dome, is beau-

straights" take a fancy to the new comer. There are but few books in the houses of our Jews, and those they possess are usually forced upon them by canvassers. . . . They are all good livers, high livers, look healthy, and live to a good old age, but they will not be Jews unless the grim tyrant Death knocks at their doors.

THE WAY IT WAS IN SAN FRANCISCO

᳁᳁ By 1849, THERE WERE already enough Jews in San Francisco to hold Yom Kippur services in a hall on the second floor of a building on Montgomery Street as well as in a tent a few blocks away on Jackson Street near the corner of Kearney. The Montgomery Street Jews were Westernized Bavarians for the most part, who considered themselves culturally and socially superior to their Jackson Street *Glaubensbrüder* (co-religionists) who were mainly from East Prussia, Posen, and other "eastern" lands. What resulted was the formation of two pioneer congregations: Emanu-El for those who looked upon themselves as *echt Deutsch* and Sherith Israel for the *"ost Juden"*—with not one but two benevolent societies to aid the needy, care for the sick, and bury the dead, one for the Germans and one for the Poles. Both congregations started out Orthodox, in keeping with the traditions these Jews brought with them from the old country; however, it wasn't long before Reform took over at Emanu-El and, in 1893, at Sherith Israel as well.

San Francisco's first rabbi, Julius Eckman, arrived on the scene in 1854, just in time to officiate at the consecrations of the synagogues each congregation had recently erected. In the fall of that year Eckman was hired to conduct services at Emanu-El. Far more of a traditionalist than a reformer, Eckman soon came under attack. "There are no innovations," one up-to-date member complained. "The synagogue services are more or less as still found in our humble villages back home." Unable or unwilling to formalize in theological terms the conception of Judaism toward which his congregation was groping, Eckman was asked to resign less than a year after his appointment. He remained in San Francisco, however, to edit a Jewish newspaper. *The Weekly Gleaner*, until his death in 1874. The following sketch was written by a Christian clergyman who knew him well.

I do not think he ever felt at home amid the hurry and rush of San Francisco. He could not adjust himself to the people. He was devout; they were intensely worldly. He thundered this sentence from the teacher's desk in the synagogue one morning: "O ye Jews of San Francisco, you have so fully given yourselves up to material things that you are losing the very instinct of immortality. Your idea of religion is to acquire the Hebrew language, *and you don't know that!*" Elijah himself was not more fearless. His belief in God and in the supernatural was startlingly vivid, the miracles of the Old Testament as real to him as the premiership of Disraeli or the financiering of the Rothschilds. There was, at the same time, a vein of ratio-

OPPOSITE, *First issue of* The Weekly Gleaner, *San Francisco, 1857. The masthead is decorated with the symbols of the Twelve Tribes of Israel.*
American Jewish Archives, Cincinnati, Ohio

nalism that ran through his thought and speech. We were speaking one day on the subject of miracles, and with his usual energy of manner he said: "There was no need of any literal angel to shut the mouths of the lions to save Daniel; the awful holiness of the prophet was enough." His face glowed as he spoke, and his voice was subdued into a solemnity of tone that told how his reverent and adoring soul was thrilled with this vision of the coming glory of redeemed humanity. He knew the New Testament by heart, as well as the Old. The sayings of Jesus were often on his lips.

Bishop O. P. Fitzgerald

AFTER RABBI ECKMAN'S departure, Emanu-El remained without a full-time rabbi until 1860, when Elkan Cohn was hired. In keeping with the wishes of his congregants, Rabbi Cohn set about removing such traces of "Orientalism" from religious services as the covering of heads, the wearing of phylacteries, and the adherence to Hebrew in much of the ritual. Not everyone was pleased with such changes. In 1864 a third of Emanu-El's membership—seventy families—seceded to organize Congregation Ohabai Shalome, leaving Rabbi Cohn free to go even further. In the 1870s, Cohn got rid of the traditional *chupah* (wedding canopy) as well as the age-old Jewish custom of burying Jews in shrouds and plain caskets. One could now go from the altar to the grave without appearing conspicuously Jewish. Even so, Jews were still excluded from some of the city's most fashionable social clubs.

OF THE NEARLY twenty thousand Jews in San Francisco at the turn of the century, only a few—the Slosses, the Gerstles, the Lilienthals—could afford huge mansions on Van Ness Avenue. There was no shortage, however, of middle-class families like the Levys of O'Farrell Street. In the following selection, Harriet Lane Levy provides an inside view of life in the Levy home around the turn of the century.

. . . Wrapped in his woolen *Schlafrock* (dressing gown), Father sat in his armchair, close to the glass-paneled doors opening into the music room. In a half circle before him sat his friends, drinking cognac from small red glasses . . . Manassah, the lantern-jawed jewel merchant; Wilzynski, the explosive wit; and B. Joseph, soft-spoken and soft-stepping. . . . These were city friends from Father's birthplace. J. Meyer had come down from Virginia City, and H. Lippman up from Santa Barbara to replenish their stocks of dry goods. . . .

On Friday afternoons he hurried away his late customer that he might attend the service in the synagogue and hasten home to usher in the Sabbath with prayer and thanksgiving. As the Passover found the house cleansed of leaven, so the Day of Atonement found his heart purified of sin. . . . Father's passionate obedience to religious observance was only one aspect of his ardor for righteousness. He wanted to be good, he wanted to do right; he wanted profoundly, above all things, to be a good man, a good father, a good citizen. . . .

*San Francisco's Sutter Street Temple.
Completed in 1866, it was the first
landmark visible to ships rounding
Telegraph Hill.*
The Bancroft Library, University of California

As if the general laws of conduct of the period were not enough to shadow the day, Mother added to them the five books of the Law and all the more recent prohibitions, evolved by the Jewish merchant class to which we belonged. "Thou shalt not" burst from her lips like an anthem. . . .

"No girl goes to a party alone with a man," Mother said. "She goes with her brother, you know that."

"But suppose she hasn't a brother?"

"Then she is unfortunate," Mother said. . . . "*Man muss manches Menschenwegen thun* (One has to do much for the sake of people)." Against the pronouncement of "*Menschenwegen*" there was no appeal.

. . . No girl with self-respect, said Mother, would enter a restaurant with a man. She could not do so without losing her reputation. I saw reputation like a coat left hanging behind in a restaurant corridor. If the restaurant were French, it was irrecoverable. . . .

"When you have cramps," I asked Mother, "where do you say that you have them?"

"Why do you have to tell that you have got them?"

"But suppose you did? You can never tell."

"Say stomach," Mother said.

"But stomach isn't where I get them. I never get pains in my stomach. I have cramps."

"Say stomach anyway," Mother commanded. . . .

I knew that there were old maids; a cousin was fast becoming one. I heard my mother reproach her on her twenty-first birthday, but that did not mean that a girl would not eventually marry; it meant only that she would have to go to the country to live, to the interior. The interior was the market for all marriageable material that could not be advantageously disposed of in the city.

San Francisco's Young Men's Hebrew Association, 1902.
San Francisco Jewish Community Center Collection, Western Jewish History Center, Judah L. Magnes Museum

Members of the Jewish "400" attending a picnic at Redwood Grove in San Rafael. The Gerstles and the Slosses spent their summers here.
Sophie Gerstle Lilienthal Collection, Western Jewish History Center, Judah L. Magnes Museum

San Francisco's YM/YWHA Symphony Orchestra, 1919.
San Francisco Jewish Community Center Collection, Western Jewish History Center, Judah L. Magnes Museum

The New Wave: Jake Pantofsky (right), an Oakland businessman from eastern Europe,
on his way home from a hunting expedition.
Pantofsky Family Collection, Western Jewish History Center, Judah L. Magnes Museum

Shopkeepers came to the city from the interior, from towns of the San Joaquin or Sacramento valleys, or from the mining towns, Grass Valley, Calaveras, or Mokelumne Hill to buy goods. Their quest often included a sentimental hope, confided to a downtown wholesale merchant. If a man's appearance was agreeable and his credit good, he would be invited to the merchant's home to dine and meet the unmarried daughters. To my way of thinking the interior was broad enough to take care of every unmated daughter. . . .

Among [my sister] Addie's many suitors were some whom she never saw, who were submitted and rejected without reaching the stage when they came to spend the evening. Others, brought by acquaintances of my parents, added sparkle to the evening's entertainment with "lively remarks." They accented Addie's accomplishments. "She baked these cookies?" "She embroidered those napkins?" Before such praise Addie withdrew more deeply into her reserve, while Mother, not to be diverted by cheap strategy, continued to examine the aspirant with proud, critical eye. . . . My parents set the highest value upon health and the outward signs of vigor. If Mother murmured, *"Blaas* [pale]" . . . the white-faced young man . . . was practically done for. . . . Father valued stability, solid qualities that insured future security. . . . Next to stability came health. . . .

Everybody agreed that August Friedlander was a fitting alliance for Addie. Although still a young man (he was twenty-six), he had a good business in a growing town across the bay. Father made inquiries of the merchants from whom August bought his goods, and they all agreed upon his integrity and good credit. . . . August's younger brother, David, who accompanied him on his visits, was short and broad and plump. August sat on the sofa, his brother on the piano stool. He smiled broadly, showing white teeth. . . . August had never heard *Il Trovatore*, he admitted to Father's chagrin; but, on the hand, while his brother was bald, August had a heavy growth of hair, and Levi Strauss, the millionaire manufacturer of I X L Overalls, told Father that he was the brains of the business.

Both Father and Mother agreed that he was better qualified than any other suitor who had yet appeared, and they encouraged him to come often. At later visits the family retired, the brother was omitted, and August and Addie conversed behind the closed folding doors.

"Well?" Father asked after a month. "What do you say?"

"I like him," Addie said, and within twenty-four hours I was hurrying to the neighbors, announcing the betrothal and spreading consternation in the homes of marriageable daughters down the two blocks.

Self-portrait by Anne Bremer. Born in San Francisco in 1872, Bremer was recognized as a leading California artist during the early years of this century.
Mills College Collection

᳕᳐ By the first world war, religious reformers had begun to reinstitute some of the old traditions abandoned during the days of Elkan Cohn and his successor, Jacob Voorsanger. A sign of this was the hiring in 1914 of Reuben Rinder, a *chazzen* with an East European Orthodox background. Well liked by his congregants, Rinder enjoyed a distinguished career as *chazzen* of Emanu-El, where he remained for over fifty years. The following account of a few memorable events from their early years in San Francisco is from an oral memoir by Rinder's wife, Rose.

First I want to give you a background of the community. It was very different than it is today. It was much more formal. Temple Emanu-El, for the most part, had only the very wealthy people in the community as members. Either they took themselves more seriously than people do today, or I thought they did. They were very formal.

The women particularly dressed more somberly than nowadays, and consequently they looked so much older to me. I was twenty-one years old and they at thirty-five or forty looked—well, they just looked old, like grandmothers. Most of them wore long black dresses and huge black hats with plumes, and veils over their faces—in fact, I began wearing a veil too.

The Temple at the time was down where 450 Sutter Street is now. It had been rebuilt after the earthquake and fire which had ruined it somewhat, but it was still a very handsome structure. There was one gratifying thing about it: It was filled almost to capacity every Saturday morning. In those days people really attended services, with their children, including their college young people who came in for the weekend, whether from Stanford or the University at Berkeley, or Mills College—they would all attend services.

After services they'd go on and have lunch at the St. Francis or the Palace Hotel and then attend a matinee. Those were the things people did in those days. So everybody came to services, and it was really very gratifying and a wonderful life then. It was all very pleasant.

Socially it was very pleasant too because the families each took turns inviting us, and we were the guests of honor in quite magnificent homes. I began feeling like Cinderella. Every night we'd go out to these places where there were butlers. So many had butlers and chauffeurs, and the cars would pick us up and I'd go to these homes and experience all these unaccustomed ways of living, and come back to my modest home.

It was all very elegant. It was certainly not what I had been accustomed to but you get used to these nice things very quickly. You begin to take them for granted.

Our entertaining was done chiefly at Passover when we had people from the Temple to *seder*, many of whom had never had a *seder* in their homes, even though they attended services. They would recall *seders* at their grandparents' homes or their parents' homes, but they themselves would not have *seders*. So they were delighted to come. We would invite them when interesting people came to the community. We would have them meet musicians and important Zionists.

Do you know this lovely house here on Washington Street where Mrs. Marcus Koshland used to live? It's supposed to be a replica of the Petit Trianon in Paris. She lived in it all alone. Her children were all married at the time. But she loved our music in the Temple and frequently brought her non-Jewish friends to services.

One day she said to my husband, "Wouldn't it be nice if we had some of this music in my home so all my non-Jewish friends could come and also

Alice B. Toklas when she still lived in San Francisco. Alice's grandfather was a California Forty-niner from Poland.
Bancroft Library, University of California

many of my Jewish friends who don't attend services. Why don't we arrange something?"

She had an organ in her home with pipes and everything constructed right into the house. So my husband arranged a program of Jewish music. And she invited about three hundred people for an afternoon. He read a paper on Jewish music, with illustrations from synagogue music and some Jewish folk songs, and it was a big success. So from then on he began giving one every year. The next one was just near Chanukah time.

It became a tradition. He would end the afternoon of music with chanting and a lighting of the Chanukah lights. It was a three-story house going up and up into the balconies and the menorahs were placed all over the house. As he chanted and lit each candle—there's a chant for each candle which he had written—a grandchild would be lighting a menorah somewhere. It was dark by then and soon the whole house was ablaze with these menorahs. Really, it was the most thrilling moment when the kindling of the lights and chanting was going on.

All the great artists would come and play there. I remember meeting Aaron Copland there. At one time during the opera season, Melchior was there. After my husband got through lighting the Chanukah lights—and he was at his best in those days—Melchior shouted, "Bravo, bravo!"

CONGREGATIONS BIG AND SMALL

As soon as the growth of a Jewish community made it possible to do so, a new congregation would come into being, and before long another and another, often as a result of disputes between Germans and Poles, Orthodox and Reformed.

INHARMONIOUS HEBREWS

September 21, 1876. As is well known to many Gentiles, there are two sects in the Jewish church, the Orthodox and the Reformed Jews. In large communities where there are a sufficient number of Israelites for more than one congregation, they form generally distinct ecclesiastical bodies, following the same general teachings of the law of Moses, but under different interpretations. In this city there has been but one congregation, and no regularly ordained priest has been established here. It does not appear that there have been any serious differences among the members of the congregation heretofore, but as the society increased in numbers a conflict became inevitable; the question of orthodoxy or heterodoxy must be settled one way or the other, and the crisis arrived yesterday.

At 6 o'clock Monday evening, the Jewish New Year's day began for the year 5637, and it was kept as a holy feast. According to the orthodox custom, however, the first two days must be kept holy, while the reformed church requires only one. It seems that Mr. M. Adamski had been asked by the Committee of Arrangements to act as reader, and he officiated accordingly the first day. Yesterday, the second day of the feast, Mr. Adamski opened his shop as usual and began business the same as on any other secular day. This act seems to have been regarded as a grave breach of the Mosaic law by the orthodox members, and they were in a state of great indignation that Adamski should profess to be a good Israelite and yet openly violate the religious law.

Consequently, when the congregation assembled in Pike's Hall on Farnam Street between Twelfth and Thirteenth Streets yesterday morning, the orthodox members were determined that Adamski should not be the reader. No sooner had be begun than he was told to stop as unworthy to act in that capacity. Mr. Jacob Myers, in company with Mr. Abraham Beiernstein, made a charge upon the venerable Adamski and drove him out of the synagogue, as also one Peddler Forman who was an assistant to Adamski in some way.

"Did you put these men out, Mr. Myers?" asked the *Herald* reporter.

"Of course we put them out. Did we want a man to read for us who came there straight from working in his shop on a holy day? No, sir. I helped to put them out and I will take the responsibility."

"Then you are an orthodox Jew?"

"Yes, indeed. I am so orthodox that I get my meat from Des Moines in order that it may be killed by a Jewish butcher."

The reporter then visited Mr. Adamski, whom he found consoling the unfortunate Forman who had got all the kicks and blows of the affair.

"What was the difficulty that occurred at the synagogue this morning, Mr. Adamski?"

"Vell, Myers thinks dat because I open my shop the day after New Years I am a great law-breaker."

"Are you not required to keep two days?"

"No, sir. One day is all that is required. I know the law as well as anyone."

"Oh, then this congregation is one of the Reformed Congregations?"

"Certainly it is."

. . . At present both factions are maintaining a watchful neutrality and the idea of calling in the aid of the law has been abandoned.

Omaha Daily Herald

Rev. M. R. Cohen, fastest mohel *in the West. From an 1872 issue of* The American Israelite.

⤳ IN SMALL TOWNS where there were not enough Jews to form a regular *minyan*, Rosh Hashonah and Yom Kippur were about the only times Jews gathered together for services, often in an upstairs hall rented from a friendly fraternal organization. These and other memories are recalled by Edna Ferber in her recollections of growing up in Ottumwa, Iowa.

Usually one of the substantial older men who knew something of the Hebrew language of the Bible, having been taught it in his youth, conducted the service. On Yom Kippur, a long day of fasting and prayer, it was an exhausting thing to stand from morning to sunset in the improvised pulpit. The amateur rabbi would be relieved for an hour by another member of the little improvised congregation. Mr. Emanuel Adler, a familiar figure to me as he sat in his comfortable home, talking with my parents, quaint long-stemmed pipe between his lips, a little black skullcap atop his baldish head as protection against drafts, now would don the rabbinical skullcap, a good deal like that of a Catholic priest. He would open on the high reading stand the Bible and the Book of Prayers containing the service for the Day of Yom Kippur; and suddenly he was transformed from a plump middle-aged German-born Jew with sad kindly eyes and a snuffy gray-brown mustache to a holy man from whose lips came words of wisdom, and of comfort, and of hope.

The store was always closed on Rosh Hashanah and Yom Kippur. Mother put on her best dress. If there were any Jewish visitors in the town at that time they were invited to the services and to dinner at some hospitable house afterward. In our household the guests were likely to be a couple of traveling salesmen caught in the town on that holy day.

    ᴖᶳ IN SETTLEMENTS that were sparse and scattered, isolated individuals and families often lost contact with Judaism and fell away; only a few, like Dr. Fred Cahan of Meadville, Missouri, managed to hold on alone.

CHILLICOTHE, MISSOURI. *Oct. 3, 1884.* Dr. Fred Cahan of Meadville, this state, was buried here in the Jewish cemetery on the evening of August 30th. The deceased was about thirty-five years old, a native of Kentucky, and a graduate of the Louisville Medical College. He came to Meadville some years ago and entered upon the practice of medicine. He soon built up a large and lucrative practice, which he had to give up on account of failing health, and opened a drug store. He was the only Jewish citizen of the place and had made for himself and his religion during all these years a most excellent record. He died there on Tuesday morning, August 26th, and there being no Jewish burial ground at Meadville, he was buried temporarily in the City Cemetery. The Rev. J. V. Willis, a Christian minister, read the Jewish burial service. On the thirtieth his remains were taken to this place where they were buried in our Jewish cemetery toward evening. Nearly all the Yehudim closed their stores in honor of the departed.

The American Israelite

    ᴖᶳ EVEN AS EARLY as 1870, there was an enormous difference between being the only Jew in a little town like Meadville and being a part of a Jewish community like the one in St. Joseph, where already there was a congregation to belong to, with a temple and a rabbi, and Jewish affairs to go to like the wedding that year that made front-page news.

January 13, 1870. Interesting as marriages always are, we have never yet had one which attracted half the attention that did the marriage at the Temple Adath yesterday afternoon of Mr. B. A. Feineman of Kansas City and Miss Bettie H. Binswanger of St. Joseph. . . . The bar, the mercantile interests, the church, the press—in fact, every rank and class of society were represented. There was a perfect crush of silks and satins and a blaze of diamonds glittering in the pale light of the evening.

At precisely quarter to five the choir opened with a voluntary composed for the occasion by Prof. Behr. The whole party reached the altar and arranged themselves in order around the semi-circle when the Rev. S. Kaufman addressed them a short welcome. After he had finished, the sublime strains of Haydn's celebrated Grand Chorus rang out from the choir.

Miss Mary Hyde sang the beautiful solos in a style that we have never heard surpassed. Prof. Behr with the violacello and Emil Hahn at the organ both executed their parts in their usual elegant taste, and Mr. A. Kaufman on the violin added much to the beauty of the rendition of the piece by his admirable executions on his instrument.

The worthy Rabbi then delivered to the young couple a brief but appropriate address. At the conclusion of the ceremony a blessing was invoked upon the newly married pair by the Rabbi, and then the Grand Hallelujah Chorus was sounded forth by the choir. We have heard many beautiful pieces of music rendered in St. Joseph, including those of the Mendelssohn Quintette Club, but we have certainly never heard anything more sublime than the rendition of this piece.

After the newly married couple had received the congratulations of hosts of friends, all sat down to one of the most magnificent suppers that has ever been prepared in St. Joseph. Two immense tables extending the full length of Kirschner's large hall, and a third extending across the end of it, literally groaned under the immense weight of the good things that had

Portland's Temple Beth Israel, built in 1864.
Oregon Historical Society

Children's Purim party, Temple Beth Israel, Portland, 1898.
Oregon Historical Society

been prepared. Turkies, ducks, geese, chickens, meats of all kinds and prepared in every way; beautiful pyramids flanked on every side by elegantly frosted cakes, pies, confections, candies—everything that the daintiest epicure could desire.

The conclusion of the feast was the commencement of the proposal of appropriate sentiments. Col. Wm. Ridenbaugh offered the following: "Kansas City and St. Joseph—may they ever be fairly and firmly united as to-night." Mr. Feineman gracefully responded that while Kansas City and St. Joseph were rivals commercially, their social interests and relations were identical, and he should heartily welcome and ever cherish the fair daughter of St. Joseph as the bride of Kansas City.

After all had feasted heartily, the beautiful notes of Prof. Rosenblatt's splendid Brass Band began to discourse sweet music and hundreds of merry feet were soon circling in the mazes of the dance. And from that time on until the first streaks of day began to tint the Eastern horizon the merriment continued unabated.

The St. Joseph Gazette

PALESTINE, TEXAS. *October 2, 1885.* Rosh Hashanah and Yom Kippur were duly celebrated here. The Jewish business houses were closed with but one or two exceptions. Services were impressively delivered at Library Hall by Mr. M. Winner, assisted by Mr. Philip Unger.

The Home Social Dramatic Club, composed almost entirely of Israelites, has been organized and will commence rehearsing at once.

All the Jewish merchants who have been East to purchase their stocks are home again.

The Social Season will soon begin here, then there will be plenty of fun for everybody.

The American Israelite

JEWISH-CHRISTIAN RELATIONS

"AIN'T YOU A JEW?"

1900. In the wilds of Tennessee a mountaineer who had just 'sperienced religion at a camp meeting was coming down the road when he met a peddler. "Say," said the converted Tennessean, "say, ain't you a Jew? I never seed a Jew but I calkalate you is one."

The peddler modestly answered the question affirmatively, ignorant of the results.

"Put your pack down," said the Tennessean. "Now I am going to knock hell out of yer," and he proceeded to do as he had threatened.

"What you hit me for?" said the peddler.

"What fer?" said his assailant, "what fer? You crucified our Lord, that's what you done."

Then the Jew explained that it had occurred nearly nineteen hundred years ago and that he had absolutely nothing to do with it.

" 'Scuse me," said the mountaineer, "I'm sorry I beat you. I was told up there at the camp meeting that the Jews had crucified the Lord and I calkerlated you was one of the men that did it. I never heard of it before today."

The Jewish Ledger

WHILE IN EUROPE the Christian myth of the Jew as a demonic figure persisted throughout the nineteenth century, in America it was not unusual for Christians either to have no preconceptions of Jews or to find in them those very qualities that they longed for most in themselves. So it was in the world of Louis Bromfield's *The Farm*, a novel of pioneer life set in a transplanted New England village in Ohio in the mid-nineteenth century.

If you were aware of anything which set the Jews apart from yourself, it was a difference in tradition, for the rich, colorful, sensual tradition of the Jews was doubly exotic against the thin, meagre background of that transplanted New England town. As a child, Johnny knew that the Jews observed Saturday as their Sunday and that on Friday nights some of them placed candles in the window, and he knew, too, that in one or two of the

Jewish houses which he entered there was a richness which elsewhere one seldom encountered—a richness of food, of custom, of music, of books, of hospitality. One never encountered that strange atmosphere of emptiness, of thrift, of barrenness which was so prevalent in the Town. . . . When one went to play in a Jewish house one found it filled to overflowing with warmth and kindliness. One never left without receiving a gift, sometimes a worn toy to which you had taken a fancy, sometimes a bouquet of flowers for your mother, sometimes a piece of *apfelstrudel,* still warm from the oven and rich scented with spices. . . .

IN SHARP CONTRAST with Bromfield's account are Mark Twain's memories of the treatment of Jews in Hannibal, Missouri, during his growing years there in the 1840s. Perhaps Twain was in a satirical mood when he wrote that the first Jews in town made "such an awful impression among us" that discussions took place over the question: "Shall we crucify them?" However, he also notes that anti-Jewish feelings were freely expressed both in the Sunday School he attended and in the local newspaper, where accounts of Jewish merchants taking advantage of non-Jews appeared frequently.

The childhood experiences of Edna Ferber and Fannie Hurst, who grew up in the Midwest fifty years later, were further complicated by the frequently held belief among Midwestern Populists in the 1890s that Jews were responsible in one way or another for the world's economic woes.

On Saturdays and on unusually busy days when my father could not take the time to come home to the noon dinner, it became my duty to take his midday meal down to him. . . . This little trip from the house on Wapello Street to the store on Main Street amounted to running the gauntlet. I didn't so much mind the Morey girl. She sat in front of her house perched on the white gatepost, waiting, a child about my age, with long, red curls, a freckled face, very light green eyes. She swung her long legs, idly. At sight of me her listlessness fled.

"Hello, sheeny!" Then variations on this. This, one learned to receive

Ottumwa, Iowa, where Edna Ferber spent her formative years.
Library of Congress

American Jewish stereotypes. From an 1872 issue of Harper's Weekly.
Museum of the City of New York

equably. Besides the natural retort to her baiting was to shout, airily, "Red Head! Wet the bed!"

But as I approached the Main Street corner there sat a row of vultures perched on the iron railing at the side of Sargent's drugstore. These were not children, they were men. Perhaps to me, a small child, they seemed older than they were, but their ages must have ranged from eighteen to thirty. There they sat, perched on the black iron rail, their heels hooked behind the lower rung. They talked almost not at all. The semicircle of spit rings grew richer and richer on the sidewalk in front of them. Vacant-eyed, they stared and spat and sat humped and round-shouldered, doing nothing, thinking nothing, being nothing. Suddenly their lackluster eyes brightened, they shifted, they licked their lips and spat with more relish. From afar they had glimpsed their victim, a plump little girl in a clean gingham frock, her black curls confined by a ribbon bow.

Every fiber of me shrieked to run the other way. My eyes felt hot and wide. My face became scarlet. I must walk carefully so as not to spill the good hot dinner. Now then. Now.

"Sheeny! Has du gesak de Isaac! De Moses! De Levi! Heh, sheeny, what you got!" Good Old Testament names. They doubtless heard them in their Sunday worship, but did not make the connection, quite. They then brought their hands, palms up, above the level of their shoulders and wagging them back and forth, "Oy-you, sheeny! Run! Go on, run!"

I didn't run. I glared. . . .

Edna Ferber

A chain of us girls were walking arm in arm in the bricked schoolyard at recess.

Suddenly one of them—I recall her name, Hazel Thompson—sang out: What religion is everybody? I'm Lutheran! Instantly the line took it up like a singing regiment. Left foot, right foot, each girl snapping out in turn: Lutheran, Catholic. Baptist. Lutheran. Presbyterian. The exception was the girl at the far end. Me. I opened my mouth to speak in turn, but no sound came. I opened my mouth again, in the silence that had fallen, unloosed my encircling arm from the girl next to me and stood apart. Suddenly I had become different.

That night at the dinner table I asked a difficult question.

Is being Jewish one's religion?

Certainly, said Mama with prompt sureness. Why do you ask such a question?

Can you be the Jewish race and be Lutheran or a Catholic the way you can be American and also be a Lutheran or a Catholic?

Of course not.

Why not?

Because you can't.

But why?

Ask your father.

Papa began to moralize. That's a mighty difficult question, Fannie, and I'm glad you are thinking about such matters. I hope you say your prayers nightly. Always be proud of your religion.

I wasn't. It was difficult to be what no one else was, even though it was never talked about.

Your mother and I aren't as observing as we might be. I think the time has come, Rose, when we should join the temple and Fannie attend Sunday school.

I don't intend to join the temple and be stuck in the back pew so I can see my rich relatives up front. Besides, aren't you the one who always says you can say your prayers as well at home as in temple?

A child should have religious training.

But I don't want to join the temple, Papa, I hastened to intervene. I can learn Bible history at school if I want to. I was just asking . . .

Since you are a great reader, Fannie, I am sure your teacher or the librarian can give you books on the subject. I don't feel competent to answer your question, except to impress upon you that the Jews are both a race and a religion, and you are both.

I'm an American.

Fannie Hurst

Noted American author Fanny Hurst. The daughter of a St. Louis shoe manufacturer, Fanny was already a successful writer when this picture was taken in St. Louis in 1914.
Library of Congress

~§ THOUGH FAR FROM UNUSUAL, overt displays of anti-Semitism were nonetheless inimical to the official—institutional—conception of the Jew in America as a distinctive, recognizable figure with an established place in society which entitled him, at the very least, to fair and courteous treatment from his Gentile peers. On the basis of this belief, the celebrated nineteenth-century Protestant clergyman Henry Ward Beecher took a congregation of self-righteous Yankee businessmen to task for treating Jews as though they "need be ashamed, in a Christian republic where all men are declared to be free and equal."

Is it that they are excessively industrious? Let the Yankee cast the first stone. Is it that they are inordinately keen in bargaining? Have they ever stolen ten millions of dollars at a pinch from a city? Are our courts bailing out Jews, or compromising with Jews? Are there Jews lying in our jails, and waiting for mercy, and dispossessing themselves slowly of the enormous wealth which they have stolen? You cannot find one criminal Jew in the whole catalogue. It is said that the Jews are crafty and cunning, and sometimes dishonest, in their dealings. Ah! what a phenomenon dishonesty must be in New York! Do they not pay their debts when it is inconvenient? Hear it, O ye Yankees! Was there ever any such thing known on the face of the earth before? Is it true that they live on that which you throw away? What a miscreant a man must be that is so closely economical! Is it true that they can make money where you go to bankruptcy? Shame on you!—not on them. Is it true that they have many among them who are untrustworthy? I suppose they must be the only people on God's earth, any portion of whom are not trustworthy! Now, I suppose there are Jews that are sometimes tempted to the devil; I suppose there are crafty men among the Jews; but I believe that for their numbers there are fewer such men among them than among us, and that of men of high and honorable dealing with enormous interests at stake, of trustworthy men in the administration of affairs, they have more in proportion to their numbers than our own or any other race-stock, in this or any other land.

11
Secular
Influences

LODGES, CLUBS, SOCIETIES

~◊ In the old world the synagogue served as a center for educational, philanthropic, and social activities. It was a tradition carried on in colonial America that persisted until the 1830s. Only then did Jewish communal life begin to expand beyond the boundaries of the synagogue as independent clubs and societies of every character and description came into being. Often the first of these were philanthropic organizations formed by native American Jews in response to the needs of a rapidly growing immigrant population. As for the immigrants, they were soon forming non-synagogue-affiliated organizations of their own which, much like the Masonic organizations on which they were modeled, provided a meeting ground for young shopkeepers and clerks in search of sociability outside a religious framework. The Independent Order of B'nai B'rith was one such organization. Founded by a group of German Jews in New York in 1843, by 1860 the order had more than fifty chapters throughout the country, which provided its members with fellowship as well as mutual insurance benefits.

In keeping with the age-old tradition of Jewish self-government, local B'nai B'rith lodges often functioned as unofficial courts of law where disputes involving members were resolved and unethical behavior condemned.

MINUTES AND CORRESPONDENCE OF DENVER LODGE, NO. 171, INTERNATIONAL ORDER OF B'NAI B'RITH

July 26th, 1876. . . . When Euphrates Lodge of Memphis first made inquiry of Denver Lodge in regard to the character, standing and habits of Jos. Gottlieb, Denver Lodge found itself in a dilemma. On the one side, Joseph Gottlieb did not enjoy a good reputation and without ever having been charged publicly or convicted of any serious offense against morality, a number of the Brethren of Denver Lodge were convinced that he was not worthy to be readmitted to the Order. On the other hand, the friends of Mr. Gottlieb, and he has such in the Lodge, claimed that he had reformed and was striving to lead a better life and that it would be unbrotherly and uncharitable to refuse him assistance when he showed an earnest

A German gymnastic society in Los Angeles to which many Jews belonged. These societies were founded on the idea of equality. Every gymnast was admonished to "bear in mind that man is the main thing, and that Christian, Jew or Mohammedan is a matter of minor importance."

desire to correct former grave mistakes. A very protracted and heated debate resulted in . . . a motion to recommend him for readmission.

Euphrates Lodge in consequence reinstated him and made him a brother again. Shortly after his reinstatement, Bro. Gottlieb made application for his third degree. In the meantime new developments arose in regard to his . . . furnishing, supporting and superintending houses of prostitution which made it evident that he had not and was not intending to become a better man and brother.

Deeming it inadvisable to advance him still further in the Order, Denver Lodge wrote to Euphrates Lodge to withhold for the present the granting of any application for higher degree. . . .

Exercise in brotherhood: Judah Magnes (last row on left) with his Oakland, California, high school baseball team, c. 1892. The first ordained rabbi born west of the Mississippi, Magnes went on to become the first chancellor of the Hebrew University at Jerusalem.

Judah L. Magnes Collection, Western Jewish History Center, Judah L. Magnes Museum

January 14, 1877. The following charge was received and read:

Brethren:

I desire it my painful duty to bring charges against a Member of our Lodge, Bro. L. Fleisher. The fact of the Matter is as follows:

After I have been unfortunate enough to lose my Business by fire some insinuation was made staining my character, but it was proved before a legal Court I was not guilty. After that transpired Brother Fleisher accused me before the Insurance agent being Guilty of Arson and not being successful in that, and now goes and brings false Witness against me and makes them swear that I have bought of him the shelving and counter that was in the Store at the same time that I have rented his store for fifty one ($51.00) dollars and now brings suit against me before a Justice of the Peace for the sum of Sixty ($60.00) dollars . . . but as I have lost my books and Papers he is trying to take advantage of me. I most respectfully ask this Lodge to take action in this charge.

Fraternally Yours,
Isaac Eppstein

The above charge was referred to the following committee—Bros. Pisko, Schayer, Hattenbach, Lowenstein and Anfenger.

February 11, 1877. Moved and Seconded that Bro. Fleisher be exonerated from all charges brought against him by Bro. Eppstein, also that it is the sense of this Lodge that Bro. E. did not bring said charges with malicious motives. Adopted.

⤳ IN 1868, B'nai B'rith established an orphan asylum in Cleveland. The following tribute, written twenty years later to commemorate the com-

B'nai B'rith's Cleveland Jewish Orphan Asylum, which for some sixty years sheltered Jewish youngsters from every section of the country.

pletion of a newer and larger building, appeared in *The Menorah*, a widely read B'nai B'rith publication in the late nineteenth century:

OUR JEWISH ORPHAN'S HOME

Back from the street, within a wreath of bowers,
   A stately mansion rears its lofty wall;
Bright sunshine falls in flecks and golden showers;
   Birds twitter in the waving tree-tops tall;
And Peace, methinks, doth keep her watch before it,
   Her snowy banner waves above its dome;
And Love and Charity do hover o'er it,
   For 'tis our newly-finished Orphan's Home.
Miriam Del Banco

Presidents, past and present, of the Portland, Oregon, section of the National Council of Jewish Women.
Oregon Historical Society/Jewish Historical Society of Oregon

*Members and friends of the Denver
section of the National Council of
Jewish Women (NCJW) on their way
to a kosher picnic, 1895. Organized
in 1893 at the Chicago World's Fair,
by 1896 NCJW included sections in
fifty American cities and two in
Canada. Among its activities were the
establishment of Jewish study groups
for its own members, Sabbath schools
for children, and a network of
immigrant aid facilities for women
and children that won recognition
from the U.S. government.*
Rocky Mountain Jewish Historical Society, Beck
Archives, Center for Judaic Studies, University of
Denver

◄§ BY THE TURN OF the century, a B'nai B'rith lodge in a far-flung place
like Portland, Oregon, often provided its members with the best entertainment in town.

PORTLAND, OREGON. *September 2, 1908.* One of the best entertainments
ever given by a local organization was that by the entertainment committee of Theodor Herzl Lodge, I.O.B.B., last Tuesday evening, consisting of
a continuous vaudeville show which included 9 numbers and lasted until
11:30 p.m. All but two numbers were rendered by members of the lodge.
P. Besserman outdid himself with an excellent recitation followed by a
characteristic story. Leo Shapirer officiated at the piano in his usual excellent manner, rendering two original selections. Al Hoppe delighted the audience with two selections on the cello. Dr. Geo. Rubenstein delivered in
French and English a selection from Hugo's *Les Huguenots*. Si San-
drowsky rendered two vocal selections which were well received. Phono-
graph records of selections by Sirota formed one of the most interesting
attractions of the evening. . . . Mr. Lerner's imitation of a Spanish dance
proved exceedingly interesting and added materially to the comedy of the
sketch. About 350 were present. The Ladies' Auxiliary were the guests of
the evening.

The Jewish Tribune

◄§ IN ADDITION TO forming their own fraternal organizations, German-
speaking Jews in America participated with German-born Gentiles in a
wide range of social and cultural activities. "Often," notes Jewish histo-

rian Henry L. Feingold in *Zion in America*, "they became the principal cultural agents of the new communities. They led the theater groups, glee clubs, gymnastic and literary societies which richly embroidered the cultural life of the German immigrants. Sometimes it seemed as if German Jews were more anxious to sustain German culture in America than their Christian brethren."

MILWAUKEE. *c. 1870.* On yesterday the various local lodges of Sons of Hermann joined in a memorial celebration of the Cheruskers' victory in the Teutoburger forest. About 800 blue-eyed sons joined in the procession from Miller's Hall on West Water Street to Quentin's Park where an address, picnic and ball were the order of the day. When the lodges reached the Park, Rev. Dr. Eppstein of the Temple Bne Jeshurun was introduced to the assembly as the orator of the day. The rabbi spoke with great earnestness and fervor, and his remarks at times elicited rapturous applause. He addressed the Sons in German, and his speech was substantially as follows:

"We are Germans by tongue; Germans by the will of reasoning our way onwards; Germans by the avowed determination to develop our mental faculties; Germans by the desire to seek knowledge and wisdom and foster them; Germans by uniting in social life; and Germans by assisting each other in times of need. By using the name of Germany's noblest son, we

The German Turnvereine, or physical-culture club, of Cincinnati, 1850. "Jews make their appearance among the rank and file and even among the leaders of the German gymnastic societies" —Turnzeitung der Cincinnati-Turngemeinde, 1851
The Cincinnati Historical Society

Scene from a Young Men's Hebrew Charity Association entertainment, Chicago, c. 1900.
Young Men's Hebrew Charity Association, Special Collections, University Library, University of Illinois at Chicago

Tableau featuring members of Chicago's Young Men's Hebrew Charity Association,
c. 1900.
Young Men's Hebrew Charity Association, Special Collections, University Library, University of Illinois at Chicago

wish not to express the idea to our fellow citizens that we will remain Germans bound by the state. We are members of this great republic, and such we will remain; hundreds of our ranks have fallen upon the battlefield of the South, in order to support the government, and no doubt hundreds of our ranks would this very day offer life and health to our adopted fatherland would it be necessary. We are Americans, but German Americans who are willing to amalgamate the good which we have brought from Europe with the good which we have found here. The name of Hermann shall be unto us the means to unite and live together for weal and woe."

Formalities over, the sons sought the shady retreats of the grove and enjoyed themselves in social intercourse. In this way the day was agreeably and profitably spent by the order and its friends. A feature that created considerable interest among the members of the local lodges was the beautiful flag to be presented to the most popular lodge, the choice to be made by ballot. The vote resulted as follows: Bne Brith, 480; sons of Hermann, 394; Harugari, 63; Druids, 96; Odd Fellows, 12; Knights of Pythias, 78. The flag was presented to the representatives of Bne Brith and was received amid great applause.

The Milwaukee Sentinel

Milton R. Hart, a Chicago Standard Club member in good standing, c. 1900.
Courtesy of The Standard Club

෫ "DISGUISE IT AS WE MAY, the extent of licentiousness indulged in by many of our young men is truly appalling; it is notoriously known that they are among the most liberal patrons . . . of infamy and vice," observed an appalled reader of *The* [San Francisco] *Hebrew* in 1864. Such conditions, coupled with a desire among German-born immigrants after the Civil War to improve their social standing, led to the creation of Jewish social institutions like the Standard Club of Chicago. Organized in 1869, when Chicago in many ways was still as rough and unruly as any frontier city, the Standard Club took pride in describing itself as an institution dedicated to "the mutual improvement of members, to be effected by social gatherings, dramatic entertainments, the establishment of a library, and pursuit of such other purposes as are generally considered to be within the scope and object of a club."

A gentlemen's club in imitation of the English model, the Standard Club endeavored to provide a group of up-and-coming Florsheims, Harts, Shaffners, Marxes, Sulzbergers, Spiegels, and Schwabs with an imposing setting for eating, card playing, and other socially acceptable activities. Located on Michigan Avenue, the original building was an impressive structure of brick and granite. On the top floor was a grand ballroom ornately decorated in keeping with the decor of the finest ballrooms of the era; in the basement were billiard tables and a bowling setup; and on the main floor was a dining room serving food as good as any in the city, a bar with every brand of liquor one could think of, and a lounge for card playing and small talk, generally in German. Of special significance was the right of each member to bring ladies, including wives and daughters, as guests—something looked upon in a Western city at this time as a sign of real social progress.

Inside San Francisco's Concordia Club.
Courtesy of the California Historical Society Library/Bernice Scharlach

New Year's Eve at The Concordia Club, 1897.
Courtesy of the Concordia-Argonaut archives/Bernice Scharlach

By the late 1870s, such clubs flourished in every significant center of Jewish population in the country, often to the detriment of Jewish organizations of a more serious nature. "We have a super-abundance of so-called Jewish social clubs in this city," noted a correspondent to *The Hebrew* in 1878, "while there is but one Jewish Literary Society in our midst, which stands on a rather weak footing owing to the slim encouragement."

DENVER. *Oct. 31, 1881.* The Standard Club will soon occupy their new building at 412 and 414 Curtis Street between 19th and 20th. The club house has a fine exterior of brick, two stories in height. The second story is ornamented with tiles decorated in mosaic designs. At the top of the facade of the building is the word "STANDARD" set in white stone.

The hall, provided with the finest and best appointed stage in Denver outside of the Tabor Opera House, will not only be used for private theatricals, etc. but will be rented to responsible and respectable amateur and professional theatrical and musical people on nights when it is not used by the club.

The reading room will be provided with all the leading papers of the country. A library fund has already been started and a large amount raised. . . . The institution, as is well known, is controlled by the Jewish people of this city.

Rocky Mountain News

⋑ EVEN BEFORE the turn of the century, prosperous Jewish immigrants and their families began moving to the outskirts of large cities, where they built elegant houses surrounded by spacious lawns and tree-shaded lanes. So many flocked to Avondale, a suburb of Cincinnati, that it soon became known as "New Jerusalem." An exclusive enclave of "old" Jewish families, Avondale had its own clubs, its own salons, its own societies, all of which endured well into the twentieth century. In the following selection, a writer for the *Jewish Daily Forward* ventures inside and comes up with a number of astute observations. The year is 1927.

Their religion is an attempt to isolate themselves from the common run of Jewish humanity. It stresses the belief that the Jews have been chosen to serve as an example to others. This exclusive character and select nature of the Jewish mission is quite in keeping with the idea of their personal and social superiority over the rest of the Jews.

Religion, however, is the weakest point of these Jews, just as worldly culture is the strongest. For being liberals and professing ideas which logically lead to a denial of all church forms and dogmas, they content themselves with a dry, perfunctory and rational formula of religion, devoid of all emotionalism, symbolism or mysticism.

Their Jewishness is no deeper than their religion. They admit that they have neglected to study and appreciate their Jewish groundings. But this they say is compensated for by their genuine interest in cultural development and social progress which are the common property of humanity and tend to the mental and spiritual assimilation of all mankind. Assimilation therefore has no terror for them. Yet strangely enough these very assimilationists who care so little about Jewishness and share practically none of the hopes and aspirations of the Jewish people persist in maintaining their Jewish identity. They stubbornly refuse to intermarry with the Gentiles and thus disappear as a racial entity. Thus the most extreme of our assimilationists have developed an attitude that is in a sense nationalistic.

But time is their greatest enemy. It is working on the side, if not of the Gentiles, then certainly of the Jews hailing from eastern Europe. These Jews are closing in upon the walls of the aristocratic Ghetto. Some of them are already inside its walls. New blood will soon be needed to keep the life-forces of the Ghetto-dwellers going. And that can come only from those brought to our shores by the most recent waves of immigration. When that happens American Jewry will witness the complete transformation and perhaps disappearance of the finest, most exclusive, most respected and most cultured Ghetto in the United States.

NEW WAYS OF LEARNING

By THE TIME Jews started coming to America in sizable numbers in the 1840s and '50s, the dominant conditions of American education had already been clearly defined as public, entirely free, and universal, with no religious instruction and no public funds for religious schools. As a result, any group that wanted full-time schools of its own had to compete out of its own resources with public schools. For a while, German-Jewish immigrants tried competing by establishing full-time religious schools in New York, Albany, Cincinnati, Chicago, Boston, Baltimore, and Philadelphia; however, such attempts invariably failed. One reason may have been that there was simply not enough money among most immigrants to provide their children with a formal education of any kind. Such was certainly the case with the Blooms of San Francisco, a family of urban Jewish pioneers who needed every penny their son Sol, the future congressman, could bring home from the California Brush Factory just to keep going.

The selection that follows is taken from *The Autobiography of Sol Bloom.*

Six days a week, rarely taking time off (and then nearly always to improve an opportunity to make extra money), I worked at the California

LEFT, *San Francisco-born prizefighter Joe Choynski, who fought Gentleman Jim Corbett for twenty-eight rounds in 1889—and lost.* RIGHT, *twenty-five years later and still friends—Joe Choynski (right) with Gentleman Jim Corbett (center) and Jack Wilson at Atlantic City, August 15, 1914.*
Mrs. Mortimer Fleishhacker, Jr.

Brush Factory. After hours I would peddle violets to theatregoers; on certain evenings I would sell newspapers, and for a time I had a regular job in the folding room of the *Chronicle*, which then was housed at the corner of Bush and Kearny Streets. This was a morning paper, and the bulldog edition started running through the press around nine in the evening; after coming off the press the papers had to be folded by hand, and I was one of the kids who performed that tedious but necessary task. On Sundays I usually worked too, at least during part of the day, peddling novelties and souvenirs to picnic and excursion crowds.

At this time I was also trying to make up for my lack of schooling by spending at least an hour daily reading and learning to write. My hours were so irregular that I seldom had any meal but breakfast with my family; I did most of my studying while eating lunch at the factory and again during my late supper at home. This unavoidable peculiarity of mine brought peculiar results. In the evening I learned Hebrew by reading, under my mother's tutelage, the Old Testament, and English through the perusal of *The Argonaut*, a local theatrical review. . . .

During the noon hour (actually a half hour) at the California Brush Factory I studied arithmetic, only this activity was in no sense a task, for I pursued it incessantly throughout the day, noting lot numbers, prices, costs, and practical calculations of all sorts that had to do with the manufacture of brushes. Before many months had passed I knew the exact specifications of every article we manufactured. I knew the precise number of holes that had to be drilled in every brush block, the amount paid at piecework rates for every single operation, and the selling price for each item, whether it was sold over the counter at retail or in job lots to dealers. With no conscious effort I made up imaginary orders in my head, and I could have set down almost instantly the price, the gross profit, and the net after wages and operating costs had been deducted. It was fun to toss the figures around while my hands were occupied with some dull routine job.

One day in the early part of 1880, about the time of my tenth birthday, Ben Figer called me into his office and began to ask me questions. He found that I knew not only specifications and costs but piecework rates—in other words, that I was able to figure payrolls.

"On Monday, Solly, I want you to start working in the office," said Mr. Figer.

At the end of the week, I found that my pay had been raised to three dollars and a half. If that seems small, even for a ten-year-old, I can give my assurance that it loomed very large in the life of a family that paid six dollars a month for the rental of their house. It was not until some months later, after I had been raised another dollar, that we felt secure enough to move from Brannan Street to a larger and more comfortable house around the corner on Sixth Street, where we had to pay ten dollars.

⚓ IN CONTRAST WITH Sol Bloom's experience is the following account by Samuel Kline of life in a Denver schoolhouse.

I attended school [in] a typical one-story, one-room school house just one block from where we lived [in Denver in the 1870s]. Our teacher, James V. Griffin, a man of but ordinary education, had his hands full. Corporal punishment was still in vogue, and when on occasion he was goaded to desperation and attempted to administer a birching to some of the larger boys, they wouldn't have it. He was no match for some of these husky fellows of sixteen or seventeen. They would wrest the switch from him and hold his hands the while they winked and made grimaces to the class. . . . One morning (it may have been St. Valentine's Day) Mr. Griffin found a letter on his desk which he tore to pieces. My curiosity aroused, I collected them carefully and that evening pieced and pasted them together. It was a comic valentine and bore this doggerel:

When birch in hand
You wildly stand
And bid the scholars tremble,
A very hog
O Pedagogue
Do you then most resemble.
To your own hide
Should be applied
That bunch of birch, old fool.
Bluster and noise
May frighten boys
But cannot teach a school.

⋙ EVEN FOR German-speaking Jews who could afford private religious instruction, the study of Judaism was likely to be considered far less important than secular considerations. So it seemed to I. J. Benjamin, a Polish *maggid* (itinerant preacher) who traveled to America in 1861 and subsequently wrote at length about his experiences throughout the country.

The mother of a little girl, a good-hearted, rather well-to-do woman, let us say, will try to impress on the young spirit of her child as much good instruction as ever she can. This private care lasts until the child is five. Then the child, it is obvious, must be sent to a public school or, what is more respectable, to a so-called "institute." Accepted by the "institute," the child begins the usual course of studies, makes the acquaintance of girls of other religions and has friends among them, and may well, without any objection or even realization of its significance, kneel during morning prayers which are arranged for those of other faiths, before classes begin. After school she studies her lessons for the next day or, like all children, plays. Upon going to bed or arising in the morning, she very likely recites for her mother some Hebrew or English prayers; but as for Judaism, the child experiences nothing and knows nothing. . . .

Her good parents have increased their wealth during these ten years and have taken the commendable resolution that their daughter should not forget all that she has learnt. Accordingly, they provide her—to complete her education—with a music teacher, a singing-teacher, a drawing-teacher, and a governess to continue the practice of French; the latter also teaches her how to sew, knit and the like; and, to give it all a final touch, they assign a teacher to give her Hebrew lessons. He must make her acquainted with the alphabet of a language in which, as a child, she should have lisped the name of God.

⋙ IF YOU WENT to "Hebrew School" at this time, chances are you learned more German than Hebrew.

B'NAI ISRAEL CONFIRMATION PROGRAM
COLUMBUS, OHIO

PART I   Prayers, Songs, Readings, Examinations

PART II   Declamations
          Miss Ida Meyer: "Good Night"
          Miss Fannie Hirschberg: "The Rainy Day"
          Misses Fannie Lehman, Sarah Hart, Tillie Steinhauser: "What
              I Love to See"
          Miss Jennie Mendel: "Rules of School"
          Master Moses Goodman: "Die beiden Hunde"
          Master Herman Hirschberg: "Kaiser Karl"
          Master Leo Philipson: "Moses und der Todte"
          Miss Bertha Strauss: "Das eitle harterzige Fraeuline"

PART III Dialogues
          "The Irishman from Cork"
          "David and Goliath"
          "The Irish Servant"

PART IV   A Song by the Scholars
          Distribution of Prizes

Ohio State Journal, March 23, 1880

IN THE SERVICE OF THE PUBLIC

Moses Alexander, governor of Idaho from 1915 to 1919. Alexander's election in 1914 created a sensation among Jews back east. "If you go west," counseled Abe Cahan from the pages of the Jewish Daily Forward, "be proud and frank, and above all be a Jew like the governor of the state of Idaho."
Library of Congress, Bain Collection

⤚ᵹ THE OPPORTUNITY FOR immigrant Jews in nineteenth-century America to play a meaningful role in public life is amply illustrated by the career of Abraham Jonas. Born in Exeter, England, in 1801, Jonas arrived in Cincinnati eighteen years later to join his brother Jonah, the first Jew to settle there (see p. 127). Both were among the incorporators of Cincinnati's pioneer synagogue in 1829. A year earlier Abraham was elected to the Kentucky State Legislature. After serving four terms, Abraham moved to Illinois, where in 1842 he ran for the state legislature and won by a wide margin. Around this time he struck up a friendship with the future representative from Springfield with whom in 1856 he was chosen by the Illinois State Convention as a presidential elector on the Fremont ticket. During 1858, and again in 1860, Jonas campaigned for his Springfield friend and was subsequently awarded the postmastership in Quincy.

In the following letter written during the heat of the 1860 presidential campaign, candidate Lincoln informs brother Jonas of his position regarding the anti-Catholic, anti-foreigner, "No Nothing" faction whose votes Lincoln needed to get elected.

July 21, 1860. . . . I suppose as good or even better men than I may have been in American or Know-Nothing lodges; but in point of fact I never was in one in Quincy or elsewhere. I was never in Quincy but one day and two nights while Know-Nothing lodges were in existence and you were with me that day and both those nights. . . . That I never was in a Know-Nothing lodge in Quincy I should expect could be easily proved by respectable men who were always in the lodges and never saw me there. An affidavit of one or two such should put the matter at rest. And now a word of caution. Our adversaries think they can gain a point if they force me to openly deny the charge, by which some degree of offense would be given to the "Americans." For this reason it must not publicly appear that I am paying any attention to the charge.

Yours truly,
A. Lincoln

Joseph Pulitzer, the half-Jewish son of a Hungarian grain dealer, during his days as a St. Louis journalist.
Library of Congress

◦◦§ ON THE WHOLE, Jews reacted to the great issues of the day exactly as their neighbors did. However, there were also those, like Ernestine Rose, who played an important role in molding public opinion. The daughter of a Polish rabbi, Ernestine came to America in 1836 and soon "commenced lecturing on the evils of the existing social system, the formation of human character, slavery, the rights of women, and other reform questions." Traveling far and wide, Ernestine addressed gatherings in New York, Massachusetts, Ohio, Michigan, South Carolina, and elsewhere. The following selection is taken from one of her many popular speeches, which were widely circulated in pamphlet form throughout the country.

WHAT IS IT TO BE A SLAVE?

It is utterly impossible for us, as finite beings, with the utmost stretch of the imagination, to conceive the depth and immensity of the horrors of slavery. I would that, instead of speaking and listening to-day, we would all sit down in perfect silence, and each and every one of us ask ourselves what is it to be a slave? . . . We have the evil among us; we see it daily and hourly before us; we have become accustomed to it: we talk about it; but do we comprehend it—do we realize it—do we feel it? What is it to be a slave? Not to be your own, bodily, mentally, or morally—that is to be a slave. Ay, even if slaveholders treated their slaves with the utmost kindness and charity; if I were told they kept them sitting on a sofa all day and fed them with the best of the land, it is none the less slavery . . . for what does slavery mean? To work hard, to fare ill, to suffer hardship? That is not slavery. For many of us white men and women have to work hard, have to fare ill, have to suffer hardship, and yet we are not slaves. Slavery is not to belong to yourself—to be robbed of yourself. There is nothing that I so much abhor as that single thing—to be robbed of oneself. We are our own legitimate masters. Nature has not created masters and slaves; nature has created man free as the air of heaven. The black man and the white man are equally children of nature. The same mother earth has created us all; the same life pervades all; the same spirit ought to animate all. Slavery deprives us of ourselves. The slave has no power to say, "I will go here, or I

Polish-born abolitionist Ernestine Rose.
The Schlesinger Library, Radcliffe College

will go yonder." The slave cannot say, "My wife, my husband, or my child." He does not belong to himself, and of course cannot claim anything whatever as his own. This is the great abomination of slavery, that it deprives a man of the common rights of humanity, stamped upon him by his Maker. . . .

❧ UTAH'S FIRST Jewish governor, Simon Bamberger, was one of many German-born Jews who became active in municipal politics in America around the turn of the century. Born in 1845 in a small town halfway between Frankfurt and Heidelberg, fourteen years later Bamberger joined a brother in Ohio before heading west to St. Louis and then on to Cheyenne, where he worked for a while managing a store at the "front" or building edge of the Union Pacific Railroad. From there Bamberger moved on to Ogden, and then to Salt Lake City where, in partnership with a Mr. Briner Cohen, he purchased a hotel which soon became the headquarters for miners who came to the city to do business.

The following account of Bamberger's subsequent activities is from Juanita Brooks's *The History of the Jews in Utah and Idaho.*

From talking to his clientele, Bamberger became interested in mining, and in 1872 purchased stock in the "Sailor Jack Mine" in the Big Cottonwood District. Later he took stock in the "Centennial Eureka" mine, from which he made a small fortune. For the remainder of his life Bamberger had mining interests in Utah and in DeLamar and Pioche, Nevada. He also built railroads, opened up a recreational center, and was involved in many other business ventures.

Governor Simon Bamberger of Utah with a group of Mormon constituents.
Special Collection, University of Utah Library, Salt Lake City, Utah

Bamberger's introduction to public life came in 1898 when he was selected to fill a position on the Salt Lake City Board of Education. Here he served for five years, during which time he demonstrated a genuine interest in the welfare of both teachers and pupils. In 1903 when it seemed that the schools would have to close early for lack of funds, Bamberger took the lead in collecting money, first by donating one-tenth of the total amount needed and then soliciting among his friends. The money was soon raised.

In the election of 1902 the Democrats drafted Bamberger to be their candidate for the state senate. The Mormon segment of the population—a very large majority—had very strong feelings about intoxicating drinks, and the fact that Bamberger himself did not use liquor or tobacco, that he did not employ men who did, that he had been engaged in enterprises that would build Utah and build character in its citizens—all counted heavily with the voters. Simon Bamberger was the only Democrat in Salt Lake County to be elected to any position that year, and he by over 2,000 votes.

For the next several years Bamberger turned his attention to his mining interests. These took him often to the East, and it was probably from friends there that he was encouraged to enter politics again, this time on a national level. In 1915 he declared himself available for the Democratic nomination for United States senator. However, after much consideration he decided instead to try for the position of governor of Utah. At the Democratic State Convention held in Ogden, 18 August 1916, Bamberger was elected to be their candidate on the second ballot. That he was nominated by B. H. Roberts, prominent Mormon historian, would mean much to the Mormon voters. Another prominent Mormon, John Henry Evans, circulated a leaflet in which he reminded all members of the laboring class that this man had shown his interest in their welfare by his acts as a legislator, that he always treated his employees as men and not as "hands," and that there had never been any need to strike among them. Even more effective was the word, not printed but carefully and skillfully passed around among the Mormon congregations, that Simon Bamberger was one of those who, during the time of their bitter persecutions, had written a letter to Congress protesting taking the franchise from Mormon men because of their religious beliefs. When the election returns came in they showed Bamberger elected by a plurality of 18,980 votes.

Edward S. Salomon, from a photograph by Matthew Brady. General Carl Schurz described Salomon as "the only soldier at Gettysburg who did not dodge when Lee's guns thundered, but stood up, smoked his cigar and faced the cannonballs." In 1870 Salomon was appointed governor of the Territory of Washington by President Ulysses S. Grant.
Library of Congress

Old ways in a new world: Denver's dean of cattle buyers, Robert Lazar Miller. Born in Vilna, for many years Miller raised cattle in Lithuania. Until he was ninety-six he continued to ride his horse daily at Denver's union stockyards. "I will live to be an old man," he would say, "because I work and because I like to work. On my horse I am a young man."

Rocky Mountain Jewish Historical Society, Beck Archives, Center for Judaic Studies, University of Denver

PART THREE
EAST EUROPEAN JEWS
1880-1930

 FOR HUNDREDS OF *years Jews had lived in eastern Europe under conditions of extreme poverty and persecution. Forced to reside within a prescribed area called the Pale, they scraped by as best they could as petty traders and craftsmen in small towns known as* shtetlach *where generations of oppression inevitably left their mark in physical debility and social paralysis. Yet they created a remarkable culture for themselves wherein religion suffused every aspect of life. Quite cut off from the ideas and achievements of the Western world, it was nonetheless a culture infused with moral and spiritual intensity. By the mid-nineteenth century a secular Yiddish culture came into being as more and more Jews turned their attention from the Talmud and the Mishnah to the works of Kant and Rousseau, Marx and Hegel, Tolstoy and Turgenev. Already the Jews of eastern Europe had begun abandoning the* shtetl *in large numbers for towns and cities in Lithuania and Russia, Galicia and Poland, where many found employment in clothing factories as seamstresses and tailors, while others went on to America.*

 When Yiddish-speaking Jews began coming over in large numbers in the 1880s, they settled either in the Lower East Side of New York or in other concentrated areas of population where there existed a growing demand for sweatshop workers in German-Jewish-owned establishments, or they moved on to smaller cities and towns, as well as to isolated settlements throughout the country. It is those Jews who went (metaphorically speaking) beyond the Lower East Side who concern us here.

 There are, of course, obvious similarities between the Jews of the Lower East Side and those who moved on—ethnic custom, Yiddish as the language of daily life, a sense of "distance" or "difference" regarding American society as a whole. But there are also significant differences.

 First, Lower East Side Jews were primarily wage earners, while Jews who went beyond were far more likely to be aspiring entrepreneurs willing to settle wherever they could go into business for themselves. So it had been in the seventeenth century and so it would remain in the twentieth for thousands upon thousands of Jewish retailers, wholesalers, and manufacturers whose descendants today make up the bulk of

America's Jewish population in the Midwest, the Far West, and the South.

Second, Yiddish secular culture, crucial to the daily experience of a Lower East Side laborer, generally had to be "imported" outside of New York. If Yiddish culture traveled at all from the American center, it came in the form of books and newspapers received by mail, an occasional lecture by a visiting Yiddish writer, or performances from time to time by a Yiddish theatrical company on tour. As a result, the immigrant Jew's dependence on the English language for information and entertainment was far greater in such places than it was "back east." This contributed to a greater degree of cultural interchange between Jew and Gentile. Thus, Jews who went west became in certain respects worldlier than their Lower East Side counterparts who, by and large, lived and worked among people pretty much like themselves.

Third, the hold of the synagogue was by no means weak on the Yiddish-speaking Jew who went west; for far from looking upon religion as an "opiate of the masses" (as the Lower East Side laborer with socialistic inclinations tended to do), he often found guidance, comfort, and even protection as a member of a shul, or synagogue, particularly in smaller cities and towns where Jews were expected to conform to the extent of expressing a belief in God and attending religious services "like everyone else."

Many of those who went west struggled to keep what they had brought with them from the old country while at the same time learning from, yielding to, criticizing, and embracing the new. There is, we are persuaded, much to admire in the conscious efforts of our mothers and fathers, our grandmothers and grandfathers, to progress to the point of providing their ainiklekh *(offspring) with a sense of the best of both worlds.*

Maxwell Street area, Chicago, c. 1900.
Chicago Historical Society

12
Beyond the
Lower East Side

SLUM AND GHETTO

≈§ WITH THE ONSET of a new wave of pogroms in czarist Russia in 1881, the Great Migration of East European Jews to America began. So many came so quickly that by 1905 there were over 600,000 Jews in New York alone, with another 200,000 in Philadelphia, Boston, and Chicago. In each of these cities—the Lower East Side in New York, the West Side of Chicago, Boston's North End, downtown Philadelphia—a Yiddish-speaking ghetto emerged,* a separate world actually, a city within a city, with a vibrant culture overshadowed by a sweatshop system plagued with wretched physical conditions, extreme exploitation, and shamefully low wages. Small wonder that people like Frieda Gass Cohen's parents dreamed of leaving the Lower East Side for the unknown world of the American West.

My parents came to the United States in 1909 from that part of Russia which became Poland after the First World War. My father was eighteen at the time, and left because he was unwilling to serve in the Russian army. He and my mother married a month prior to leaving the country and escaped from Russia through the woods where people were waiting to lead them into Germany and then to a port to come in steerage to the United States. They were chased through the forest by dogs and police but they made it. They went to New York rather than to another port because my father had an uncle living there. My mother and father stayed in New York for two years. He and his brother who came over with him tried at first to make a living by fixing roofs, and then by working in sweat shops as tailors. He and my uncle would get up around 5 in the morning and cover a distance of around fourteen miles on foot so that they would not pay the five cents on the subway. When they would get to the place where they

---

* See *World of Our Fathers* (Harcourt Brace Jovanovich, 1976) and *How We Lived* (St. Martin's/Marek, 1979), both by Irving Howe and Kenneth Libo.

were supposed to work, they would sometimes wait three or four hours and then be told, "Sorry, no work today," and have to pick up their sewing machine (you had to own your own sewing machine in those days) and go back home.

Their first child was born in New York—a boy. After the baby was bitten by a rat in their tenement flat, they decided to leave the filth and the dirt of New York and go where they could see some sky. At that time my mother had a sister, Mrs. Lorber, who had emigrated to Portland because her husband was a European cabinet maker and B. P. Johns was bringing woodworkers to Portland to work in their plant. So my mother and father left New York, much to the chagrin of my father's uncle who was so afraid that my father was coming to a land of no Jewish knowledge, certainly to a much smaller Jewish community, and they were very fearful of what would become of them in this vast expanse out here.

My mother, like other Jewish housewives, packed a week's worth of food, and she and my Dad and an infant and my uncle came across the country with all their belongings while she was pregnant and settled in South Portland in 1911. My parents found Portland much more to their liking than New York, and that of course is why they stayed here where all the surviving five children were born. All attended school and all lived here until our various marriages. At that time upper South Portland housed practically every Jewish person in the city. There were very few that lived any place else. It was really a teeming place for the Jews. They never had to go out of the neighborhood to do their shopping. All of their Jewish grocery stores were in the area as well as two or three kosher meat markets. The children grew up in the neighborhood and more or less stayed in the neighborhood all the time they were growing up.

ᏭᏥ WHILE MOST Yiddish-speaking immigrants who traveled west (or south) went on their own, others went as a result of the efforts of organizations created by German Jews ostensibly to relieve overcrowded conditions in the East. The Industrial Removal Office was one such institution. Organized in 1901, it sent tens of thousands of Jewish immigrants to towns and cities throughout America. Five years later the Galveston Plan was instituted by the wealthy German-Jewish financier Jacob Schiff to divert Jewish emigration from New York, Boston, Philadelphia, and Baltimore where "the great congestion prevails, to the great American 'Hinterland,' where a constant demand for labor exists. . . ." Deeply concerned with the proclivity of ghettoized Jews to hold on to the old ways, Schiff hoped to hasten the dissolution of the Eastern ghettos by making it easier for newcomers to settle elsewhere.

The following recollection is by one of many East European Jewish immigrants who came via Galveston to Omaha, and stayed.

There was a committee, a Jewish committee, to deliver you to the United States, a society. So we paid in I don't know how much (after all, I was just a kid) to come to Galveston, Texas.

The same committee furnished a meal or two and then asked us do we have any relations where we want to go. Well, we didn't know anybody. All my father knew was that New York was a city and California a state. So my father mentioned New York.

"We can't take you to New York," they told him. "There are too many of our people there already."

"How about California?"

Well, they said the same thing—we can't take you there. My father looked around on the map and saw Omaha, Nebraska. So they took us to Omaha where a committee of one met us.

"The first thing you have to do," this man said, "is to have a house." So they found us a house, a little dump, with no stove, no dishes, no nothing. Anyway, we told the committee man how much money we had and he took us to a second-hand store and we picked up a few things—a bed, a second-hand stove—everything was second-hand. But the stove didn't work and we had so many bed bugs we couldn't sleep.

We went back to the committee man and told him, "Give us our money back and we will return the furniture."

"Oh," he says, "We don't do business that way in the United States. You bought it, you bought it." And that was that.

Joe W. Gotsdiner

&ᖚ ATHOUGH NOT AS crowded as the Lower East Side, ghettos outside New York shared many of the same problems, not the least of them being a built-in resistance on the part of the community at large to recognize its own culpability in creating and perpetuating slum conditions. This and other shortcomings are reflected in the following front-page newspaper article written by William Allan White when he was a twenty-five-year-old reporter for *The Kansas City Star.*

February 21, 1893. McClure Place is right in the heart of Kansas City between McGee and Grand Avenue on Nineteenth Street. It consists of three rows of one story tenements, running from Nineteenth to Twentieth north and south, with sixty-six houses in each row and three rooms and a hallway in each house. The houses are "attached" and each tenement is provided with a water pipe and sink, and improved sanitary sewer connections. Two of these rows open on a narrow court perhaps twenty feet wide and the third row faces McGee. There is a front and a back door to each house and one window in the kitchen and one in the front room.

About three-fourths of the apartments are occupied and the population of the neighborhood is composed almost entirely of Russian Jews. Policeman Whitsett, who has the place on his beat, says that 500 is not an extravagant estimate of the number of people housed in McClure Place. The ground space covered by the residence is less than a block. In the houses themselves dirt rules unquestioned despite the water facilities. In the chief sleeping room of the tenements there is no window. And in the summer the rooms running through the building from east to west are arranged so that the north and south winds that are most frequent in this latitude never stir the foul and putrid air.

To look down the court in the evening at sundown there appears to be at least a thousand children all under 8 years swarming in the filthy, muddy area. These children all look alike, and all are uniformly dirty. A reporter for the *Star* visited many of these apartments yesterday and in all asked one question: "Where do you dump your slops?" In only one case was the answer other than "in the alley." The one exception was, "Out in front." There are two main alleys to McClure Place, each running the entire distance of the block north and south from Nineteenth to Twentieth. These alleys are a trifle more than six feet wide, and only for a few moments at high noon does the sun get an opportunity to dry the reeking pools of filth.

The police officers say that the occupation of the male population of McClure is largely that of rag pickers and junkmen's assistants.

❧ THE FOLLOWING DESCRIPTIONS of Pittsburgh and Cincinnati are by the Yiddish poet and dramatist Peretz Hirshbein and the Yiddish journalist and socialist Borach Charney Vladeck.

As you approach Pittsburgh you might think that the earth has been burning there since ancient days, pouring forth smoke for generations, and that the people who appear from time to time in the billows of smoke, in the light of the yellow flames, are occupied in extinguishing the fire which began because of God's curse.

But in reality it was people who lit the fire and who watch over it day and night so that it should not be put out. And the ring of steel which echoes from the flickering darkness is the gigantic noise of a hammer. There they are forging happiness for the country. Whole forests of high chimneys pour smoke into the world and from time to time a golden yellow flame torn from the chimneys drives the billowing smoke away. But soon the flame is suffocated in thick black smoke.

Pittsburgh is the mother who feeds a large part of the world with steel and iron. She cooks and burns the raw material in her belly so that the world will be able to digest it.

I spent five days in Pittsburgh and for five days I did not see the light of the sun. It sometimes seemed to me that a dark nightmare had descended upon the entire region. As for the people who were then around me, I do not see them as they were, but in the reflection of my oppressed mood and of my heated brain.

Peretz Hirshbein, translated from the Yiddish by Eleanor Robinson

January 7, 1912. Cincinnati is the birthplace of our President [William Howard Taft]; its citizens have named her the Queen City. As a frump is to a queen so is this city to our President.

In the center all is dark, dank, uninviting. Its health matches its appearance. It is second only to New York as a breeding ground for tuberculosis.

In 1911 alone more than one thousand people died of this dread illness.

The moral welfare of the city is hardly better. Last year there were 157 murders, twice the average of a city its size. In addition, prostitution is rife and appears to be the foulest in the nation.

West of Pennsylvania, Cincinnati has the oldest Jewish community in the nation. Its Russian Jewish population, however, is only a few decades old. Numbering 30,000 people, half of them live in the worst neighborhood in the city. It is nothing short of a ghetto, a Tenderloin, a marketplace for cheap labor.

Walking through this area is a heartache. Everywhere you look you see misery, sloth, dirt. As Jews continue streaming in, the filth becomes even worse, with young men squandering their days in saloons and young women turning to prostitution in ever-increasing numbers.

Borach Charney Vladeck, *The Jewish Daily Forward*

⤐ FEAR MUST HAVE stalked the hearts of these Jews as they struggled to make a place for themselves in the wilderness of an Omaha or Kansas City slum or a Pittsburgh or Cincinnati ghetto. Foreigners without a land of their own to go back to or a language or culture known to non-Jews, they often had no one to turn to for assistance of any kind but themselves.

The following selections are taken from the memoirs of Abraham Bisno, the first president of the Chicago Cloak Makers' Union—one of the forerunners of the International Ladies' Garment Workers Union.

. . . We got to Chicago in about July, 1882, and rented three rooms over at Canal and Twelfth streets. There were then cloak factories in Chicago who sent work out to tailors to be made up at home. They furnished the cloth, cut and trimmed, and the samples to be copied, and we would carry the cloth home to make up there. These were the first sweatshops established by the Jewish immigrants in Chicago. I was to do the machine sewing, Father the hand sewing, with Mother's help, and Brother, who was very incompetent in tailoring, was doing odd jobs such as pressing and a little sewing. . . .

We lived in a building in the rear of a lot, above a stable. The building in front contained a store downstairs, where there was a rag shop. The owners lived upstairs. Both front and rear buildings and the yard were full of rags, junk, rats, and vermin, besides manure from the horses. It was an old frame shack, dilapidated beyond belief. Our first years of immigrant life were not happy for us. . . .

At fifteen I first began to learn to read. Both in Jewish and English . . . Jewish I learned when there was no work and a man who peddled Jewish stories loaned them out weekly to me for five cents a week. He persuaded me to learn to read these stories because they were great romances. An agent of a Jewish newspaper got me to subscribe to a weekly paper. In those years I was very ignorant. I practically knew nothing of what was happening in the United States, and outside of my work and my family experiences, knew very little. . . .

MISS MORCELLE MORT JN, French,
933 Customhouse Street.
Annie Robert, French, 933 Customhouse.
MISS EMMA JOHNSON, French,
923 Customhouse Street,
Vina Allison, French, Earl Nestley, French, Rosa Orlanos, Solidad Avaiga, 923 Customhouse.
MISS ALICE CHAPINS, French,
1021 Customhouse Street.
Pansy Martin, Malvina La Blanc, Anetta Smith, Lizzetta Duran, 1021 Customhouse.
MISS BLANCH WHITE, French,
1416 Customhouse Staeet.
Loula Bell, 1416 Customhouse.

The JEW COLONY. "J."
MISS FANNY GOLD, "J",
812 Bienville Street.
Jessie Clark, Jennie York, Gussie Smith, Minnie Green, 812 Bienville.
MISS MIDGET ASHLEY, "J",
814 Bienville Street.
Jennie Hickey, "J", Lizzie Wemer, Becky Schwartz, 822 Bienville.
MISS ROSIE BLANCHARD, "J",
829 Bienville Street.
Lizzie Simons, Etta Cohn, 829 Bienville.
MISS JENNIE GOLDSTEIN, "J",
923 Bienville Street.
Ida Meyers, "J", 823 Bienville.
MISS IDA ARONSON, "J", 826 Bienville.
Ollie Meyers, "J", 826 Bienville.
MISS LENA FRIEDMAN, "J",
830-832 Bienville Street.
Rose Smith, "J", 830-832 Bienville.
MISS LAURA MILLER, "J",
833 Bienville Street.
Minnie Lonergan, "J", 833 Bienville.

A page from The Blue Book, *a guide to New Orleans's red-light district, 1907. The terms "The* JEW COLONY" *and "J" were dropped from later editions, some say because it was bad for business.*

A boy friend of mine took me to Halsted and Harrison streets, where a company of actors played stock drama. Here, for ten cents, on a Saturday afternoon, our one day of rest, I would enter a new world. I waited all week for Saturday to come around. I knew how to read English only slightly. I learned it very slowly. Occasionally I would decipher advertisements distributed on bills in our neighborhood. On these ads there were pictures of the wares to be sold and so I was able to associate the English word with the picture next to it.

. . . I had a sex urge for years before, but was never able to buy satisfaction before. Now, with money, I was able to have my first experience in a whore house. This first experience left such a mark on my mind that I visited those places regularly once or twice a week after. . . . The problem with me was not whether I ought to do it at all, but the opportunity to get a chance at it was my difficulty. . . .

I remember once I . . . made friendly approaches to a Jewish prostitute who was very young, not more than seventeen, who liked me very much, and whom I liked very much. I told her so. She then naturally asked me the same question that most of the girls asked, "Will you come again?" I said, "I might, and might not." . . . I finally formed the resolution to be loyal and to visit the same girl regularly. For several months I did until I found in the same house some girl that attracted me from the point of view of desire very strongly and I broke my resolutions. I was very much worried and felt a great sense of contempt for myself.

✒ WHILE THE JEW from eastern Europe who remained a laborer found little incentive to leave the big city ghettos of the East where his major source of employment, the sweatshop industry, was most heavily concentrated, it was not unusual for a person thinking of going into business for himself to travel to cities and towns farther south and west where greater opportunities existed for self-employment. Thus, in New York in 1900, there were more Russian Jews working in sweatshops than in all other fields of employment combined, whereas in Chicago at roughly the same time only one in eight Russian Jews were sweatshop workers, and even they were already dreaming of going into business for themselves in burgeoning Polish and Lithuanian neighborhoods (far larger than any in the East) where Gentiles accustomed to doing business with Jews in Europe felt all the more comfortable doing so in a foreign land. Bisno comments:

Among the peddlers and small store-keepers in Chicago, the rag peddlers form the largest group. Most of them are very poor and hard working; they earn a precarious livelihood. I am told there are about 2,000. Very few of their children follow in their footsteps; most work in stores and some in factories. . . .

Some 95 per cent of the peddlers own their own horse and wagon; some of them, however, are so poor that they live partially on charity. The majority work in the city, but a portion ply their trade in the neighboring country towns.

Third Street, Milwaukee, c. 1905.
Local History & Marine Room of the Milwaukee
Public Library

*Inside Max Trushinsky's grocery
store, 622 North Tenth Street,
Milwaukee, 1916. Sam Trushinsky,
the little boy on the left, recalls this
photo being taken by a traveling
photographer who charged just 25
cents for his services.*
Local History & Marine Room of the Milwaukee
Public Library

Closely related to the above are the old iron dealers and peddlers. In fact, a rag dealer will often also deal in old iron, furniture, clothing, etc. But the old iron dealer is a sort of merchant, buying and selling iron and metal only. There are several hundred of these. Their earnings are higher than those of the rag peddlers. A number own their own homes and are quite prosperous. In their case the children are generally absorbed into other occupations.

The iron yard owners are a prosperous class. Some are reputed to be worth over $200,000. They do an extensive business. They are generally former iron or junk dealers.

Dealers in old bottles buy their goods from the rag peddlers. Their business has been developed only in the past few years. . . . Of the fruit and market peddlers there are about 1,000. Their average earnings are very low. . . . Some develop into grocery store keepers. Very few of the children of these follow the occupation of their fathers.

ঙ্গ GERMAN-SPEAKING JEWS, who had arrived earlier and were by now integrated into American society, tended to look upon Yiddish-speaking immigrants as socially and culturally inferior to themselves. As a result, two distinct communities developed—one German, the other East European—with little connecting them at first aside from organizations set up by the Germans to provide their *ost-Judische Glaubensbrüder* (East European Jewish co-religionists) with food, clothing, housing, and employment. Conflicts frequently arising between insensitive donors and overly sensitive recipients only widened the gulf.

Later, more sophisticated organizations were created by Germans together with eastern Europeans (who brought with them a rich institutional life) to take care of such problems as malnutrition, education, and Americanization. Yet no matter how much was done, poverty and suffering did not go away. Even after the peak years of East European migration, sizable numbers of immigrant Jews and their families remained in desperate need of assistance.

MINUTES OF RELIEF COMMITTEE OF THE
OMAHA JEWISH WELFARE FEDERATION

1924. Man, woman and three children. Man peddling bread. Son 16 feeble-minded, unable to hold on to a job. Woman sick, needs necessities for the sick room which husband is unable to supply. Asks for $3 per week help until husband can provide.

Man, wife and three children. Peddler, unable to earn living due to injuries to leg two years ago. Recommend he be placed on relief budget until work can be found for him.

Man, wife and three children, ages 12, 10 and 3. Peddler incapacitated by injury to jaw by horse. Says "Horses and children are starving." Gave him $5 for feed for horses so that he may provide for children. Recommend that he temporarily be placed on the relief budget until the weather permits him to peddle.

Man, woman and nine children. . . . Man peddling out of the city and has not been heard from for a week. Upon woman's request sent one ton of coal. Child, age 5, took sick Saturday, and upon recommendation of Dr. Grodinsky, sent to Wise Memorial Hospital. Family income at present insufficient.

Girl 22. Two years in this country. Mentally and physically not well. Subject to deportation. Relatives in this city either cannot or will not help her any further. A brother in Chicago is willing to take care of her. Recommend that she be sent to Chicago, if consent is granted by Chicago Federation.

Man, woman and seven children. Tailor. Oldest boy, 21, earning $15 weekly; two girls ages 17 and 15 earning each $6 per week at the Rialto Theater. Man asks his rent be paid. Recommend the request be denied.

Man, woman and three children, boys aged 5, 6 and 8. Woman just returned from the National Jewish Hospital. Father and husband repeated deserter, now also returned. The children have been boarded out by us. Woman requests aid in reestablishing the family. In order to do that, work for the husband is necessary. He now ekes out a precarious existence doing odd jobs whenever he is hungry.

Deserted woman and three children, ages 9, 11 and 14. Woman received $7.50 per week from us in addition to rent, fuel and clothing. A position in a home is awaiting the oldest child, Jennie, aged 16, but mother refuses to let the girl work. Investigating Committee recommends that woman's allowance be reduced.

Man, woman and seven children, oldest age 14. Man milk peddler, unable to earn enough for the support of the family. Our allowance is $5 per week, plus coal. Recommend that allowance be continued till spring.

◆§ AS MUCH AS East European Jews resented German Jews for their condescending ways, at the same time they admired them as fellow Jews for their achievements and their sacrifices. When on April 15, 1912, the sinking of the *Titanic* took the lives of the philanthropist and department store owner Isidor Straus and his wife, Ida, who chose to die beside her husband rather than save herself with the women and children on the lifeboats of the sinking liner, Yiddish-speaking Jews both in America and in Europe did not hesitate to commemorate Ida's heroism.

CHURBN TITANIC

Ot shteyen, mit veyen,
Di toyznde in noyt.
Un veysn az shtoysn
Vet sey tsum grunt der toyt.
Ot shrayt men: "geyt sey retn
In shiflech, froyen, shnel,
Nit vagn zol batretn
Kayn man gor yene shtel."
Doch hert a froyen zele
Vos ken a zog ton dan:
"Ich gey nit fun der shtele,
Ich starb do mit mayn man. . . ."
Zoln ern kleyn un groys,
Dem nomen *ida shtroys.*

THE *TITANIC'S* DISASTER

There stand in agony
The thousands helpless,
Knowing that death will cast them
To the bottom of the sea.
There is shouting: "Rescue them,
Into the boats, women, quickly!
Let no man dare to step into the boats
Meant for women and children."
Yet listen to one woman
Who dared to say just then:
"I'll not move from this spot,
I'll die here with my husband. . . ."
May young and old honor
The name of Ida Straus.

S. Smulewitz,
translated by Ruth Rubin

American Jewish Historical Society, Waltham,
Massachusetts

SMALL-TOWN PROSPECTS

THE LIFE EASTERN European Jewish immigrants found and made for themselves in small towns in America was significantly different from the life of those who clustered in city slums and ghettos. Initially, these Jews were far more self-conscious than their big-city brethren of being strangers, outsiders in an English-speaking world, with no *shul,* no *rebbe,* no circle of friends, no organized Jewish community to find comfort in or to turn to for guidance and support. Yet for some there were also compensations.

THE COMPLAINT OF THE COUNTRY JEW

February 10, 1905. Ten weeks ago Mr. David Blaustein, superintendent of the Educational Alliance, determined to see at close range some of the communities of the West and South, in order to secure a fresh impression of conditions. He traveled to Madison, Wisconsin, thence through Kentucky, through Alabama, Mississippi, down to New Orleans, and north to Washington, returning to New York after an absence of about six weeks. In an interview with Mr. Blaustein he gave a few impressions of his trip.

Q. What is your opinion generally speaking of the small communities of the West and the South?

A. I had not traveled far in the West before I was struck by the signs of dissatisfaction among the Jews of the smaller cities. Almost everywhere I found small Jewish groups prospering in every outer circumstance, but hiding beneath their prosperity a regret for life in larger cities. The desire for a more Jewish social life; the longing for the more interesting, more diversified life in the larger centers of Jewish population; the impression that slowly and inexorably their traditions and customs are doomed to disappear, to be replaced by alien conceptions of life—was in one form or the other the general complaint of all the provincial Jews I met and conversed with.

In spite of their prosperity, they feel the need of some social or religious center where they can live in harmony with their ideals. The Jew has always had an ideal. He may be a socialist: then his ideal is the co-operative commonwealth. He may be an individualist: his ideal will then be a superior society where right shall be recognized without law. He may be an orthodox Jew: his ideal then is to bring up his children with knowledge of the Law in which they shall live and have their being. But what shall they do—these dwellers in humdrum cities, without social centers, without a press, without the means of communicating with their fellows, untouched by those waves of progress that reach the larger groups first, and, finally, after much buffeting, approach the outer limits of society?

The Jew will not live in the sameness of the provincial city, eating and sleeping, eating and sleeping, from day to day, with no other interest in life, as so many other people do. He desires something more, and therefore, though his worldly possessions be assured, he finds that he would rather live within the walls of a large city, in spite of its discomforts, risking his life in the fierce competitive struggle, rather than live in comparative ease and somnolence in the small country town.

The Russian Jews especially felt themselves beyond the pale of civilization. They read the Yiddish papers eagerly, but that does not bring them any nearer to the source of Jewish life. The Jewish young man or woman, natives of their cities, are becoming commonplace citizens, and knowing this, the parents feel that they were unfair to their children to keep them away from opportunities.

I spoke with one man in a southern state. He was making a good living, but was discontented. He said: "If I were in New York, evenings I could go to the Yiddish theaters, hear a lecture, visit people whose conversation I enjoy, join a club, enter some movement: in short, after working hours be a man. Here I have nowhere to go, no one to talk with, nothing to do with myself."

The American Hebrew

꿁 HOW SUCCESSFUL were other small-town Jewish merchants in "fitting in?" According to Harry Golden, in the South they were indeed quite successful.

There have been cases where the schools have been closed an hour earlier for his funeral, in some towns they have flown the flag at half-mast on the Court House building, and high school trophies have been presented in his memory. . . . The editor calls on him as part of his regular rounds, and once a month or so, he may ask the Jewish merchant for a "wise saying by one of the rabbis" for the editorial page. . . . The Jewish merchant takes his regular turn as president of Rotary, Kiwanis, Lions, Retail Merchants, Country Club, Chamber of Commerce, and Community Chest. And it is precisely his "conspicuousness" that gives him a security and allows him a relaxation that would be the envy of his co-religionists of the metropolitan areas of the North, or for that matter, of the larger urban centers of the South.

◆§ So it was in Harry Golden's South, as well as in Medford, Oregon, where the following incident took place.

We used to close on Rosh Hashonah and Yom Kippur. I had a sign, "We open after sunset." At that time the sun went down 6:30 or 7 o'clock. At about 7 when I came down to the store there was a line of about 15 or 20 people.

So one guy says to me—he happens to be a Jewish salesman—"Did you advertise a sale?"

"No," I says, "today is Yom Kippur."

He didn't even know what was Yom Kippur.

There was another fellow who came over to talk to me. His name was Applegate from the country around there. He spent with me about $300. "We came into Medford about 10 o'clock this morning," he said to me, "and I says to my wife, 'we are going to wait till they open up because if they respect their religion and give up the business for a day, we are going to wait.' "

I did more business that evening than I did on a normal Saturday all day.

Harry Rubenstein

◆§ Just as revealing are the experiences of Isaac Goldstein of Jonesboro, Arkansas, as described by his son Hymie:

Dad made clothes for people like the Falstaff Brewery officials and the owners of the Lennox and Mayfair hotels in St. Louis. He made clothes for Judge Martineau who became Governor of Arkansas. He made Senator T. H. Caraway's suit to go to Washington. He made suits for the best dressed men in Little Rock, Memphis and St. Louis. He also had Cotton Belt and Frisco Railroad contracts to make the uniforms for all the railroad men—conductors, brakemen and porters. One of Dad's good friends was Mr. McGraw who was Vice President and General Manager of the Cot-

Nathan Colman's Coal and Milk Depot, Deadwood, South Dakota, in the days when Deadwood had a Jewish mayor, a Jewish-owned bank, and a Jewish-operated mining company. Nathan Colman, whose name is spelled incorrectly on the awning, is the man in the vest.
American Jewish Archives, Cincinnati, Ohio

Sol (Eye) Berg Men's Store, El Paso, Texas.
El Paso Public Library

ton Belt Railroad. He had a private car on the *Cotton Belt* and Dad and I
used to ride up and down with him. . . .

. . . I remember one time Mayor Herbert Bosler was in the tailor shop
with Chief of Police Charlie Craig. We were making uniforms for the police department and Mayor Bosler told my Dad, "Goldie, you have so
many friends I believe you could go out on the street and shoot a man and
they'd turn you loose." My dad was a 32nd degree Mason, a Shriner, an
Elk and a Colonel on the Kentucky Governor's staff. He was proud to be a
member of these organizations. They meant a lot to him. . . . My father
loved visiting with railroad people. He'd go down and meet the trains
every morning rain or shine, and he'd stay at the shop every night until the
trains came in just to see his railroad buddies. Some of the conductors
when coming into Jonesboro would say, if Dad was on the train, "Jonesboro, Jonesboro, Arkansas—Home of Isaac Goldstein."

ᕗᔓ NOT EVERYONE WAS so lucky. In the following selection, Abraham
Isaacson describes a world in which an established "better class" looked
upon Jews as "foreigners" who were tolerated only as long as they did
what they were expected to do. Yet even here there were compensations.

When I came to Clarksdale, Mississippi in 1913 the town had a population of about five thousand people consisting of an equal number of whites
and blacks. The majority of the white people were farmers and planters
who owned considerable acreage in the country but who chose to live in
the city for the conveniences and advantages that the town offered which
could not be had in the rural districts. Of course those farmers and planters did not do the actual farm work; that was done by Negro labor from
sun up to sun down.

Others in town included doctors, dentists, office holders at the court
house . . . and about twenty five or thirty families of Jewish storekeepers,
peddlers, junk dealers, etc., a few Greeks that had a monopoly on the restaurant and fruit business, also a few Syrian families engaged in peddling,
and a few Italian families engaged in small grocery stores where bootleg
whiskey was the main line and groceries a side line.

The real Southerners were the aristocracy and the others—the "foreign" element—were tolerated as long as they behaved themselves and
acted in a meek manner towards the "Better Class." Of course, at that
time the aristocracy of the town would have nothing to do with the foreign
element, unless there was some competition over some electoral office.
Then the various candidates for that office would come around to visit
those foreigners who were naturalized, but when the election was over you
didn't see them until another election. . . .

Throughout the Western territory where I traveled, I found a good
many good sized towns where a Jew was not to be seen, yet through the
Delta, where I made it to almost each town, village and railway station

during my travels, I found a Jewish family in business in every one of them. The reason for that condition is based on the fact that this part of the country has a larger Negro population than any other part. Moreover, the average Negro has a grudge against the native white man whom he blames for all the bad luck and poverty that sticks to him. As it is, the Negro would rather patronize a store operated by a foreigner than the one owned by a native American. Then again the native white man regards agriculture as his inherited right of occupation and regards storekeeping as a lower occupation fit only for New England Yankees and Jews; hardly any respectable Southern gentleman in those days would stoop down to store-keeping as a means of making a living, and thus that occupation was left to the foreigner—Jews, Chinamen, Italians, Syrians and so on. Occasionally, a native white man who lost at farming by being shiftless would take a plunge and open up some kind of small business, but generally he didn't make any success at it, his competitors having the advantage of more frugal living, sticking out longer hours at the store and selling goods a little bit cheaper.

Also the Negro customer would rather trade with the Jew for there he could bargain for a reduced price and get the satisfaction that he made the storeman come down from the original price. In fact, quite often they did buy their goods cheaper through the bargaining process, and by matching wits with the foreign storekeeper, than if they would have bought their goods from the native American's store.

Jewish Cemetery, El Paso, Texas.
El Paso Public Library

When I came to the Delta, I found out that it was the custom of the majority of the storekeepers to buy goods on credit from the wholesalers, then sell it to the retail trade for cash, pocket the money thus realized from the sales and go broke, that is declare bankruptcy. It was not unusual for a merchant to open up again under his wife's name and then when that name was dragged in the bankruptcy court, they would open again on the name of some other member of the family. That was the condition of the dry goods business when I came to the Delta thirty years ago and was going on until during the last ten years credits tightened up.

≈§ EAST EUROPEAN JEWS were by no means oblivious or insensitive to what was happening to the Negro in small towns throughout the South at this time. The following poem was written by Yehoash (1872–1927), a widely read Yiddish writer in his day, whose lyrics are characterized by a striving for truth and a longing for the power to do good.

LYNCHING

"Father of my soul,
Where can I find You?"

Defiler!
Look at your work—
A black body striped with blood,
A face of pitch with turned-up eyes,
A red, swollen tongue
Between gleaming teeth.

"Father of my soul,
And Master of all bodies,
Where can I find You?"

Blasphemer!
He who trembles
In the blue webs
Of your holy dusk,
He who clouds himself in your tears by night,
In your song by day,
He who shudders in the roe
Of your unborn desires,
He who calls you, tears at you, makes you greater—
Has become flesh,
Has become a black body

With thick lips and matted curls;
And your nails
You have buried in his ribs,
Stuck knives in his breast,
Spat at him, a dying man,
And let him swing
On a tree.

Translated from the Yiddish
by Eleanor Robinson

❧ VERY FEW IMMIGRANT Jews became wealthy during the period of East European migration, and even for those who did, the climb to success was often as slow as it was unpredictable. For E. J. Stern, a New Mexico millionaire, it took close to two decades to get into the right business. The following recollection is from a 1980 interview with Stern in Las Cruces, New Mexico, where, over the years, Stern's generosity and countless good deeds have enriched the lives of thousands of people of diverse cultural and racial backgrounds.

"Our Temple's First Boy Scout Troupe," Congregation B'nai Israel, Little Rock, Arkansas.
Congregation B'nai Israel, Little Rock, Arkansas/ Charles H. Elias

I arrived in New York City in January, 1903 from Hungary with the total sum of $2.50 left over from my journey. The second day I was here I obtained employment with Rosette and Company, a travel agency. Their business was to import foreign citizens to this country. They hired me because I had a background in four foreign languages. My native language was Hungarian. My second language was German. Number Three was French. And Number Four was the Slovenian language. My salary was four dollars a week, and out of that four dollars I had to buy all my necessities and pay for my room and buy my meals.

Now, they had a branch office in Wilkes-Barre, Pennsylvania, and promoted me to five dollars a week to go there. After six months I saved up enough money to pay for my transportation to El Paso. My uncle was there. I thought I could get financial assistance from him to improve my future life. I arrived on a Saturday and the next morning I went to his home and knocked on his door. My uncle came out and discussed matters with me right on the front porch. I spent with him about two hours in conversation, but I was not invited to come in and spend any further time with him.

Hence, I went out and got me a place to stay in a small accommodation hotel at a price of fifty cents a night. The day following the good Lord helped me get a job with a company that was operating a general store. It consisted, Number One, of all food needs for all families, Number Two, all clothing needs for all families, and, Number Three, all medical needs for all families. This concern, the Joe Nation Company, was a very successful operation. They had many ranches of their own and plenty of money.

My first job was delivering purchases made by various families to their homes with a horse and wagon. They trained me and for some reason continued to train me until I obtained knowledge of their twelve delivery routes and eventually was promoted to other jobs. My first one was to train new employees for certain routes that were vacated by other employees leaving the job. My next job was contacting Chinese restaurants for necessary merchandise they were in need of. I remained with that one company for six years, from January of 1904 to 1910 when I applied for a job with the State Insurance Company of Denver and subsequently sold insurance by going with a horse and buggy from house to house, community to community, in southern Colorado and northern New Mexico.

In Trinidad, where I spent some time, I run into a person, a young girl from the State of Nebraska. Her name was Mabelle Lull. We finally got acquainted enough to go to a city on the Colorado–New Mexico border where there was an attorney that had an office to make marriages. Anyway we went there and got a certificate and got married.

Just about six miles north of Trinidad I acquired a small acreage with a house on it and we made that our home for a while. Then we decided, my wife and I, to make a change. So we disposed of our belongings in Colorado and moved to Las Vegas, New Mexico, and with the little money we had we filed on a homestead. At that time you could only file on a quarter

*Olympic Athletic Club boxing match
between Baker and McKenna.
Pueblo, Colorado, December 1, 1911.*
Rocky Mountain Jewish Historical Society, Beck
Archives, Center for Judaic Studies, University of
Denver. Photo reproduced by Gay Lasher and the
May Company, courtesy of May D&F.

section, so we filed on a quarter section, 160 acres, and built a small shack on it. We decided to improve what we could on this acreage, but to do so required some finance and ours was very limited. However, there were two young men in the neighborhood looking for employment. So I employed them and gave them orders for the improvements I wanted on that homestead, and that gave me freedom to continue in my insurance operation.

We stayed on that place up to two years in order to get a property right to that homestead; then we sold it for $2,000. With outside savings we had about $2,600. During that period I had seen a large ad for a general store operation in New Mexico. That brought me to Las Cruces to check on that little store. I contacted the owner, but we could not get together. I guess the main reason was because my finances were so limited. However, I relocated to Las Cruces in 1916 and got myself a job with a downtown store. It was owned by some Jewish operators in El Paso. The store was not operated in a proper manner and they were losing money. I worked for them for about a year and improved the operation very much.

With the savings I had brought with me plus a little I accumulated over a period of a few years I had enough money I felt to go into business for myself, and believe you me that's exactly what I did. I leased some ground in 1920 with an option to purchase and put up a small building for an operation of my own which I called the Popular Dry Goods Company. I operated that store for seven years. Then in 1928 I built a two-story structure which I called The White House. At this time I began developing farmland in the Rio Grande Valley. By using concrete ditch irrigation and employing over fifty farmhands on 1,600 acres I became quite successful.

PEOPLE OF THE SOIL

IT TOOK OVER two thousand years of denial and persecution, restriction and hostility to transform Jews from men and women of the soil into city folk, from a people working their own land to a dispersed population of urban toilers. By the late nineteenth century the transformation was all but complete, and nowhere was the change more striking than in czarist Russia. Yet out of tragedy arose new causes, new dreams—or rather, variations on old dreams—among a new breed of Russian-Jewish intellectuals who yearned for change. Some became revolutionists dedicated to improving conditions at home. Others sought freedom in exile, either in Palestine or America. Calling themselves *Am Olem*, the Eternal People, they talked of forming utopian farm colonies.

One such group arrived in New York in 1882. Before the year was out, most of them were on their way to a colony in Oregon they called New Odessa. In 1883, a hundred or so settlers erected a large two-story building where they lived as one big family. Their goal: to become self-sufficient by raising wheat, oats, beans, and peas on two hundred acres of land. (Expenses were kept to a minimum: when a daily food budget of 5 cents per person rose to 8 cents, the colonists reproached themselves for wasting what little money they had.) Like most other immigrant Jewish farm colonies in America, the New Odessa experiment failed, yet while it lasted a spirit of freedom and happiness prevailed. One of the most festive occasions in its short history was a wedding that took place in 1885.

On Sunday we had been lounging on our beds most of the morning, taking a late breakfast at ten o'clock and going back upstairs to lounge again or to read the philosophers of evolution, of progress, and social emancipation. About two in the afternoon I descended to the kitchen to enquire for dinner. To my surprise I found several of the women very busy making dried apple pies and custards—great novelties, the usual dinner at New Odessa being bean soup and hard baked biscuits. I was told that there was to be a wedding. It was a very sudden affair, a surprise to everybody as well as myself; a young man and woman had made up their minds to enter into matrimony, and it was to be done at once.

There was an immediate bustle and hurry; every man in the community

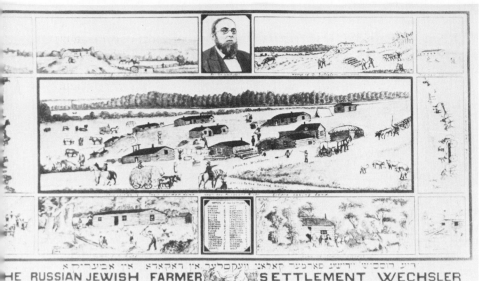

HE RUSSIAN JEWISH FARMER SETTLEMENT WECHSLER
BURLEIGH COUNTY DAKOTA TERRITORY.

A North Dakota Jewish farm colony that failed. Organized in the early 1880s by Judah Wechsler, a Reform rabbi with a pulpit in St. Paul, the colony of roughly fifty East European Jewish families disbanded after a destructive drought in 1886.
American Jewish Archives, Cincinnati, Ohio

tried to find the suit of clothes in which he left Russia. Two or three young girls went into the woods for flowers, and the rafters of the hall, upstairs and down, were soon hung with the flowering branches of the tulip tree. White cloths instead of oil cloths were spread upon the dining table. The pies were inscribed in paste with the initials of the bridegroom and bride.

The brothers and sisters had been gathered a few moments on the benches in the dining room when the bride and bridegroom entered. Both parties were young, perhaps twenty-two; the young man well educated, well read in philosophic and romantic literature, and rather good looking. The bride is noted for her kind disposition, or what might be called her womanliness; but having her hair cut short, her aspect was that of a strong-minded female. She was very nicely dressed, wore a wreath of white flowers, and looked charming enough to make any man happy.

Both the groom and bride were embraced by the associates, the kissing being entirely different from the kissing done on similar occasions by English or Americans. Each in turn took the groom and bride in his or her arms; the lips were pressed together again and again with a long, deep, and almost solemn emotion—such kisses as English-speaking people exchange only at moments of direst tragedy or the most passionate exaltation. These kisses are, I think, peculiar to the Russian Jews: at least, I have never seen other races kiss with such effusion. After the embraces were finished, the groom, giving his arm to the bride, led her to the head of the table where they sat down side by side, facing the company. . . .

When the dishes were washed and stored away, all repaired to the upper room, where the bridal party seated themselves. When all are settled in their places, an associate of the Community steps forward and announces that he will marry the couple again. The serious tones of his voice awe even the children to quiet, and there is a hushed silence in the room when he commences:

THE REFORM ADVOCATE.
("The Jews of Chicago.")

DEVOTED TO

The Jewish Agriculturists' Aid Society of America.

MOTTO AND EMBLEM:

"HE THAT TILLETH HIS LAND
WILL HAVE PLENTY OF BREAD"

Published at CHICAGO 204 Dearborn St.

Vol. XXVII, 14th Year   June 4, 1904.   No. 15.

Youth! dost thou take her as thy bride?
The simple Yes your lives hath tied.
Maiden! shall he thy husband be?
Yes? Then thou ceasest to be free. . . .

The ball is the next thing in order. Alas, the society has no instrumental music. The particular favorite of the people seemed to be the American country quadrille. This was danced again and again, with, it seemed to me, every possible variety of blunder. Altogether the ball was a very rude affair. At quite an early hour, the new couple retired from the scene to the shanty assigned them close to the hall. The ball went on, and the writer went to bed. And when he awoke very early in the morning, the festivities were only concluding, for he saw some of the brothers stealing gently to rest. . . .

The Overland Monthly

◆§ SOMETIMES THE EFFORTS of an individual succeeded where collective enterprise failed. Harry Turnoy's life as a North Dakota farmer is a case in point. A cheese merchant in Russia, one day Harry read in a Yiddish newspaper of a worldwide movement to help Jews like himself become farmers in America. Though his wife pleaded with him not to leave her and the children behind, Harry's mind was made up. He would go to America, and as soon as he could he would send for his family.

From Russia, Harry traveled to New York, and from New York to Chicago, where he visited with a young brother who had emigrated to America several years before. His brother urged him to go into peddling, but Harry would have none of it. Making money, getting rich—that was not as important as showing the world what a Jew could do in America with his bare hands and a little piece of earth to call his own.

The government gave Harry a quarter section of virgin soil in Burleigh County, North Dakota, with the proviso that he live on it, improve it, make it productive. Assuming Harry lived up to his agreement, the land would be his in five years, after which he could leave, rent it, sell out, or stay put.

After filing a claim at the Burleigh County courthouse, Harry set about making it valid by building a crude shack from whatever bits and pieces of scrap material he could find. Then he started to dig a well and build a fence. When winter came and the land lay locked and frozen, he went to the nearest coal mine where he worked until spring. Then back to the land, working feverishly, from daybreak till dusk.

Though Harry had no training as a carpenter, it didn't stop him from doing what had to be done. A few discarded railroad ties served as the framework for a house and barn. With a plow he cut squares of earth, held together by the roots of the tall grass, and made a roof. Out of boards discarded by neighbors he made a floor. He planted a garden, he cleared the fields. And when it was dark he set the dough to rise and kneaded it into loaves to bake the following morning. With his one horse and mule he put in a crop of wheat and oats that first spring.

THE FOLLOWING ACCOUNT is by a Jewish homesteader's wife who also journeyed to North Dakota.

I had never ridden in a wagon. I climbed up on the seat, wrapped my baby in her shawl, and drove off into the unbroken prairies. The road was a rude wagon trail. Here and there we passed a sod cabin or shanty and saw a patch of plowed ground. Toward dark we drove into a buffalo hole. The horses unhitched themselves and my husband, holding the lines, was obliged to follow them as they hurried across the prairie.

It was after midnight when we finally reached Harrisburg. An escort with a lantern saw us to a house built the previous spring. Here I learned to make bread with dried yeast and flap jacks and biscuits and pies. One day a Mr. Mendelson brought in a crate of pork and asked me, a pious Jewess, to cook it. In time I consented.

We had only one near neighbor, the Seligers, another Jewish family. Their cabin was so poorly built that during our first real blizzard they were afraid to spend the night there. Mr. Seliger came to our place and asked if he might have the team to bring his wife and baby, but the storm was such that a team couldn't have found its way.

My husband advised him to keep to the plowed ground which ran from his door to ours. He returned home and late that night came to our place almost frozen. He had let go of his wife and baby for just a bit and had been searching for them since mid-afternoon.

The storm lasted three days. When it cleared mother and baby were found about fifty feet from their house frozen to death. A few days later a sleigh full of men and women came from somewhere. We heated water and thawed the bodies sufficient to fit in a home-made coffin. I remember that beautiful baby to this day. The frost glistened on her cheeks making her look like a wax doll.

That fall my second baby was born. It was in September. The weather turned cold and the wind blew from the north. I was so cold that during the first night they moved my bed by the stove and pinned sheets around it to keep the draft out. And so I lived through my first childbirth in the prairies.

Sarah Thal

◆✦ IN THE FOLLOWING ACCOUNTS of life on the Dakota plains, the Yiddish poet and playright Peretz Hirshbein and the Yiddish novelist Isaac Raboy contrast the world as it is with the world as it should be.

There is no song in the fields of North America, and therefore it is sad there.

The horses drag their heavy plowshares. The farmer walks after them silently, thinking his thoughts, and in silence clods of earth fall beside the plowshares. No songs are sung about the corn or wheat or the seeds that are sewn in the freshly plowed warm earth. No song is heard about the green grass when it peeps forth from the ground. Without song the grain is cut and taken to the barn or threshed in the field. The people go about their work coldly and silently. The hay is scythed from the meadows and dried in heaps and no song is sung. And the apple, the pear and the golden orange hang silently among the green leaves. And when the time comes they are plucked from the trees. The branches are shaken and the fruit falls silently to the earth. They are packed in boxes and carried to cities far, far

Another Jewish farm colony that failed. Established near the tiny village of Cotopaxi, Colorado, in 1882 by Emanuel H. Saltiel, owner of the Cotopaxi Silver Mine, "it was the poorest place in the world for farming," according to Idel Grimes, a seventeen-year-old settler. In order to stay alive, some of the settlers were forced to work in Saltiel's silver mine while others dug ditches for the Denver and Rio Grande Railroad before moving on to Denver, the Dakotas, and California.

Both, American Jewish Historical Society, Waltham, Massachusetts

away. And no one sings about it. They only think about the money.

It is sad in the fields of North America, because there are no women there.

Here a woman's place is in the kitchen or the factory but not in God's blessed field. In this country field work is done by men whose mouths are filled with shag-tobacco. Women know nothing of going about with sickles on their shoulders and looking through the grain to see if their loved ones will appear in the golden sea of sheathes. They do not come into the fields at dawn to ask the wonder flowers if their lovers' hearts still belong to them. They never carry heavy bundles of hay on their heads to the hay stacks where they would feel the glances of young men on their naked feet. There is no love play in the corn fields, and in the wheat fields love does not sing of unhappy hearts. From the threshhold of the farmhouse to the edge of the field is man's dominion. It is he who plants the vegetables for the house, and when they turn ripe it is he who picks them and carries them into the house to his wife who stands by the oven and watches the pots. The man milks the cow and carries the bucket of milk into the house. Mother Earth is in his dominion, and therefore it is sad in the fields for our people.

Peretz Hirschbein,
translated from the Yiddish by Eleanor Robinson

Riding home in a wagon from town, Ike and his boss saw a lot of people coming on foot from the other direction. They turned out to be Indians with their wives and children.

First came the squaws carrying big bundles of bedclothes. Some of them had little children tied with sheets on their backs. Every woman who carried a child on her back also had a bundle on her head.

After the women came the bigger children—girls and boys, all of them dressed alike in long leather coats. Under the coats appeared white linen shirts. The children's feet were bare, as were their mothers'.

Behind them walked the fathers and the young men. They seemed worried with their gloomy faces.

The Indians were walking on the road, but soon they turned off to enter a field where wild grass was growing.

Why did the Indians leave the path, Ike asked himself. Isn't the prairie theirs just as much as ours.

As the Indians went by Ike lifted his hat to greet them, but none of them responded. They gave no sign.

"There goes the Red Peril," said Ike's boss.

Long after this the words "Red Peril" rang in Ike's ears. He could not understand why these peaceful Indians should be looked upon this way.

A whole revolution took place in his mind. Ike began asking himself a lot of questions: Who posed the bigger danger for the country? Wasn't his

Jewish farmer Isaac Roet, Harding County, South Dakota, c. 1910.
American Jewish Historical Society, Waltham, Massachusetts

boss more dangerous than these Indians who had been driven from their land? Why was such injustice carried out against a peaceful people? Why did they have to live on reservations as if they were exiles with no means of communication among themselves, no possibility of leading their own way of life? This was by no means the first injustice Ike had witnessed.

Isaac Raboy,
translated from the Yiddish by Eleanor Robinson

☙ IN 1900, a group of wealthy American Jews founded the Jewish Agricultural Society to help East European immigrants become "free farmers on their own soil." Eight years later the Society began publishing *The Jewish Farmer*, the first Yiddish agricultural periodical in the world, and for a long time the only one. Its objectives were "to provide for the non-English reading Jewish farmer expert advice on agricultural subjects not otherwise available; to supply him with a publication to which he can turn for sympathy and encouragement; to furnish him with a medium for the expression of his feelings and aspirations; to bring him inspiration by keeping him in touch with his fellow tillers of the soil." *The Jewish Farmer* received a hearty reception. Before long it was being read in every state in the Union.

Gravestone in a cemetery at Devil's Lake, North Dakota, site of the Wechsler colony.
American Jewish Archives, Cincinnati, Ohio

April, 1912. It seems to be a prevalent notion that the Jewish immigrant prefers settling in the congested cities of the eastern seaboard to living in the more sparsely populated regions of the West and Middle West. While this is in a measure true, not only of Jewish but of non-Jewish immigrants as well, there has in recent years been an increasing tendency on the part of Jews to move toward the West, either to take up commercial pursuits or to return to the more fundamental calling of agriculture.

Out of a total of 334 loans granted by the Jewish Agricultural Society last year, 111 were to farmers in the Middle Western and Western States. In amount these loans aggregated $82,218.26 out of a total of $256,000.07 for all states. These figures show that the work in the interior and Western states forms an important part of the Society's activities. . . .

March, 1923. We were at festivities incident to a *Syum Hasefor*—the dedication of a new Torah. The community is small and has no synagogue or social hall of any kind. Divine services are held at the house of the most prominent Jewish member, who is entrusted with the custody of the scrolls. These he keeps in a little closet in the living-room which also serves as the place of worship. This celebration is staged in the largest room in the building which is the so-called summer kitchen, that is, an enclosure which can hardly be dignified by the term "room," closed in by rough pine boards so crudely placed together as to leave innumerable crevices—a makeshift used for cooking and dining purposes in the summer, so as to keep the house free from the heat of the stove, and incidentally also to free a room in the main house for summer guests. Here the ceremonies attendant upon the occasion were held, addresses by invited guests delivered, and refreshments served.

February, 1932. In 1900 when the Jewish Agricultural Society first began to function there were less than 1,000 Jewish farmers in the United States. Today we have a Jewish population of over 100,000 deriving their sustenance in whole or in part from the farm. Every state in the union has its quota of Jewish tillers of the soil.

May, 1959. The Petaluma Jewish farm community of California developed to become the largest west of the Delaware River. It had its start when an emigrant from a Lithuanian farming village, Sam Melnick, came by chance there in 1904 and decided to remain. He bought seven acres, built a small shack and a poultry house, bought 500 pullets and became

Price 25 cts. per year.　　　3 cts. per Copy.

דער אידישער פֿאַרמער

THE JEWISH FARMER

May 1912.
Vol. V., No. 5.

ביזר. נום. 27 וויזום א מאשין צו זעעזו סוום באטיזטס.

PUBLISHED BY
The Jewish Agricultural and Industrial Aid Society
174 Second Avenue, New York City, U. S. A.

the first Jewish poultry farmer in Petaluma and probably in all of California. Later he became one of the leading poultrymen in the area with a
flock of 16,000.

Sam Melnick's farm venture became known in the immigrant circles of
San Francisco and a slow trickle to Petaluma began. Four families settled
there in 1907–08. The accretion of new settlers continued; by 1917 there
were 25 families on farms. About 40 additional families settled there during 1917–1921.

Nearly all of the first group of settlers had come to Petaluma by way of San Francisco from the large eastern and midwestern cities. They were mostly working people or small businessmen with little or no farm experience and limited means. The older farmers who had credit in the bank endorsed notes for the newcomers, vouched for them at the feed companies and hatcheries and instructed them in the practical phases of poultry farming. The Hebrew Free Loan Society of San Francisco was liberal with loans to needy farmers. In 1925 a $14,000 community center was erected with the aid of a $5,000 donation from Mrs. Abraham Haas.

The depression of the early '30s, when eggs sold as low as 12 cents a dozen, weeded out some of the farmers who were over-burdened with debts. The vast majority, however, survived. In 1935 the 90 Jewish farmer families of Petaluma were the pioneers in starting to raise broilers and fryers. This proved to be a profitable enterprise and most of the farmers switched from eggs to fryer production.

During the Second World War the Jewish farmers established a cooperative poultry dressing plant which operated successfully. By the end of the war the number of Jewish farm families grew to 175. Petaluma had become one of the important Jewish farm settlements in the U.S.

We had friends here in Petaluma, quite a number of them in the egg business. And they said, "You listen to us. You are preparing to take in chickens. Take in the hen chicken. It is steadier. People have to eat eggs every day of the week. The price may go up and down a little bit, but there is a steady market for it. Sometimes you can make even a nice profit, and it's easier too."

Then we had friends who were specializing in raising chickens for meat—like fryers and roasters. And they would say like this: "Listen to me. You'll be better off to raise meat birds. You're a slave to the chicken when you're on a hen ranch. Not like us. We fill the containers just like a cafeteria and they eat. You don't have to cater to them. Only twice a day you go in to see that everything is in order, that nothing is spilled. In the meantime, you drive out to the Russian River, you go to the bay, you visit friends. Heaven on earth. So listen to us. We're better off. They are slaves."

And each one had his own way: "You see the chicken house? You know why there is sickness? Because there are drafts. There is here a crack in the wall. You stuff it up with papers. No draft! The chickens have an even temperature and they'll be all right."

"How come there are so many sicknesses around?"

"Oh, there are viruses in the air; birds are flying in . . ."

Well, I listened to all these stories, and then I went to the famous agricultural college at Davis. There I heard an entirely different story. "Sicknesses," they said, "come not because there is some air coming in, but because there is not enough. They are choking one right on top of the other because the air is contaminated. What you have to do when you are building your chicken houses is to build them so that they should be almost open."

That was the instructor of poultry, a fellow by the name of Virgil Stratten. I took Virgil's advice, and I was ahead of the game.

Did I like farming? I said right in the beginning I don't like chickens, I don't like the smell of them. It's still true. But it's also true that there are certain pleasures connected with it. To plug a leak in a roof, and add things, and work on the outside. I really enjoyed it.

Also, there was the proximity to the beauty that we were surrounded by. And proximity, by the way, to the city. Going out there for a concert, or opera, or ballet. This was our life.

Sam Rapoport

&ε JEWS WHO SUCCEEDED at farming sometimes became legendary figures—like Isadore Bolten, a Russian Jew who made his mark in southern Wyoming in the early years of this century.

One day my partner, Jack White, and I were building fences along the road and a little fellow came walking up the road with a brown derby hat on. He didn't talk very good English, but he made himself known and said he was coming in and he wanted to get some free land. Well, we directed him on up the road, we didn't want him to take up land near our claims, and he went up to what we call the "rimrock country." This is a high ledge of rock. He got a surveyor and located the corners and filed a homestead. He had nothing to live on except his labor and he wanted a job. . . . The railroad was building at that time and they were grading and he got a team of mules and went on with a grading outfit. He worked with the graders and saved his money and he was a very intelligent fellow and it was a pleasure to talk to him because he could tell you quite a story about Russia, where he came from. . . .

That summer he took his team down and worked for me on the ranch for $40 a month and his board . . . but he saved his money. A few years after that came hard times and you couldn't sell sheep and there was a fellow by the name of N. N. Chapman at Craig who was a big sheep operator and a pretty hard dealer and he had about a thousand what we called broken-mouth ewes. Those were ewes that were not expected to winter and he wanted to sell them, so he told Isadore [the "little fellow"] he would sell them and he could take them through the winter and he could lamb them out in the spring and he asked for so much down and the balance when they lambed, but Chapman didn't think they would ever winter. Nobody else did either and they might never have wintered but it was a very light winter and . . . Isadore got out and he wintered those sheep and they all had lambs and the price came up and he made his first $1,000 right

RIGHT, Canadian Jewish farm colonists near Edenbridge in the northern part of Saskatchewan, c. 1930. Organized by a group of Lithuanian Jews without any previous agricultural experience, the colony spread across a bridge on both sides of the Carrot River, hence the name "Yidn bridge" or "Jews Bridge." BELOW, The Chazan of Edenbridge behind his tractor.

Both, Library of the Jewish Theological Seminary of America

there. . . . He then went into the sheep business a little further. Every time he bought a bunch of sheep he made a little money. . . .

When he was wintering his sheep over at Rawlins he used to spend his evenings at the public library. There was a widow over there whose husband had been a shoe man . . . in Rawlins. Well, when this smart little Jewish boy would come into the library and get books, she cast her eye on him and decided she wanted him and gave him a Cadillac car. In a little while they got married. He told me, and I'm sure it's true, although she had quite a little money . . . he never used her money. He let her keep her money for what she wanted and he told me that everything he made was made with his own money and I believe it was so.

I was practicing law at the time and he was very much concerned about his name and he wanted to go to court and have his name changed. His real name when he came over was Israel Boloten and he thought the word "Israel" was very Jewish and he wanted it changed to Isadore. I don't know whether he got a lot of good out of changing it, but at any rate, we went to court and he was changed from Israel Boloten to Isadore Bolten. . . .

Among other things, he had his eye on his social standing in the community and he wanted to join the Masonic Lodge in Hayden. Well, a Masonic Lodge is a Lodge that doesn't like to take Catholics and they don't like to take Jewish people generally, but Isadore got acquainted with everybody and finally a petition went around to be broad-minded and to take Isadore in. So he was taken in. He got a large size Masonic ring, which he figured would give him a kind of prestige of dealing on the square. He was a member of the Lodge—I think until he died, although I don't know whether he kept up his attendance or not.

Farrington R. Carpenter

ᴈᵹ NOT EVERYONE was as lucky as Isadore Bolten, certainly not the protagonist of the following story by the Yiddish writer Boruch Glassman, who went no farther west than upstate New York, only to return to the Lower East Side bitterly disappointed.

VALHALLA

I

It was my first year as an immigrant and there was a great hunger in my belly.

It was summer and the slack season. I went round whole mornings and whole afternoons on the Bowery from one employment agency to another looking for work, but I didn't find any.

My eyes scanned the blackboards with notices: dishwashers, bakers, cooks, unskilled laborers for railroad work. I was mesmerized by the swimming letters written with thin lime water on dirty panes of glass: stonemasons, builders, cement workers. . . . I tried everything. But I had no luck.

So I continued to live on the Bowery where I spent whole days eating nothing but bananas.

Nice fruit, bananas. "Cheap as bananas." My pockets were always full of them. Two or three for a penny. I bought them overripe and spotted. After a while you get sick of their soft sweetness. But you can outwit your hunger with them.

II

Along the whole length of a large windowpane of an employment agency around Delancey Street and the Bowery appeared a large sign: "150 laborers required today, immediately, for work out of town."

Considerable numbers of unemployed workers were streaming towards the agency. Giants: Irish, Germans, Scandinavians. Medium and small: Greeks, Italians, Jews. And among the last named, myself.

Since they wanted 150 "Today, Immediately," I began to feel hopeful. Why shouldn't I be one of them? And what was more, it was already late in the morning. The crowd around me numbered some 40 to 50 people. My heart started beating. Where would they find 150 people today? I shoved and was shoved by the crowd nearer and nearer to the large green entrance.

Inside in a big office everything happened too quickly. We were put in a line, a long loopy line like a snake. A short, plump, red-faced man seated at a desk quickly dealt with the applicants. I saw that unemployed people without any money at all were quickly taken on. Candidates with a few dollars in their pockets, on the other hand, were put in a separate group to the left.

Heads quickly fell from the snaky line—the tongue of the short, plump, red-faced man cut them off sharply, as if with a knife. Before I had time to look around, the little man glanced sharply at me:

"Do you have any money? I mean for a train ticket."

"No." My heart throbbed. "I got sixty cents in my pocket. Does that count as money?"

"Well, it doesn't matter. We'll lay it out. They'll give you food there as well. On credit, that is. You'll work it off."

My heart almost burst for joy. He asked again, cuttingly, "Relations . . . Do you have any friends or relatives in New York? I mean in case . . ."

"No."

"Allright. Go to the right. The truck will take you to the railroad."

III

I felt very cheerful. First, on account of the great hunger in my belly which would soon be satisfied at regular intervals; second, because of the enchanting name of the place we were going to—Val-hal-la.

We arrived in the evening. From the train we went straight to our barracks. We hardly had a chance to see the village. In the dark blue of the night we saw—not saw but felt—many ditches and heaps of earth along the way, as if we were looking at a battlefield. The drowsing concrete mixers, the excavators, the machines with broad shiny beaks for digging—in the darkness they could easily be taken for cannons and tanks.

We hungrily licked up the last trace of spaghetti and tomato sauce from our greasy tin plates and remained hungry. The large wooden building where we had been brought in to eat looked like a military mess. In the second part of the building there was a counter. Workers who had money in their pockets went there to get something extra to eat and drink.

After supper a supervisor took from me one ticket from the company booklet which I had been given when I arrived. When I was given a pair of overalls I lost another ticket. A bed—I lost another. You couldn't make a move without a ticket.

We slept in a long wooden building where there were several hundred black iron bunks. My neighbor in the next bed was a skinny Syrian with reddish eyes discolored by sickness and a fearfully wrinkled face. For a long, long time he tossed on his bed. The electric lamps in the room were extinguished suddenly without warning, as if in a hospital. A column of moonlight shone in a nearby window. When the Syrian saw me looking at him, he whispered painfully, "Me no like this place."

IV

Upstate, north of New York, in the many branches and chains of the Catskill Mountains, fresh streams well up from the mountain depths.

At that time giant aqueducts were being dug from the Catskill Mountains across a distance of more than a hundred miles to New York to provide the millions living in the giant city with fresh mountain water. And this aqueduct was to go through Valhalla as well.

Whole days, from early morning till evening, we spent in the excavations. I hardly had a chance to look at the place with the enchanting name: Valhalla. . . .

At the machines worked mechanics who were "real" Americans. They had little contact with the unskilled laborers in the barracks. Most of them were natives of Valhalla. We "foreigners" stood for days on end in wetness, bent double over our spades. We developed swollen feet and rheumatism. Most of the older workers had tall, rubber boots but we, the army of new arrivals, had only our thin city shoes. The damp soaked into them. By evening we were broken men. We were shuddering. Some of us had fever. We were generously supplied with aspirin—the only thing that we got for nothing here.

Above the excavation walked a tall, blond foreman in high red-leather boots with a pointed stick in his hand. I didn't like the way he made the stick whistle in the air like a lion tamer. I began grumbling to the workers in the ditches, saying we should ask for work boots, but my sharp tongue didn't help me. However bad my own English was, the other workers—Italians, Greeks and Syrians—understood even less. They looked at me with confused smiles. Some stammered in agreement, "All right boss."

V

On the first Saturday evening, when the accounts were made for food, bed, overalls, transportation, laundry, barbershop, a piece of soap, and so on, it turned out that I owed the company $3.

I had been counting on a few dollars in my pocket to get something nice and tasty to eat in the canteen, and after that to go and look at Valhalla. Valhalla! And now I was bitterly disappointed. I went to the foreman: "Next week you must at least give me a pair of boots," I said angrily.

He told me to hand him the coupon book. He leafed through it and immediately gave it back.

"No good. You haven't got enough. You've overdrawn. Wait a week and we'll see then."

"But by next week I may be sick. We stand in water all day."

He looked me up and down with a smile.

"If not, I'll lose my job."

"Good-by and good luck," said the foreman indifferently. "But first work off what you owe us. . . . Next!"

I went away with pain in my heart. It was a frosty night in late October. The dry mountain air refreshed me at once. The stars were shining and I felt their beauty luring me to stay in Valhalla. I began walking rapidly and soon found myself at the railroad station.

My heart missed a beat. On the platform stood my neighbor from the barracks—the Syrian. Had he been sent to stop me from getting away? And even if not, how could I get on the train while he was watching. I felt desperate.

"Me no like this place. Bah! Suckers."

His face became even more wrinkled and distorted.

"No good place. Me go home."

Out of joy I shook his hand so hard that he shouted in pain. If I had not been such a bashful person I would have held the hand of my Syrian comrade during the whole journey home.

Boruch Glassman,
translated from the Yiddish by Eleanor Robinson

REFORMERS AND ORGANIZERS

◄§ IN ORDER TO stay alive, East European Jews were forced to accept employment under intolerable conditions in sweatshops in New York, Philadelphia, Chicago, and other large cities. It was not uncommon in such places for men and women to sit bent over sewing machines from eleven to fifteen hours a day, six and even seven days a week and receive as little as $4 in pay. Sweatshop workers labored continuously, fearing that if they stopped they might fall behind and be replaced by others just as desperate for work. At first they had no way of protecting themselves. As a result many were literally worked to death.

Improvements came only after immigrants like Sidney Hillman organized unions to combat the evils of a cold and ruthless system. As a boy growing up in Lithuania, Hillman rejected the rigors of religious orthodoxy for the promise of democratic socialism. With the outbreak of the 1905 Russian Revolution, young Hillman joined the *Bund*, a radical Jewish organization committed to restructuring society along cooperative lines. After being arrested twice, he fled to England, and from there went on to America.

Arriving in Chicago in 1907, Hillman found work as a clerk at Sears, Roebuck and Company (whose president, Julius Rosenwald, was a Jew) at a salary of $8 a week. After being laid off during the slack season, Hillman became an apprentice cutter at Hart, Schaffner & Marx, one of the largest manufacturers of men's clothing in America. Controlled by German Jews, the company employed between eight and ten thousand workers who lived in almost constant fear of being fired. When a strike was finally called in 1910 in exasperation over the way workers were being treated, Hillman walked out. The following selection is taken from Hillman's testimony before the U.S. Commission on Industrial Relations shortly before the founding in 1914 of the Amalgamated Clothing Workers Union of America (ACWU), a union Hillman headed for thirty-one years.

I remember at Sears-Roebuck's shop the constant fear of the employee of being discharged without cause at all. There really was no cause at all, sometimes. The floor boss, as we called him, did not like a particular girl or a man, and out they went. I remember especially the panic of 1907 when the employees were in constant fear of "Who will be thrown out?" I remember we tried, all of us, to get into the good graces of the floor boss. . . .

When I worked for Hart, Schaffner & Marx the conditions prevailing were practically the same. The man directly in charge was the boss and everything else. As a matter of fact, in most instances the working people do not know who is the head of the firm, only the people who are directly above them. . . .

The strike occurred some time in October when five girls walked out. I remember we made fun of it—five girls working against Hart, Schaffner & Marx—but somehow the girls managed to take out the men after a while. There really were no definite demands—the demands were that conditions must be changed. . . .

After eighteen weeks of strike we settled an agreement, submitted everything to arbitration, and the board of arbitration settled all the grievances that there were at that time and also established some method for settling grievances in the future. We appointed Clarence Darrow to represent us and the firm appointed Mr. Carl Mayer to represent them. . . .

The most essential part in the agreement, in my opinion, is the last paragraph. It introduces really what I call the new principle in our organization, that if the workers are to be disciplined for any violation, they themselves partly should be the judges, agreeing themselves to a certain agreement. [Now] the people really feel themselves a little more like men and women. Before that there was not a feeling like that in any shop.

Julius Rosenwald, president for many
years of Sears, Roebuck and Co.
Chicago Historical Society

Kohlberg Brothers cigar factory,
El Paso, c. 1915.
El Paso Public Library

October 20, 1913, English-Yiddish issue of the Chicago American, *reporting a Chicago protest meeting against the murder trial of Mendel Bailis, charged by the Russian government with the blood libel of a Christian boy. Jane Addams, pictured here, was the main speaker.*
Chicago Jewish Archives, Spertus College of Judaica

FOR JEWISH ANARCHISTS like Emma Goldman and Alexander Berkman, peaceful negotiation between workers and owners was a farce. To gain a free life, the toiler must declare, not a strike but "an open declaration of war." The following selection is from Emma's memoir, *Living My Life.*

News from Pittsburgh announced that trouble had broken out between the Carnegie Steel Company [in Homestead] and its employees organized in the Amalgamated Association of Iron and Steel Workers . . . one of the biggest and most efficient labour bodies of the country. . . . Andrew Carnegie . . . had temporarily turned over the entire management to the company's chairman, Henry Clay Frick, a man known for his enmity to labour. . . . [Frick] declared that henceforth . . . he would not treat with the employees collectively, as before. He would close the mills, and the men might consider themselves discharged. Thereafter they would have to apply for work individually, and the pay would be arranged with every worker separately. Frick curtly refused the peace advances of the workers' organizations, declaring that there was "nothing to arbitrate." Presently the mills were closed. "Not a strike, but a lockout," Frick announced. It was an open declaration of war. . . .

Far away from the scene of the impending struggle, in our little ice-cream parlour in the city of Worcester [Mass.], we eagerly followed developments. To us it sounded the awakening of the American worker, the long-awaited day of his resurrection. The native toiler had risen, he was beginning to feel his mighty strength, he was determined to break the chains that had held him in bondage so long, we thought. Our hearts were filled with admiration for the men of Homestead. . . .

One afternoon a customer came in for an ice-cream, while I was alone in the store. As I set the dish down before him, I caught the large headlines of his paper: "LATEST DEVELOPMENTS IN HOMESTEAD—FAMILIES OF STRIKERS EVICTED FROM THE COMPANY HOUSES—WOMAN IN CONFINE-MENT CARRIED OUT INTO STREET BY SHERIFFS." I read over the man's shoulder Frick's dictum to the workers: he would rather see them dead than concede to their demands. . . . The brutal bluntness of the account, the inhumanity of Frick towards the evicted mother, inflamed my mind. Indignation swept my whole being. . . .

Sasha was the first on his feet. "Homestead!" he exclaimed. "I must go to Homestead!" I flung my arms around him, crying out his name. I too would go. "We must go tonight," he said; "the great moment has come at last!" Being internationalists, he added, it mattered not to us where the blow was struck by the workers; we must be with them. We must bring them our great message and help them see that it was not only for the moment that they must strike, but for all time, for a free life, for anarchism. Russia had many heroic men and women, but who were there in America? Yes, we must go to Homestead, tonight! . . .

That evening we were especially busy. We had never before had so many customers. By one o'clock we had sold out everything. Our receipts were seventy-five dollars. We left on an early morning train. . . .

A few days [later] the news was flashed across the country of the slaugh-ter of steel-workers by Pinkertons. . . . We were stunned. . . . Sasha broke the silence. "Frick is the responsible factor in this crime," he said; "he must be made to stand the consequences." It was the psychological mo-ment for an *Attentat*; the whole country was aroused, everybody was con-sidering Frick the perpetrator of a cold-blooded murder. A blow aimed at Frick would re-echo in the poorest hovel, would call the attention of the whole world to the real cause behind the Homestead struggle. It would also strike terror in the enemy's ranks and make them realize that the pro-letariat of America had its avengers. . . . Sasha . . . had waited for this sub-lime moment to serve the Cause, to give his life for the people. He would go to Pittsburgh.

"We will go with you!" Feyda and I cried together. But Sasha would not listen to it. He insisted that it was unnecessary and criminal to waste three lives on one man. . . .

In the early afternoon of Saturday, July 23 [1892] Fedya rushed into my room with a newspaper. There it was, in large black letters: "YOUNG MAN BY THE NAME OF ALEXANDER BERGMAN SHOOTS FRICK—ASSASSIN OVER-POWERED BY WORKING-MEN AFTER DESPERATE STRUGGLE."

Working-men, working-men overpowering Sasha? The paper was lying! He did the act for the working-men; they would never attack him. . . .

In [our] group I found everybody elated over Sasha's act. . . . The group decided that the next issue of the *Anarchist*, its weekly paper, should be entirely devoted to our brave comrade, Alexander Berkman, and his heroic deed. I was asked to write an article about Sasha. Except for a small contribution to the *Freiheit* upon one occasion, I had never written for publication before. I was much worried, fearing I should not be able to do justice to the subject. But after a night's struggle and the waste of several pads of paper, I succeeded in writing an impassioned tribute to "Alexander Berkman, the avenger of the murdered Homestead men."

⋙ IN 1922, a group of immigrant Jewish clothing workers in Los Angeles organized Local 278 of the Amalgamated Clothing Workers Union of America. The following selection from *The Advance*, a weekly publication of the ACWU, traces its emergence and growth as an effective bargaining agent.

October 27, 1922. Local 278 of Los Angeles held a special meeting . . . addressed by Brother A. Plotkin. The work of the organization is being carried on under difficult circumstances. Members have not yet done their duty in the matter of paying dues and the morale of the Local is not at the level that the active members believe it ought to be. . . .

February 2, 1923. Recently Local 278 has acquired a new lease on life. Brother Plotkin has been chosen business agent and Sister Sarah Cornblath has been elected recording secretary. . . . As Los Angeles is in many ways the center for contracting shops, contact has been established with some of the contractors with a view of getting them to associate and of ultimately arranging an understanding between them and the Union. . . .

February 23, 1923. The negotiations with the contractors who do about three quarters of the work in the men's clothing industry in this city regarding the formation of a contractors' association are still continuing. . . .

April 6, 1923. Negotiations between Business Agent Plotkin and the firm of Topper, Roth and Knewbow resulted in an understanding by which the firm agreed not to discriminate in any way against Union members and settle all differences with the shop committee through the shop chairman, or failing in that with the official of the Local. Negotiations with the committee ended in the following additions to the agreement:

1. That no Union member may be dismissed after the two weeks probationary period, without reasonable cause.

2. That the Union shall be free to complete the organization of shops.

3. That temporary help shall be taken on only after an explicit agreement with the shop chairman.

May 4, 1923. On Wednesday April 25, Locals 273 and 278 called out the 200 clothing workers who make men's clothing in this city. The call followed the refusal of the manufacturers to confer with Brother Plotkin and the other representatives of the workers on the demands of the Union for this market.

. . . They require the recognition of the Union, the establishment of Union Standards and conditions in the shops, and a wage increase of 20 per cent. Upon the refusal of the employers even to consider these demands, the workers were called out and at ten o'clock in the morning of April 25th, 95 per cent of them left the shops.

One hour before the walkout Brothers Plotkin and Golub were arrested on the suspicion of Criminal Syndicalism. Freed from arrest on a writ of habeas corpus after twenty-one hours in jail, Brother Plotkin was re-arrested on April 27th on a charge of vagrancy.

May 11, 1923. In this market the organization after a three day strike secured from the contractors a ten per cent wage increase, time and a half for overtime, and "the same shop relations that existed prior to the strike." . . .

The membership of the organization as a result of the successful organization work conducted by Brothers Plotkin and Golub and the Los Angeles Locals has been more than doubled within ten days.

Brothers Plotkin and Golub are still under $500 bail as "vagrants."

◄§ THE FOLLOWING REPORTS from *Justice*, a weekly publication of the International Ladies' Garment Workers Union edited for many years by Leon Stein, were written during the days of lockouts, Communist agitation, and the 48-hour week.

March 20, 1932. The Collinsville, Ill. shop which I visited last week consists of about 450 girls, the majority of them very young. They are manufacturing a cheap cotton apron and some cheap washable dresses.

On my first visit, Wednesday, March 11, I talked matters over with the officers of the local City Central Labor body, and they gave me to understand that no matter what we may do, they don't want the shop driven out of the city as they are very much interested in seeing that the girls have employment, but are willing to help us organize a local if the girls would be willing to join the Union. They suggested that we pay a visit to the superintendent of the firm.

I happened to know the man as he was formerly a garment cutter in St. Louis. I explained to him my mission and he told me, as I expected he would, that conditions are not bad and that girls in St. Louis were not getting higher wages for similar work. I also found out while there that the mayor was in the shop at that time looking over sanitary conditions and trying, besides, to effect some improvements in working conditions. So we went back to the City Hall and waited for the mayor. I had to return the next day as he was too busy, and that day was the day set for the meeting with the workers of the shop. On Thursday, the mayor explained to me that while he does not object to organizing the girls into a union, his own mission is to get for them an increase in wages, while he would leave the subject of organizing to the workers themselves.

The meeting in the evening was a big one. About 250 of the workers were present in addition to about 50 others—fathers, husbands, brothers. The mayor told the girls what he was trying to achieve for them and it seemed that they were very pleased with his remarks. There was also there a speaker representing the A. F. of L., who told them of my mission, and it seemed that his talk was very well received. I had Bro. Cohen, manager of the St. Louis office of the *Forward* with me and he was also invited to speak.

Then the fun began. Collinsville is supposed to be a hotbed of the so-called "communist miners' union," and they invited their friends from St. Louis to come over and help them break up the meeting. So just as we started to take up the question of organizing a local, these fellows began to bombard us with such nice epithets like "scab," "bosses' agents," "fakers," etc. They were yelling all over the place that the only thing to do was for the girls to "go out on strike at once and not to listen to any of these fakers." It almost came to a riot, and the meeting naturally was broken up. As I was ready to leave the hall about fifty girls came over excusing themselves that it wasn't their fault that we were so badly insulted; that they were interested in organizing a union that would help them get better conditions. They also told the mayor that they appreciated his efforts and hoped that he would continue to help them get better conditions. They decided that another meeting should be called within two weeks, and I had to promise them that I would come to address the meeting again.

Brother Ben Gilbert

Sept. 1932. There are in Portland, Ore. some 400 cloakmakers employed in four large shops.

At one time both work conditions and earnings in the Portland cloak shops were fair, but in the past three or four years conditions there have grown worse from season to season. Wages were slashed time and again, the 48-hour week was substituted for the 44-hour week, in some shops section work was introduced, until finally piece-work became established. Shortly before Local 70 was organized things had come to such a pass that one of the local manufacturers could boast that "labor was the most insignificant item on the production budget," and another manufacturer actually charged his workers rent for the privilege of occupying chairs in his shops.

These conditions, naturally, had bred a lot of discontent, but unfortunately there was no one in Portland cloak circles to translate this discontent into a sensible and clear-cut movement along trade union lines. Last year Brother Solomon Richards, of Local 8, San Francisco, came to Portland. Richards is an old and tried trade union man with a great deal of experience. He had worked in Portland several years ago when conditions were still fair; he knew a good many workers and the workers in turn knew and respected him.

Brother Richards decided to start an ILGWU local in Portland and at the end of a few months about half of the cloakmakers had joined. The local decided to demand the abolition of piece-work, the restoration of the wage-cuts, and a 44-hour work-week. As the manufacturers refused to confer with the Union on these demands and began instead to divide the work in shifts as if serving notice on the workers that they would eventually be locked out entirely, the Portland local decided to retaliate immediately by calling out on strike the 125 workers employed in the Modish Cloak Co. After one week, the strike was won, and the strikers returned to the shop after having been granted all the major points in dispute, leaving only a few minor points to arbitration.

The next step was the organization of the remaining shops. Within a few days after the Modish settlement, the 70 workers employed in the Pacific Cloak Co.'s shop were called out, and this strike was also won after less than two weeks of striking though the firm proved very obstinate at the start and refused to deal with the Local's representatives. The terms of the Pacific shop settlement are the same as in the Modish. The fact that the ILGWU Office in New York has not only promised help to the strikers but actually forwarded assistance in addition to instructing the writer to come from San Francisco and to help in organizing and leading the strike produced a splendid impression on the local workers.

D. Gisnet, Special Organizer

❧ IN ADDITION TO trade unions, trade associations paralleling East European *hebrot* were formed by Yiddish-speaking owners of their own businesses. Grocers, butchers, bakers, house painters, shoe repairers, peddlers, junk dealers—all had their own organizations.

June 29, 1909. Thirteen Omaha peddlers have organized in Omaha to form a union. A document filed with the county clerk Monday afternoon states their purpose as follows:

"The organization's duty shall be to protect each member and to help one another in case of distress and when lawfully engaged in his business and not when himself looking for trouble. Members shall be taken in only such which are settlers of Omaha and own their own teams. And all such business to transact officers shall be elected for 6 months as follows: president, vice president, secretary, treasurer and three trustees."

The charter members are P. Flionsky, J. Birk, H. Kalman, F. Foodman, H. Sakaloff, I. Morgan, M. Sokaloff, A. Zeatky, V. Brookstein, J. Finkelsten, A. Zeggman, and L. Green whose names are signed in Hebrew.

The Omaha Bee

❧ IMMIGRANT JEWS also formed their own political groups to protect themselves in ways that would have been impossible in eastern Europe.

PEDDLERS WANT PROTECTION

May 16, 1899. The small boys of the town who have been amusing themselves by throwing stones at peddlers and ragpickers had better watch out. The Jewish Arapahoe Democratic Society met yesterday and passed resolutions asking for an ordinance protecting its members from molestation while in pursuit of any lawful occupation. A heavy penalty will be established and any little urchins caught interfering in any manner with any member of this society will be given a big dose of the medicine of the law.

The Denver Times

&ᴢ IN THE OLD COUNTRY, Jews took care of their own and by so doing ful-
filled their moral obligation to act justly and generously toward those
worse off than themselves. The tradition, called *tsedaka*, was adapted
successfully to American conditions, largely through the efforts of people like Dr. Charles Spivak. Himself an immigrant, in the fall of 1903
Dr. Spivak met with a group of "lungers" in a downtown Denver synagogue to organize the Jewish Consumptives' Relief Society (JCRS), an
extraordinary institution to which Dr. Spivak devoted the rest of his life.
The following recollection was written by Dr. Spivak in 1909.

The fame of Colorado as a health resort for those afflicted with tuberculosis has been well known ever since the first prairie schooner wended its
way westward. It thus came about that the Denver Jewish district was vir-
tually flooded with many hopeless and helpless poor who dragged their
weary steps along its streets and mutely appealed to the passer-by. To relieve the situation the old method of house to house collection for a particular needy one had become a daily feature in the streets of the Ghetto.
The familiar red bandana handkerchief, the traditional "schnorr" symbol,
was a familiar sight in those days. The results, however, were utterly inadequate in spite of the utmost effort among the poor people from whom the
collecting was done. . . .

The meeting of the synagogue was well attended. As a result a permanent organization was effected which assumed the now well known title of
the Jewish Consumptives' Relief Society. It was practically fathered by the
poor consumptives themselves, who initiated the movement and stimu-

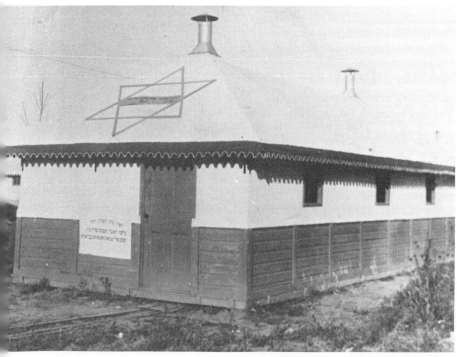

*Tent synagogue, Jewish
Consumptives' Relief Society,
Denver, c. 1930.*
Rocky Mountain Jewish Historical Society, Beck
Archives, Center for Judaic Studies,
University of Denver

lated others to continue the work. The young organization undertook first of all to canvass the city of Denver for contributions before appealing to the country at large. When a thousand dollars were collected a stirring appeal was broadcast over the country through the Jewish press and by letter to lodges, societies and congregations and individuals. As all the patients come from other places than Denver, it was but just that the country at large contribute to their support.

To take care of patients in advanced stages was at that time a revolutionary undertaking. The movement therefore encountered quite a little opposition in the beginning. Yet time and experience have proved the wisdom of this measure. Starting in September, 1904, with eight tents and a little wooden shack which served as a dining room, kitchen, office and medical treatment center, it gradually added new tents and new buildings from year to year as its income increased. Its income is not derived from rich endowments, but from the three- and five-dollar membership dues, and contributions from lodges, societies, congregations and fraternal orders. At the present time the list of members and donors is close to 20,000, evidencing the affection with which it is regarded by the middle and poorer classes of the Jewish population of this country.

The Sanatorium operates its own dairy, all the milk given to the patients being supplied by the Sanatorium's own cows. There is also a large hennery which furnishes a considerable number of the eggs consumed. The St. Louis Ladies' Auxiliary is now having an artesian well drilled on the grounds which will give an abundant supply of pure water.

During the six years of its activity the J.C.R.S. Sanatorium has taken care of more than a thousand unfortunate sufferers. Many of these have been restored to a life of health and usefulness, while the lives of others have been prolonged and their sufferings mitigated. The membership and the management are all actuated by the "Leit motif" of the Society, the slogan that calls the recruits to battle against the White Plague, i.e.: "He who saves one life is considered as if he preserved the whole world."

⋙ THE FOLLOWING selections are from *Hatikvah*, a magazine published monthly by the patients of Denver's JCRS Sanatorium.

It has always been a puzzle to me that attention is paid only to the physical condition of the patient, while his mental demands are entirely ignored. I have had the misfortune of spending a round year in a large Eastern Municipal Sanatorium; and just think, the same institution that takes care of 700 patients did not even have one shelf of books to start a library. In this same sanatorium I had a fight with a visiting doctor who took a book away from me I received from a friend of mine.

"Doctor," I demanded, "I cannot lie here all day long doing nothing but looking into the sky. Give me the book, doctor."

The doctor smiled. "Forget the books," and with great assurance he added, "Just rest and see how much good it will do you."

From the Municipal I went to another sanatorium kept up by the Jews and for the Jews. Here were a few bookcases and about 200 nicely bound volumes under lock—not for use.

From then on I spoke to many a patient, and I am sorry to state that only a small number of sanatoriums have libraries.

M. Lune

IN THE COLORADO MOUNTAINS

Tall, black, mountain walls
Fence in the image of the sun;
Through thick waves of cloud
Struggle the last flames.

Colors and new shapes,
Emerge and quickly disperse;
Giant hands hidden in the mountain
Draw the curtains swiftly. . . .

There is a lightning flash.
Swords are drawn from scabbards.
A wild cry resounds
From the entrails of the rocks.

The valleys round about
Feel a dreadful tumult,
And on my face falls warmly
The first drop from the sky. . . .

Now comes the quiet evening hour
With gold and stripes of purple,
And summer day with summer night
Kissing, are betrothed.

Now the mountains turn blue and large,
The valley turns darker, smaller,
And from somewhere breathes
A melody without notes.

The scent of meadow flowers
Rises like incense.
And the world rests and makes itself holy
In silent eveningshine.

Yehoash,
translated from the Yiddish
by Eleanor Robinson

THE TERM "ZIONISM" was coined in 1893 by Nathan Birnbaum, a political and philosophical writer. Four years later Theodor Herzl, the father of political Zionism, called for the establishment for the Jewish people of a national home in Palestine guaranteed by public law. Initially, Herzl's call evoked little more than a faint echo from Jews in America.

*A picnic sponsored by the Hebrew
Progressive Club of Greeley,
Colorado, 1921.*
Rocky Mountain Jewish Historical Society, Beck
Archives, Center for Judaic Studies,
University of Denver

Even after American Jewry was "stirred" by the bloody Russian pogroms of 1903, Zionism attracted little attention. With a Jewish population in America of 1,500,000 in 1905, the total Zionist membership of
25,000 amounted to no more than a tiny dissident movement composed
primarily of recent arrivals from eastern Europe.

The following account of the birth and growth of Zionism in Kansas
City is in many ways typical of developments in small and medium-sized
cities throughout America in subsequent years.

There was . . . a Ladies Zion Club organized in 1901 by Mrs. Helen
Leavitt, a native of Russia who had come to Kansas City in 1892 and who
was prominent in Orthodox society and well-known in Jewish philanthropic circles. It had thirty-five members initially, and seventy-five by
1908. Reportedly, the society was "the largest shareholder in the West of
the Zionist movement," holding shares sold at that time by the Jewish Colonial Trust, an English-chartered bank, to help finance colonization and
development in Palestine.

Another major Zionist group in Kansas City was the Poale (Labor)
Zion-Zeire Zion Labor Zionist Organization formed in 1908 by Arye Shes-
kin, a carpenter; Israel Gorman, a cleaner; Robert Bader, a tailor; and Dr.
Alexander Lehman, a dentist. This group, like Poale Zion groups elsewhere in America, participated in general Jewish communal and cultural
causes as well as supporting Zionist aims.

Hadassah, the Women's Zionist Organization of America, was also an
important Zionist group in the area in the pre–World War I period. It was
in 1912 that several chapters of the Daughters of Zion, a new national
women's organization, united to form Hadassah; in 1913, Henrietta Szold,
the national president, visited Kansas City. She inspired a group of women
meeting at the home of Mrs. A. H. Lehman to take up her call to send and
maintain nurses in Palestine and to help supply the medical needs of the
population. . . .

The activities of Hadassah proliferated in the early 1920s, as did the membership, which was up to six hundred by 1923. The Hadassah Medical Organization campaigns proceeded smoothly as did other activities, including penny and milk funds, support for infant welfare stations, a sewing circle to make garments needed in Palestine and educational activities.

For all elements of the Kansas City Jewish community, the highlight of 1928 was undoubtedly the visit in April of Dr. Chaim Weizmann, in connection with the United Palestine Appeal Campaign chaired by Jacob Harzfeld. A mass meeting was held at Ivanhoe Temple, and Izler Solomon played a musical interlude. Wiezmann's speech reiterated the historical situation; stated that it was necessary to be cautious with the Arabs but that Palestine was safe, secure and peaceful; he emphasized that Kansas City Jews did not need to feel obligated to go to Palestine.

Among other speakers who arrived from time to time to address Kansas City audiences was Goldie Myerson, later Golda Meir, who spoke in behalf of the local Histadrut campaign on March 12, 1929, at the YM-YMHA. On this visit she stayed with Bessie Zoglin, chairman of the Histadrut campaign between 1927 and 1930, and was so impressed with Mrs. Zoglin's abilities that she asked her to form a local chapter of Pioneer Women.

According to one old-timer, the climate for political Zionism was rather unfavorable at this time in Kansas City. The concept of a state, in any event, seemed remote. It appears that if there were a predominant Zionist ideology in the Kansas City Jewish community at all, it was that of Ahad Ha'am, with its emphasis on the spiritual, moral and cultural elements in

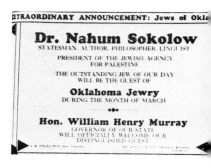

Zionist meeting, Omaha, 1916.
National Council of Jewish Women,
Omaha Section

Jewish nationalism. This emphasis remained throughout the 1930s, although the idea of a place of refuge and safe haven became more widely stressed as Hitler came to power in Germany and the horrors of the decade began to unfold. That these events would make a Jewish state imperative was realized by very few.

Carla L. Klausner

Football heroes Morris Hillman (left) and Ernie Kaplan of the Judeas, a team sponsored by a pioneer Jewish community house on Minneapolis's North Side.

&ᔑ EVEN BEFORE THE turn of the century, pioneer Jewish social workers were calling for the creation of "educational alliances" to build bridges between the circumscribed world of the immigrant Jew and the world outside. A number of leaders in this movement—David Blaustein, Boris Bogen, Jacob Billikopf—were themselves immigrants. Largely through their efforts, the Educational Alliance movement developed into an Americanizing agency for immigrants as well as a Judaizing agency for their children who, as a result of American influences in the school and on the street, were in danger of becoming separated from their Jewish roots. Pragmatic in outlook, committed to no single religious or political philosophy, the Educational Alliance was as much a night school and a social center as a political and cultural forum for everything from Zionism to Shakespeare.

ST. LOUIS JEWISH EDUCATIONAL ALLIANCE REPORTS

February 23, 1906. That Zionism is practical seemed to be proven by the decision of an appreciative audience at the last meeting of the Bention Literary Society. "There can be no home for a Jew but a Jewish one," said Mr. Levitt, first affirmative, and Mr. Sam Siff, second affirmative, admirably followed up this line of thought. The negative which had on its side Mr. Shifen and Mr. Rotman spoke well, but were not successful in convincing the audience that Palestine is dry, unfertile and wholly unfitted for colonization.

The Night School and Industrial School have opened and a large attendance is reported. There is no excuse for a foreigner not learning English for books and tuition are free and everyone is welcome.

The Legal Aid Department has started. Free legal advice is given to those in trouble and the bureau will endeavor to keep many petty quarrels from being aired in the courts.

A class in Telegraphy will be started within a few weeks.

March 24, 1911. The Shakespeare Club was addressed at its meeting Saturday night by Mr. Henry Sayers who gave an account of his visit to the Globe Theatre and to the birthplace of Shakespeare. . . . The class which is one of the oldest in the building and whose membership is made up of doctors, teachers and university students, is at the present time reading *King Lear.*

The "Hazomir," a Hebrew singing society, gave a concert in the auditorium of the Alliance, of Hebrew, Russian and English songs. . . .

May 5, 1911. Mr. Schlechter was agreeably surprised the other day when he was notified by a committee of the Knights of Columbus that a new five hundred dollar piano had been voted to the Educational Alliance by the Carnival Committee. It seems that this piano was bought for the purpose of having it voted to the most popular organization. The Alliance won out after a close contest with a Catholic educational institution.

March 29, 1912. The Yiddish Dramatic Club gave a fine interpretation of Jacob Gordin's one-act sketch, *The Debtor,* Sunday evening. The auditorium was packed to its capacity. Preparations are being made for a recital where Mr. David A. Jones, the well-known elocutionist, will give his rendition of Israel Zangwill's play *The Melting Pot.*

April 12, 1912. "Shall Women Vote?"—On this timely subject Prof. Mangold of Washington University, author of *Child Problems,* is to speak Saturday evening. The prospective lecture is attracting a great deal of attention, so if you wish to have a seat come early Saturday evening and hear the lecture and take part in the discussion.

May 3, 1912. Mrs. Leonard has arranged a visit for the Mothers' Club at the Child Welfare Exhibit at the Colosseum for Saturday afternoon, May 4. Mothers of children who attend the Sabbath School have also been invited. Mrs. Leonard is to explain in Yiddish as much of the exhibit as can be seen in an afternoon. Do not forget to look at the Settlements exhibit. You will find the Alliance well represented.

October 24, 1913. A series of lectures entirely new in St. Louis is planned for the season. These lectures will be given by Rabbi Rabinowitz in Yiddish and will deal with great men in Jewish history. The parents of our boys and girls will thus have an opportunity to become more closely attached to the Alliance.

Club House in Boyle Heights, the Lower East Side of Los Angeles, c. 1925.
Howard Shorr, Theodore Roosevelt High School, Los Angeles

Kapores—a traditional ceremony of atonement on the eve of Yom Kippur.
Painting by Ben-Zion.
Courtesy of Ben-Zion

13
Enclaves of Yiddishkeit

A MIXTURE OF MEMORIES

AS LONG AS there were enough Yiddish-speaking Jews in an American city or town to form a neighborhood of their own, it was possible to a surprising degree to recreate the look and the feel of an East European *shtetl* wherein the values of *Yiddishkeit*, far from being abandoned or forgotten, provided direction and meaning to the lives of young and old alike, particularly for people like Frieda Gass Cohen, who remembers the immigrant Jewish neighborhood of South Portland, Oregon, as a place of warmth and comfort during her growing years—an oasis of tenderness and concern in the midst of a cold and often brutal world.

We would go to school, come home from school, go to Hebrew School and come home from Hebrew School from Monday through Thursday, never on Fridays, and again on Sunday. In between, on Friday evening and Saturday morning, we attended Sabbath services, and if you did not show up, on Sunday Mr. Chenochovsky the Hebrew School teacher would take a big gold ring and slam it on the table until your teeth would chatter. All of my life-long associations come out of that neighborhood. The Chenochovskys, the Nepoms, the Rosenfelds—within five minutes I could be at the home of twenty friends. Any evening we wanted to see fifty or a hundred Jewish kids we would go to the Neighborhood House, a distance of eight blocks, and find anyone we wanted. We walked it like you would walk from your living room to your kitchen. We went to Hebrew School there, we swam in the pool, we used the gymnasium. It was a very necessary part of the Jewish community at that time.

Our family lived in a group so close-knit that you seldom did anything or bought anything or had anything without calling your aunts and your uncles and telling them just what had occurred. No celebration ever took place without the whole neighborhood practically. In my mother's home there must have been on any Saturday night thirty, forty or fifty people who walked in unexpectedly. They would come after *Shabbes* [the Sabbath]—it didn't matter how many. Rabbi Fain would come and the Chenochovskys and the three Rosenfeld brothers and their wives, and of

*Where Portland's immigrant Jews
and their families settled, c. 1910.*
Oregon Historical Society

*Bergman's Dairy Store, Portland,
1927.*
Oregon Historical Society

course my aunts and uncles. It didn't matter how many—they all sat down. There was room for everybody, there was food for everybody. All these people would sit around in our dining room. It seemed the walls must have been made of rubber because no matter how many people there were somehow they all found room around the table. And the discussions that went on—everything from Jewish problems to political problems to present-day problems. These people were for the most part knowledgeable, and of course when they came they all brought their children with them. If it were summer time we played outside until it got too late and then we all came inside and sometimes would sit around and listen and sing the songs they sang. . . .

I always felt that if I awoke from a deep sleep after a long time and then dropped into my mother's house on a Friday, I would know it was Friday because of the smell of my mother's house with the baking and the cooking and the gefillte fish and the fresh chicken soup. My mother would get up Friday morning and go from our house to buy some fresh fish from Mrs. Levine. Then she would go across the street to Benzie Skomak and have him slaughter a fresh chicken for her. She might even stop at Schnitzer's butcher shop on the way back and pick up a piece of fresh meat, and then she would come home and pluck the chicken over the garbage can and take it down the basement and then open it and soak it and salt it and cook it for *Shabbes*. It would all get done plus the baking, plus some fresh *lokshen* [noodles] because my brother Dave did not like *lokshen* that was made in the fall and hung to dry. When my father came home, at first he would clip off a piece of gefillte fish and tell my mother it was good, it was worth it. We all sat down Friday night which was one of the few nights we did sit down together. From that moment when she *benscht licht* [blessed the candles] until Saturday night, my mother did not turn on the lights or turn on the stove or do anything else. She had done her preparation and done it well.

  WHILE FOR SOME Portland was a *goldeneh medina*, for others like Israel Boxer, a young immigrant immersed in Yiddish culture, it was a place that could drive you *meshugga*.

I had an older brother in Portland who was in the junk business who wrote to us in New York that Portland was the *goldeneh medina*, that gold grows here on the trees. But when I came here I wanted to die. In New York I went to lectures every night, it was wonderful. But here the Jews were such *goys*, so terribly dumb. People just didn't understand Jewish life. When you came into a Jewish home you didn't see a Jewish book. They didn't know what a *menorah* is. No *mizzuzahs*, no intention of being a Jew. I tell you I found a bunch of *goyim*. I cried here for two years. No Jewish words you could talk like New York. No Jewish boys from Odessa to sing Jewish songs, Russian songs, to recite poetry and tell stories. To get a job I had to work on *Shabbes* and I wouldn't work on *Shabbes*. On *Shabbes* I had to go to *shul*. All my life I did and I wouldn't give it up. There was a Reform Temple here on 14th and Taylor Streets, but a Jewish

boy born in orthodoxy not to have my cap on in the *shul*—I wanted to die. I couldn't do it. I just want to remind you of one thing: you had to be pretty brave, you had to be strong like the Bible says. Not to have strong muscles but to have a strong head or you could go *meshugga*. Lots of boys did.

May 31, 1916
To the Editor of *Der Yiddisher Geist*
Portland, Oregon

As I am a long-time resident of this city, I ask you to be so kind as to raise the question of the need for an orthodox rabbi in Portland. That a community of 8,000 Jews—may they multiply—should not have an orthodox rabbi is nothing short of the most despicable badge of shame that diminishes us in the eyes of the *goyim*. The *goyim* know that the Reform are but a small percentage of the Jews of Portland. So how does it look that we remain without our own rabbi.

As if this were not enough, the *goyim* are saying that we don't have the slightest bit of shame for our own children who can't help but notice the chaos that reigns within our midst. How does it look that our older children search among strangers for discipline and order whereas by us they see only strife, backbiting and bitterness. Is it any wonder they become Christian Scientists and soon talk their parents into believing that Christian Science is not really *goyish*. There are no crosses, they argue. They just sing a few songs and that's all.

And why should they not turn away from us? Is there a rabbi here to tell them otherwise?

With respect,
M. Borenstein

THE "we" and "they" referred to in the following recollection by Sarah J. Schwartz of Columbus, Ohio, are the "uptown" German Jews and the "downtown" East European Jews.

"We" lived south of Main, in our special enclave or neighborhood. It wasn't a ghetto, in the accepted meaning of the word, for our neighbors were white, Catholic, and Protestant—and black—and for the most part, we lived among them in peace and harmony. It was our special kind of neighborhood. Main Street was its northern boundary, Livingston Avenue its boundary on the south. It extended west to Seventh Street and east to Parsons. With few exceptions, we lived clustered about our synagogues, the kosher butchers, the Jewish bakeries—yes, and even the *mikveh,* or *ritual bath,* which was in Shapiro's Bath House, on Donaldson, down the street from the Beth Jacob Synagogue. Washington Avenue was our main "drag," our own High Street.

"They" lived north of Main, on Rich, Bryden, Franklin—near their own Temple on 18th and Bryden. Even then, some were moving eastward, to Bexley, a new development out in the country.

We rarely crossed "the tracks"—Main Street—and they rarely crossed over in our direction. When, at the age of four, I went to preschool—the original "head start" program, at the Jewish Welfare Board building—my teacher, Miss Brevord, was assisted by volunteers from the German Jewish community. How I admired them—hair combed high in pompadours, long black skirts, white blouses, a gold brooch at the throat, a long gold chain with a gold watch hanging from their necks. We loved them.

When "Pop" Schonthal (also known as "Daddy" Schonthal), a wealthy industrialist, gave his palatial mansion on Rich Street as a center or settlement house for the immigrants, we crossed Main Street, to go there for cooking and sewing lessons, our brothers to play basketball in the converted garage "gym," our parents for English and citizenship classes. . . .

But we, the Russian immigrants, also took care of our own. My aunt was president of the Ezras Noshim Society—the Ladies Aid, forerunner of the Jewish Family Service. She rode around, seated proudly in the back of her big, black Packard with the oval isinglass windows, driven by Ernest, her big, black chauffeur, whom we children loved. He would let us sit in the car (what a thrill!) as she and her friends delivered baskets of coal, Passover supplies, groceries, and sundries to needy families.

And we had an Hachnosis Orchim Society, in a little house at the corner of Livingston and Lehman, a shelter for transient Jews, where a poor man coming through Columbus could get a room for the night, a kosher meal—and bus or railroad fare to the next town.

And we had a Ladies Free Loan Society, where a member who paid twenty-five cents a month to belong could borrow up to fifty dollars, to be repaid, without interest, at the rate of one dollar per month. Many a poor man depended on this small, interest-free loan, to buy a horse when his died, to buy the produce he peddled, or for other emergencies, like shoes for his children.

Jefferson and 12th Streets, Chicago, c. 1906.
Chicago Historical Society

And we had the Voliner Society, ostensibly restricted to men from the Volynhia *gibernia* in the Ukraine, but to which even Litvaks could belong. It was a quasi-social, self-help organization, and my father was paid fifty dollars a year to be its secretary.

And we had the Jewish National Fund, and we children would scour the neighborhood, blue boxes in hand, to collect the pitifully small donations to help redeem the Land of Israel. On Flower Day we sold the little blue and white flower of the JNF, convinced that we were personally responsible for Israel's redemption, dunam by dunam. One of my most unpleasant—and almost only—anti-Semitic incidents happened when I was selling flowers, this time real roses, at a downtown hotel for the JNF. I was a brash teenager, and as I pinned a rose to the lapel of an older gentleman, he handed me a dollar and asked me what the money was for. When I told him it was to buy land in Palestine for the Jewish people, he grabbed the dollar from my hand and tore the rose from his lapel! Naturally, I cried, not so much for the slight, but for the dollar lost to the Fund.

◆§ BECAUSE EAST EUROPEAN rabbis were slow to join the migration, even as late as 1920 less than half of America's immigrant congregations had rabbis. As for those that did, the following accounts by Nathan Pelkovitz, the son of a Columbus, Ohio, rabbi, and Art Rosenbaum, a distinguished writer for the *San Francisco Examiner,* document the important role such people played in the immigrant Jewish world.

Our house was used as more than a parsonage. It was a wailing wall, a refuge for the disturbed, a hostel for visiting mendicants and collectors for *yeshivot.* But more important, the rabbi was busy in *kashruth* [dietary laws]—examining the entrails of chickens surrounded by the *shulchan aruch* [a sixteenth-century legal compendium] code to see if he couldn't tease out a verdict of "kosher" while the poor housewife stood apprehensive that the fowl was flawed; in marital affairs, ranging from counselor to president of a Jewish divorce court; in business affairs, since it was still not uncommon for civil disputes about money matters to be taken to the rabbi as arbiter in a *din torah* [court]. . . . The week before Passover congregants would troop in on a dual mission—to sell their *chometz* [leavened food] and chat about communal affairs and to purchase the jug of sacramental concord grape wines (sometimes also muscatel and for favored folk my mother would make a gift of her homemade honey-based mead). At *Pesach* [Passover] time the rabbi became the wine merchant and a most welcome source of income it was for the clergyman who lived on the edge.

Nathan Pelkovitz

Rabbi Gold was apparently a very handsome man. I couldn't tell exactly because he had a long beard which was not common in those days. I recall when he was on the pulpit the almost athletic manner with which he would draw his long *tallis* around him, from one shoulder to his other shoulder. It was kind of a sweeping gesture. It had a nobility to it. You felt he was an extension of the hand of God.

When he started his lectures or sermons he would stand there and move his lips for two to three minutes and you couldn't tell exactly what he was saying. It was a half whisper. You knew he was speaking but you couldn't quite make out the words. Pretty soon you caught a word, and then another word, usually something provocative like "We shouldn't"—something like that—and you'd wonder what it was we shouldn't do. Then he'd start to come up through a medium voice and then, five to ten minutes into the sermon, he would go into his real act. Those words would pour out. Any time you see a movie and you hear the voice of the Lord or Moses or, in some cases, Jesus Christ—that great penetration, he had it. Fifteen or twenty minutes into his sermon they were crying in the balconies while the people down below were saying "Amen, Amen."

Most of the time there were two major themes. One was objecting to the people not inside the synagogue who were being carried away from the faith. The other was that we must support this synagogue, and you're the ones to do it, and we will have a collection. This was the whole point—to bring it to such a frenzy that you would want to pledge. I remember once or twice some of the boys would get excited too and we'd pledge five dollars.

You could say in one sense it was a harangue. But in another sense it was pretty holy to us. Everyone agreed that just to be able to go in there and hear him for half an hour was worth the price of admission. I say it in that sense today but I don't believe anybody ever made that statement in that way at that time. All I know is that whenever we were away from the temple, talking to anybody else regarding Jewishness, it was standard to say, "*We* have the greatest rabbi in the world, Rabbi Gold." Yet now that I think about it I can't remember a word that he said.

Art Rosenbaum

CHEVRA, SHUL, CHEDER

✒️ *CHEVRA* (SOCIETY), *shul* (synagogue), *cheder* (elementary school)—institutions that lay at the very core of Jewish life in eastern Europe—played an important role for a time in the lives of Yiddish-speaking Jews in America, even for those who peddled or kept their stores open on *Shabbes.* As much a men's club as a house of worship, the *shul* in America was where one went to escape being a lonely peddler or a beleagured family man. In some places, as soon as there were enough Jews for a *minyan*, services would be held, and before long meetings on a regular basis of various *shul*-affiliated societies—a *chevra kadisha* to take care of the dead, *bikur cholim* to visit the sick, *gemilath chasodim* to make small loans to those temporarily in distress. Initially meetings would be held in a store or someone's house. A bit later members might meet in a reconverted church before building a synagogue of their own. By then, in all likelihood, a new *chevra* would come into being, often as a result of an argument between competing factions over such important matters as who sits where and for how much.

FROM THE MINUTE BOOKS OF CONGREGATION BETH HAMEDROSH, HAGODOL, OMAHA

April 19, 1897—A mass meeting was called in our synagogue at 1315 Douglas Street to organize a new *chevra.* Ike Demoratsky made a motion that Mr. Kulakofsky should be appointed temporary chairman for this meeting and this was agreed upon. It was suggested that the new synagogue be called Beth Hamedrosh Hagodol and after debating back and forth this was decided. It was moved and seconded that the temporary secretary Horwich with two other people be appointed a committee to go to a lawyer for advice on how to incorporate or organize the *chevra* in a manner which would both be best for the organization and least expensive. Brothers Demoratsky and Kendis were also appointed. At the same meeting it was suggested that nominations and appointment of regular officers for the *chevra* be made for a term of six months. Brother Michel Kulakofsky was appointed president by acclamation; brother Abraham Monsky, vice president; Moshe Horwich, secretary; Jacob Kendis, treasurer—all by acclamation. Harris and Horwich were appointed superintendents of the cemetery while Aaron Rubenstein and Al Miller were nominated to be trustees, with

וְאִלּוּ בִּשָּׂר

רִזְבְּבּוֹי

שׁוֹמְרֵי שַׁבָּת יִקְרָא

תברה ש״ם

דבית הכנסת

החדש

נתימרהבשנת

תרנ'זפה

יאצעסטער

כארי

 וגבור

Title page of a congregational register, or pinkes, Rochester, New York, c. 1900.
Karp Family Collection/Museum of American Folk Art

Rubenstein as first trustee and Miller as second trustee. The officers were to assume their positions at the conclusion of this meeting. Harris moved and Kendis seconded a motion that regular dues should be 40¢ per month until July 1. The motion was unanimously accepted.

May 16, 1897—A regular meeting was called to order by President Kula-kofsky. . . . The following bills were presented for payment—insurance $10.80, gas $4.15, books $2.92, collections to the *shamas* 80¢—total $19.61. . . . Income at this meeting $21.05, outgo $19.61, leaving a grand total of $55.73 in the treasury. No further business, meeting adjourned.

Sept. 26, 1897—Special meeting. All officers present. It was moved by a member in good standing that the seats in the new synagogue should be appraised at four different prices—seats on the east wall, no less than $75; first row bench opposite east wall, no less than $50; four rows from east to west and north and south, no less than $40; corners of the four benches, $50; remaining seats, no less than $35, and the corners $40. The motion was carried.

May 8, 1898—A communication was accepted from the young children who have started a Zionist lodge—they request permission to hold their meetings in our synagogue. The communication was accepted and it was decided that they should be permitted to hold their meetings in our synagogue gallery without payment with the consideration that they should keep order in the gallery.

July 16, 1900— . . . It was moved and seconded that the cantors for the next high holidays should be from the city of Omaha and not from any other town. . . . It was further moved and seconded that brother Michel Kilakofsky should write to the man from Clarinda, Iowa about the $7 expense that the synagogue has incurred to bury his child and he should be asked to pay for it.

Oct. 28, 1900—Minutes of preceding meeting read and objection was raised to correct the minutes which state that the rabbi was to be given $10 to officiate in the closing of the book. It should read rather that the synagogue should spend $10 and ask the rabbi to say something at the closing of the book and if the rabbi would refuse then to ask Mr. Bramson to say it. The correction was approved. . . . It was also moved and seconded to re-

East Los Angeles's Talmud Torah Synagogue at 114 Rose Street, 1917.
Security Pacific National Bank Photograph Collection/Los Angeles Public Library

consider the motion that was passed at an earlier meeting that the synagogue should not accept any donations from the women, but that some
women could make donations to the synagogue from time to time. The
motion was accepted and the minutes were then approved as corrected.

June 14, 1903—A motion was made and seconded that a *hazzan* [cantor]
be hired for the high holidays and if the *hazzan* pleases the committee he
should be hired on an annual basis. An amendment was made to the motion to interview the Denver *Hazzan* to see if he would be satisfied with
$300 for the high holidays with the arrangement for $400 for an entire
year. . . . It was moved and seconded to appoint a committee to see the
Denver *Hazzan*.

Sept. 17, 1904— . . . Brother Adler presented a claim that seat No. 21 had
been sold to Brother Stein for $100 and that Brother Stein claimed he
bought the seat for $75. Brother Adler wishes to pay $95 for the seat if
Brother Stein would give it up. The question was presented to Brother
Stein and he decided to give the seat up as a gesture of good will in order
to maintain peace in the organization. Seat No. 21 was therefore given to
Brother Adler for $95. . . .

Feb. 28, 1909— . . . Objections were raised by good standing brothers that
since many people are moving from the area of the synagogue, it remains
extremely difficult to assemble a quorum for sabbath services. Those who
live far from the current location are not able to come and must therefore
go to strange synagogues. The *chevra* therefore should seek to secure a location which would be able to accommodate everyone. A motion was
made and seconded that our synagogue be given over to real estate people
for sale for the best price obtainable. . . . The motion was carried.

> Translated from the Yiddish
> by J. Lewis Yager

❧ A *CHEDER* (Jewish elementary school) in America often started out as
nothing more than a place over someone's store or in a basement where
an ill-paid, overworked, and untrained *melamed* (teacher) taught a
bunch of restless kids just enough *ivre* (Hebrew) to get through their *bar
mitzvahs* and say *Kaddish* (prayer for the dead). Only gradually did the
cheder develop into a Hebrew School where formal instruction in religion and the Hebrew language took place, sometimes with noticeable
success in communities large enough to attract first-rate teachers. In the
following selection, one such teacher describes a model Hebrew School
system in Detroit in the 1920s.

Our course is a seven year course. The pupil is first taught to read and
instructed in the elements of writing. Meanwhile he is made familiar with
a small vocabulary of Hebrew words such as the meaning of the classroom
routine and ordinary conversation. This method is followed because it is
one of the aims of the Hebrew Schools to connect their studies with the

*Class portrait, Yeshiva Eitz Chaim,
Denver, c. 1915.*
Rocky Mountain Jewish Historical Society, Beck
Archives, Center for Judaic Studies, University of
Denver

synagogue from the very first. . . . When he enters the third year the pupil begins the study of the Bible with Genesis. By this time 60 to 70 per cent of the words are already known to him. They continue to use advanced readers and they keep up their language studies all the way through school till graduation. . . .

Even those teachers who are students of the Bible and are well acquainted with modern criticism teach it in the traditional sense. We meet with no difficulty as far as the children are concerned, doubtless because they come from orthodox and conservative homes where there is faith. Maybe if they came from other classes we would have difficulties. As it is we teach the Bible in the full orthodox belief—everything the Bible says—not merely in a metaphorical sense but the plain meaning of the words. For instance, the crossing of the Red Sea by the children of Israel; we do not tell the children about tides or any of the other theories of modern criticism. Children are naturally religious. They love the stories of Moses and the crossing of the Red Sea and how the waters divided. . . .

We have been established only seven years but already in 1924 we had fifteen graduates, in 1925 we had 25 and this year 33. All these, with the exception of one or two who left the city, are now enrolled in our high school and are continuing their studies. Just multiply these numbers by 10 and you will see how certain it is that Jewish leadership in 10 years will be recruited from among our graduates. Eleven girls are now preparing for teaching positions with us.

As to which is the most important—Yiddish or Hebrew—as a language and as a literature, without question Hebrew. Hebrew has been the language of the Jewish people from its inception. Hebrew will replace Yiddish in the future. From Palestine where it is now, as it has always been, the language of the country, it will spread throughout the world. In America, with immigration practically cut off from eastern Europe, Yiddish is bound to disappear but Hebrew will take its place. The future belongs to Hebrew.

Detroit Jewish Chronicle

A BISL FRAYLAKHS (A BIT OF FUN)

&§ WHAT A TREAT it was for an immigrant Jew far away from the Lower East Side and all it represented when Yiddish culture came to him in the form of a theatrical company, bringing with it a touch of Moscow, New York, Philadelphia. For someone in Denver or St. Louis yearning for a more diversified Jewish lifestyle, joining other Jews in a rented theater to see a Yiddish play once or twice a year was an event not to be missed.

RUSSIAN JEWS ENTERTAINED BY A DRAMA IN THEIR LANGUAGE

February 20, 1899. Diana Hall was filled last night by exiles from the czar's domain who were again given a picture of life in the land of the oppressor in a play *Golus Russland*, a five act drama in Yiddish. It was given under the auspices of the Hebrew Women's Council, the proceeds to be given to the night school in Colfax and the library at 1415 Larimer Street. The school is for the instruction of the Jewish children.

The scene of the play is laid in Moscow and in New York. The cast is helped considerably in the songs by the rich soprano voice of Miss Anna Goldschmitt of Philadelphia. Her renditions of the Jewish Friday night hymn brought down the house. The costumes were gorgeous and the play was remarkably well staged.

The Denver Times

A NEW IMPORTANT YIDDISH PLAY AT THE VICTORIA THEATRE

December 26, 1913. Mme. Keny Lipzin, recognized as the greatest Yiddish tragedienne, will appear next Monday evening, December 29th, at the Victoria Theatre, 3631 Delmar, for one performance in the newest and best Yiddish play *Damaged Children.*

While the theme of the great play *Damaged Children* is on the same order as the English play *Damaged Goods*, its story and its plots are entirely different, and all those who have witnessed both plays frankly admit

The celebrated Vilna Troupe starring in Tog und Nakht (Day and Night), *Chicago, 1925.*
American Jewish Historical Society, Waltham, Massachusetts

that *Damaged Children* is more satisfactory: it has a better moral, while the story is more interesting and undoubtedly is bound to please almost everybody.

Damaged Children was produced for the first time in Chicago, since the last part of November continuously, and has attracted the largest crowds in the history of Yiddish theatre in Chicago. Hundreds and hundreds of men and women could not be accommodated at the large Empire Theatre in Chicago and many went three or four times before they could gain admission.

The Company, on their way East, are unable to play in this city more than one performance.

St. Louis Jewish Voice

YIDDISH THEATER IN DENVER

September 13, 1922. Mr. and Mrs. Josephson and their wonder sons, Sol and Sam, with a first class Yiddish New York Company, will open at the Palm Theatre Sunday evening, September 24, 1922 in the greatest musical comedy drama in 4 acts, entitled *Genendel in America* with 10 songs.

The cast includes Mr. A. R. Mason, the young lover, Mr. Widman, the character actor, Miss Lipolsky, the juvenile character actress, and Madam Estherfield the character actress well known both in Russia and America.

Denver Jewish News

THE FOLLOWING EXCERPT is from a biography by Jack Bernardi of his parents, Berel and Laina, who toured America as a Yiddish acting team for over twenty years.

Boris Thomashefsky arranged for Berel Topf to be engaged at Bernstein's theater in Pittsburgh for the season.

Before he left, Thomashefsky said, "What kind of name is *Topf* for an actor? Listen, why not take the letter *i* from the Hebrew alphabet, add it to your first name in English, Bernard, and we get Bernardi. And now, Berel, go in good health, and begin a successful career in America."

In Pittsburgh, Berel Bernardi was the featured comedian. He would make his appearance in an ill-fitting police uniform with a billy club hanging from a loose belt around a long coat and a police hat on sideways. With a wispy mustache and a chin beard pasted to his face, he would look dumbly out to the audience.

As the orchestra vamped the first two bars, he would explain that he was tired of being nagged by his wife and that he had joined the police force to put a little fear into her. Just then his name was yelled out off stage by his wife, the *yente*.

His knees started buckling.

"I'll be right there," he called into the wings, then turned to the audience. "She hasn't seen the uniform yet."

He began singing: "Sheriff bin ich fin dem shtetl, Judge, policeman bin ich alain/ Az der prisoner vil nit gehn in station/ Tih ich ihm a toiveh in gai alain."

Berel Bernardi was engaged in Chicago at Glickman's Theater for the 1901–02 season.

In one comic role, Berel entered a doctor's office for an examination.

Hanging his coat on an imaginary nail in the wall, he turned away as the coat fell to the floor. The doctor asked him to remove his vest, which he did—revealing another. He kept removing vest after vest, until finally he was seen in his undershirt.

*Yiddish actress Bertha Kalich starring
in an English-language play in Kansas
City, Missouri, 1907.*
Missouri Valley Room, Kansas City (Missouri)
Public Library

Doctor: "Say 'Ah.' "
Berel: "Ooh."
Doctor: "No, 'Ah.' "
Berel: "Oh."
Doctor: "Stick your tongue out."
Berel does so.
Doctor: "Stick it out more."
Berel: "That's all I got."

◄§ THE FOLLOWING ANSWERS to the question "What Does It Mean To Be
Americanized?" appeared in *The Jewish Daily Forward* in 1911.

A person who comes to the Yiddish theater *after* having eaten instead of
bringing along bread, herring and other delectables.

T. Pushkin. Chicago

Someone who wears diamond rings on both hands, gold-rimmed glasses
and is proud of a fat salary.

A. Weiss. Toronto, Ontario

An *oysgegrinteh* is one who makes her husband wash the dishes and mop the floor while she goes to the movies with a boarder.

B. Schmulivitz. Wilmington, Delaware

He who finally stops putting his mouth into the receiver when using a telephone.

T. Plotkin. Charleston, West Virginia

A person who is not ashamed to admit to being a Jew.

B. Brodsky. Charlotte, North Carolina

Someone who speaks the complex language of real estate and mortgages but doesn't have a hundred dollars to his name.

I. Gordon. Little Rock, Arkansas

One who reads in Monday's *Forward* the news that has already appeared in Sunday's English press but insists that he gets all of his information straight from the *New York Times*.

Z. Pinsker. Pierre, South Dakota

JOURNEYS OUTWARD

◄§ IN THE EARLY YEARS of this century, Marcus Ravage, a young immigrant from Romania, left the Lower East Side to study medicine at the University of Missouri. A sweatshop intellectual, Ravage was amazed to discover how little the Lower East Side had taught him about America. Back in the ghetto everyone had looked upon him as quite Americanized. Only now did it dawn on him that he was a stranger in a land utterly beyond his experience and understanding. At first Ravage was so confused that he couldn't make up his mind whether he liked or hated "Middle America." On the one hand, he had to admire "the heartiness, the genuineness, and the clean-cut manliness" of this new world. Yet at the same time he was dismayed by "a cool-headedness, a practical indifference to things of the spirit, which the 'intelligent' of the Lower East Side in me revolted against." Despite, or perhaps because of, such feelings Ravage soon entered upon an intellectual adventure just as exciting, in its own way, as anything he had experienced back east.

Most of the conversation at the table and around the campus was about athletics. I wanted to talk about socialism, and found that these university men knew as little about it, and had as dark a dread of it, as the clodpate on the East Side. Religion was taboo. They went to church because it made them feel good, as they put it; and there was an end. They took their Christianity as a sort of drug. Sex, too was excluded from sane conversation, although there was no objection to it as material for funny stories. I went to one or two football and basketball games—I could not afford very many—and liked them. But I could not, for the life of me, say an intelligent word about them. The chatter around me about forward passes and goals and fumbles might just as well have been in a foreign language, for all I got out of it. When Missouri won a hard victory over Texas I caught the enthusiasm and joined in the shirt-tail parade, wondering, in the meantime, what my intellectual friends in New York would have thought. . . .

I made heroic efforts to become an adept in sports, not so much because the subject interested me, but because I did not greatly relish being taken for a fool. There could be very little doubt but that my tablemates had made up their minds that I was one. No one else that they had ever seen or heard of could sit through a meal the way I did without opening his mouth, and that while the calendar was crowded with "events" of every kind. Moreover, I knew but one way to make friends with people, and that was by the East Side method of discussion. There was no help for it; I was in the enemy's country and I must submit to his tradition and his customs or die. If he refused to talk about poetry and Nietzsche and the Russian revolution and the Scandinavian drama and the class struggle, I ought, at any rate, to be thankful that there was at least one topic he was interested in. It was not his fault that I had been sewing sleeves when I ought to have been playing ball, and that I had gone to the wrong kind of a school for my secondary training, where I had been made into a grind and a bore and a disputatious fanatic. . . .

Besides, the institution of sport had begun to interest me. No one but an intellectual snob could remain at Missouri for any length of time without perceiving that the enthusiasm of the ball-field was something more than a mere fad or a frivolous pastime. It was a highly developed cult, sprung out of the soil and the native spirit, and possessed of all the distinguishing characteristics of its type. It had a hierarchy and a liturgy and a symbolic ritual of its own. What was on first impression taken to be but an *argot* was in reality a very exact sacred tongue, in a class with the choice Hebrew which my rabbi's wife in Vaslui insisted on talking on Saturdays. A football match in full swing had all the solemnity and all the fervor and color of a great religious service . . . a significant national worship, something akin to the high mass and the festival of Dionysus.

⊷§ THE DISPERSION OF immigrant Jews in America began the very day they left their enclaves to explore other worlds more pleasing in appearance, such as the one described in the following selection from Myron Brinig's moving account of Jewish life in Minnesota and Montana, *Singermann*.

On Sundays, Moses did not peddle his fruits and vegetables. This was the day the family went picnicking. Up early in the morning, Rebecca and Moses would carry out the food and place it in the wagon. Joseph and Louis would harness the horses and David would turn the garden hose on the brightly painted wagon until it sparkled in the sunshine. It was fun to give the horse a bath, especially in hot weather. His eyes were soft with gratitude and he tossed his long gray mane with an ecstatic, sensuous pleasure.

If there was not a baby in the house, or one on the way, Rebecca would accompany her husband and children on these picnics. Louis was fascinated watching her dress. First, she would struggle into a bony corset, and Louis had to pull the strings behind as hard as he could, while Rebecca groaned and fretted at the tightness of it. Louis could never understand why his mother wore a corset if it gave her so much pain. The corset was an American innovation that Rebecca had taken to at the suggestion of Mrs. Rosen, her next-door neighbor. "You should not to go out on the street without a corset," Mrs. Rosen warned Rebecca. "All the people will laugh on you and say, 'Look, look on the Greenhorn!' " But the corset was not nearly so fascinating as the bustle. This was the inflated wire pad, the shape of a halfmoon, that Rebecca wore to give her skirt a fashionable bulge. It made her look like a restrained kangaroo hopping along. . . .

Stiff in front and bulging behind, Rebecca would be ready to start on the picnic, and then the children would whoop with laughter and wrestle one another in the curiously empty wagon. Moses was in good humor on those days, for relaxation always put him in a happy mood. He loved the outdoors, the rutted roads and the free sweep of the sky. He loved the sound of the horse's hoofs clogging against the road and raising clouds of dust. He would draw Rebecca's attention to the greenness of the leaves, the colors of certain wildflowers, the songs of birds. And Rebecca would nod her head; and sometimes she would weep seeing how all the strain and irritation had gone out of Moses, and there was only goodness in him.

The wagon would bump and rattle over the railroad tracks of the Northern Pacific, the Chicago, Milwaukee, the Great Northern. The rails were burning steel that rushed away into a wistful infinity. After several hours of riding, the Singermann family would reach an elevation of land and see before them the Mississippi, the stolid, sluggish river with its tiny islands and numberless contrary currents. Moses halted the horse and rose from his seat, scratching himself with a slow, expansive delight. Yawning prodigiously, he unharnessed the horse while Rebecca burst open the bundles containing food, knives, forks, spoons, and a red tablecloth. The boys kicked off their shoes and ran shouting with freedom to the river's brim, while Rebecca called after them to be careful. . . .

Rachel was uninterested in the river. She had brought a book along, one by Marie Corelli, and though she could not as yet read with full comprehension, she was absorbed away from the picnic, the red tablecloth, the Mississippi. She was particularly interested in the tall, beautiful heroes who strode so splendidly from the front to the back of the book, leaving behind them the unalterable footprints of words.

Under the trees, the Singermanns ate their dinner, sometimes chicken, sometimes gefilte fish, and always dishes of sliced tomatoes and cucumbers. Moses brought along bottles of beer and wine, and he would take long, earnest gulps of the wine and taste it with all his senses before swallowing. Rebecca often joined him drinking beer, but the wine went to her head quickly and she rarely tasted it. . . .

The day creeps slowly across the sky, staining the clouds with rose-colored wounds, and there is twilight in Minnesota, above the Mississippi. Rebecca clears away the remains of the dinner and rouses Moses who has fallen asleep against a tree. He rises complainingly, sniffing at the sweet night air, the cool river air. Below them, the lights on the many docks flicker on and off like so many mischievous eyes; and river boats, with their huge paddle wheels, cast off rivulets of gray foam as they whistle their way down the Mississippi. . . .

On their way home to the house on Sixth Street, Moses raises his voice in a song and the children join him. If he has drunk too much wine, he takes off Rebecca's funny, lopsided hat and twirls it around and around on the end of his finger, until Rebecca rebukes him with a sentence of Yiddish, half anger, half laughter. She almost loves her husband in those moments, they are so few in his life of bustle and toil. She looks forward to these picnic days when he drinks too much wine. . . . Tomorrow he will be sullen again, immersed in his peddling, without a kind word for her and snapping impatiently at the children.

Some Sundays they go out to Minnehaha Falls. Sometimes there are the lakes to be visited, Harriet and Minnetonka. It is great fun to watch the lovers out in rowboats, the men in their high, stiff collars perspiring over the oars, the girls, prim and genteel, sitting upright against cushions, tucking their ankles out of sight.

When it rains on the lakes, thousands of diamonds appear gleaming and glittering on the water. When the sun breaks through the rain, the world of every day is forgotten, and an eerie splendor takes possession of Harriet and Minnetonka. How softly the word falls on the ears. Min-ne-tonk-a. In the old days Indian braves swam these lakes from end to end while laughing maidens waved from the shore, their white teeth showing like brief lightnings.

These days are so brief to the Singermann children, sweet, swift songs in the harassed monotony of their youth. The next morning means imprisonment in the schoolroom, and after school the peddler's wagon. But it is not the same wagon of yesterday. Now it is a vehicle of labor, of hardship and strain. The romance and color are gone. There is even a different sound to the horse's hoofs plop-plopping over the streets. Today, he is just a hard-working horse drawing a load of potatoes and green onions and cabbages. But yesterday we stood on the shore and watched the rain fall softly upon the waters of Minnetonka.

&ʒ LIKE OTHER immigrant groups, Jews tended to live in the older parts of a city for only as long as it took them to save enough money to move into better homes in newer sections of town. There, more often than not, the old ways were replaced by a conflicting set of standards, as was the case with Ruth S. Hurwitz, whose recollections of her life as "a Hoosier twig" follow.

Shortly after I entered high school the family acquired a substantial, many-roomed brick house on East Main Street, then *the* residential street of New Albany. It had five large porches, the two front ones decorated with wrought iron, reminiscent of Spanish-type homes in New Orleans. Two of our side-porches we screened, the upper one becoming a good sleeping porch. Our front lawn did not boast that typically Victorian zoological specimen, a cast-iron deer; but our next-door neighbors, the Baldwins, had two; and just up the street, at the "Depauw mansion," two Trafalgar-like lions awed the passersby. It was our backyard that drew everybody's envy. Here my brother Julius had a good clay tennis court laid out. Since he provided all guests with the latest in racquets from New York, the best of tennis balls, and large Turkish towels with a shower in the barn, the court was a popular place, particularly on Sundays and holidays when a contingent of Louisville youths regularly appeared for speedy sets of tennis with my brothers until dusk.

As my four years at high school were drawing to a close I debated "What College?" Credits from our school would admit me to the State University or other mid-Western universities. But I was bent on going East to college. Just then *The Ladies Home Journal* began to run a series on Eastern women's colleges. For no reason except that I liked the pictures of Wellesley better than those of other colleges, and preferred to be near Boston rather than New York or Philadelphia, I decided on Wellesley. My sister Bertha now decided she too was going to college. We sought out Professor Abraham Flexner, of Louisville, owner and principal of one of the first progressive schools in the country. Here my sister prepared for Wellesley during part of a year, and I followed her in 1905.

Attendance at this school brought me into daily association with the upper-class youths of Louisville, whose grandparents and great grandparents had given to city and state the names of streets, counties and institutions, whose fathers owned its great tobacco plants, distilleries, and the wholesale businesses that lined the Ohio River. Needless to say, I had little enough social relationship with these gilded young Kentuckians. Indeed their presence outside school and sport hours was almost wholly demanded at balls and hops and the late afternoon *thés dansants* for debutantes then coming into vogue. Nevertheless, one spring day I invited three of the school's lions and a girl classmate nearer to my own social level for an afternoon of tennis at New Albany.

Before their arrival I was as much in a dither as though my guests were to be the Prince of Wales and his entourage. What if it suddenly began to teem? What if Rick our young Negro houseboy should be in jail? Perhaps the pineapple frappe and the angel food cake that I made myself would suddenly turn to fizzle. In the tub I suddenly remembered to my horror that this was the afternoon for Aunt Dvorie's fortnightly visit. Heaven be praised, Aunt Dvorie was not on the trolley with the tennis party. But two of my young gentlemen were openly critical of the court. It was too short by at least a foot.

Suddenly I heard Aunt Dvorie's voice. No Southern lady's gentle drawl was hers. My aunt lived in a crowded, ghetto-like neighborhood in Louisville, and her English was not only broken, it was shattered. When at supper that evening my brother Julius asked me how the big party went I answered ruefully, "Catch me ever again inviting those snobs to play here!" But in my heart I realized that the lives of the young Kentuckians were utterly different from mine. Aunt Dvorie belonged, whether I liked it or not, to the pattern of my life.

⋧ THE DREAM OF becoming independent, the desire to come into one's own, the need to pass from the enclosed Jewish family into a new way of life with new possibilities of experience—for a Jew brought up in an immigrant milieu in the 1920s and '30s, the Second World War was instrumental in transforming such yearnings into poignant realities.

The army pressed one into physical closeness with hundreds of men, some from distant, alien parts of the country; the army, knowing its business, broke down persuasions of privacy, shame, and fastidiousness; the army imposed hardship and humiliation. Still, it didn't quite break one's spirit if one struggled shrewdly enough to keep it, so that even in recurrent stretches of depression, while zombying through close-order drill or lying empty on a bunk, I would still feel a bit of satisfaction at having stayed in the ranks and not having wanted to become an officer. Finally the army brought a lengthy exposure to solitude, that straining of nerves and pin's worth of knowledge which comes from being locked into one's self.

Army ways are mysterious and opaque: why it sent me to places where there was no active fighting I would never discover. I learned nothing about the dangers men in combat face, and little of those intimations of solidarity they are said to enjoy. Whether one lived or died, fought in the mud of Europe or dozed in an Alaskan barrack, was largely a matter of chance. Idling or shuffling papers in a headquarters company, picking up cigarette butts on parade grounds, standing guard like an iced scarecrow, seeing over and over again the syphilis horror film with its well-profiled chancres, taking basic training three times (once as an "armament specialist," though I hardly knew the difference between a machine gun and a howitzer)—to get past this bulking tedium was to be driven to a severity of inwardness that nothing in my previous years could have prepared me for. Yet others had it far worse.

My last two years in the army I spent at Fort Richardson, a post near Anchorage, Alaska. It was a landscape at once beautiful and barren. In the distance rose great mountain peaks, forever white; in the foreground lay a stubbled, chill terrain. During the long winter the days last no more than six hours. The cold reached thirty below, ripping into one's flesh like a drill, hard and dry. Nature here was pronounced sublime, but I found it without solace; the wonders of Alaska were not for a soldier's condition. I would wear three or four layers of outer clothing, puffed out like a clown, though in fairness I'll admit I never got sick. The germs, we used to say, were too clever to follow us up there.

All that bleakness and cold, also the stripped-down familiarities of the barrack, imposed a new order of awareness—perhaps in the way a prisoner studies a crack in the wall, bugs on the ground. Divisions of time grew blurred, then fell into neglect. Having no end of time while living in fear of its end, we did not know how to deal with mere days and weeks. One learned to attend the longer rhythms, living in the sweep of months—or sometimes, in a heightened moment, from the spark of a thought, the pang of a letter. But which day of the week it was—how could that matter if all were alike in their boredom.

By any obvious calculation I was lucky to be up there in Alaska, away from the killing, safe and sluggish, almost indifferent to ego, sex, or thought of the future. I had only to get through a minimal routine: occasional details assigned by a sergeant; Monday morning hikes across the snow; aimless fussing with blanket corners for Saturday inspection; faked urgencies of some dimwit lieutenant about keeping rifles oiled. No one cared much anymore. In this refrigerated asylum it was only natural that army standards relax to a slouchy humaneness. . . .

Evenings were hard. Loneliness came to a pitch, the very presence of the other men in the barrack serving only to aggravate my sense of being cut off from life. About half an hour before "lights out" a saddened hush would fall across the barrack, as if everyone were slipping back into memory. During spring and summer the Alaskan evenings are splashed with sun, and one July evening we played baseball after midnight, an ecstatic game with wild shouts bearing thoughts of home and freedom. But the long months of cold also meant long hours of darkness, and there was little to do but lie evening after evening on one's bunk, dozing or reading. . . .

I made friends with a Southern boy who slept in the next bunk, a good-hearted, unworldly Baptist. We used to talk about racial equality, cultural difference, sometimes religion, talk softly and carefully like scouts feeling out terrain. Some of the other men would come by to listen and that was all right, sanctioned by the code of the barrack. But they rarely interfered, since it was understood that our mild disputes constituted a bond that it would be tactless to violate.

The strongest impression during those years was made by the Southerners. I had never been south of Washington, D.C., and thought all Southern whites were bigots and reactionaries (as many were). Almost by instinct I saw them as threatening, certainly beyond the reach of my understanding. Yet I was repeatedly struck by the ways in which even the least educated Southerners, hard-spirited as they might seem, still were in command of language, still could reach to a coarse or even obscene sort of oral poetry, a *debased* poetry, such as Northerners had either lost or never possessed. And though I could never learn to feel at ease with them, I was sometimes stunned by their gift for tenderness, breaking past the invisible lines of separation we all felt it necessary to preserve, and speaking openly of loneliness, lostness, yearning. I did not understand this and perhaps still don't, but it left a mark on my memory and enlarged my learning: it helped me unlearn a little the things I had already learned.

Irving Howe

By any of *the usual or conventional standards, the American Jewish experience has been a spectacular success. The evidence is familiar enough and can be put very briefly:*

- *an astonishing rise in socioeconomic position, so that there barely remains a Jewish working class and the bulk of the Jewish population now consists of medium-level businessmen, professionals, and white-collar workers;*
- *a heartening decline of prejudice against Jews, with anti-Semitism having ceased to be "respectable" since the Second World War—though pockets of discrimination and subterranean hostility survive;*
- *a community with political influence and strength notably larger than its size might warrant, mainly as a result of the readiness of many Jews to participate in political life, especially primaries, and to contribute generously to parties and candidates;*
- *an internal structure of extremely complex (some would say baroque) institutional life, the best parts of which, in the tradition of* tsedaka *(communal responsibility), are devoted to a wide range of philanthropy and welfare;*
- *an active and often fruitful participation in American cultural life;*
- *a strong commitment to providing political and financial support to Israel.*

Seen through the rosy lens of communal pride, all of this adds up to one of the few Jewish victories in an age of unprecedented disaster. Yet most American Jews seem to regard their condition as uncertain; they seldom feel quite secure; and insofar as they remain Jews they experience—perhaps they must experience—some nervousness. For precisely at this moment of strength and comfort, the Jewish community in America also finds itself in a situation of growing, if not quite acknowledged, crisis.

It is an irony beyond understanding, and for some beyond bearing, that the eased life of the American Jews should have coincided with the most terrible events in the entire history of the Jews. How can any sensitive, indeed, any sane person reconcile our condition in America with our awareness that only a few decades ago six million Jews were systematically exterminated in gas cham-

bers? Must this not create a kind of moral schizophrenia, a ferment of guilt beneath the surface of consciousness? I know of no way to cope with this problem, except either to live with its pain or expel it from our awareness. Day by day no one can keep it in the forefront of his or her mind; yet neither can anyone, I should think, quite put it out of mind. We Jews are a haunted people.

There are other problems, deriving from life in America itself. Precisely the very successes within America these past several decades serve to expose, perhaps even to intensify, weaknesses and failures of the Jewish community.

The experience of American Jews has, to a very considerable extent, been that of an immigrant subculture. Without yielding to that smugness which sometimes mars contemporary Jewish life, I think it fair to say that no other ethnic or immigrant group has made so much out of an experience, has improvised so rich a cultural and intellectual milieu, as have the Jews during their decades of adaptation. For the Jews, the immigrant experience was a way of fulfilling the high promise of that secular Jewishness which began to spring up in eastern Europe during the late nineteenth century. It was a way of making substantial, sometimes brilliant contributions to the culture of Yiddishkeit— literature, theater, intellectual and social thought. But the immigrant experience is reaching its end. In the smaller cities and towns of the country, it is all but over; in the few largest cities it hangs on by a thread.

Seen in historical retrospect, the culture of Yiddish has been a victim of the whole of modern history—both the murderous rage of the totalitarian states and the subtle enticements of the liberal democracies. We can now mark out, roughly, a phase of Jewish history, say, the past two hundred years, in which Yiddish culture flourished across a span of several continents—and then declined. My own view is that this phase of Jewish history will come to be seen as one of the most vital in the whole history of our people. But neither will nor nostalgia can prevent it from reaching its termination.

For some thoughtful Jews, those who want to remain "Jewish Jews" but in all seriousness cannot yield themselves to religious faith, the result is a sense of profound discomfort, perhaps even desperation. What kept them tied to the Jewish past was not so much the commandments of faith or the commitment to nationality, but the experience of living in a rich and coherent culture, one that possessed its own language and common manners, styles, and values. Where can such Jews find an adequate substitute? Many try to subsist on a steadily thinning diet of nostalgia; others on political activities in behalf of Israeli survival or American liberalism, both urgent but neither sufficient; and some go back to the synagogue, more out of a wish for social warmth and aesthetic consolation than a genuine search for faith.

So the problem of self-definition, at least for those who cannot find comfort in religion, grows more acute each day. In part this is due to a shared feeling that assimilation—though a genuine possibility and, for a small minority, an accomplished fact—is morally sterile and culturally uninteresting. But despite all the hand-wringing about assimilation within the Jewish community, the real problem is something else: it is the gradual attrition, the wearing down or thinning out of Jewish distinctiveness, the loss of moral and spiritual content even as the institutional shells of communal life grow more imposing.

The organized portions of American Jewry have tried to cope with such problems by focusing most of their attention on help to Israel. This has, in fact, become the "civil religion" of American Jews—a public activity undertaken with the fervor customarily associated with religious faith. Israel has brought new meaning to Jewish life; new perceptions of a collective self; and a major alternative to assimilation, though not one that many American Jews have chosen to take. Yet I think reflective persons would agree that no matter how central to our immediate concerns, Israel cannot serve as the substance of, or a substitute for, a living Jewish experience. That Israel must be helped, nurtured, and protected is a premise of Jewish life in America. But if one can establish oneself as a Jew simply by "working for Israel," then it becomes a little too easy to put aside those irksome spiritual and intellectual problems that life has imposed on American Jews, especially that large segment which, in fact if not always appearance, is secular in outlook. Working for Israel has been a necessity, yet it has left a growing mound of intellectual debts that must sooner or later be paid.

There remains the option of Judaism as religion, whether traditional or not. A large number of American Jews, perhaps half the total population, maintain a membership in a temple or synagogue. They often send their children to Jewish schools, mostly on Sundays or in the afternoons but a growing minority to day schools. They attend some religious services, a small number fairly frequently, a larger number only on the high holidays. Many temples have learned to adapt themselves to these half-religious, somewhat religious, and nonreligious Jews. No great demands are made on them for signs of faith or exercises in learning. Especially in the smaller cities and towns, which cannot sustain a network of Jewish secular institutions, the temple is often the only agency through which to express a Jewish identification—it is that or nothing. One can understand why some nonreligious Jews in the smaller cities and towns join a temple, perhaps with a certain uneasiness, even though they have no religious vocation.

A tremendously wide range of feelings and attitudes can be found among temple congregants. The cynical belong for convenience, the sentimental for nostalgia. There are also serious and thoughtful groups seeking, and sometimes finding, the grounds for renewed faith. My impression—and about such mat-

ters there can only be impressions—is that many American Jews affiliated to the temples are probably confused and uncertain. Others are tepid and indifferent. From the confusion and uncertainty something good might yet arise. Yet I think the more serious rabbis, those who still believe their main task is to serve as guardians of faith, would agree with me that religious conviction is not very strong among most American Jews. And this—despite the multiplication of temple buildings and committees and banquets—is what accounts for the sense of hollowness one often detects in the American Jewish community.

Several years ago the gifted writer Hillel Halkin, born in the United States but now a permanent resident of Israel, published a book in which he argued that, with the tragic loss of the Jewish communities in eastern Europe and the disintegration of the immigrant subculture in America, there remained only two viable long-range options for Jews who wished to resist assimilation: either to live in Israel as a member of a Jewish nation, whether or not one adheres to a Jewish congregation; or to engage oneself seriously with religion in the Diaspora. Since, he argued, the latter choice seemed unlikely for the majority of American Jews, Israel is the only long-range choice open to nonreligious Jews who wish to remain Jews. I have deliberately emphasized the qualifier long-range since obviously there are all sorts of mixed and intermediary states that for the immediate future remain open to Jews. But, despite my initial reluctance to accept Halkin's argument, I do not see how it can finally be denied. Those of us who, in all seriousness and goodwill, cannot declare ourselves believers and who respect the faith enough not to pretend that we share it, must therefore find ourselves in severe difficulties—at least insofar as we try to think about these matters and are not content with slogans and phrases. But for the American Jewish community as a whole, I don't think this dwindling minority of confirmed secular Jews constitutes nearly so great a difficulty as does the far larger number of those neither fervent in Jewish faith nor steeped in Jewish learning and culture, those who go to, or drop in at, the temple with a sort of residual attachment. Or, for that matter, those who don't go, or drop in. Always, it's the lukewarm who are the problem.

I have been speaking here of long-range trends, problems, directions. But even if all I have said is true—surely an implausible proposition—it is true only with respect to historical direction. Beset though it is by the kinds of crises I've merely sketched, and not, or not often enough, sufficiently engaged with trying to confront them, the American Jewish community nevertheless survives in all its human aspiration and confusion, energy and doubt.

The theologian Emil Fackenheim has written that a Jew "is anyone who by his descent is subject to Jewish fate." (Perhaps anyone, also, who chooses to be subject to Jewish fate?) No doubt deliberately, he offers an encompassing defi-

nition: it can include the Lubavitcher Rebbe, Menachem Begin, Noam Chomsky, Lenny Bruce, myself, and in extreme circumstances I hope we will never know, Barry Goldwater. The value of Fackenheim's definition is that it places the emphasis squarely on shared experience, a community visible and invisible, resting on common memories that support a possibility of common fate. At the very least, this comes to that sense of shared situation and response which Freud called "the hidden secret of a common psychic structure."

There are some—too many—for whom that "secret" has become the occasion for smugness, philistinism, self-congratulation. But there are others—not enough—for whom it sets off deeply earnest inquiries into history, community, value, meaning. Even in the most bland of Jewish communities you can find serious people intensely concerned with the problems of self-scrutiny and self-awareness. There are groups of young people, some in the haverot *(religious or secular communities), who seem to me intensely admirable in their effort to find out what it means for them to be Jews. There are serious religious thinkers, and even a few surviving secular Jewish thinkers too.*

For the moment it may suffice to stress common memory and shared experience. These may not, in the long run, be enough to maintain a vital Jewish life in America. But in the short run, the sense of a vibrant past—some of which shines out in the pages of the book that Mr. Libo has put together—sustains many Jews in America. What will yet come of it I cannot say. That there has been in America, as still more in all the countries from which American Jews came, a multitude of rich and sustaining Jewish traditions, I can say. Life lived intensely, at the fine edge of consciousness, is always a problem, always an inducement to probe and wonder. The hope for Jewish renewal in America depends upon steadily asking what Jewish existence means, what it has been, and what it should be. Only if the questions were to end would the heart stop beating.

We wish to thank the following for permission to quote from the sources listed:

Amalgamated Clothing and Textile Workers Union for reports published in *The Advance*.

American Jewish Archives, Cincinnati, Ohio, for the diaries of Abraham Kohn, Sigmund Schlesinger; the memoirs of Abraham Isaacson, Julius Ochs, Philip Sartorius, Raphael Jacob Moses, and Anna Freudenthal Solomon; the letter books of Solomon Sonnenschein; the letters of Rebecca Samuel and Meyer Josephson; and the Minute Books of the Hebrew Benevolent Association of Jefferson, Texas.

American Jewish Historical Society, Waltham, Massachusetts, for the letters of Abigail Franks and Hayim Gratzer; the letters of Moses Albert Levy in PAJHS, No. 46; the letters of Bernhard Marks in PAJHS, No. 44; the letters of Maj. Louis A. Gratz in PAJHS No. 38; the Minute Books of Congregation Shearith Israel in PAJHS, No. 21; the memoir of Isaac Gomez, Jr., in PAJHS No. 11.

Mrs. Herbert Asbury for Herbert Asbury's profile of Jacob Hays in *The New Yorker*.

Mrs. Thomas Barnett for the interview with Israel Boxer by Laurie Rogoway for the Oral History Project of the Jewish Historical Society of Oregon.

Ira M. Beck Memorial Archives, Rocky Mountain Jewish Historical Society, Center for Judaic Studies, University of Denver for Minutes and Correspondence of Denver Lodge, No. 171, International Order of B'nai B'rith.

Myron Brinig for *Singermann*.

Farrington R. Carpenter for Oral History Interview, July 11–12, 1970. Interviewed by Herbert P. White. Denver Public Library, Western History Department.

Frieda Gass Cohen for interview with Frieda Gass Cohen. Conducted by Molly Mae Pierri for the Oral History Project of the Jewish Historical Society of Oregon.

Columbia University Press for *Portrait of Henry Sienkiewicz*, translated and edited by Charles Morley. Copyright © 1959 Columbia University Press, New York.

John Cumming for *Little Jake of Saginaw*.

Doubleday & Company, Inc., for *920 O'Farrell Street* by Harriet Lane Levy. Copyright 1937, 1947 by Harriet Lane Levy.

Joyce Engelson for correspondence to David Abrams of San Antonio, Texas.

The estate of Edna Ferber for *A Peculiar Treasure* by Edna Ferber. Copyright © 1960 by Edna Ferber.

Mrs. Louis E. Freudenthal and Elsa F. Altshool for the memoir of Wolff Freudenthal.

Carol Gendler, Director, Omaha Jewish History Project, for the correspondence of Adolphus Gladstone; the Omaha Jewish Welfare Committee Minute Book; the Minute Books of Congregation Beth Hamedrosh Hagodol, translated by J. Lewis Yager.

Harcourt Brace Jovanovich, Inc., for *A Margin of Hope*, © 1982 by Irving Howe.

Harper & Row, Publishers, Inc., for *An American in the Making* by M. E. Ravage, copyright 1917 by Harper & Row, Publishers, Inc., renewed 1945 by Mark Eli Ravage; for *Mark Twain's Autobiography*, copyright 1924 by Clara Gabrilowitsch, renewed 1954 by Clara Clemens Samossoud; for *The Farm* by Louis Bromfield, copyright 1933 by Louis Bromfield, renewed 1961 by Hope Bromfield Stevens.

Hastings House, Publishers, Inc., for *Copper Camp*. Copyright © 1970, 1943.

The Historical Society of Pennsylvania for Gratz correspondence from the Etting Papers.

Holt, Rinehart & Winston, Inc., for *Baruch: My Own Story* by Bernard M. Baruch. Copyright © 1957 by Bernard M. Baruch.

The Jewish Community Foundation of Greater Kansas City for "The Zionist Spectrum" by Carla L. Klausner in *Mid-America's Promise: A Profile of Kansas City Jewry*.

The Jewish Publication Society of America for *Letters of Rebecca Gratz* edited by Rabbi David Philipson and copyrighted by the Jewish Publication Society of America.

Justice/ILGWU for reports published in *Justice*.

Kenneth Kann for the interview with Joe Rapoport by Kenneth Kann.

Alfred A. Knopf, Inc., for *Living My Life* by Emma Goldman. Copyright 1931 by Alfred A. Knopf, Inc. Reprinted by permission of the publisher.

The Library Company of Philadelphia for correspondence to and from Barnard and Michael Gratz.

Congregation Mikveh Israel of Philadelphia for the Minute Books of Congregation Mikveh Israel and letters of Gershom Mendes Seixas and Hayman Levy.

Montana Historical Society, Helena, Montana, for Isadore Strasburger Papers, Small Collections 805, Archives Program.

W. W. Norton & Company, Inc., for *My Father, The Actor* by Jack Bernardi. Copyright © 1971 by W. W. Norton & Company, Inc.

National Council of Jewish Women, Omaha Chapter, for the interview with Joe Gotsdiner.

The Ohio Historical Society for Nathan Pelkovitz's memoir in *Jews and Judaism in a Midwestern Community: Columbus, Ohio, 1840–1975* by Marc Lee Raphael.

El Palacio for Nathan Bibo's memoir.

The Oral History Project of the Jewish Historical Society of Oregon for the following interviews: Israel Boxer by Laurie Rogoway; Frieda Gass Cohen by Molly Mae Pierri; Harry Rubenstein by Lora Meyer.

Elizabeth Romenofsky for the Elizabeth Ramenofsky collection at the American Archives, and for *The Solomons of Arizona: From Charcoal to Banking*, a chronicle of the family of Anna and Isadore E. Solomon and their contributions to the development of a frontier outpost in southeastern Arizona to the county seat of Graham County from 1876 to 1920, published by Westernlore Press, 1984.

Theodore N. Rubenstein for the interview with Harry Rubenstein by Lora Meyer for the Oral History Project of the Jewish Historical Society of Oregon.

Ruth Rubin for *Churbn Titanic* in *Voices of a People* by Ruth Rubin. Jewish Publication Society of America, Philadelphia, Pa., 1983.

Simon & Schuster for *Pioneer Women: Voices from the Kansas Frontier*. Copyright © 1981 by Joanna L. Stratton.

Roger W. Straus for *Under Four Administrations* by Oscar Straus.

Mrs. Arthur Hays Sulzberger for Julius

Ochs's autobiography.

The Regional Oral History Office, Bancroft Library, University of California and the Western Jewish History Center, Judah L. Magnes Museum for Rose Rinder, "Music, Prayer and Religious Leadership: Temple Emanu-El, 1913–1969." Oral interview conducted by Malca Chall, 1971.

The University of Wisconsin Press for *Abraham Bisno: Union Pioneer.*

Harris Newman III for *Sixty Years in Southern California* by Harris Newmark.

Western Epics, Inc., Salt Lake City, for *The History of the Jews in Utah and Idaho* by Juanita Brooks.

The Western Jewish History Center, Judah L. Magnes Museum and the American Jewish Congress for the oral interview with Art Rosenbaum conducted by Jane Field, 1977.